W9-CUC-623

The Brontës

LONGMAN CRITICAL READERS

GENERAL EDITOR

STAN SMITH

Research Professor in Literary Studies, The Nottingham Trent University

TITLES AVAILABLE

MARY EAGLETON, Feminist Literary Criticism
GARY WALLER, Shakespeare's Comedies
JOHN DRAKAKIS, Shakespearean Tragedy
RICHARD WILSON AND RICHARD DUTTON, New Historicism and Renaissance Drama
PETER WIDDOWSON, D. H. Lawrence
PETER BROOKER, Modernism/Postmodernism
RACHEL BOWLBY, Virginia Woolf
FRANCIS MULHERN, Contemporary Marxist Literary Criticism
ANNABEL PATTERSON, John Milton
CYNTHIA CHASE, Romanticism
MICHAEL O'NEILL, Shelley
STEPHANIE TRIGG, Medieval English Poetry
ANTONY EASTHOPE, Contemporary Film Theory
TERRY EAGLETON, Ideology
MAUD ELLMANN, Psychoanalytic Literary Criticism
ANDREW BENNETT, Readers and Reading
MARK CURRIE, Metafiction
BREAN HAMMOND, Pope
STEVEN CONNOR, Charles Dickens
REBECCA STOTT, Tennyson
LYN PYKETT, Reading *Fin de Siècle* Fictions
ANDREW HADFIELD, Edmund Spenser
SUSANA ONEGA AND JOSÉ ANGEL GARCÍA LANDA, Narratology: An Introduction
TESS COSSLETT, Victorian Women Poets
BART MOORE-GILBERT, GARETH STANTON AND WILLY MALEY, Postcolonial Criticism
ANITA PACHECO, Early Women Writers
JOHN DRAKAKIS AND NAOMI CONN LIEBLER, Tragedy
ANDREW MICHAEL ROBERTS, Joseph Conrad
JOHN LUCAS, William Blake
LOIS PARKINSON ZAMORA, Contemporary American Women Writers: Gender, Class, Ethnicity
THOMAS HEALY, Andrew Marvell
JANE STABLER, Byron
STEVE ELLIS, Chaucer: The Canterbury Tales
RICHARD KROLL, The English Novel, Volume I, 1700 to Fielding
RICHARD KROLL, The English Novel, Volume II, Smollett to Austen
CRISTINA MALCOLMSON, Renaissance Poetry
HARRIET DAVIDSON, T. S. Eliot
JEREMY TAMBLING, Dante
KIERNAN RYAN, Shakespeare: The Last Plays
RICHARD WILSON, Christopher Marlowe
NIGEL WOOD, Jonathan Swift
JENNIFER BIRKETT AND KATE INCE, Samuel Beckett
RICHARD DUTTON, Ben Jonson
DAVID DUFF, Modern Genre Theory

The Brontës

EDITED AND INTRODUCED BY

PATRICIA INGHAM

An imprint of **Pearson Education**

London · New York · Toronto · Sydney · Tokyo · Singapore · Hong Kong · Cape Town
New Delhi · Madrid · Paris · Amsterdam · Munich · Milan · Stockholm

PEARSON EDUCATION LIMITED

Head Office:
Edinburgh Gate
Harlow CM20 2JE
Tel: +44 (0)1279 623623
Fax: +44 (0)1279 431059

London Office:
128 Long Acre
London WC2E 9AN
Tel: +44 (0)20 7447 2000
Fax: +44 (0)20 7240 5771
Website: www.history-minds.com

First published in Great Britain in 2003

© Pearson Education, 2003

ISBN 0 582 32727 X

British Library Cataloguing in Publication Data
A CIP catalogue record for this book can be obtained from the British Library

Library of Congress Cataloging-in-Publication Data
A CIP catalogue record for this book can be obtained from the Library of Congress

All rights reserved; no part of this publication may be reproduced, stored
in a retrieval system, or transmitted in any form or by any means, electronic,
mechanical, photocopying, recording, or otherwise without either the prior
written permission of the Publishers or a licence permitting restricted copying
in the United Kingdom issued by the Copyright Licensing Agency Ltd,
90 Tottenham Court Road, London W1P 0LP. This book may not be lent,
resold, hired out or otherwise disposed of by way of trade in any form
of binding or cover other than that in which it is published, without the
prior consent of the Publishers.

10 9 8 7 6 5 4 3 2 1

Set in 9.5/12.5pt Stone Serif by Graphicraft Limited, Hong Kong
Produced by Pearson Education Asia Pte Ltd
Printed in Malaysia, PA

The Publishers' policy is to use paper manufactured from sustainable forests.

Contents

Acknowledgements

I should like to thank Jenny Harrington and Shannon Russell for their help in preparing this Reader. I am also grateful to the staff of St Anne's College Library for their generous cooperation.

PUBLISHER'S ACKNOWLEDGEMENTS

We are grateful to the following for permission to reproduce copyright material:

Eastern Michigan University Press for 'Gendered and Layered Narrative in *Wuthering Heights* and *The Tenant of Wildfell Hall*' by N.M. Jacobs published in *Journal of Narrative Technique* vol.16 no.3 (1986); Modern Language Association of America for 'The Profession of the Author: Abstraction Advertising and *Jane Eyre*' by Sharon Marcus published in *PMLA* vol.10 no.2 (1995); Palgrave Publishers Limited for an extract from *Myths of Power: A Marxist Study of the Brontës* by Terry Eagleton 1998; Papers on Language & Literature for 'The Other Case: Gender and Narrator in Charlotte Brontë's *The Professor*' by Annette R. Federico and 'Edward Rochester and the Margins of Masculinity in *Jane Eyre* and *Wild Sargasso Sea*' by Robert Kendrick both published in *Papers on Language & Literature* vol.30 no.4 Fall 1994 (© 1994 by The Board of Trustees, Southern Illinois University Edwardsville); Pearson Education Limited for *'Shirley'* from *Charlotte Brontë* by Penny Boumelha (1990); Rice University for 'Siblings and Suitors in the Narrative Architecture of *The Tenant of Wildfell Hall*' by Tess O'Toole and 'Gothic Desire in Charlotte Brontë's *Villette*' by Toni Wein both published in *Studies in English Literature* vol.39 no.4 Autumn 1999; Routledge Inc., part of The Taylor & Francis Group, for a chapter by S. Meyer published in *The New Nineteenth Century: Feminist Readings of Under-read Victorian Fiction* ed. B.L. Harman and S. Meyer (1996); The University of Chicago Press for 'The Sultan and the Slave: Feminist Orientalism and the Structure of *Jane Eyre*' by Joyce Zonana published in *Signs* vol.18 no.3 (1993); University of North Texas for 'Diaries and Displacement in *Wuthering Heights*' by Rebecca Steinitz published in *Studies in the Novel* vol.32 no.4 Winter 2000 (© 2000 by the University of North Texas); The University of Wisconsin Press for 'The Surveillance of a Sleepless Eye: the Constitution of Neurosis in *Villette'* by Sally Shuttleworth published in *One Culture Essays in Science and Literature* ed. George Levine (© 1988); and Yale University Press for extracts from *The Madwoman in the Attic: The Woman Writer and the Nineteenth-century Literary Imagination* by Sandra Gilbert and Susan Gubar (©1979 by Yale University and 1984 by Sandra M. Gilbert and Susan Gubar).

In some instances we have been unable to trace the owners of copyright material and we would appreciate any information that would enable us to do so.

For Gabriele Taylor

Introduction

Issues

In the past fifty years, interpretation of the Brontës' work has effortlessly accommodated aspects of modern criticism which would have been unintelligible to the earliest reviewers. Feminist, Marxist, postcolonialist, psychological and postmodernist critics have all found issues that resonate with their concerns. The early reviews, by contrast, seem innocent in their approach. If closely examined, however, in the social context of the 1840s they reveal that the reviewers recognise in the texts issues that later critics have since unpacked with varying degrees of skill. Such reviewers were working without a clear sense of the nature of the genre but with a perceived need to rank works for the benefit of the reader according to well-understood conventions as to the sayable and the unspeakable. In an elitist society, ranking was the natural thing for the elite to provide; and in a patriarchal society it was equally natural that different standards prevailed for women and men as authors.

From the first there was much curiosity as to the identity of the 'Bells' with their deliberately androgynous first names, Currer, Ellis and Acton. This began an interest in the authorship of the novels which was to blossom later in a variety of forms. While their identity was still unknown, Elizabeth Rigby remarked when reviewing *Jane Eyre* that it must be by a man because it gets domestic details wrong. If it is written by a woman 'we have no alternative but to ascribe it to one who has, for some sufficient reason, long forfeited the society of her own sex'.[1] Her comment hints at sexual misdemeanour and presumably makes inferences from Jane's passion for Rochester. When G.H. Lewes only guessed that the author was a woman, he praised it extravagantly as 'soul speaking to soul'. Once he knew it was by a woman, he changed his mind: 'A more masculine book, in the sense of vigour, was never written . . . Indeed that vigour often amounts to coarseness . . . That same over masculine vigour is found in *Shirley*'.[2] Another reviewer solved the problem by deciding that 'the said Currer . . . divides the authorship . . . with a brother and sister'.[3]

There were other guesses as to whether this evidently hermaphrodite text was written by a man or woman, a fact which indicates that it was felt to be subversive of the idea of separate spheres or an attack on domestic ideology that later critics were to elaborate.

As this excited discussion among contemporaries shows, the issue of gender was raised in Brontë criticism from the earliest days. It was fostered by the centrality of female protagonists in five of the sisters' novels. Each replaced heroes with heroines who, instead of maturing in *Bildungsroman* fashion into creatures of modesty, timidity, restraint, self-deprecation and dependence, show signs of unfeminine qualities. It is the 'spirit of self-reliance' which several critics found most distasteful. This is seen not only in *Jane Eyre* but even in Helen Huntingdon in *The Tenant of Wildfell Hall* who runs away from a drunken and unfaithful husband. The problem for those who disliked these aspects of the novels was that nonetheless many of them found that they made a powerful impact. These confused responses are best illustrated by the reaction to *Wuthering Heights*. The work, violent in itself, evoked violence in the shocked reviewers. One described himself as 'shocked, disgusted, almost sickened by details of cruelty, inhumanity and the most diabolical hate and vengeance'. But he also found that it was 'impossible to begin and not finish'.[4] Another felt it 'inexpressibly painful' yet '[it] seizes us with an iron grasp'.[5] The same critic admits that despite its 'disgusting coarseness of language' and its portrayal of 'unbridled passions' and 'hideous unhumanities', readers are 'spellbound' by the 'immense power of the book'.[6]

Much of the hostility provoked by this and the other novels relates to the treatment of gender but there are occasionally signs of a deeper unease. By some it was felt that society as a whole was under threat. A reviewer in *The Athenaeum* in 1849 claimed that Shirley Keeldar and Caroline Helstone 'suffer from the malady of unrest and dissatisfaction – on the prevalence of which among women of the nineteenth century so many protests have been issued, so many theories of "emancipation" have been set forth'.[7] The threat lurking in women's restlessness is expanded upon by Margaret Oliphant, writing on *Jane Eyre*:

Here is your true revolution. France is but one of the Western Powers; woman the half of the world. Talk of a balance of power which may be adjusted by taking a Crimea, or fighting a dozen battles – here is a battle which is always going forward – a balance of power only to be decided by single combat, deadly and uncompromising.[8]

Eugene Forçade writes in 1849 of conservative critics who felt that *Jane Eyre* 'bore the accent of revolt against certain social conventions . . . [and]

those writers who stand guard over the traditional values of English society were harsh in their denunciation of such tendencies'.[9]

Certainly, Forçade is right in his understanding of the connection between the roles currently ascribed to women and men and a social order in which there was a divinely ordained place for everyone. These places required the subordination of one sex to another and one class to another. It was left to the ineffably superior Elizabeth Rigby to spell out the link between *Jane Eyre* and social anarchy at the end of 1848, the year of Chartism at home and revolution abroad:

Altogether the autobiography of Jane Eyre is pre-eminently an anti-Christian composition. There is throughout a murmuring against the comforts of the rich and against the privations of the poor, which as far as each individual is concerned is a murmuring against God's appointment . . . There is that pervading tone of ungodly discontent which is at once the most prominent and the most subtle evil which the law and the pulpit, civilized society in fact at the present day has to contend with. We do not hesitate to say that the tone of mind and thought which has overthrown authority and violated every code human and divine abroad, and fostered Chartism and rebellion at home, is the same which has written Jane Eyre.[10]

These were the issues which the early critics bequeathed to their later successors. They include the construction of gender and its corollaries self-hood and identity; social class in a capitalist society; and the connection between the social order and religion. Only the inherent colonialism in *Jane Eyre* remained to be discovered. All three sisters were seen from the first to be subversive of the social order, but it was left to the late-twentieth-century critics to relate their subversions to the context with which they engaged. Meantime, when the necessary rankings were made, Charlotte took first place until the late nineteenth century.

By the 1880s, however, in the developing climate of aestheticism, Emily's strange novel, 'a fragment, yet of colossal proportion, and bearing evidence of some great design',[11] began to seem more interesting than Charlotte's. Strangeness was now sought; eccentricity and individuality were valued. By now, as the legal position of women improved, the daring nature of Charlotte's critique of the gender hierarchy was diminished. In 1883, Algernon Swinburne, a poet with a taste for the unconventional and for sado-masochism, took up Emily's cause and argued for her superiority: 'From the first we breathe the fresh dark air of tragic passion and presage; and to the last the changing wind and flying sunlight are in keeping with the stormy promise of the dawn',[12] possibly attracted by the 'emotional primitivism, violence and lack of a conventional moral standpoint'.[13] Swinburne claims the novel as a cry for liberty, comparable with *King Lear* or Aeschylus' *Eumenides*. He attributes 'genius' to Emily, a word which began to be automatically triggered by her name. In 1899, Mary Ward echoed Swinburne's evaluation, seeing *Wuthering Heights* as a work of superior power to Charlotte's and Shakespearean in its force. She too saw the two protagonists striving for liberty and 'the exaltation of the Self'.[14] This was a view of the novel that went down well in the early twentieth century, particularly in the post-war period of the 1920s and 1930s. Meantime, *Jane Eyre* had declined to the status of a great love story, particularly in the hands of film-makers who, by the 1930s, had produced some dozen versions of it.

Transition: Virginia Woolf

This trend towards the processing of *Jane Eyre* into camera-fodder was flouted by Virginia Woolf in 1929 in *A Room of One's Own*. In this essay she rehabilitated Charlotte's work in strikingly modern terms in the year after that in which women over the age of 21 were given the right to vote. In doing so, she laid the foundation for subsequent feminist criticism. Focusing on the needs of a woman writer for time of her own and a room of her own in order to write, she surveys female authors of the past. She only briefly mentions Emily, though in an interesting parallel between women and the working class: 'Yet genius of a sort must have existed among women as it must have existed among the working classes. Now and again an Emily Brontë or a Robert Burns blazes out and proves its presence.'[15]

Charlotte is the subject of a more extended and analytical account even though the account reverts to the practice of ranking to reinstate Charlotte at the top of the list in spite of her flaws. Woolf's essay gives a vivid account of how Charlotte evokes a perception of women's consciousness in the early nineteenth century. She places her firmly in a patriarchal society, and adds 'since a novel has this correspondence to real life, its values are to some extent those of real life. But it is obvious that the values of women differ very often from the values which have been made by the other sex; naturally this is so. Yet it is the masculine values that prevail'.[16] Consequently, as men have determined, women have been defined in their relation to men. Woolf sees this as changing in the early-nineteenth-century novel where the representation of women begins to become more varied and complicated in response to existing circumstances. She translates the early reviewers' bewilderment at the contradictions this change involved into a more intelligible form:

The whole structure, therefore, of the early nineteenth century novel was raised, if one was a woman, by a mind which was slightly pulled from the straight, and made to alter its clear vision by deference to external authority.[17]

In keeping with current critical practice, Woolf reads such novels as flawed by this inconsistency:

The writer was meeting criticism; she was saying this by way of aggression, or that by way of conciliation. She was admitting that she was 'only a woman', or protesting that she was 'as good as a man'. She met that criticism as her temperament dictated, with docility and diffidence, or with anger and emphasis. It does not matter which it was; she was thinking of something other than the thing itself. Down comes her book upon our heads. There was a flaw at the centre of it.[18]

As she applies this description to Charlotte's novels, she sees in them 'an acidity which is the result of oppression, a buried suffering smouldering beneath her passion, a rancour which contracts these books, splendid as they are, with a spasm of pain'.[19]

It is impossible to overestimate the significance of Woolf's prescient account on which post-1970s feminist criticism relies. The terms of her description are attributable to the traditional desire for flawless works, but nonetheless she finds the novels, contradictions and all, splendid. As the fading of 1950s organicist New Criticism subtracted from critical thinking the idea of internal contradictions as weaknesses, there remained Woolf's perception of the nature of Charlotte's work. This proved an important starting point.

POST-1970s CRITICISM

Femininity, class and colonialism

By the 1970s, many critics were looking at literature not in order to alter the 'canon' but to see the social meaning of literary texts. In doing so they took account of the fact established by linguists in the early decades of the century that language was not a transparent medium but loaded with the values and assumptions of the society it came from. One characteristic of the early instances of this kind of criticism is that they engage with a single issue. Marxists looked for the implications of how social class was represented; feminists gave their priority to the issue of gender; and post-colonialists read for the subject of race. By the 1980s the subjection of women in Victorian novels was seen to figure these other forms of oppression. This meant that Charlotte's novels in particular had relevance to all these varieties of critics as they sought not to evaluate and rank literary works but to tease out their meaning. The first three essays chosen here demonstrate the rather territorial attitude among critics that prevailed at the time.

The first of these is taken from Terry Eagleton's *Myths of Power* in which the lives of women in the Brontë texts are the medium, not the message. In this work, which was to qualify markedly in an introduction to a later edition, Eagleton continues the practice of ranking Charlotte and Emily. Although he speaks of the authors as 'socially insecure women', he is concerned with them, as his expansion of this phrase indicates, as 'members of a cruelly oppressed group'. He adds that their 'victimized condition reflected a more widespread exploitation'.[20] The exploitation he has in mind is not the male victimisation of women but the oppression of one social class by another in a rigidly hierarchical society. This is the context to which he returns the text, ignoring the fact that both writers and protagonists are women. He summarises the Brontës' social position in Marxist terms, presumably thinking of them in their fictional characters as governesses:

They felt, on the one hand, a fierce petty bourgeois bitterness for those idle gentry whose pampered offspring they were required to enlighten; they experienced on the other hand a patronizing distaste for the vulgar philistinism of the *nouveau riche*.[21]

He complicates this by arguing that, since their family was professional, not commercial, they felt culturally superior to those who had risen into the middle class through commercial and financial success. This combination of self-perceptions is said also to be mixed with 'a blunt exasperated criticism of the traditional gentry' which connects these women to 'the plain, taciturn, hard-headed world of the old yeomanry and the new industrial capitalists'.[22] At this time, Eagleton had not entirely abandoned the notion of unity as a requirement for literary success. Consequently his essay involves a comparison of the relative merits of Charlotte and Emily in their representation of the class system. The outcome is that he finds Emily's novel superior because it confronts the contradictions inherent in this class-based society but maintains 'a coherence of vision'.[23] Charlotte's work, by contrast, is a 'contradictory amalgam of smouldering rebelliousness and prim conventionalism'.[24]

This is almost a rewording of Woolf's account of the fluctuations in Charlotte's novels. But, unlike Woolf, Eagleton sees only their social class, as he has described it, as the issue which causes the women to feel the hunger, rebellion and rage that Matthew Arnold spoke of. Because they are governesses or private tutors, they are trapped in an ambiguous position: they are servants required to be subservient and deferential but as upper servants and teachers they are necessarily possessed of an imagination and culture that divides the self. He reads Charlotte's work as fudging this issue and Emily's as confronting it uncompromisingly.

Eagleton's volume, which he later recognised as gender-blind, was both innovative and influential. It begins to reinstate the Brontës' work in a specific context of which it constitutes a part. His concentration on class brings out the social structures inherent even in *Wuthering Heights*, a novel that in the past had been regarded as freakishly timeless. As he points out in his second edition, his critique predates the rise of feminist criticism in which the construction of femininity in a particular period is the message not the medium. One such influential work not yet published when Eagleton wrote *Myths of Power* sets out exclusively to dismantle patriarchal ideology. Sandra Gilbert and Susan Gubar's *The Madwoman in the Attic: The Woman Writer and Nineteenth-century Literary Imagination* shows that the authors continue the practice of discussing the Brontës' lives alongside their novels. They, too, aim to re-place the texts in a specific historical context which reclaims them for feminist as opposed to class-based criticism.

Gilbert and Gubar take as a motif the way that women relate to a 'patriarchal theory of literature' which has a long history. They wish to show how in such circumstances women writers struggle towards 'literary autonomy'.[25] They make the case for such struggles by looking back in a general way on early women writers, but Charlotte's work in particular is the focus of attention. Much of their discussion is more rhetorically based than was later to be the case with critics who were also context-orientated, such as the New Historicists. Within these terms, Gilbert and Gubar make a passionate and striking case. But if Eagleton is gender-blind, they are class-blind. There is little mention of social structures in their discussion of Jane Eyre's and Lucy Snowe's experience. It is hinted at briefly by implication when Jane is spurned by Blanche Ingram and the other society ladies. They focus instead on underlining the two women's sense of claustrophobic oppression which is echoed in other texts by women at the time. They do, however, share with Woolf and Eagleton a view of the victims' experience of the splitting of self as a consequence of oppressive circumstances. This is recognised in the alternation of the sense of oppression captured, say, by the red room in *Jane Eyre* with the rejection of the compliance that creates it.

Some later feminist critics pursue questions of self and subjectivity through the use of psychologically based criticism which involves accepting some theory of how selfhood is attained. In such work the mirror in which the subject sees herself imaged is a central feature. Gilbert and Gubar anticipate this when they draw attention to the mirror images in *Jane Eyre* which reflect Jane back to herself. The first is in the red room where the terrified child sees herself in the mirror as an alienated figure. Later there is a similar episode when Bertha Mason intrudes into Jane's room at night: 'Jane first clearly perceives her terrible double when Bertha puts on the wedding veil . . . At that moment Jane sees "the reflection of the visage and features quite distinctly in the dark oblong glass", sees them as distinctly as if they were her own'.[26] For Bertha, the two critics argue convincingly, is Jane's alter ego, the madwoman in the attic of patriarchal tyranny who gives this name to their book: 'on a figurative and psychological level it is suspiciously clear that the specter of Bertha is still another – indeed the most threatening avatar of Jane'.[27] Accordingly, every violent act perpetuated by Bertha that shatters the life at Thornfield is seen to figure Jane's repressed feelings of rebellion against the very limitations on her gender that she has internalised. The tearing of her wedding veil by Bertha is translated as the eruption of Jane's hidden anger at the mastery that Rochester claims over her.

The two conflicting aspects of Jane herself are also interpreted as figured by the two men whose relationships with her try to impose definition on her. Rochester equals fire – and all that implies, St John Rivers is a figure of the reason and logic by means of which Jane exerts control over her fiery self. Pursuing the image, Gilbert and Gubar cite her thoughts on what it would be like to be the wife of the priggish missionary and accompanying him to India. In considering this, Jane recognises that if she were to do so, she would be forced 'to keep the fire to my nature continually low . . . though the imprisoned flame consumed vital after vital'.[28] Similarly, the destruction of Thornfield by the fire Bertha lights is read as the fiery Jane's attempt to destroy Rochester's dominance and her own servitude. The authors are uncertain how to read the end of the narrative: as compromise or conquest? But they are tempted to argue that some figurative hint of optimism about the future holding a marriage of equals lies in the few closing images suggesting the healing power of nature.

The account of Bertha is strikingly written but involves a double paradox. She is supposed to represent Jane's dark side which fosters her rebellion against male dominance. Yet the fire which blinds and cripples Rochester is said to lead not just to Bertha's death but to the death of Jane's dark side which fortunately allows her to return (submit?) to him. A further contradiction in this text concerns the oppression of a woman who fails to qualify as a person, let alone a member of the female sex. For all the literal and metaphorical stress on Bertha's darkness, indicating that she is physically and morally sub-human, Gilbert and Gubar fail to see this as racism: her race apparently erases her humanity and gender. Later post-colonialist critics were to see this as a blindness more insidious than gender-blindness. It is for them the single issue. By sealing off Bertha from the other women in the text, Charlotte, they believe, writes an oppressive text. The essay given here by Joyce Zonana argues for *Jane Eyre* and earlier feminist critics along with it as racist: prepared to accept unquestionably that the non-white races are inferior, placed in the scheme of things closer to animals than to humanity. How can it be a cry for human equality when this lies at its core? Zonana characterises this use of eastern races as 'feminist orientalism'. She makes her case not figuratively but by applying logic to the images of the harem, of which several exist in the novel, to describe the Jane Eyre–Rochester relationship. When, against her wishes, he loads her with fine clothes and jewels, Jane is resentful: 'I thought his smile was such as a sultan might, in a blissful and fond moment, bestow on a slave his gold and gems had enriched'.[29] She feels degraded by what might appear to be a reward for anticipated sexual favours. Later Rochester is shown representing his relationship with Jane as that between a sultan and a slave in his harem: 'I would not exchange this one little English girl for the Grand Turk's whole seraglio – gazelle eyes, houri forms and all'.[30] He jokes in the same commercial terms of bargaining for 'so many tons of flesh and such an assortment of black eyes'.[31] Earlier critics were content to see the sultan–slave figure as an effective way of symbolising the status of women in the West. Zonana reads it differently, regarding such imagery as

a rhetorical strategy (and form of thought) by which a speaker or writer neutralizes the threat inherent in feminist demands and makes them palatable to an audience that wishes to affirm its occidental superiority.[32]

By this she implies that comparison between the condition of women in the West with those in an eastern harem means that the feminist desire to change that condition can be represented as 'a conservative effort' to slough off orientalism and 'make the West more like itself'.[33] Zonana follows Gilbert and Gubar in looking back at earlier women writers, but this is to trace a long lineage of 'feminist orientalism' that Charlotte Brontë inherits. Far from finding *Jane Eyre* a radical text, Zonana reads Charlotte as a feminist racist among many others. For Zonana, race erases questions of class and gender.

An approach which recognises but does not share in the competitiveness of critics preoccupied with one type of oppressive system rather than another is found in Penny Boumelha's book *Charlotte Brontë* from which the next extract is taken. She deals with all three types of interpretation discussed so far by allowing the texts to dictate the internal relationships between them. She points out that in *Jane Eyre* there is racism implicit in the fact that there is no reference to the slave trade on which the fortunes of all the central characters in the novel are based. Jane Eyre herself receives by inheritance just such a fortune which allows her to return to her proper place in society. Boumelha summarises the central problem of the novel as 'the apparently blithe predication of the liberty and happiness of the few upon the confinement and suffering of the many'.[34]

Her chapter on *Shirley* given here relates the two issues of gender and class by showing how working-class women are disadvantaged by both, erased and rendered voiceless. The chapter also extends the consideration of these subjects to take in other aspects of the novel as well as the figurative. This includes notably a detailed response to its language and critically to the intertextuality of the novel. Much of this analysis reveals how Shirley Keeldar and Caroline Helstone rewrite canonical male texts between themselves. By doing this they are able to use works such as the Bible and Shakespeare's plays as a means of imagined escape into work, adventure and freedom, in place of the tomb-like domesticity which entraps them. Boumelha shows how they extend the narrow horizons imposed by the concept of separate spheres into alternative worlds as they transform or interpret afresh what they read. In doing this, the two women sweep through past literature like a nineteenth-century Gilbert and Gubar, reading old texts from a female viewpoint. In this way, Boumelha's treatment is more comprehensive than most, though, like feminists in general, it remains vividly close to the texts.

All the post-1970s criticism discussed so far attempts, to varying degrees, to relate the Brontës' representation of femininity to its contemporary context, though early feminists took a simplistic view of the relationship between text and reality. A far more detailed and tightly argued approach to such a context is found in Sally Shuttleworth's seminal essay 'The constitution of neurosis in *Villette*'. Here she relates Lucy Snowe's mental and emotional movement towards selfhood to the ideas and language of nineteenth-century discourses on psychological medicine. This choice is not random: Shuttleworth is able to demonstrate Charlotte's familiarity with the literature of this particular discipline and her use of its language and ideas in *Villette*. She bases her method on the theories of New Historicists who argue that for too many centuries western philosophy accepted as fact a politically motivated construction of Reason. It is a construction which can be used to create a society willingly compliant with what is represented as reasonable because they have internalised the values it assumes. The concept is linked with the organisation of power and dominates all representational systems, including medicine and literature. There are other, sometimes complementary, representational systems that might have been chosen and later critics have pursued these.

Psychological medicine in the nineteenth century is shown in this account to deploy a definition of insanity in terms of reason and unreason. This led easily to the conclusion that since men were governed by reason and women by emotion, the latter were more vulnerable to crossing the border into insanity, a view with which Lucy Snowe is at least partly collusive because she has accepted it. Women's vulnerability was further increased by the physiology which determined that their nature should be governed by their reproductive function. It was therefore necessary to keep them under surveillance by external means and crucially by the encouragement of self-censorship. Shuttleworth demonstrates how Lucy attempts to control her own self-definition in the teeth of pressures of medical, institutional and religious surveillance. Under the stress of this she succumbs at first to an assumption that her mental turmoil means that she is unstable or neurotic. Later she characterises her infatuation with Dr John as the pathological state of monomania of 'chaste eroticism' which, through the repression of sexual desire, can lead to insanity. Lucy's attempt at such repression, in compliance with what she has internalised as reasonable, culminates in her symbolic burial of the doctor's prosaic letters. However, such acts alternate with rebellious impulses which find inspiration in the passionately imaginative acting of the tragic actress Vashti. As a result she begins to accept the value of imagination and emotion as against Reason. Shuttleworth sees the novel as a slow progress towards a control of selfhood by breaking 'the hierarchy of outer and inner life upon which definition of "the Real" (and sanity) depend according to the dictates of "Reason"'. She also points out that the intended marriage of equals between Lucy Snowe and M. Paul is never put to the test but left in abeyance. Lucy's emotional history is 'a challenge to the normative psychological definitions of "The Real"'.[35] Others have followed in Shuttleworth's tracks to relate *Villette* fruitfully to other contemporary discourses such as phrenology. Hers is a vividly illuminating account of the insights that such contextualising produces.

Authors and authorship

So far the subject of authorship has appeared only as a linking thread through successive periods. The curiosity about the identity of Currer, Acton and Ellis Bell was transferred, once the Brontës' names became public, to the sisters themselves and their lives. The connection between the lives and the novels was assumed to be apparent and fairly direct. This idea was reinforced by the fact that six of the novels had first-person narrators. Of these, William Crimsworth, Lucy Snowe, Gilbert Markham, Agnes Grey and Lockwood are all represented as authors of their own narratives. There is some equivocation about *Jane Eyre* since the title page claims that the work is edited by Currer Bell; and in the case of *The Professor* there is an opening sentence allegedly written by his friend, Charles, describing the text as the contents of a letter from Crimsworth. The interest in the Brontës flourished through succeeding decades until by the time of Virginia Woolf the traditional view of women writers as suited mainly to domestic fiction became an issue for protofeminists. Woolf's essay had a powerful effect, and by the time of *The Madwoman in the Attic* a more radical view of women's capacity for authorship had developed.

Recent criticism has focused on the issue, arguing in effect that the Brontës' novels confront the contemporary construction of women writers. This approach is illustrated by Susan Meyer's essay on *Agnes Grey*, an apparently conventional text. Meyer demonstrates that it is itself a form of social resistance to the patriarchal tradition. She reads the novel as challenging the silencing of women. The idea that women should be sparing of speech has a long history, but in nineteenth-century conduct books and other writing the idea of silence as womanly perfection is prominent. Sarah Ellis, a contemporary of the Brontës, wrote several such books in the early 1840s in which she discusses at length the kind of conversation that women should aspire to. They should facilitate rather than take a prominent role in it. They should not ride hobby horses or complain or make themselves prominent. Florence Nightingale later made sardonic reference to such instructions. But conduct books were only a very visible manifestation of the public silencing of women by excluding them from Parliament and the professions where they had no place. Meyer interprets *Agnes Grey* as in part an attack on this silencing both of women and of the supposedly inferior classes. Agnes herself belongs to a declassed group since she is the daughter of a woman who married 'beneath' her. On her husband's death, Mrs Grey's family are willing to restore her and her daughter to their own rank only if she will denounce her unfortunate marriage. Instead, Agnes becomes a governess or upper servant to support herself and her mother. She is now a member of the inferior sex and an inferior class. As Meyer reads it, the novel represents a contrast between the limitations on her speech imposed by her employers and the unrestrained way that she talks back in her narrative. She is instructed to acknowledge her social inferiority by prefixing Mr and Miss to the names of her troublesome young pupils. She is not to raise her voice to them nor is she to tell their mother of their faults. But her own account makes clear that the children behave barbarously, torturing birds and disparaging servants and local villagers to their faces by describing them as stupid and animal-like. Publicly Agnes submits, but privately she records and criticises these habits freely in her diary.

Meyer, however, believes that this resistance is countered by the conclusion of the novel which reverts to a conservative construction of a 'good' woman, since, when Agnes marries the clergyman Weston (whom no one else in her employer's family has recognised for the true Christian he is), she and her mother are restored to the class to which they belong. Agnes achieves the security of a middle-class status and home. The lack of ostentation in her new life is an implicit criticism of the feckless and indulgent families she has worked for. But, like Oliver Twist, she is the only one to escape from a life of inferiority shared by servants and working-class villagers. Once Weston has proposed, Agnes's protest ends and she appears ready to accept the prevailing ideology. Like his faithful dog, she too sees Weston as her master. She returns to the domestic hearth and silence with the words 'And now I think I have said sufficient'.[36] This compromise leaves her companions in distress where they were, as Oliver Twist left those in the workhouse.

A more precise attempt to read the treatment of authorship in a Brontë novel in a nineteenth-century context is made by Sharon Marcus in her article on abstraction and advertising in *Jane Eyre*. She points to a change in the construction of authorship which, as a result of changes in the material circumstances of publishing, distanced the reader from author and publisher. Improvements in printing, more rapid methods of book production and transport, and developments in advertising combined with a growing reading public to turn authorship into a more abstract affair, remote from readers. This effect is seen as part of the wider development in capitalist society of a process of alienation between government and governed, evident in increasing bureaucracy and the widespread reporting of social issues in terms of statistics. This abstraction of the process of communicating with readers is described by Marcus as normatively masculine in its mechanical economic logic. Because of this change, authorship is at odds with the contemporary femininity in which body, not mind, is seen to determine self.

Within this framework Marcus uses a Lacanian theory of the nature of such alienation as authorship is now seen to represent. The Lacanian view offered is that alienation is a positive, not a necessarily negative, state. On this reading, Jane Eyre, like Charlotte Brontë, recurrently suppresses her material being and so is able to trespass on masculine territory by rendering herself invisible. Charlotte wills her own invisibility by retreating behind the pseudonym Currer Bell. She retreats still further by describing the narrative as 'edited' by Bell. In effect she exploits the alienation and abstraction of authorship for her own purposes so that she and her fictional character 'cover' for each other. As the narrative progresses, Jane disembodies herself behind initials or a false name. When advertising her services or planning to advertise them in this way, she can become 'an economic actor'. She is 'the apparent author of her fate only when she alienates herself into writing, into advertisements and into an abstract professional body'.[37] Marcus does not see this abstraction into the marketplace as all gain for abstractee. Instead she believes that the rejection of the physical self is a demonstration that the split subject of Jane to which critics have referred is the necessary product of an imperial capitalist society for a radical woman author.

A reading of authorship that is similarly context-specific but very different in its approach to a novel by Charlotte is Toni Wein's article on intertextual connections between *Villette* and the Gothic text *The Monk* by Matthew Gregory 'Monk' Lewis (1796). Her piece is typical of a tendency in the 1990s to draw on the terminology of deconstruction without basing the critique itself on Derrida's theories. She makes almost metaphorical use of the terms 'substitution' and 'deferral' thought by deconstructionist critics to be the kinds of words describing slippage that have been devalued for too long by western philosophy. Wein argues for their relevance both to Charlotte Brontë's function as an author and to the structure of *Villette* itself. She reads the novel as a feminist rewriting of Charlotte's first novel *The Professor*, published after her death. This rewriting is, she implies, a bold reappropriation of a masculine text in a calculated slippage. She takes *The Monk* as a masculine text, not because the author is male but because of its construction. *The Professor* has a male first-person narrator for whom Charlotte substitutes a female as she turns a two-volume novel into the required three. Substitution as part of the plot is described in terms of female sexuality; and this is where deferral comes into Wein's interpretation. She believes that there is a sequence of deferral in the events of the narrative that invokes a female logic of desire. This replaces Lewis's masculine account in *The Monk* of what constitutes a 'sustained arousal of attentions until the narrative climax is reached'.[38] Lucy Snowe pursues the pattern of emotional deferral as she negotiates her relationship first with Dr John and then with M. Paul and at times with both.

The essay makes a close analysis of Lewis's novel as a story of substitutions. The central male, Ambrosio, substitutes a series of women for each other as his sexual partner but is haunted and possessed by the ghost of a female figure, a nun. Brontë appropriates the nun as one of Lucy's alter egos, using her to disembody sexual desire which is what she represents and again involves deferral. To Ambrosio, women, Wein argues, are simply counters seen as substitutable for one another in an economy of exchange. Through her revision, Charlotte erases and overrides the representation of women in commercial terms. Wein also equates the significance of Lewis's representation of women with the views expressed both by Charlotte's father Patrick and by the poet Robert Southey on the subject of the unsuitability of authorship for women. Both asserted that the domestic was a woman's natural and best role and that it was not the business of her life to aspire to be an author. The essay shows Charlotte claiming a right to such a career by engaging in it in order to twist a masculine text into a blatantly female narrative. The essays on authorship argue that Charlotte and Anne deploy skilful foot-work as they challenge the patriarchal tradition of authorship on its own ground.

Masculinity

By the 1980s the preoccupation with gender had extended its range to include masculinity as well as femininity, the gay as well as the straight. The trend shows up in Brontë studies in the shape of critiques of how the sisters represent masculinity. Two essays on this topic are included here. The one by Annette R. Federico starts in the obvious place with *The Professor* where the narrator is a man, William Crimsworth. Like other protagonists in Charlotte's *Jane Eyre* and *Villette*, he is a tutor – for most of the time in a girls' school in Belgium. He provides a parallel and a con-trast to both Jane Eyre and more particularly Lucy Snowe. The contrast lies in his reactions to his circumstances compared with hers. Federico aims to illuminate the culture's construction of gender by examining not its consequences for women but its consequences for men. She argues that the theory of separate spheres and all its baggage has costs for men as well as for women: it imposes limitations on the aspects of self they are supposed to possess. These taboo qualities are the opposites of their natural characteristics of fixity, dominance, confidence, competitiveness and stoicism. What they must repress are compassion or fellow-feeling, and respect for others' emotional sensibilities. Federico points out that Crimsworth possesses all the approved masculine traits and material circumstances. They derive from his upbringing and his public-school education which has left him with influential friends who will write effective letters of recommendation to potential employers. He is easily mobile and can take advantage of this to change his circumstances and, whatever these are, he maintains an unshakeable sense of his own super-iority and autonomy. Even his poverty at the opening of the novel is the result of masculine pride: his rich uncles will finance him only if he disowns his less well-born mother; he refuses their offer. At this point, though virtually enslaved as the employee of his vicious brother Edward, he retains an unshaken sense of superiority as to class and gender. His middle-class standing, even under pressure, asserts itself in the shabby treatment of servants. He does not equate Edward's other workers with himself and shows no signs of compassion or feeling for them. Federico believes that, in suppressing any softer emotions, he is like his blustering mentor, Hunsden, who can only turn what appear to be his homosocial feelings into sneering jokes. Federico does not recognise/examine the nature of this relationship; no doubt others will.

It is as a stereotypically masculine figure that William Crimsworth surveys his female Belgian pupils: he does so by assessing their physical attractions in sexist terms. Federico's argument is that Crimsworth is gradually introduced to fine feminine qualities in an English teacher, Frances Henri, and absorbs them from her. He also learns from the infatuation of Madame Reuter whose flattery turns to slavish adulation. He has seen tyranny in his brother Edward and felt its impact, but he now finds that the possession of a slave is turning him into the kind of tyrant he abhors: 'There was at once a sort of low gratification in receiving this luscious incense from an attractive and still young worshipper; and an irritating sense of degradation in the very experience of such pleasure'.[39] In recognising the sexually stimulating effect of power, Crimsworth is shaken in his belief in his fantasy that he is god-like. Throughout his experiences with these two different women, the portrait of his sensitive and gentle dead mother acts as both reproach and inspiration. She represents for him, at crucial moments, those supposedly feminine qualities that he learns to foster in himself. Federico sees signs of these in his positive treatment of Frances's wish to teach after their marriage and his hope that his own son will be compassionate and openly affectionate. The conclusion drawn is that what Brontë reveals by interrogating the construction of gender is the 'moral and emotional immunity' it involves for men.

The idea of 'feminising' men, used skilfully here, is fairly traditional. A more innovative approach to the nature of masculinity by Charlotte Brontë is found in Robert Kendrick's article on *Jane Eyre* and Jean Rhys's *Wide Sargasso Sea* (1966) which is its prequel. Rhys's novel is one of many dramatic and filmed adaptations, musical settings, as well as imitations, parallels and allusions to Charlotte's work. The article is original in both method and interpretation: Kendrick reads *Wide Sargasso Sea* and *Jane Eyre* in that order as a single text, with the later narrative representing events which lead up to Bertha's incarceration in the Thornfield attic. He believes that only in this way can the reader understand the depth and potential of Brontë's ethical revision of masculine subjectivity in *Jane Eyre*.

The essay draws on the Lacanian-based model of subjectivity in which self-identity is split internally since it is formed by an idea of dialectic of self and other than self because it is dependent on the other to reflect the desired identity and confirm it. Looked at in this framework, Rochester's masculinity is unstable. As a son of the landed gentry, he has strong claims to be a gentleman; but as a younger son, he has neither estate nor money to support these claims. In the new society, Jamaica, these lacks are even more apparent and he tries to meet them by marrying Antoinette, the wealthy daughter of an ex-slave-holder and his Creole wife. He needs a wife who will restore him to his proper standing but Antoinette is not such a wife because her status, like his, is unstable in her own community: she belongs to neither white nor Creole community. Though Rochester tries to turn her into a normal pretty English wife and renames her Bertha, he cannot accept her as a wife and an equal, especially when he discovers a genetic inheritance of madness and alcoholism.

He breaks away from her in disgust and, on returning to England, has no other resource to try to reassert himself as a member of the landed gentry with her money than to imprison her out of sight in the attic. Even there, however, her presence naggingly reminds him of his fractured subjectivity in all its uncertainty. In Kendrick's account, Rochester needs Jane Eyre as his refined English wife; she will not serve when only a governess to act as his reflecting other. So he remains unstable, volatile, bitter, uncertain of holding his proper place. Kendrick argues that the marriage of Rochester and Jane is ambiguous since Charlotte Brontë provides only a provisional solution which leaves open the question of the power hierarchy between the two. He finds his evidence in Rochester's final verbal acceptance of divine justice which, Kendrick claims, leaves open the question of who is to be master. In relating the novel to a later work, the essay opens the way to the use of film and other adaptations as a source of fresh interpretations and insights.

Form and structure

Early reviews of the Brontës' novels make only superficial comments on the way they are constructed. Their references treat the subject as a matter of aesthetic pleasure or a question of plausibility and both these approaches assume a reflectionist model of literature. In the twentieth century, formalist writers went to the other extreme and focused on form above all else. They aimed to describe the characters of different genres and discourses and in doing so drew attention to them in a way that has been useful to later approaches. These critics included those concerned with the social meaning of texts, who were interested in considering how their formal features affected their significance. This much of formalism has generally been taken on board: the next essays chosen are three which deploy analyses of the structural aspects of narratives as prominent parts of their interpretations. The third of them also suggests that *Wuthering Heights* has an innovative structure, a feature that increases the potential of novelists' techniques.

Given their convoluted structures, it is not surprising that *The Tenant of Wildfell Hall* and *Wuthering Heights* have attracted this kind of discussion. Like *Jane Eyre* and *Villette*, both follow in the Gothic tradition of sensational plots but, unlike Charlotte's work, they involve details of much brutality. Jacobs's article reads them as more radical than *Jane Eyre* and *Villette* in their treatment of gender, for, she believes, although Charlotte criticised domestic ideology, she finally 'eroticized the very dominance/submission dynamic from which she longed to escape'.[40] By contrast, Emily and Anne are said to go beyond the categories of gender formulated by their culture and see them as 'a ragged and somewhat ridiculous masquerade'.[41] This critique, she believes, is largely effected by the structuring of each of the novels.

The domestic ideal was supposedly typified by the middle-class home, where peace and order reigned. Both Emily and Anne's novels have such a place at their centre. But surrounding each is a framing narrative which examines and exposes the nature of that central core. Far from being ideal havens supporting a sturdy social framework, these interiors are sites of unfailing male violence in *Wuthering Heights*, and of dissipation, drunkenness, open adultery and physical brutality against women in *The Tenant of Wildfell Hall*. Jacobs emphasises that the frames which surround these lurid accounts are not a means of detaching the reader from the horrors. Instead they offer not picture frames but alternative pictures of the male narrators, Markham and Lockwood. The organisation of the novels into these double structures makes comparison between the two parts inevitable. An innocent reading might start from the assumption that a contrast is implied between the two, but the texts soon dispel this idea. The narrators are not benign domestic figures who throw the infamy of Heathcliff and Huntingdon into relief. On the contrary, Gilbert Markham is revealed as a man who shows the same masculine characteristics as Helen's first husband: he is vain, arrogant, domineering and hot-tempered. He treats women as inferiors, there to serve and flatter him. In subjecting Helen's brother to an unprovoked attack through a fit of jealousy, he shows a violence more extreme than Heathcliff's. His characteristics are precisely those which have produced the domestic hell in which Helen finds herself once married to Huntingdon. Her first and second husbands share the same 'masculinity'.

A similar strategy is discernible in *Wuthering Heights* which frames its violent interior with an apparently innocent narrator faced with such behaviour. In fact, Jacobs believes, Lockwood colludes with it by shutting his eyes to what is really going on. Hence the ridiculous assumption to which at first he clings that Heathcliff is a hospitable host and the Heights a cosy refuge. His capacity to remain uninvolved mirrors his reaction to the woman he fell in love with before coming to the Grange: when she 'looked a return' he 'shrank icily into [him]self, like a snail'. His reaction to a sight of the pretty second Catherine is to size her up as a possible partner. Violence seems to pass him by and he does not altogether disapprove of Hareton striking the girl. Though he appears mild, his dream of the first Catherine's ghost reveals his capacity for violence as he wrenches her wrist along broken glass until it bleeds. Jacobs concludes from this that Lockwood embodies the very ideology that justifies the violence. She also sees it as significant that in both novels it is women who strip away the frame that conceals the true state of affairs in these middle-class homes: Helen describes the horrors in her diary and Nelly Dean tells the details to Lockwood. It is this revelation of what really lies behind society as currently organised that Jacobs reads into the structure of the two novels. She also argues somewhat controversially that both novels end with some version of domestic harmony in the marriages of Helen and Gilbert Markham and of Hareton and Catherine, without clearly weighing these against the rest of the narratives.

O'Toole's essay on *The Tenant of Wildfell Hall* is in effect a critique of Jacobs's. She discusses 'the narrative architecture of the novel' and, like Jacobs, examines it in terms of comparisons implied by the structure. But, for her, there is a double comparison to be made in the parallels between the relationship of Helen and her brother and those she has with Huntingdon and Markham, both of whom treat her badly, though in different ways. The significance of the comparisons these visibly offer is said to be the superiority of the relationship between female and male siblings rather than that between heterosexual lovers. This reading does not assume, as Jacobs does, that Markham is a New Man when he marries or that he has been redeemed from his vices by reading Helen's diary. Although his attitude to her has changed, his attitude to women in general remains the same for it is an extension of himself that he proposes to care for his wife. The implication is that she chooses as a second husband a man as capable of mistreating her as the first.

O'Toole argues that the marriage to Gilbert is not the place to look for a positive alternative to the Huntingdons' marriage. That is to be found in the familial relationship to which Helen returns with her son when in flight from her first husband. She goes back to her brother and reassumes the family name. It is Frederick who treats her with the care a husband is supposed to show. Significantly he does not respond with violence or a desire for revenge when Markham attacks him. He reveals, at least in his relationship with Helen, a different kind of masculinity, but that, O'Toole believes, is the point. Although the brother–sister relationship temporarily redeems a compromised domestic sphere, it is not implied that this bond is a panacea for all the ills that undermine marital domesticity. It merely facilitates an uneasy account of how men relate to women with whom they are in sexual partnership.

In the third of these essays, Rebecca Steinitz also bases her reading on analysis of the structure of *Wuthering Heights*. Where Jacobs interprets it through a comparison between Lockwood and the men at the Heights, Steinitz focuses on the diaries of Lockwood and the first Catherine. This essay also draws on Emily's diary fragments to consider the potential of diaries as a fictional device. Steinitz resists the common practice of merging these diaries into all other references to texts in the novel and argues for them as important structural elements in their own right. The two mirror the separate spheres to which their two writers belong. Lockwood is the cool and detached observer and, as its author, apparently the controlling force in the novel. On the other hand, Catherine's diary is a small material object, written in a childish hand and defaced by time. Its condition signals her marginality but is, by contrast with Lockwood's, a record of vivid subjective experience. Psychologically as well as physically, it is the inner text to Lockwood's outer.

Steinitz moves on to consider the nature and potential of diaries generally. She argues that earlier novels used diaries as a way of marking and ordering time, particularly when there were daily entries. She characterises two forms of time: the 'tick tick tick' of daily recording and the 'tock' or peal of occasional time, marking the insertion of only significant events.[42] Both suggest an open-ended sequence that precludes closure. But in addition to what it offers in the way of dealing with time, a diary is an apparent opportunity for writers to realise desires on the blank sheets of the future. Steinitz sees this desire in *Wuthering Heights* as a struggle to find a place. The struggle may be physical, as in Lockwood's need of a bed for the night or for the ownership of the Heights itself, or an emotional search such as that of Catherine and Heathcliff. On this reading, each individual finds herself or himself displaced; and as with the open-ended diary, displacement never ends. Diaries are thus an attempt to control place as much as time. Steinitz argues that the diary becomes a place of one's own, 'but its very status reveals how psychologically, textually and materially, one's own place can never be secured'.[43] There is, of course, here an allusion to the endless deferral that deconstruction deploys. Emily is seen as reshaping the cultural significance of diaries in a way that extends their potential use in fiction, since they are the site where time and place intersect.

PATTERNS OF CRITICISM

The essays in this volume are an illustration of the many and varied readings that have been offered for the Brontës' novels. The texts have been a rich source of social meanings for critics who looked for them. This is not surprising since they are usually expanding on the subversiveness already recognised by the earliest reviewers. But the essays are not so conflicting as might at first appear, except in so far as Marxist, feminist and post-colonialist critics privilege one strand in the novels over the others.

In unearthing the issues of class, gender and race, most critics have seen themselves as relating a novel to its social context. Marxists produce an analysis of the Brontës' capitalist society to provide a matrix which explains their treatment of class. Feminists give accounts of the nineteenth-century construction of gender in order to dismantle it or to demonstrate that a text partly does this. Post-colonialists disinter the racism inherent in the treatment of non-Europeans in the Brontës' writing, as well as in critics' readings. All see themselves as clarifying the treatment of these issues in the novels but, as has long been recognised, meaning is the joint product of text and reader. And readers as well as texts have contexts. The later interpretations included here are possible only for readers whose take on a novel is determined by their own contexts.

Since evaluation of texts and ranking are no longer critical issues, interpretations, as Zonana's article shows, are ammunition in ideological conflicts. In any attempt to predict the prospects for future Brontë criticism, it is necessary to speculate tentatively about possible launching pads for future debates. Some of the essays included here may point to such areas. Kendrick's and Federico's articles broach the subject of gender studies now expanded into the construction of masculinity and sexuality. Another related area is that of homosexual ties, as exemplified by Crimsworth and Hunsden in *The Professor*; and the triangular relationships between Heathcliff, Edgar Linton and Catherine Earnshaw; Gilbert Markham, Frederick Lawrence and Helen Huntingdon. Similarly, further exploration of class issues as seen from a late capitalist society, or race as constructed from a new imperialist position seems possible for the future. At the same time, the use of prequels, sequels and film adaptations as a way of challenging other readers' ideological positions also seems a likely way forward. Certainly there seems no reason to expect a drying up of new readings for novels which have proved such fertile ground for many modern approaches.

NOTES

1. Miriam Allott, *The Brontës: The Critical Heritage* (London: Routledge & Kegan Paul, 1974), p. 111.
2. Ibid., p. 163.
3. Ibid., p. 98.
4. Ibid., p. 228.
5. Ibid., p. 223.
6. Ibid., pp. 233–4.
7. Ibid., p. 123.
8. Ibid., p. 313.
9. Ibid., p. 143.
10. Ibid., pp. 109–10.
11. Ibid., p. 226.
12. Ibid., p. 439.
13. Lucasta Miller, *The Brontë Myth* (London: Jonathan Cape, 2001), pp. 209–10.
14. Allott, p. 457.
15. Virginia Woolf, *A Room of One's Own* (London: Hogarth Press, 1929), pp. 209–10.
16. Ibid., p. 110.
17. Ibid., p. 111.
18. Ibid., p. 111.
19. Ibid., p. 110.
20. Terry Eagleton, *Myths of Power: A Marxist Study of the Brontës*, 2nd edn (Basingstoke: Macmillan, 1988), p. 8.
21. Ibid., p. 11.
22. Ibid., p. 11.
23. Ibid., p. 98.
24. Ibid., p. 16.
25. Sandra Gilbert and Susan Gubar, *The Madwoman in the Attic: The Woman Writer and Nineteenth-century Literary Imagination* (New Haven, Conn.: Yale Univ. Press, 1979), p. 16.
26. Ibid., p. 362.
27. Ibid., p. 359.
28. Ibid., p. 366.
29. Joyce Zonana, 'The Sultan and the Slave: Feminist Orientalism and the Structure of *Jane Eyre*', *Signs* 18.3 (1994): 16.
30. Ibid., p. 596.
31. Ibid., p. 597.
32. Ibid., p. 594.
33. Ibid., p. 594.
34. Penny Boumelha, *Charlotte Brontë* (Hemel Hempstead: Harvester Wheatsheaf, 1990), p. 62.

35. Sally Shuttleworth, *Charlotte Brontë and Nineteenth Century Psychology* (Cambridge: Cambridge University Press, 1996), p. 332.

36. Susan Meyer, '"Words on Great Vulgar Sheets": Writing and Social Resistance in Anne Brontë's *Agnes Grey*' in Susan Meyer (ed.) *The New Nineteenth Century: Feminist Readings of Underread Victorian Fiction* (New York: Garland, 1996), p. 15.

37. Sharon Marcus, 'The Profession of the Author: Abstraction, Advertising and *Jane Eyre*', *PMLA* 110.2 (1996): 209.

38. Toni Wein, 'Gothic Desire in Charlotte Brontë's *Villette*', *Studies in English Literature* 39.4 (1999): 735.

39. Annette R. Federico, 'The Other Case: Gender and Narration in Charlotte Brontë's *The Professor*', *Papers on Language and Literature* 30.4 (1994): 340.

40. N.M. Jacobs, 'Gendered and Layered Narrative in *Wuthering Heights* and *The Tenant of Wildfell Hall*', *Journal of Narrative Technique* 16.3 (1986): 204.

41. Ibid., pp. 204–5.

42. Rebecca Steinitz, 'Diaries and Displacement in *Wuthering Heights*', *Studies in the Novel* 334.2 (2000): 409.

43. Ibid., p. 408.

CHAPTER ONE

Wuthering Heights

TERRY EAGLETON

Terry Eagleton was until recently Wharton Professor of English at the University of Oxford and is now Professor of English at Manchester University. He is one of the foremost literary critics of the day. His gradual changes in approach and increasing interest in the development of literary and cultural theory are reflected in the many works he has written, including *Criticism and Ideology*, *Marxism and Literary Criticism*, *The Rape of Clarissa*, *The Function of Criticism* and, most recently, *The Idea of Culture*. The chapter here is from an early book, *Myths of Power: A Marxist Study of the Brontës* (1975). The account of *Wuthering Heights* is more singlemindedly Marxist in its concentration on class struggle than his later works. He recognises this himself in his introduction to a second edition of the work in 1988. It stands as a classical Marxist reading, all the more striking for its account of the social classes represented by a narrative previously regarded as relatively isolated from class issues and society generally. It reads the tangled lives of the Earnshaws and the Lintons as a clash between the traditional yeoman economy and rising capitalists. He sees Heathcliff as an outsider who becomes a pitiless capitalist landlord who aims to avenge himself on both groups.

   At this stage in his work, Eagleton evaluates texts in a way he was later to abandon, and so sees *Wuthering Heights* as superior to Charlotte Brontë's novels in its refusal to compromise and provide an optimistic outcome for the narrative.

Reprinted from *Myths of Power: A Marxist Study of the Brontës*, 2nd edn (Basingstoke: Macmillan, 1988), pp. 97–121.

I f it is a function of ideology to achieve an illusory resolution of real contradictions, then Charlotte Brontë's novels are ideological in a precise sense – myths. In the fabulous, fairy-tale ambience of a work like *Jane Eyre*, with its dramatic archetypes and magical devices, certain facets of the complex mythology which constitutes Victorian bourgeois consciousness find their aesthetically appropriate form. Yet 'myth' is, of course, a term more commonly used of *Wuthering Heights*; and we need therefore to discriminate between different meanings of the word.

For Lucien Goldmann, 'ideology' in literature is to be sharply distinguished from what he terms 'world-view'. Ideology signifies a false, distortive, partial consciousness; 'world-view' designates a true, total and coherent understanding of social relations. This seems to me a highly suspect formulation: nothing, surely, could be more ideological than the 'tragic vision' of Pascal and Racine which Goldmann examines in *The Hidden God*. Even so, Goldmann's questionable distinction can be used to illuminate a crucial difference between the work of Charlotte and Emily Brontë. Charlotte's fiction is 'mythical' in the exact ideological sense I have suggested: it welds together antagonistic forces, forging from them a pragmatic, precarious coherence of interests. *Wuthering Heights* is mythical in a more traditional sense of the term: an apparently timeless, highly integrated, mysteriously autonomous symbolic universe. Such a notion of myth is itself, of course, ideologically based, and much of this chapter will be an attempt to de-mystify it. The world of *Wuthering Heights* is neither eternal nor self-enclosed; nor is it in the least unriven by internal contradictions. But in the case of this work it does seem necessary to speak of a 'world-view', a unified vision of brilliant clarity and consistency, in contrast to the dominant consciousness of Charlotte's novels. Goldmann's distinction is valuable to that limited extent: it enforces an appropriate contrast between the elaborated impersonality of Emily's novel, the 'intensive totality' of its world,[1] and Charlotte's tendentious, occasionally opportunist manipulation of materials for ideological ends, her readiness to allow a set of practical interests to predominate over the demands of disinterested exploration. If *Wuthering Heights* generally transcends those limits, it is not in the least because its universe is any less ideological, or that conflictive pressures are absent from it. The difference lies in the paradoxical truth that *Wuthering Heights* achieves its coherence of vision from an exhausting confrontation of contending forces, whereas Charlotte's kind of totality depends upon a pragmatic integration of them. Both forms of consciousness are ideological; but in so far as Emily's represents a more penetrative, radical and honest enterprise, it provides the basis for a finer artistic achievement. *Wuthering Heights* remains formally unfissured by the conflicts it dramatises; it forges its unity of vision from the very imaginative heat those conflicts generate. The book's genealogical structure is relevant here: familial relations at once provide the substance of antagonism and mould that substance into intricate shape, precipitating a tightly integrated form from the very stuff of struggle and disintegration. The genealogical structure, moreover, allows for a sharply dialectical relation between the 'personal' and 'impersonal' of a sort rare in Charlotte: the family, at once social institution and domain of intensely interpersonal relationships, highlights the complex interplay between an evolving system of given unalterable relations and the creation of individual value.

One is tempted, then, to credit Goldmann's dubious dichotomy between ideology and world-view to this extent: that if 'ideology' is a coherence of antagonisms, 'world-view' is a coherent perception of them.* An instance of such coherent perception may be found in Emily Brontë's early essay, 'The Butterfly':

All creation is equally insane. There are those flies playing above the stream, swallows and fish diminishing their number each minute: these will become in their turn, the prey of some tyrant of air or water; and man for his amusement or his needs will kill their murderers. Nature is an inexplicable puzzle, life exists on a principle of destruction; every creature must be the relentless instrument of death to the others, or himself cease to live.[2]

This, clearly enough, is ideological to the point of prefiguring Social Darwinism; but it is difficult to imagine Charlotte having written with this degree of generalising impersonal poise, this fluent projection of fearful private vision into total, lucid statement. Charlotte, indeed, seems to have recognised something of this difference with her sister. 'In some points', she once wrote, 'I consider Emily somewhat of a theorist; now and then she broaches ideas which strike my sense as much more daring and original than practical.'[3] Defining the issue as a contrast between theory and practice seems significant: the cautious empiricist greets the totalising visionary with a mixture of respect and reservation. It certainly seems true of Charlotte that her *imaginative* daring is not coupled with any equivalent moral or intellectual boldness. Hunsden, Rochester, Shirley, Paul Emmanuel: all combine a civilised moderation with their Romantic radicalism, which could hardly be said of Heathcliff. Heathcliff, as Lockwood finds to his cost, is precisely *not* a rough diamond; he conceals no coy Hunsden-like affection beneath his barbarous behaviour.

* A coherence which is partial, limited, defined as much by its absences and exclusions as by its affirmations, and so (*pace* Goldmann) ideological.

The difference between Charlotte and Emily can be expressed another way. The spite, violence and bigotry which in *Wuthering Heights* are aspects of the narrative are in parts of Charlotte's fiction qualities of the narration. *Wuthering Heights* trades in spite and stiff-neckedness, but always 'objectively', as the power of its tenaciously detailed realism to survive unruffled even the gustiest of emotional crises would suggest. Malice and narrowness in Charlotte's work, by contrast, are occasionally authorial as well as thematic, so that characters and events are flushed with the novelist's ideological intentions, bear the imprint of her longings and anxieties. This, as I have argued, is less true of *Jane Eyre*, where a subtler epistemology grants the objective world its own relative solidity: we feel the menacingly autonomous existence of Brocklehurst, Mrs Reed, even Bertha, as we do not with Père Silas, Madame Walravens or Job Barraclough. Because these figures are so directly the spontaneous precipitates of authorial fantasy, they have both the vividness and the vacuity of Lucy Snowe's dazed perceptions. We are almost never at a loss what to think about a Charlotte character, which could hardly be said of *Wuthering Heights*. No mere critical hair-splitting can account for the protracted debate over whether Heathcliff is hero or demon, Catherine tragic heroine or spoilt brat, Nelly Dean shrewd or stupid. The narrative techniques of the novel are deliberately framed to preserve these ambivalences; those of Charlotte Brontë allow us fairly direct access to a single, transparent, controlling consciousness which maintains its dominance even when its bearer is in practice subdued and subordinated.

I have said that *Wuthering Heights* remains unriven by the conflicts it releases, and it contrasts as such with those Charlotte works which are formally flawed by the strains and fictions of their 'content'. Charlotte's fiction sets out to reconcile thematically what I have crudely termed 'Romance' and 'realism' but sometimes displays severe structural disjunctions between the two; *Wuthering Heights* fastens thematically on a near-absolute antagonism between these modes but achieves, structurally and stylistically, an astonishing unity between them. Single incidents are inseparably high drama and domestic farce, figures like Catherine Earnshaw contradictory amalgams of the passionate and the pettish. There seems to me an ideological basis to this paradoxical contrast between the two sisters' works. Charlotte's novels, as I have suggested, are ideological in that they exploit fiction and fable to smooth the jagged edges of real conflict, and the evasions which that entails emerge as aesthetic unevennesses – as slanting, overemphasis, idealisation, structural dissonance. *Wuthering Heights*, on the other hand, confronts the tragic truth that the passion and society it presents are not fundamentally reconcilable – that there remains at the deepest level an ineradicable contradiction between them which refuses to be unlocked, which obtrudes itself as the very stuff and secret of experience. It is, then, precisely the imagination capable of confronting this tragic duality which has the power to produce the aesthetically superior work – which can synchronise in its internal structures the most shattering passion with the most rigorous realist control. The more authentic social and moral recognitions of the book, in other words, generate a finer artistic control; the unflinchingness with which the novel penetrates into fundamental contradictions is realised in a range of richer imaginative perceptions.

The primary contradiction I have in mind is the choice posed for Catherine between Heathcliff and Edgar Linton. That choice seems to me the pivotal event of the novel, the decisive catalyst of the tragedy; and if this is so, then the crux of *Wuthering Heights* must be conceded by even the most remorselessly mythological and mystical of critics to be a social one. In a crucial act of self-betrayal and bad faith, Catherine rejects Heathcliff as a suitor because he is socially inferior to Linton; and it is from this that the train of destruction follows. Heathcliff's own view of the option is not, of course, to be wholly credited: he is clearly wrong to think that Edgar 'is scarcely a degree dearer [to Catherine] than her dog, or her horse'.[4] Linton lacks spirit, but he is, as Nelly says, kind, honourable and trustful, a loving husband to Catherine and utterly distraught at her loss. Even so, the perverse act of *mauvaise foi* by which Catherine trades her authentic selfhood for social privilege is rightly denounced by Heathcliff as spiritual suicide and murder:

'*Why* did you betray your own heart, Cathy? I have not one word of comfort. You deserve this. You have killed yourself. Yes, you may kiss me, and cry; and ring out my kisses and tears: they'll blight you – they'll damn you. You loved me – then what *right* had you to leave me? What right – answer me – for the poor fancy you felt for Linton? Because misery and degradation, and death, and nothing that God or Satan could inflict would have parted us, *you*, of your own will, did it. I have not broken your heart – *you* have broken it; and in breaking it, you have broken mine.'[5]

Like Lucy Snowe, Catherine tries to lead two lives: she hopes to square authenticity with social convention, running in harness an ontological commitment to Heathcliff with a phenomenal relationship to Linton. 'I *am* Heathcliff!' is dramatically arresting, but it is also a way of keeping the outcast at arm's length, evading the challenge he offers. If Catherine is Heathcliff – if identity rather than relationship is in question – then their estrangement is inconceivable, and Catherine can therefore turn to others without violating the timeless metaphysical idea Heathcliff embodies. She finds in him an integrity of being denied or diluted in routine social relations; but to preserve that ideal means reifying him to a Hegelian essence, sublimely untainted by empirical fact. Heathcliff, understandably, refuses to settle for this: he would rather enact his essence in existence by becoming Catherine's lover. He can, it seems, be endowed with impressive ontological status only at the price of being nullified as a person.

The uneasy alliance of social conformity and personal fulfilment for which Charlotte's novels works is not, then, feasible in the world of *Wuthering Heights*; Catherine's attempt to compromise unleashes the contradictions which will drive both her and Heathcliff to their deaths. One such contradiction lies in the relation between Heathcliff and the Earnshaw family. As a waif and orphan, Heathcliff is inserted into the close-knit family structure as an alien; he emerges from that ambivalent domain of darkness which is the 'outside' of the tightly defined domestic system. That darkness is ambivalent because it is at once fearful and fertilising, as Heathcliff himself is both gift and threat. Earnshaw's first words about him make this clear: ' "See here, wife! I was never so beaten with anything in my life: but you must e'en take it as a gift of God; though it's as dark almost as if it came from the devil." '[6] Stripped as he is of determinate social relations, of a given function within the family, Heathcliff's presence is radically gratuitous; the arbitrary, unmotivated event of his arrival at the Heights offers its inhabitants a chance to transcend the constrictions of their self-enclosed social structure and gather him in. Because Heathcliff's circumstances are so obscure he is available to be accepted or rejected simply for himself, laying claim to no status other than a human one. He is, of course, proletarian in appearance, but the obscurity of his origins also frees him of any exact social role; as Nelly Dean muses later, he might equally be a prince. He is ushered into the Heights for no good reason other than to be arbitrarily loved; and in this sense he is a touchstone of others' responses, a liberating force for Cathy and a stumbling-block for others. Nelly hates him at first, unable to transcend her bigotry against the new and non-related; she puts him on the landing like a dog, hoping he will be gone by morning. Earnshaw pets and favours him, and in doing so creates fresh inequalities in the family hierarchy which become the source of Hindley's hatred. As heir to the Heights, Hindley understandably feels his social role subverted by this irrational, unpredictable intrusion.

Catherine, who does not expect to inherit, responds spontaneously to Heathcliff's presence; and because this antagonises Hindley she becomes after Earnshaw's death a spiritual orphan as Heathcliff is a literal one. Both are allowed to run wild; both become the 'outside' of the domestic structure. Because his birth is unknown, Heathcliff is a purely atomised

individual, free of generational ties in a novel where genealogical relations are of crucial thematic and structural importance; and it is because
he is an internal *émigré* within the Heights that he can lay claim to a relationship of direct personal equality with Catherine who, as the daughter
of the family, is the least economically integral member. Heathcliff offers
Catherine a friendship which opens fresh possibilities of freedom within
the internal system of the Heights; in a situation where social determinants are insistent, freedom can mean only a relative independence of
given blood-ties, of the settled, evolving, predictable structures of kinship.
Whereas in Charlotte's fiction the severing or lapsing of such relations
frees you for progress up the class-system, the freedom which Cathy
achieves with Heathcliff takes her down that system, into consorting
with a 'gypsy'. Yet 'down' is also 'outside', just as gypsy signifies 'lower
class' but also a social vagrant, classless natural life-form. As the eternal
rocks beneath the woods, Heathcliff is both lowly and natural, enjoying
the partial freedom from social pressures appropriate to those at the
bottom of the class-structure. In loving Heathcliff, Catherine is taken
outside the family and society into an opposing realm which can be
adequately imaged only as 'Nature'.

The loving equality between Catherine and Heathcliff stands, then,
as a paradigm of human possibilities which reach beyond, and might
ideally unlock, the tightly dominative system of the Heights. Yet at the
same time Heathcliff's mere presence fiercely intensifies that system's
harshness, twisting all the Earnshaw relationships into bitter antagonism.
He unwittingly sharpens a violence endemic to the Heights – a violence
which springs both from the hard exigencies imposed by its struggle with
the land, and from its social exclusiveness as a self-consciously ancient,
respectable family. The violence which Heathcliff unwittingly triggers
is turned against him: he is cast out by Hindley, culturally deprived,
reduced to the status of farm-labourer. What Hindley does, in fact, is
to invert the potential freedom symbolised by Heathcliff into a parody of
itself, into the non-freedom of neglect. Heathcliff is robbed of liberty in
two antithetical ways: exploited as a servant on the one hand, allowed to
run wild on the other; and this contradiction is appropriate to childhood,
which is a time of relative freedom from convention and yet, paradoxically, a phase of authoritarian repression. In this sense there is freedom
for Heathcliff neither within society nor outside it; his two conditions are
inverted mirror-images of one another. It is a contradiction which encap-
sulates a crucial truth about bourgeois society. If there is no genuine
liberty on its 'inside' – Heathcliff is oppressed by work and the familial
structure – neither is there more than a caricature of liberty on the 'outside',
since the release of running wild is merely a function of cultural

impoverishment. The friendship of Heathcliff and Cathy crystallises under the pressures of economic and cultural violence, so that the freedom it seems to signify ('half-savage and hardy, and free'[7]) is always the other face of oppression, always exists in its shadow. With Heathcliff and Catherine, as in Charlotte's fiction, bitter social reality breeds Romantic escapism; but whereas Charlotte's novels try to trim the balance between them, *Wuthering Heights* shows a more dialectical interrelation at work. Romantic intensity is locked in combat with society, but cannot wholly transcend it; your freedom is bred and deformed in the shadow of your oppression, just as, in the adult Heathcliff, oppression is the logical consequence of the exploiter's 'freedom'.

Just as Hindley withdraws culture from Heathcliff as a mode of domination, so Heathcliff acquires culture as a weapon. He amasses a certain amount of cultural capital in his two years' absence in order to shackle others more effectively, buying up the expensive commodity of gentility in order punitively to re-enter the society from which he was punitively expelled. This is liberty of a kind, in contrast with his previous condition; but the novel is insistent on its ultimately illusory nature. In oppressing others the exploiter imprisons himself; the adult Heathcliff's systematic tormenting is fed by his victims' pain but also drains him of blood, impels and possesses him as an external force. His alienation from Catherine estranges him from himself to the point where his brutalities become tediously perfunctory gestures, the mechanical motions of a man who is already withdrawing himself from his own body. Heathcliff moves from being Hindley's victim to becoming, like Catherine, his own executioner.

Throughout *Wuthering Heights*, labour and culture, bondage and freedom, Nature and artifice appear at once as each other's dialectical negations and as subtly matched, mutually reflective. Culture – gentility – is the opposite of labour for young Heathcliff and Hareton; but it is also a crucial economic weapon, as well as a product of work itself. The delicate spiritless Lintons in their crimson-carpeted drawing-room are radically severed from the labour which sustains them; gentility grows from the production of others, detaches itself from that work (as the Grange is separate from the Heights), and then comes to dominate the labour on which it is parasitic. In doing so, it becomes a form of self-bondage; if work is servitude, so in a subtler sense is civilisation. To some extent, these polarities are held together in the yeoman-farming structure of the Heights. Here labour and culture, freedom and necessity, Nature and society are roughly complementary. The Earnshaws are gentlemen yet they work the land; they enjoy the freedom of being their own masters, but that freedom moves within the tough discipline of labour; and because the social unit of the Heights – the family – is both 'natural' (biological) and an economic system, it acts to some degree as a mediation between Nature and artifice, naturalising property relations and socialising blood-ties. Relationships in this isolated world are turbulently face-to-face, but they are also impersonally mediated through a working relation with Nature. This is not to share Mrs Q.D. Leavis's view of the Heights as 'a wholesome primitive and natural unit of a healthy society';[8] there does not, for instance, seem much that is wholesome about Joseph. Joseph incarnates a grimness inherent in conditions of economic exigency, where relationships must be tightly ordered and are easily warped into violence. One of *Wuthering Heights'* more notable achievements is ruthlessly to de-mystify the Victorian notion of the family as a pious, pacific space within social conflict. Even so, the Heights does pin together contradictions which the entry of Heathcliff will break open. Heathcliff disturbs the Heights because he is simply superfluous: he has no defined place within its biological and economic system. (He may well be Catherine's illegitimate half-brother, just as he may well have passed his two-year absence in Tunbridge Wells.) The superfluity he embodies is that of a sheerly human demand for recognition; but since there is no space for such surplus within the terse economy of the Heights, it proves destructive rather than creative in effect, straining and overloading already taut relationships. Heathcliff catalyses an aggression intrinsic to Heights society; that sound blow Hindley hands out to Catherine on the evening of Heathcliff's first appearance is slight but significant evidence against the case that conflict starts only with Heathcliff's arrival.

The effect of Heathcliff is to explode those conflicts into antagonisms which finally rip the place apart. In particular, he marks the beginnings of that process whereby passion and personal intensity separate out from the social domain and offer an alternative commitment to it. For farming families like the Earnshaws, work and human relations are roughly coterminous: work is socialised, personal relations mediated through a context of labour. Heathcliff, however, is set to work meaninglessly, as a servant rather than a member of the family; and his fervent emotional life with Catherine is thus forced outside the working environment into the wild Nature of the heath, rather than Nature reclaimed and worked up into significant value in the social activity of labour. Heathcliff is stripped of culture in the sense of gentility, but the result is a paradoxical intensifying of his fertile imaginative liaison with Catherine. It is fitting, then, that their free, neglected wanderings lead them to their adventure at Thrushcross Grange. For if the Romantic childhood culture of Catherine and Heathcliff exists in a social limbo divorced from the minatory world of working relations, the same can be said in a different sense of the genteel culture of the Lintons, surviving as it does on the basis of material conditions it simultaneously conceals. As the children spy on the Linton family, that concealed brutality is unleashed in the shape of bull-dogs brought to the defence of civility. The natural energy in which the Lintons' culture is rooted bursts literally through to savage the 'savages' who appear to threaten property. The underlying truth of violence, con-tinuously visible at the Heights, is momentarily exposed; old Linton thinks the intruders are after his rents. Culture draws a veil over such brute force but also sharpens it: the more property you have, the more ruthlessly you need to defend it. Indeed, Heathcliff himself seems dimly aware of how cultivation exacerbates 'natural' conflict, as we see in his scornful account of the Linton children's petulant squabbling; cultivation, by pampering and swaddling 'natural' drives, at once represses serious physical violence and breeds a neurasthenic sensitivity which allows selfish impulse free rein. 'Natural' aggression is nurtured by both an excess and an absence of culture – a paradox demonstrated by Catherine Earnshaw, who is at once wild and pettish, savage and spoilt. Nature and culture, then, are locked in a complex relation of antagonism and affinity: the Romantic fantasies of Heathcliff and Catherine, and the Romantic Linton drawing-room with its gold-bordered ceiling and shimmering chandelier, both bear the scars of the material conditions which produced them – scars visibly inscribed on Cathy's ankle. Yet to leave the matter there would be to draw a purely formal parallel. For what distinguishes the two forms of Romance is Heathcliff: his intense communion with Catherine is an uncompromising rejection of the Linton world.

The opposition, however, is not merely one between the values of personal relationship and those of conventional society. What prevents this is the curious impersonality of the relationship between Catherine and Heathcliff. Edgar Linton shows at his best a genuine capacity for tender, loving fidelity; but this thrives on obvious limits. The limits are those of the closed room into which the children peer – the glowing, sheltered space within which those close, immediate encounters which make for both tenderness and pettishness may be conducted. Linton is released from material pressures into such a civilised enclave; and in that sense his situation differs from that of the Heights, where personal rela-tions are more intimately entwined with a working context. The relation-ship of Heathcliff and Catherine, however, provides a third term. It really is a personal relationship, yet seems also to transcend the personal into some region beyond it. Indeed, there is a sense in which the unity the couple briefly achieve is narrowed and degutted by being described as 'personal'. In so far as 'personal' suggests the liberal humanism of Edgar, with his concern (crudely despised by Heathcliff) for pity, charity and humanity, the word is clearly inapplicable to the fierce mutual tearings of Catherine and Heathcliff. Yet it is inadequate to the positive as well as the destructive aspects of their love. Their relationship is, we say, 'onto-logical' or 'metaphysical' because it opens out into the more-than-personal, enacts a style of being which is more than just the property of two individuals, which suggests in its impersonality something beyond a merely Romantic-individualist response to social oppression. Their rela-tionship articulates a depth inexpressible in routine social practice, transcendent of available social languages. Its impersonality suggests both a savage depersonalising and a paradigmatic significance; and in neither sense is the relationship wholly within their conscious control. What Heathcliff offers Cathy is a non- or pre-social relationship, as the only authentic form of living in a world of exploitation and inequality, a world where one must refuse to measure oneself by the criteria of the class-structure and so must appear inevitably subversive. Whereas in Charlotte's novels the love-relationship takes you into society, in *Wuthering Heights* it drives you out of it. The love between Heathcliff and Catherine is an intuitive intimacy raised to cosmic status, by-passing the mediation of the 'social'; and this, indeed, is both its strength and its limit. Its non-sociality is on the one hand a revolutionary refusal of the given language of social roles and values; and if the relationship is to remain unabsorbed by society it must therefore appear as natural rather than social, since Nature is the 'outside' of society. On the other hand, the novel cannot realise the meaning of that revolutionary refusal in social terms; the most it can do is to *universalise* that meaning by intimating the mysteriously impersonal energies from which the rela-tionship springs.

Catherine, of course, *is* absorbed: she enters the civilised world of the Lintons and leaves Heathcliff behind, to become a 'wolfish, pitiless' man. To avoid incorporation means remaining as unreclaimed as the wild furze: there is no way in this novel of temporising between conformity and rebellion. But there is equally no way for the revolutionary depth of relationship between Heathcliff and Catherine to realise itself as a histor-ical force; instead, it becomes an elusive dream of absolute value, an incomparably more powerful version of Charlotte's myth of lost origins. Catherine and Heathcliff seek to preserve the primordial moment of pre-social harmony, before the fall into history and oppression. But it won't do to see them merely as children eternally fixated in some Edenic infancy: we do not see them merely as children, and in any case to be 'merely' a child is to endure the punitive pressures of an adult world. Moreover, it is none of Heathcliff's fault that the relationship remains 'metaphysical': it is Catherine who consigns it to unfulfilment. Their love remains an unhistorical essence which fails to enter into concrete existence and can do so, ironically, only in death. Death, indeed, as the ultimate outer limit of consciousness and society, is the locus of Catherine and Heathcliff's love, the horizon on which it moves. The absolutism of death is prefigured, echoed back, in the remorseless intensity with which their relationship is actually lived; yet their union can be achieved only in the act of abandoning the actual world.

Catherine and Heathcliff's love, then, is pushed to the periphery by society itself, projected into myth; yet the fact that it seems *inherently* convertible to myth spotlights the threshold of the novel's 'possible consciousness'. I take that phrase from Lukács and Goldmann to suggest those restrictions set on the consciousness of a historical period which only a transformation of real social relations could abolish – the point at which the most enterprising imagination presses against boundaries which signify not mere failures of personal perception but the limits of what can be historically said. The force Heathcliff symbolises can be truly realised only in some more than merely individualist form; *Wuthering Heights* has its roots not in that narrowed, simplified Romanticism which pits the lonely rebel against an anonymous order, but in that earlier, more authentic Romantic impulse which posits its own kind of 'transindividual' order of value, its own totality, against the order which forces it into exile. Heathcliff may be Byronic, but not in the way Rochester is: the novel counterposes social convention not merely with contrasting personal life-styles but with an alternative world of meaning. Yet it is here that the limits of 'possible consciousness' assert themselves: the offered totalities of Nature, myth and cosmic energy are forced to figure as asocial worlds unable to engage in more than idealist ways with the society they subject to judgement. The price of universality is to be fixed eternally at a point extrinsic to social life – fixed, indeed, at the moment of death, which both manifests a depth challengingly alien to the Lintons and withdraws the character from that conventional landscape into an isolated realm of his own.

Nature, in any case, is no true 'outside' to society, since its conflicts are transposed into the social arena. In one sense the novel sharply contrasts Nature and society; in another sense it grasps civilised life as a higher distillation of ferocious natural appetite. Nature, then, is a thoroughly ambiguous category, inside and outside society simultaneously. At one level it represents the unsalvaged region beyond the pale of culture; at another level it signifies the all-pervasive reality of which culture itself is a particular outcropping. It is, indeed, this ambiguity which supplies the vital link between the childhood and adult phases of Heathcliff's career. Heathcliff the child is 'natural' both because he is allowed to run wild and because he is reduced as Hindley's labourer to a mere physical instrument; Heathcliff the adult is 'natural' man in a Hobbesian sense: an appetitive exploiter to whom no tie or tradition is sacred, a callous predator violently sundering the bonds of custom and piety. If the first kind of 'naturalness' is anti-social in its estrangement from the norms of 'civilised' life, the second involves the unsociality of one set at the centre of a world whose social relations are inhuman. Heathcliff moves from being natural in the sense of an anarchic outsider to adopting the behaviour natural to an insider in a viciously competitive society. Of course, to be natural in both senses is at a different level to be unnatural. From the viewpoint of culture, it is unnatural that a child should be degraded to a savage, and unnatural too that a man should behave in the obscene way Heathcliff does. But culture in this novel is as problematical as Nature. There are no cool Arnoldian touchstones by which to take the measure of natural degeneracy, since the dialectical vision of *Wuthering Heights* puts culture into question in the very act of exploring the 'naturalness' which is its negation. Just as being natural involves being either completely outside or inside society, as roaming waif or manipulative landlord, so culture signifies either free-wheeling Romantic fantasy or that well-appointed Linton drawing-room. The adult Heathcliff is the focus of these contradictions: as he worms his way into the social structure he becomes progressively detached in spirit from all it holds dear. But *contradiction* is the essential emphasis. Heathcliff's schizophrenia is symptomatic of a world in which there can be no true dialectic between culture and Nature – a world in which culture is merely refuge from or reflex of material conditions, and so either too estranged from or entwined with those conditions to offer a viable alternative.

I take it that Heathcliff, up to the point at which Cathy rejects him, is in general an admirable character. His account of the Grange adventure, candid, satirical and self-aware as it is, might itself be enough to enforce this point; and we have in any case on the other side only the self-confessedly biased testimony of Nelly Dean. Even according to Nelly's grudging commentary, Heathcliff as a child is impressively patient and uncomplaining (although Nelly adds 'sullen' out of spite), and the heart-rending cry he raises when old Earnshaw dies is difficult to square with her implication that he felt no gratitude to his benefactor. He bears Hindley's vindictive treatment well, and tries pathetically to keep culturally abreast of Catherine despite it. The novel says quite explicitly that Hindley's systematic degradation of Heathcliff 'was enough to make a fiend of a saint';[9] and we should not therefore be surprised that what it does, more precisely, is to produce a pitiless capitalist landlord out of an oppressed child. Heathcliff the adult is in one sense an inversion, in another sense an organic outgrowth, of Heathcliff the child. Heathcliff the child was an isolated figure whose freedom from given genealogical ties offered, as I have argued, fresh possibilities of relationship; Heathcliff the adult is the atomic capitalist to whom relational bonds are nothing, whose individualism is now enslaving rather than liberating. The child knew the purely negative freedom of running wild; the adult, as a man vehemently pursuing ends progressively alien to him, knows only the delusory freedom of exploiting others. The point is that such freedom seems the only kind available in this society, once the relationship with Catherine has collapsed; the only mode of self-affirmation left to Heathcliff is that of oppression which, since it involves self-oppression, is no affirmation at all. Heathcliff is a self-tormentor, a man who is in hell because he can avenge himself on the system which has robbed him of his soul only by battling with it on its own hated terms. If as a child he was outside and inside that system simultaneously, wandering on the moors and working on the farm, he lives out a similar self-division as an adult, trapped in the grinding contradiction between a false social self and the true identity which lies with Catherine. The social self is false, not because Heathcliff is only apparently brutal – that he certainly is – but because it is contradictorily related to the authentic selfhood which is his passion for Catherine. He installs himself at the centre of conventional society, but with wholly negative and inimical intent; his social role is a calculated self-contradiction, created first to further, and then fiercely displace, his asocial passion for Catherine.

Heathcliff's social relation to both Heights and Grange is one of the most complex issues in the novel. Lockwood remarks that he looks too genteel for the Heights; and indeed, in so far as he represents the victory of capitalist property-dealing over the traditional yeoman economy of the Earnshaws, he is inevitably aligned with the world of the Grange. Heathcliff is a dynamic force which seeks to destroy the old yeoman settlement by dispossessing Hareton; yet he does this partly to revenge himself on the very Linton world whose weapons (property deals, arranged marriages) he deploys so efficiently. He does this, moreover, with a crude intensity which is a quality of the Heights world; his roughness and resilience link him culturally to Wuthering Heights, and he exploits those qualities to destroy both it and the Grange. He is, then, a force which springs out of the Heights yet subverts it, breaking beyond its constrictions into a new, voracious acquisitiveness. His capitalist brutality is an extension as well as a negation of the Heights world he knew as a child; and to that extent there is continuity between his childhood and adult protests against Grange values, if not against Grange weapons. Heathcliff is subjectively a Heights figure opposing the Grange, and objectively a Grange figure undermining the Heights; he focuses acutely the contradictions between the two worlds. His rise to power symbolises at once the triumph of the oppressed over capitalism and the triumph of capitalism over the oppressed.

He is, indeed, contradiction incarnate – both progressive and out-dated, at once caricature of and traditionalist protest against the agrarian capitalist forces of Thrushcross Grange. He harnesses those forces to worst the Grange, to beat it at its own game; but in doing so he parodies that property-system, operates against the Lintons with an unLinton-like explicitness and extremism. He behaves in this way because his 'soul' belongs not to that world but to Catherine; and in that sense his true commitment is an 'outdated' one, to a past, increasingly mythical realm of absolute personal value which capitalist social relations cancel. He embodies a passionate human protest against the marriage-market values of both Grange and Heights at the same time as he callously images those values in caricatured form. Heathcliff exacts vengeance from that society precisely by extravagantly enacting its twisted priorities, becoming a darkly satirical commentary on conventional mores. If he is in one sense a progressive historical force, he belongs in another sense to the super-seded world of the Heights, so that his death and the closing-up of the house seem logically related. In the end Heathcliff is defeated and the Heights restored to its rightful owner; yet at the same time the trends he epitomises triumph in the form of the Grange, to which Hareton and young Catherine move away. Hareton wins and loses the Heights simul-taneously; dispossessed by Heathcliff, he repossesses the place only to be in that act assimilated by Thrushcross Grange. And if Hareton both wins and loses, then Heathcliff himself is both ousted and victorious.

Quite who has in fact won in the end is a matter of critical con-tention. Mrs Leavis and Tom Winnifrith both see the old world as having yielded to the new, in contrast to T.K. Meier, who reads the conclusion as 'the victory of tradition over innovation'.[10] The critical contention reflects a real ambiguity in the novel. In one sense, the old values have triumphed over the disruptive usurper: Hareton has wrested back his birthright, and the qualities he symbolises, while preserving their authen-tic vigour, will be fertilised by the civilising grace which the Grange, in the form of young Catherine, can bring. Heathcliff's career appears from his perspective as a shattering but short-lived interlude, after which true balance may be slowly recovered. In a more obvious sense, however, the Grange has won: the Heights is shut up and Hareton will become the new squire. Heathcliff, then, has been the blunt instrument by which the remnants of the Earnshaw world have been transformed into a fully-fledged capitalist class – the historical medium whereby that world is at once annihilated and elevated to the Grange. Thrushcross values have entered into productive dialogue with rough material reality and, by virtue of this spiritual transfusion, ensured their continuing survival; the Grange comes to the Heights and gathers back to itself what the Heights can yield it. This is why it will not do to read the novel's conclusion as some neatly reciprocal symbolic alliance between the two universes, a symmetrical symbiosis of bourgeois realism and upper-class cultivation. Whatever unity the book finally establishes, it is certainly not symmetrical: in a victory for the progressive forces of agrarian capitalism, Hareton, last survivor of the traditional order, is smoothly incorporated into the Grange.

There is another significant reason why the 'defeat' of Heathcliff cannot be read as the resilient recovery of a traditional world from the injuries it has suffered at his hands. As an extreme parody of capitalist activity, Heathcliff is also an untypical deviation from its norms; as a remorseless, crudely transparent revelation of the real historical character of the Grange, he stands askew to that reality in the very act of becoming its paradigm. It *is* true that Heathcliff, far from signifying some merely ephemeral intervention, is a type of the historically ascendant world of capital; but because he typifies it so 'unnaturally' the novel can move beyond him, into the gracefully gradualistic settlement symbolised by the union of Hareton and young Catherine. Heathcliff is finally fought off, while the social values he incarnates can be prised loose from the self-parodic mould in which he cast them and slowly accommodated. His undisguised violence, like the absolutism of his love, come to seem features of a past more brutal but also more heroic than the present; if the decorous, muted milieu of the Grange will not easily accommodate such passionate intensities, neither will it so readily reveal the more unpleasant face of its social and economic power. The 'defeat' of Heathcliff, then, is at once the transcending of such naked power and the collapse of that passionate protest against it which was the inner secret of Heathcliff's outrageous dealings.

We can now ask what these contradictions in the figure of Heathcliff actually amount to. It seems to me possible to decipher in the struggle between Heathcliff and the Grange an imaginatively transposed version of that contemporary conflict between bourgeoisie and landed gentry which I have argued is central to Charlotte's work. The relationship holds in no precise detail, since Heathcliff is not literally an industrial entrepreneur; but the double-edgedness of his relation with the Lintons, with its blend of antagonism and emulation, reproduces the complex structure of class-forces we found in Charlotte's fiction. Having mysteriously amassed capital outside agrarian society, Heathcliff forces his way into that society to expropriate the expropriators; and in this sense his machinations reflect the behaviour of a contemporary bourgeois class increasingly successful in its penetration of landed property. He belongs fully to neither Heights nor Grange, opposing them both; he embodies a force which at once destroys the traditional Earnshaw settlement and effectively confronts the power of the squirearchy. In his contradictory amalgam of 'Heights' and 'Grange', then, Heathcliff's career fleshes out a contemporary ideological dilemma which Charlotte also explores: the contradiction that the fortunes of the industrial bourgeoisie belong *economically* to an increasing extent with the landed gentry but that there can still exist between them, socially, culturally and personally, a profound hostility. If they are increasingly bound up objectively in a single power-bloc, there is still sharp subjective conflict between them. I take it that *Wuthering Heights*, like Charlotte's fiction, needs mythically to resolve this historical contradiction. If the exploitative adult Heathcliff belongs economically with the capitalist power of the Grange, he is culturally closer to the traditional world of the Heights; his contemptuous response to the Grange as a child, and later to Edgar, is of a piece with Joseph's scorn for the finicky Linton Heathcliff and the haughty young Catherine. If Heathcliff exploits Hareton culturally and economically, he nevertheless feels a certain rough-and-ready *rapport* with him. The contradiction Heathcliff embodies, then, is brought home in the fact that he combines Heights violence with Grange methods to gain power over both properties; and this means that while he is economically progressive he is culturally outdated. He represents a turbulent form of capitalist aggression which must historically be civilised – blended with spiritual values, as it will be in the case of his surrogate Hareton. The terms into which the novel casts this imperative are those of the need to refine, in the person of Hareton, the old yeoman class; but since Hareton's achievement of the Grange is an ironic consequence of Heathcliff's own activity, there is a sense in which it is the capitalist drive symbolised by Heathcliff which must submit to spiritual cultivation. It is worth recalling at this point the cultural affinities between the old yeoman and the new industrial classes touched on by David Wilson;[11] and F.M.L. Thompson comments that by the early 1830s a depleted yeomanry were often forced to sell their land either to a large landowner, or to a local tradesman who would put a tenant in.[12] On the other hand, as Mrs Gaskell notes, some landed yeomen turned to manufacture. Heathcliff the heartless capitalist and Hareton the lumpish yeoman thus have a real as well as an alliterative relation. In so far as Heathcliff symbolises the dispossessing bourgeoisie, he links hands with the large capitalist landowner Linton in common historical opposition to yeoman society; in so far as he himself has sprung from that society and turned to amassing capital outside it, still sharing its dour life-style, he joins spiritual forces with the uncouth Hareton against the pampered squirearchy.

In pitting himself against both yeomanry and large-scale agrarian capitalism, then, Heathcliff is an indirect symbol of the aggressive industrial bourgeoisie of Emily Brontë's own time, a social trend extrinsic to both classes but implicated in their fortunes. The contradiction of the *novel*, however, is that Heathcliff cannot represent at once an absolute metaphysical refusal of an inhuman society and a class which is intrinsically part of it. Heathcliff is both metaphysical hero, spiritually marooned from all material concern in his obsessional love for Catherine, and a skilful exploiter who cannily expropriates the wealth of others. It is a limit of the novel's 'possible consciousness' that its absolute metaphysical protest can be socially articulated only in such terms – that its 'outside' is in this sense an 'inside'. The industrial bourgeoisie is outside the farming world of both Earnshaws and Lintons; but it is no longer a *revolutionary* class, and so provides no sufficient social correlative for what Heathcliff 'metaphysically' represents. He can thus be presented only as a conflictive unity of spiritual rejection and social integration; and this, indeed, is his personal tragedy. With this in mind, we can understand why what he did in that two years' absence has to remain mysterious. The actual facts of his return, as an ambitious *parvenu* armed with presumably non-agrarian wealth and bent on penetrating agrarian society, speak eloquently enough of the real situation of the contemporary bourgeoisie; but it is clear that such social realities offer no adequate symbolism for Heathcliff's unswerving drive, which transcends all social determinants and has its end in Catherine alone. The novel, then, can dramatise its 'metaphysical' challenge to society only by refracting it through the distorting terms of existing social relations, while simultaneously, at a 'deeper' level, isolating that challenge in a realm eternally divorced from the actual.

It seems clear that the novel's sympathies lie on balance with the Heights rather than the Grange. As Tom Winnifrith points out, the Heights is the more homely, egalitarian place; Lockwood's inability at the beginning of the book to work out its social relationships (is Hareton a servant or not?) marks a significant contrast with the Grange. (Lockwood is here a kind of surrogate reader: we too are forestalled from 'reading off' the relationships at first glance, since they are historically moulded and so only historically intelligible.) The passing of the Heights, then, is regretted: it lingers on in the ghostly myth of Heathcliff and Catherine as an unbanishable intimation of a world of hungering absolution askew to the civilised present. Winnifrith declares himself puzzled by Mrs Leavis's point that the action of Hareton and Catherine in replacing the Heights' currant-bushes with flowers symbolises the victory of capitalist over yeoman, but Mrs Leavis is surely right: flowers are a form of 'surplus value', redundant luxuries in the spare Heights world which can accommodate the superfluous neither in its horticulture nor in its social network. But though the novel mourns the death of Wuthering Heights, it invests deeply in the new life which struggles out of it. In so far as Heathcliff signifies a demonic capitalist drive, his defeat is obviously approved; in so far as his passing marks the demise of a life-form rougher but also richer than the Grange, his death symbolises the fleeing of absolute value over the horizon of history into the sealed realm of myth. That death, however tragic, is essential: the future lies with a fusion rather than a confrontation of interests between gentry and bourgeoisie.

The novel's final settlement might seem to qualify what I have said earlier about its confronting of irreconcilable contradictions. *Wuthering Heights* does, after all, end on a note of tentative convergence between labour and culture, sinew and gentility. The culture which Catherine imparts to Hareton in teaching him to read promises equality rather than oppression, an unemasculating refinement of physical energy. But this is a consequence rather than a resolution of the novel's tragic action; it does nothing to dissolve the deadlock of Heathcliff's relationship with Catherine, as the language used to describe that cultural transfusion unconsciously suggests:

'Con-*trary*!' said a voice as sweet as a silver bell – 'That for the third time, you dunce! I'm not going to tell you again. Recollect or I'll pull your hair!'

'Contrary, then', answered another, in deep but softened tones. 'And now, kiss me, for minding so well.'

'No, read it over first correctly, without a single mistake.' The male speaker began to read; he was a young man, respectably dressed and seated at a table, having a book before him. His handsome features glowed with pleasure, and his eyes kept impatiently wandering from the page to a small white hand over his shoulder, which recalled him by a smart slap on the cheek, whenever its owner detected such signs of inattention. Its owner stood behind; her light, shining ringlets blending, at intervals, with his brown locks, as she bent to superintend his studies; and her face – it was lucky he could not see her face, or he would never have been so steady. I could; and I bit my lip in spite, at having thrown away the chance I might have had of doing something besides staring at its smiting beauty.[13]

The aesthetic false moves of this are transparently dictated by ideological compromise. 'Sweet as a silver bell', 'glowed with pleasure', 'shining ringlets', 'smiting beauty': there is a coy, beaming, sentimental self-indulgence about the whole passage which belongs more to Lockwood than to Emily Brontë, although her voice has clearly been confiscated by his. It is Jane and Rochester in a different key; yet the difference is as marked as the parallel. The conclusion, while in a sense symbolically resolving the tragic disjunctions which precede it, moves at a level sufficiently distanced from those disjunctions to preserve their significance intact. It is true that *Wuthering Heights* finally reveals the limits of its 'possible consciousness' by having recourse to a gradualist model of social change: the antinomies of passion and civility will be harmonised by the genetic fusion of both strains in the offspring of Catherine and Hareton, effecting an equable interchange of Nature and culture, biology and education. But those possibilities of growth are exploratory and undeveloped, darkened by the shadow of the tragic action. If it is not exactly true to say that Hareton and Catherine play Fortinbras to Heathcliff's Hamlet, since what they symbolise emerges from, rather than merely imposes itself upon, the narrative, there is none the less a kernel of truth in that proposition. Hareton and Catherine are the products of their history, but they cannot negate it; the quarrel between their sedate future at Thrushcross Grange and the spectre of Heathcliff and Catherine on the hills lives on, in a way alien to Charlotte's reconciliatory imagination.

There is another reason why the ending of *Wuthering Heights* differs from the ideological integration which concludes Charlotte's novels. I have argued that those novels aim for a balance or fusion of 'genteel' and bourgeois traits, enacting a growing convergence of interests between two powerful segments of a ruling social bloc. The union of Hareton and Catherine parallels this complex unity in obvious ways: the brash vigour of the petty-bourgeois yeoman is smoothed and sensitised by the cultivating grace of the squirearchy. But the crucial difference lies in the fact that the yeomanry of *Wuthering Heights* is no longer a significant class but a historically superannuated force. The transfusion of class-qualities in Charlotte's case rests on a real historical symbiosis; in *Wuthering Heights* that symbolic interchange has no such solid historical foundation. The world of the Heights is over, lingering on only in the figure of Hareton Earnshaw; and in that sense Hareton's marriage to Catherine signifies more at the level of symbolism than historical fact, as a salutary grafting of the values of a dying class on to a thriving, progressive one. If Hareton is thought of as a surrogate, symbolic Heathcliff, then the novel's ending suggests a rapprochement between gentry and capitalist akin to Charlotte's mythical resolutions; if he is taken literally, as a survivor of yeoman stock, then there can be no such historical balance of power. Literally, indeed, this is what finally happens: Hareton's social class is effectively swallowed up into the hegemony of the Grange. Symbolically, however, Hareton represents a Heathcliff-like robustness with which the Grange must come to terms. It is this tension between literal and symbolic meanings which makes the ending of *Wuthering Heights* considerably more complex than the conclusion of any Charlotte Brontë novel. Read symbolically, the ending of *Wuthering Heights* seems to echo the fusion of qualities found in Charlotte; but since the basis of that fusion is the absorption and effective disappearance of a class on which the novel places considerable value, Emily's conclusion is a good deal more subtly shaded than anything apparent in her sister's work.

Wuthering Heights has been alternately read as a social and a metaphysical novel – as a work rooted in a particular time and place, or as a novel preoccupied with the eternal grounds rather than the shifting conditions of human relationship. That critical conflict mirrors a crucial thematic dislocation in the novel itself. The social and metaphysical are indeed ripped rudely apart in the book: existences only feebly incarnate essences, the discourse of ethics makes little creative contact with that of ontology. So much is apparent in Heathcliff's scathing dismissal of Edgar Linton's compassion and moral concern: 'and that insipid, paltry creature attending her from *duty* and *humanity*! From *pity* and *charity*! He might as well plant an oak in a flower-pot, and expect it to thrive, as imagine he can restore her to vigour in the soil of his shallow cares!' The novel's dialectical vision proves Heathcliff both right and wrong. There *is* something insipid about Linton, but his concern for Catherine is not in the least shallow; if his pity and charity are less fertile than Heathcliff's passion, they are also less destructive. But if ethical and ontological idioms fail to mesh, if social existence negates rather than realises spiritual essence, this is itself a profoundly social fact. The novel projects a condition in which the available social languages are too warped and constrictive to be the bearers of love, freedom and equality; and it follows that in such a condition those values can be sustained only in the realms of myth and metaphysics. It is a function of the metaphysical to preserve those possibilities which a society cancels, to act as its reservoir of unrealised value. This is the history of Heathcliff and Catherine – the history of a wedge driven between the actual and the possible which, by estranging the ideal from concrete existence, twists that existence into violence and despair. The actual is denatured to a mere husk of the ideal, the empty shell of some tormentingly inaccessible truth. It is an index of the dialectical vision of *Wuthering Heights* that it shows at once the terror and the necessity of that denaturing, as it shows both the splendour and the impotence of the ideal.

NOTES

1. See Lukács, *The Historical Novel* (London: Merlin Press, 1962), esp. chs 1–2.
2. Quoted by J. Hillis Miller, *The Disappearance of God* (Cambridge, Mass., 1963), p. 163.
3. Quoted by Leavis, *Lectures in America* (London: Chatto and Windus, 1969), p. 127.
4. *Wuthering Heights*, edited by C.K. Shorter, with Introduction by M.A. Ward, Haworth edition (1898), reprinted by AMS Publications (1973), ch. 14, p. 155.
5. Ibid., ch. 15, p. 168.
6. Ibid., ch. 4, p. 36.
7. Ibid., ch. 12, p. 130.
8. Leavis, p. 99.
9. Ibid., ch. 8, p. 66.
10. *Brontë Society Transactions*, no. 78 (1968).
11. *Modern Quarterly Miscellany*, no. 1 (1947).
12. F.M.L. Thompson, *English Landed Society in the Nineteenth Century* (London: Routledge, 1963), p. 233.
13. Ibid., ch. 32, pp. 319–20.

CHAPTER TWO

A Dialogue of Self and Soul: Plain Jane's Progress

SANDRA M. GILBERT AND SUSAN GUBAR

The authors of *The Madwoman in the Attic: The Woman Writer and the Nineteenth-century Literary Imagination* (1979) are both distinguished feminist critics: Sandra Gilbert is a Professor at the University of California, Davis; and Susan D. Gubar a Distinguished Professor of English and Women's Studies at Indiana University. They have also collaborated on *No Man's Land: The Place of the Woman Writer in the Twentieth Century*, *Sex Changes* and *Letters from the Front* with the aim of using feminist criticism to understand the achievements of British and American women in modern times. More recently they have also co-authored a collection of poetry, *Mother Songs* (1995), for and about mothers. *The Madwoman in the Attic* was a landmark in feminist criticism. It focuses almost exclusively on the issue of gender in relation to women, though it refers briefly to the ambiguous class position of governesses such as Jane Eyre. The authors analyse the intertwined processes of female rebellion and repression in the narrative and highlight in particular the reading of Bertha Mason, the mad wife, as the symbol of Jane's repressed passion. This was later to become an accepted interpretation of Bertha. In relating the novel to Charlotte Brontë the writer, they see the text as ultimately half-optimistic for women's future in the prospect of a marriage of equals. Others were to read the ending as a compromise with contemporary patriarchal ideals of marriage.

Reprinted from *The Madwoman in the Attic: The Woman Writer and the Nineteenth-century Literary Imagination* (New Haven, Conn.: Yale University Press, 1979), pp. 336–71.

[. . .] Unlike many Victorian novels, which begin with elaborate expository paragraphs, *Jane Eyre* begins with a casual, curiously enigmatic remark: 'There was no possibility of taking a walk that day.' Both the occasion ('that day') and the excursion (or the impossibility of one) are significant: the first is the real beginning of Jane's pilgrim's progress toward maturity; the second is a metaphor for the problems she must solve in order to attain maturity. 'I was glad' not to be able to leave the house, the narrator continues: 'dreadful to me was the coming home in the raw twilight . . . humbled by the consciousness of my physical inferiority' (ch. 1).[1] As many critics have commented, Charlotte Brontë consistently uses the opposed properties of fire and ice to characterize Jane's experiences, and her technique is immediately evident in these opening passages.[2] For while the world outside Gateshead is almost unbearably wintry, the world within is claustrophobic, fiery, like ten-year-old Jane's own mind. Excluded from the Reed family group in the drawing room because *she* is not a 'contented, happy, little child' – excluded, that is, from 'normal' society – Jane takes refuge in a scarlet-draped window seat where she alternately stares out at the 'drear November day' and reads of polar regions in Bewick's *History of British Birds*. The 'death-white realms' of the Arctic fascinate her; she broods upon 'the multiplied rigors of extreme cold' as if brooding upon her own dilemma: whether to stay in, behind the oppressively scarlet curtain, or to go out into the cold of a loveless world.

Her decision is made for her. She is found by John Reed, the tyrannical son of the family, who reminds her of her anomalous position in the household, hurls the heavy volume of Bewick at her, and arouses her passionate rage. Like a 'rat,' a 'bad animal,' a 'mad cat,' she compares him to 'Nero, Caligula, etc.' and is borne away to the red-room; to be imprisoned literally as well as figuratively. For 'the fact is,' confesses the grownup narrator ironically, 'I was [at that moment] a trifle beside myself; or rather *out* of myself, as the French would say . . . like any other rebel slave, I felt resolved . . . to go all lengths' (ch. 1).

But if Jane was 'out of' herself in her struggle against John Reed, her experience in the red-room, probably the most metaphorically vibrant of all her early experiences, forces her deeply into herself. For the red-room, stately, chilly, swathed in rich crimson, with a great white bed and an easy chair 'like a pale throne' looming out of the scarlet darkness, perfectly represents her vision of the society in which she is trapped, an uneasy and elfin dependent. 'No jail was ever more secure,' she tells us. And no jail, we soon learn, was ever more terrifying either, because this is the room where Mr Reed, the only 'father' Jane has ever had, 'breathed his last.' It is, in other words, a kind of patriarchal death chamber, and here

Mrs Reed still keeps 'divers parchments, her jewel-casket, and a miniature of her dead husband' in a secret drawer in the wardrobe (ch. 2). Is the room haunted, the child wonders. At least, the narrator implies, it is realistically if not gothically haunting, more so than any chamber in, say, *The Mysteries of Udolpho*, which established a standard for such apartments. For the spirit of society in which Jane has no clear place sharpens the angles of the furniture, enlarges the shadows, strengthens the locks on the door. And the deathbed of a father who was not really her father emphasizes her isolation and vulnerability.

Panicky, she stares into a 'great looking glass,' where her own image floats toward her, alien and disturbing. 'All looked colder and darker in that visionary hollow than in reality,' the adult Jane explains. But a mirror, after all, is also a sort of chamber, a mysterious enclosure in which images of the self are trapped like 'divers parchments.' So the child Jane, though her older self accuses her of mere superstition, correctly recognizes that she is doubly imprisoned. Frustrated and angry, she meditates on the injustices of her life, and fantasizes 'some strange expedient to achieve escape from insupportable oppression – as running away, or, if that could not be effected, never eating or drinking more, and letting myself die' (ch. 2). Escape through flight, or escape through starvation: the alternatives will recur throughout *Jane Eyre* and, indeed, as we have already noted, throughout much other nineteenth- and twentieth-century literature by women. In the red-room, however, little Jane chooses (or is chosen by) a third, even more terrifying, alternative: escape through madness. Seeing a ghostly, wandering light, as of the moon on the ceiling, she notices that 'my heart beat thick, my head grew hot; a sound filled my ears, which I deemed the rushing of wings; something seemed near me; I was oppressed, suffocated: endurance broke down.' The child screams and sobs in anguish, and then, adds the narrator coolly, 'I suppose I had a species of fit,' for her next memory is of waking in the nursery 'and seeing before me a terrible red glare crossed with thick black bars' (ch. 3), merely the nursery fire of course, but to Jane Eyre the child a terrible reminder of the experience she has just had, and to Jane Eyre the adult narrator an even more dreadful omen of experiences to come.

For the little drama enacted on 'that day' which opens *Jane Eyre* is in itself a paradigm of the larger drama that occupies the entire book: Jane's anomalous, orphaned position in society, her enclosure in stultifying roles and houses, and her attempts to escape through flight, starvation, and – in a sense which will be explained – madness. And that Charlotte Brontë quite consciously intended the incident of the red-room to serve as a paradigm for the larger plot of her novel is clear not only from its position in the narrative but also from Jane's own recollection of the experience at crucial moments throughout the book: when she is humiliated by Mr Brocklehurst at Lowood, for instance, and on the night when she decides to leave Thornfield. In between these moments, moreover, Jane's pilgrimage consists of a series of experiences which are, in one way or another, variations on the central, red-room motif of enclosure and escape.

* * *

Like the protagonist of Bunyan's book, Jane Eyre makes a life-journey which is a kind of mythical progress from one significantly named place to another. Her story begins, quite naturally, at *Gateshead*, a starting point where she encounters the uncomfortable givens of her career: a family which is not her real family, a selfish older 'brother' who tyrannizes over the household like a substitute patriarch, a foolish and wicked 'stepmother,' and two unpleasant, selfish 'stepsisters.' The smallest, weakest, and plainest child in the house, she embarks on her pilgrim's progress as a sullen Cinderella, an angry Ugly Duckling, immorally rebellious against the hierarchy that oppresses her: 'I know that had I been a sanguine, brilliant, careless, exacting, handsome, romping child – though equally dependent and friendless – Mrs Reed would have endured my presence more complacently,' she reflects as an adult (ch. 2).

But the child Jane cannot, as she well knows, be 'sanguine and brilliant.' Cinderella never is; nor is the Ugly Duckling, who, for all her swansdown potential, has no great expectations. 'Poor, plain, and little,' Jane Eyre – her name is of course suggestive – is invisible as air, the heir to nothing, secretly choking with ire. And Bessie, the kind nursemaid who befriends her, sings her a song that no fairy godmother would ever dream of singing, a song that summarizes the plight of all real Victorian Cinderellas:

> My feet they are sore, and my limbs they are weary,
> Long is the way, and the mountains are wild;
> Soon will the twilight close moonless and dreary
> Over the path of the poor orphan child.

A hopeless pilgrimage, Jane's seems, like the sad journey of Wordsworth's Lucy Gray, seen this time from the inside, by the child herself rather than by the sagacious poet to whom years have given a philosophic mind. Though she will later watch the maternal moon rise to guide her, now she imagines herself wandering in a moonless twilight that foreshadows her desperate flight across the moors after leaving Thornfield. And the only hope her friend Bessie can offer is, ironically, an image that recalls the patriarchal terrors of the red-room and hints at patriarchal terrors to come – Lowood, Brocklehurst, St John Rivers:

> Ev'n should I fall o'er the broken bridge passing,
> Or stray in the marshes, by false lights beguiled,
> Still will my Father, with promise and blessing
> Take to His bosom the poor orphan child.

It is no wonder that, confronting such prospects, young Jane finds herself 'whispering to myself, over and again' the words of Bunyan's Christian: 'What shall I do? – What shall I do?' (ch. 4).[3]

What she does do, in desperation, is burst her bonds again and again to tell Mrs Reed what she thinks of her, an extraordinarily self-assertive act of which neither a Victorian child nor a Cinderella was ever supposed to be capable. Interestingly, her first such explosion is intended to remind Mrs Reed that she, too, is surrounded by patriarchal limits: 'What would Uncle Reed say to you if he were alive?' Jane demands, commenting, 'It seemed as if my tongue pronounced words without my will consenting to their utterance: something spoke out of me over which I had no control' (ch. 4). And indeed, even imperious Mrs Reed appears astonished by these words. The explanation, 'something spoke out of me,' is as frightening as the arrogance, suggesting the dangerous double consciousness – 'the rushing of wings, something . . . near me' – that brought on the fit in the red-room. And when, with a real sense that 'an invisible bond had burst, and that I had struggled out into unhoped-for liberty,' Jane tells Mrs Reed that 'I am glad you are no relation of mine' (ch. 4), the adult narrator remarks that 'a ridge of lighted heath, alive, glancing, devouring, would have been a meet emblem of my mind' – as the nursery fire was, flaring behind its black grates, and as the flames consuming Thornfield also will be.

*   *   *

[. . .] It is, of course, her eagerness for a new servitude that brings Jane to the painful experience that is at the center of her pilgrimage, the experience of *Thornfield*, where, biblically, she is to be crowned with thorns, she is to be cast out into a desolate field, and most important, she is to confront the demon of rage who has haunted her since her afternoon in the red-room. Before the appearance of Rochester, however, and the intrusion of Bertha, Jane – and her readers – must explore Thornfield itself. This gloomy mansion is often seen as just another gothic trapping introduced by Charlotte Brontë to make her novel saleable. Yet not only is Thornfield more realistically drawn than, say, Otranto or Udolpho, it is more metaphorically radiant than most gothic mansions: it is the house of Jane's life, its floors and walls the architecture of her experience.

Beyond the 'long cold gallery' where the portraits of alien unknown ancestors hang the way the specter of Mr Reed hovered in the red-room, Jane sleeps in a small pretty chamber, harmoniously furnished as Miss Temple's training has supposedly furnished her own mind. Youthfully optimistic, she notices that her 'couch had no thorns in it' and trusts that with the help of welcoming Mrs Fairfax 'a fairer era of life was beginning for me, one that was to have its flowers and pleasures, as well as its thorns and toils' (ch. 11). Christian, entering the Palace Beautiful, might have hoped as much.

The equivocal pleasantness of Mrs Fairfax, however, like the ambiguous architecture of Thornfield itself, suggests at once a way in which the situation at Thornfield reiterates all the other settings of Jane's life. For though Jane assumes at first that Mrs Fairfax is her employer, she soon learns that the woman is merely a house*keeper*, the surrogate of an absent master, just as Mrs Reed was a surrogate for dead Mr Reed or immature John Reed, and Miss Temple for absent Mr Brocklehurst. Moreover, in her role as an extension of the mysterious Rochester, sweet-faced Mrs Fairfax herself becomes mysteriously chilling. 'Too much noise, Grace,' she says peremptorily, when she and Jane overhear 'Grace Poole's' laugh as they tour the third story. 'Remember directions!' (ch. 11).

The third story is the most obviously emblematic quarter of Thornfield. Here, amid the furniture of the past, down a narrow passage with 'two rows of small black doors, all shut, like a corridor in some Bluebeard's castle' (ch. 11), Jane first hears the 'distinct formal mirthless laugh' of mad Bertha, Rochester's secret wife and in a sense her own secret self. And just above this sinister corridor, leaning against the picturesque battlements and looking out over the world like Bluebeard's bride's sister Anne, Jane is to long again for freedom, for 'all of incident, life, fire, feeling that I . . . had not in my actual existence' (ch. 12). These upper regions, in other words, symbolically miniaturize one crucial aspect of the world in which she finds herself. Heavily enigmatic, ancestral relics wall her in; inexplicable locked rooms guard a secret which may have something to do with *her*; distant vistas promise an inaccessible but enviable life.

Even more importantly, Thornfield's attic soon becomes a complex focal point where Jane's own rationality (what she has learned from Miss Temple) and her irrationality (her 'hunger, rebellion and rage') intersect.[4] She never, for instance, articulates her rational desire for liberty so well as when she stands on the battlements of Thornfield, looking out over

51

the world. However offensive these thoughts may have been to Miss Rigby – and both Jane and her creator obviously suspected they would be – the sequence of ideas expressed in the famous passage beginning 'Anybody may blame me who likes' is as logical as anything in an essay by Wollstonecraft or Mill. What is somewhat irrational, though, is the restlessness and passion which, as it were, italicize her little meditation on freedom. 'I could not help it,' she explains,

the restlessness was in my nature, it agitated me to pain sometimes. Then my sole relief was to walk along the corridor of the third story, backwards and forwards, safe in the silence and solitude of the spot, and allow my mind's eye to dwell on whatever bright visions rose before it.

And even more irrational is the experience which accompanies Jane's pacing:

When thus alone, I not unfrequently heard Grace Poole's laugh: the same peal, the same low, slow ha! ha! which, when first heard, had thrilled me: I heard, too, her eccentric murmurs; stranger than her laugh. (ch. 12)

Eccentric murmurs that uncannily echo the murmurs of *Jane's* imagination, and a low, slow ha! ha! which forms a bitter refrain to the tale *Jane's* imagination creates. Despite Miss Temple's training, the 'bad animal' who was first locked up in the red-room is, we sense, still lurking somewhere, behind a dark door, waiting for a chance to get free. That early consciousness of 'something near me' has not yet been exorcised. Rather, it has intensified.

*   *   *

Many of Jane's problems, particularly those which find symbolic expression in her experiences in the third story, can be traced to her ambiguous status as a governess at Thornfield. As M. Jeanne Peterson points out, every Victorian governess received strikingly conflicting messages (she was and was not a member of the family, was and was not a servant).[5] Such messages all too often caused her features to wear what one contemporary observer called 'a fixed sad look of despair.'[6] But Jane's difficulties arise also, as we have seen, from her constitutional *ire*; interestingly, none of the women she meets at Thornfield has anything like that last problem, though all suffer from equivalent ambiguities of status. Aside from Mrs Fairfax, the three most important of these women are little Adèle Varens, Blanche Ingram, and Grace Poole. All are important negative 'role-models' for Jane, and all suggest problems she must overcome before she can reach the independent maturity which is the goal of her pilgrimage.

The first, Adèle, though hardly a woman, is already a 'little woman,' cunning and doll-like, a sort of sketch for Amy March in Louisa May Alcott's novel. Ostensibly a poor orphan child, like Jane herself, Adèle is evidently the natural daughter of Edward Rochester's dissipated youth. Accordingly, she longs for fashionable gowns rather than for love or freedom, and, the way her mother Céline did, sings and dances for her supper as if she were a clockwork temptress invented by E.T.A. Hoffman. Where Miss Temple's was the way of the lady and Helen's that of the saint, hers and her mother's are the ways of Vanity Fair, ways which have troubled Jane since her days at Gateshead. For how is a poor, plain governess to contend with a society that rewards beauty and style? May not Adèle, the daughter of a 'fallen woman,' be a model female in a world of prostitutes?

Blanche Ingram, also a denizen of Vanity Fair, presents Jane with a slightly different female image. Tall, handsome, and well-born, she is worldly but, unlike Adèle and Céline, has a respectable place in the world: she is the daughter of 'Baroness Ingram of Ingram Park,' and – along with Georgiana and Eliza Reed – Jane's classically wicked stepsister. But while Georgiana and Eliza are dismissed to stereotypical fates, Blanche's history teaches Jane ominous lessons. First, the charade of 'Bridewell' in which she and Rochester participate relays a secret message: conventional marriage is not only, as the attic implies, a 'well' of mystery, it is a Bridewell, a prison, like the Bluebeard's corridor of the third story. Second, the charade of courtship in which Rochester engages her suggests a grim question: is not the game of the marriage 'market' a game even scheming women are doomed to lose?

Finally, Grace Poole, the most enigmatic of the women Jane meets at Thornfield – 'that mystery of mysteries, as I considered her' – is obviously associated with Bertha, almost as if, with her pint of porter, her 'staid and taciturn' demeanor, she were the madwoman's public representative. 'Only one hour in the twenty four did she pass with her fellow servants below,' Jane notes, attempting to fathom the dark 'pool' of the woman's behavior; 'all the rest of her time was spent in some low-ceiled, oaken chamber of the third story; there she sat and sewed . . . as companionless as a prisoner in her dungeon' (ch. 17). And that Grace is as companionless as Bertha or Jane herself is undeniably true. Women in Jane's world, acting as agents for men, may be the keepers of other women. But both keepers and prisoners are bound by the same chains. In a sense, then, the mystery of mysteries which Grace Poole suggests to Jane is the mystery of her own life, so that to question Grace's position at Thornfield is to question her own.

Interestingly, in trying to puzzle out the secret of Grace Poole, Jane at one point speculates that Mr Rochester may once have entertained

'tender feelings' for the woman, and when thoughts of Grace's 'uncome-
liness' seem to refute this possibility, she cements her bond with Bertha's
keeper by reminding herself that, after all, '*You* are not beautiful either,
and perhaps Mr Rochester approves you' (ch. 16). Can appearances be
trusted? Who is the slave, the master or the servant, the prince or
Cinderella? What, in other words, are the real relationships between the
master of Thornfield and all these women whose lives revolve around
his? None of these questions can, of course, be answered without reference to the central character of the Thornfield episode, Edward Fairfax
Rochester.

* * *

Jane's first meeting with Rochester is a fairytale meeting. Charlotte
Brontë deliberately stresses mythic elements: an icy twilight setting out
of Coleridge or Fuseli, a rising moon, a great 'lion-like' dog gliding through
the shadows like 'a North-of-England spirit, called a "Gytrash" which . . .
haunted solitary ways, and sometimes came upon belated travellers,' followed by 'a tall steed, and on its back a rider.' Certainly the Romanticized
images seem to suggest that universe of male sexuality with which
Richard Chase thought the Brontës were obsessed.[7] And Rochester, in a
'riding-cloak, fur-collared, and steel-clasped,' with 'a dark face . . . stern
features and a heavy brow' himself appears the very essence of patriarchal
energy, Cinderella's prince as a middle-aged warrior (ch. 12). Yet what are
we to think of the fact that the prince's first action is to fall on the ice,
together with his horse, and exclaim prosaically 'What the deuce is to
do now?' Clearly the master's mastery is not universal. Jane offers help,
and Rochester, leaning on her shoulder, admits that 'necessity compels
me to make you useful.' Later, remembering the scene, he confesses that
he too had seen the meeting as a mythic one, though from a perspective
entirely other than Jane's. 'When you came on me in Hay Lane last night,
I . . . had half a mind to demand whether you had bewitched my horse'
(ch. 13). Significantly, his playful remark acknowledges *her* powers just as
much as (if not more than) *her* vision of the Gytrash acknowledged *his*.
Thus, though in one sense Jane and Rochester begin their relationship as
master and servant, prince and Cinderella, Mr B. and Pamela, in another
they begin as spiritual equals.

As the episode unfolds, their equality is emphasized in other scenes
as well. For instance, though Rochester imperiously orders Jane to
'resume your seat, and answer my questions' while he looks at her
drawings, his response to the pictures reveals not only his own Byronic
broodings, but his consciousness of hers. 'Those eyes in the Evening Star
you must have seen in a dream . . . And who taught you to paint wind?

... Where did you see Latmos?' (ch. 13). Though such talk would bewilder most of Rochester's other dependents, it is a breath of life to Jane, who begins to fall in love with him not because he is her master but in spite of the fact that he is, not because he is princely in manner, but because, being in some sense her equal, he is the only qualified critic of her art and soul.

Their subsequent encounters develop their equality in even more complex ways. Rudely urged to entertain Rochester, Jane smiles 'not a very complacent or submissive smile,' obliging her employer to explain that 'the fact is, once for all, I don't wish to treat you like an inferior . . . I claim only such superiority as must result from twenty years difference in age and a century's advance in experience' (ch. 14). Moreover, his long account of his adventure with Céline – an account which, incidentally, struck many Victorian readers as totally improper, coming from a dissipated older man to a virginal young governess[8] – emphasizes, at least superficially, not his superiority to Jane but his sense of equality with her. Both Jane and Charlotte Brontë correctly recognize this point, which subverts those Victorian charges: 'The ease of his manner,' Jane comments, 'freed me from painful restraint; the friendly frankness . . . with which he treated me, drew me to him. *I felt at [these] times as if he were my relation rather than my master*' (ch. 15, italics ours). For of course, despite critical suspicions that Rochester is seducing Jane in these scenes, he is, on the contrary, solacing himself with her unseduceable independence in a world of self-marketing Célines and Blanches.

His need for her strength and parity is made clearer soon enough – on, for instance, the occasion when she rescues him from his burning bed (an almost fatally symbolic plight), and later on the occasion when she helps him rescue Richard Mason from the wounds inflicted by 'Grace Poole.' And that these rescues are facilitated by Jane's and Rochester's mutual sense of equality is made clearest of all in the scene in which only Jane of all the 'young ladies' at Thornfield fails to be deceived by Rochester in his gypsy costume: 'With the ladies you must have managed well,' she comments, but 'You did not act the character of a gypsy with me' (ch. 19). The implication is that he did not – or could not – because he respects 'the resolute, wild, free thing looking out of' Jane's eyes as much as she herself does, and understands that just as he can see beyond her everyday disguise as plain Jane the governess, she can see beyond his temporary disguise as a gypsy fortune-teller – or his daily disguise as Rochester the master of Thornfield.

This last point is made again, most explicitly, by the passionate avowals of their first betrothal scene. Beginning with similar attempts at disguise and deception on Rochester's part ('One can't have too much of such a very excellent thing as my beautiful Blanche') that encounter causes Jane in a moment of despair and ire to strip away her own disguises in her most famous assertion of her own integrity:

'Do you think, because I am poor, obscure, plain, and little, I am soulless and heartless? You think wrong! – I have as much soul as you, – and full as much heart! And if God had gifted me with some beauty, and much wealth, I should have made it as hard for you to leave me, as it is now for me to leave you. I am not talking to you now through the medium of custom, conventionalities, or even of mortal flesh: – it is my spirit that addresses your spirit; just as if both had passed through the grave, and we stood at God's feet equal, – as we are!' (ch. 23)

Rochester's response is another casting away of disguises, a confession that he has deceived her about Blanche, and an acknowledgment of their parity and similarity: 'My bride is here,' he admits, 'because my *equal* is here, and my *likeness*.' The energy informing both speeches is, significantly, not so much sexual as spiritual; the impropriety of its formulation is, as Mrs Rigby saw, not moral but political, for Charlotte Brontë appears here to have imagined a world in which the prince and Cinderella are democratically equal, Pamela is just as good as Mr B., master and servant are profoundly alike. And to the marriage of such true minds, it seems, no man or woman can admit impediment.

* * *

But of course, as we know, there is an impediment, and that impediment, paradoxically, pre-exists in both Rochester and Jane, despite their avowals of equality. Though Rochester, for instance, appears in both the gypsy sequence and the betrothal scene to have cast away the disguises that gave him his mastery, it is obviously of some importance that those disguises were necessary in the first place. Why, Jane herself wonders, does Rochester have to trick people, especially women? What secrets are concealed behind the charades he enacts? One answer is surely that he himself senses his trickery is a source of power, and therefore, in Jane's case at least, an evasion of that equality in which he claims to believe. Beyond this, however, it is clear that the secrets Rochester is concealing or disguising throughout much of the book are themselves in Jane's – and Charlotte Brontë's – view secrets of inequality.

The first of these is suggested both by his name, apparently an allusion to the dissolute Earl of Rochester, and by Jane's own reference to the Bluebeard's corridor of the third story: it is the secret of masculine potency, the secret of male sexual guilt. For, like those pre-Byron Byronic heroes the real Restoration Rochester and the mythic Bluebeard (indeed, in relation to Jane, like any experienced adult male), Rochester has specific and 'guilty' sexual knowledge which makes him in some sense her 'superior.' Though this point may seem to contradict the point made earlier about his frankness to Jane, it really should not. Rochester's apparently improper recounting of his sexual adventures *is* a kind of acknowledgment of Jane's equality with him. His possession of the hidden details of sexuality, however – his knowledge, that is, of the *secret* of sex, symbolized both by his doll-like daughter Adèle and by the locked doors of the third story behind which mad Bertha crouches like an animal – qualifies and undermines that equality. And though his puzzling transvestism, his attempt to impersonate a *female* gypsy, may be seen as a semi-conscious effort to reduce this sexual advantage his masculinity gives him (by putting on a woman's clothes he puts on a woman's weakness), both he and Jane obviously recognize the hollowness of such a ruse. The prince is inevitably Cinderella's superior, Charlotte Brontë saw, not because his rank is higher than hers, but because it is *he* who will initiate *her* into the mysteries of the flesh.

That both Jane and Rochester are in some part of themselves conscious of the barrier which Rochester's sexual knowledge poses to their equality is further indicated by the tensions that develop in their relationship after their betrothal. Rochester, having secured Jane's love, almost reflexively begins to treat her as an inferior, a plaything, a virginal possession – for she has now become his initiate, his 'mustard-seed,' his 'little sunny-faced . . . girl-bride.' 'It is your time now, little tyrant,' he declares, 'but it will be mine presently: and when once I have fairly seized you, to have and to hold, I'll just – figuratively speaking – attach you to a chain like this' (ch. 24). She, sensing his new sense of power, resolves to keep him 'in reasonable check': 'I never can bear being dressed like a doll by Mr Rochester,' she remarks, and, more significantly, 'I'll not stand you an inch in the stead of a seraglio. . . . I'll [prepare myself] to go out as a missionary to preach liberty to them that are enslaved' (ch. 24). While such assertions have seemed to some critics merely the consequences of Jane's (and Charlotte Brontë's) sexual panic, it should be clear from their context that, as is usual with Jane, they are political rather than sexual statements, attempts at finding emotional strength rather than expressions of weakness.

Finally, Rochester's ultimate secret, the secret that is revealed together with the existence of Bertha, the literal impediment to his marriage with Jane, is another and perhaps most surprising secret of inequality: but this time the hidden facts suggest the master's inferiority rather than his superiority. Rochester, Jane learns, after the aborted wedding ceremony, had married Bertha Mason for status, for sex, for money, for everything but love and equality. 'Oh, I have no respect for myself when I think of that act!' he confesses. 'An agony of inward contempt masters me. I never loved, I never esteemed, I did not even know her' (ch. 27). And his statement reminds us of Jane's earlier assertion of her own superiority: 'I would scorn such a union [as the loveless one he hints he will enter into with Blanche]: therefore I am better than you' (ch. 23). In a sense, then, the most serious crime Rochester has to expiate is not even the crime of exploiting others but the sin of self-exploitation, the sin of Céline and Blanche, to which he, at least, had seemed completely immune.[9]

* * *

That Rochester's character and life pose in themselves such substantial impediments to his marriage with Jane does not mean, however, that Jane herself generates none. For one thing, 'akin' as she is to Rochester, she suspects him of harboring all the secrets we know he does harbor, and raises defenses against them, manipulating her 'master' so as to keep him 'in reasonable check.' In a larger way, moreover, all the charades and masquerades – the secret messages – of patriarchy have had their effect upon her. Though she loves Rochester the man, Jane has doubts about Rochester the husband even before she learns about Bertha. In her world, she senses, even the equality of love between true minds leads to the inequalities and minor despotisms of marriage. 'For a little while,' she says cynically to Rochester, 'you will perhaps be as you are now, [but] . . . I suppose your love will effervesce in six months, or less. I have observed in books written by men, that period assigned as the farthest to which a husband's ardor extends' (ch. 24). He, of course, vigorously repudiates this prediction, but his argument – 'Jane: you please me, and you master me [because] you seem to submit' – implies a kind of Lawrentian sexual tension and only makes things worse. For when he asks 'Why do you smile [at this], Jane? What does that inexplicable . . . turn of countenance mean?' her peculiar, ironic smile, reminiscent of Bertha's mirthless laugh, signals an 'involuntary' and subtly hostile thought 'of Hercules and Samson with their charmers.' And that hostility becomes overt at the silk warehouse, where Jane notes that 'the more he bought me, the more my cheek burned with a sense of annoyance and degradation . . . I thought his smile was such as a sultan might, in a blissful and fond moment, bestow on a slave his gold and gems had enriched' (ch. 24).

Jane's whole life-pilgrimage has, of course, prepared her to be angry in this way at Rochester's, and society's, concept of marriage. Rochester's loving tyranny recalls John Reed's unloving despotism, and the erratic nature of Rochester's favors ('in my secret soul I knew that his great kindness to me was balanced by unjust severity to many others' (ch. 15)) recalls Brocklehurst's hypocrisy. But even the dreamlike paintings that

Jane produced early in her stay at Thornfield – art works which brought her as close to her 'master' as Helen Graham (in *The Tenant of Wildfell Hall*) was to hers – functioned ambiguously, like Helen's, to predict strains in this relationship even while they seemed to be conventional Romantic fantasies. The first represented a drowned female corpse; the second a sort of avenging mother goddess rising (like Bertha Mason Rochester or *Frankenstein*'s monster) in 'electric travail' (ch. 13); and the third a terrible paternal specter carefully designed to recall Milton's sinister image of Death. Indeed, this last, says Jane, quoting *Paradise Lost*, delineates 'the shape which shape had none,' the patriarchal shadow implicit even in the Father-hating gloom of hell.

Given such shadowings and foreshadowings, then, it is no wonder that as Jane's anger and fear about her marriage intensify, she begins to be symbolically drawn back into her own past, and specifically to reexperience the dangerous sense of doubleness that had begun in the red-room. The first sign that this is happening is the powerfully depicted, recurrent dream of a child she begins to have as she drifts into a romance with her master. She tells us that she was awakened 'from companionship with this baby-phantom' on the night Bertha attacked Richard Mason, and the next day she is literally called back into the past, back to Gateshead to see the dying Mrs Reed, who reminds her again of what she once was and potentially still is: 'Are you Jane Eyre? . . . I declare she talked to me once like something mad, or like a fiend' (ch. 21). Even more significantly, the phantom-child reappears in two dramatic dreams Jane has on the night before her wedding eve, during which she experiences 'a strange regretful consciousness of some barrier dividing' her from Rochester. In the first, 'burdened' with the small wailing creature, she is 'following the windings of an unknown road' in cold rainy weather, straining to catch up with her future husband but unable to reach him. In the second, she is walking among the ruins of Thornfield, still carrying 'the unknown little child' and still following Rochester; as he disappears around 'an angle in the road,' she tells him, 'I bent forward to take a last look; the wall crumbled; I was shaken; the child rolled from my knee, I lost my balance, fell, and woke' (ch. 25).

What are we to make of these strange dreams, or – as Jane would call them – these 'presentiments'? To begin with, it seems clear that the wailing child who appears in all of them corresponds to 'the poor orphan child' of Bessie's song at Gateshead, and therefore to the child Jane herself, the wailing Cinderella whose pilgrimage began in anger and despair. That child's complaint – 'My feet they are sore, and my limbs they are weary; / Long is the way, and the mountains are wild' – is still Jane's, or at least the complaint of that part of her which resists a marriage of inequality. And though consciously Jane wishes to be rid of the heavy problem her orphan self presents, 'I might not lay it down anywhere, however tired were my arms, however much its weight impeded my progress.' In other words, until she reaches the goal of her pilgrimage – maturity, independence, true equality with Rochester (and therefore in a sense with the rest of the world) – she is doomed to carry her orphaned alter ego everywhere. The burden of the past cannot be sloughed off so easily – not, for instance, by glamorous lovemaking, silk dresses, jewelry, a new name. Jane's 'strange regretful consciousness of a barrier' dividing her from Rochester is, thus, a keen though disguised intuition of a problem she herself will pose.

Almost more interesting than the nature of the child image, however, is the *predictive* aspect of the last of the child dreams, the one about the ruin of Thornfield. As Jane correctly foresees, Thornfield *will* within a year become 'a dreary ruin, the retreat of bats and owls.' Have her own subtle and not-so-subtle hostilities to its master any connection with the catastrophe that is to befall the house? Is her clairvoyant dream in some sense a vision of wish-fulfilment? And why, specifically, is she freed from the burden of the wailing child at the moment *she* falls from Thornfield's ruined wall?

The answer to all these questions is closely related to events which follow upon the child dream. For the apparition of a child in these crucial weeks preceding her marriage is only one symptom of a dissolution of personality Jane seems to be experiencing at this time, a fragmentation of the self comparable to her 'syncope' in the red-room. Another symptom appears early in the chapter that begins, anxiously, 'there was no putting off the day that advanced – the bridal day' (ch. 25). It is her witty but nervous speculation about the nature of 'one Jane Rochester, a person whom as yet I knew not,' though 'in yonder closet . . . garments *said* to be hers had already displaced [mine]: *for not to me appertained that . . . strange wraith-like apparel*' (ch. 25, italics ours). Again, a third symptom appears on the morning of her wedding: she turns toward the mirror and sees 'a robed and veiled figure, so unlike my usual self that it seemed almost the image of a stranger' (ch. 26), reminding us of the moment in the red-room when all had 'seemed colder and darker in that visionary hollow' of the looking glass 'than in reality.' In view of this frightening series of separations within the self – Jane Eyre splitting off from Jane Rochester, the child Jane splitting off from the adult Jane, and the image of Jane weirdly separating from the body of Jane – it is not surprising that another and most mysterious specter, a sort of 'vampyre,' should appear in the middle of the night to rend and trample the wedding veil of that unknown person, Jane Rochester.

Literally, of course, the nighttime specter is none other than Bertha
Mason Rochester. But on a figurative and psychological level it seems
suspiciously clear that the specter of Bertha is still another – indeed the
most threatening – avatar of Jane. What Bertha now *does*, for instance,
is what Jane wants to do. Disliking the 'vapoury veil' of Jane Rochester,
Jane Eyre secretly wants to tear the garments up. Bertha does it for her.
Fearing the inexorable 'bridal day,' Jane would like to put it off. Bertha does
that for her too. Resenting the new mastery of Rochester, whom she sees
as '*dread* but adored' (italics ours), she wishes to be his equal in size and
strength, so that she can battle him in the contest of their marriage. Bertha,
'a big woman, in stature almost equalling her husband,' has the necessary
'virile force' (ch. 26). Bertha, in other words, is Jane's truest and darkest
double: she is the angry aspect of the orphan child, the ferocious secret self
Jane has been trying to repress ever since her days at Gateshead. For, as
Claire Rosenfeld points out, 'the novelist who consciously or unconsciously
exploits psychological Doubles' frequently juxtaposes 'two characters,
the one representing the socially acceptable or conventional personality,
the other externalizing the free, uninhibited, often criminal self.'[10]

It is only fitting, then, that the existence of this criminal self imprisoned in Thornfield's attic is the ultimate legal impediment to Jane's
and Rochester's marriage, and that its existence is, paradoxically, an
impediment raised by Jane as well as by Rochester. For it now begins
to appear, if it did not earlier, that Bertha has functioned as Jane's dark
double *throughout* the governess's stay at Thornfield. Specifically, every
one of Bertha's appearances – or, more accurately, her manifestations –
has been associated with an experience (or repression) of anger on Jane's
part. Jane's feelings of 'hunger, rebellion, and rage' on the battlements,
for instance, were accompanied by Bertha's 'low, slow ha! ha!' and
'eccentric murmurs.' Jane's apparently secure response to Rochester's
apparently egalitarian sexual confidences was followed by Bertha's attempt
to incinerate the master in his bed. Jane's unexpressed resentment at
Rochester's manipulative gypsy-masquerade found expression in Bertha's
terrible shriek and her even more terrible attack on Richard Mason. Jane's
anxieties about her marriage, and in particular her fears of her own alien
'robed and veiled' bridal image, were objectified by the image of Bertha in
a 'white and straight' dress, 'whether gown, sheet, or shroud I cannot tell.'
Jane's profound desire to destroy Thornfield, the symbol of Rochester's
mastery and of her own servitude, will be acted out by Bertha, who burns
down the house and destroys *herself* in the process as if she were an agent
of Jane's desire as well as her own. And finally, Jane's disguised hostility
to Rochester, summarized in her terrifying prediction to herself that 'you
shall, yourself, pluck out your right eye; yourself cut off your right hand'

(ch. 27) comes strangely true through the intervention of Bertha, whose melodramatic death causes Rochester to lose both eye and hand.

These parallels between Jane and Bertha may at first seem somewhat strained. Jane, after all, is poor, plain, little, pale, neat, and quiet, while Bertha is rich, large, florid, sensual, and extravagant; indeed, she was once even beautiful, somewhat, Rochester notes, 'in the style of Blanche Ingram.' Is she not, then, as many critics have suggested, a monitory image rather than a double for Jane? As Richard Chase puts it, 'May not Bertha, Jane seems to ask herself, be a living example of what happens to the woman who [tries] to be the fleshly vessel of the [masculine] *élan*?'[11] 'Just as [Jane's] instinct for self-preservation saves her from earlier temptations,' Adrienne Rich remarks, 'so it must save her from becoming this woman by curbing her imagination at the limits of what is bearable for a powerless woman in the England of the 1840s.'[12] Even Rochester himself provides a similar critical appraisal of the relationship between the two. 'That is *my wife*,' he says, pointing to mad Bertha,

'And *this* is what I wished to have . . . this young girl who stands so grave and quiet at the mouth of hell, looking collectedly at the gambols of a demon. I wanted her just as a change after that fierce ragout . . . Compare these clear eyes with the red balls yonder – this face with that mask – this form with that bulk . . .' (ch. 26)

And of course, in one sense, the relationship between Jane and Bertha is a monitory one: while acting out Jane's secret fantasies, Bertha does (to say the least) provide the governess with an example of how not to act, teaching her a lesson more salutary than any Miss Temple ever taught.

Nevertheless, it is disturbingly clear from recurrent images in the novel that Bertha not only acts *for* Jane, she also acts *like* Jane. The imprisoned Bertha, running 'backwards and forwards' on all fours in the attic, for instance, recalls not only Jane the governess, whose only relief from mental pain was to pace 'backwards and forwards' in the third story, but also that 'bad animal' who was ten-year-old Jane, imprisoned in the red-room, howling and mad. Bertha's 'goblin appearance' – 'half dream, half reality,' says Rochester – recalls the lover's epithets for Jane: 'malicious elf,' 'sprite,' 'changeling,' as well as his playful accusation that she had magically downed his horse at their first meeting. Rochester's description of Bertha as a 'monster' ('a fearful voyage I had with such a monster in the vessel' (ch. 27)) ironically echoes Jane's own fear of being a monster ('Am I a monster? . . . is it impossible that Mr Rochester should have a sincere affection for me?' (ch. 24)). Bertha's fiendish madness recalls Mrs Reed's remark about Jane ('she talked to me once like something mad or like a fiend') as well as Jane's own estimate of her mental state ('I will hold to the principles received by me when I was sane, and not mad – as I am now' (ch. 27)). And most dramatic of all, Bertha's incendiary tendencies recall Jane's early flaming rages, at Lowood and at Gateshead, as well as that 'ridge of lighted heath' which she herself saw as emblematic of her mind in its rebellion against society. It is only fitting, therefore, that, as if to balance the child Jane's terrifying vision of herself as an alien figure in the 'visionary hollow' of the red-room looking glass, the adult Jane first clearly perceives her terrible double when Bertha puts on the wedding veil intended for the second Mrs Rochester, and turns to the mirror. At that moment, Jane sees 'the reflection of the visage and features quite distinctly in the dark oblong glass,' sees them as if they were her own (ch. 25).

For despite all the habits of harmony she gained in her years at Lowood, we must finally recognize, with Jane herself, that on her arrival at Thornfield she only '*appeared* a disciplined and subdued character' (italics ours). Crowned with thorns, finding that she is, in Emily Dickinson's words, 'The Wife – without the Sign,'[13] she represses her rage behind a subdued facade, but her soul's impulse to dance 'like a Bomb, abroad,' to quote Dickinson again,[14] has not been exorcised and will not be exorcised until the literal and symbolic death of Bertha frees her from the furies that torment her and makes possible a marriage of equality – makes possible, that is, wholeness within herself. At that point, significantly, when the Bertha in Jane falls from the ruined wall of Thornfield and is destroyed, the orphan child too, as her dream predicts, will roll from her knee – the burden of her past will be lifted – and she will wake. [. . .]

*   *   *

Far and lonely indeed Jane wanders, starving, freezing, stumbling, abandoning her few possessions, her name, and even her self-respect in her search for a new home. For 'men are hard-hearted, and kind angels only / Watch'd o'er the steps of a poor orphan child.' And like the starved wanderings of Hetty Sorel in *Adam Bede*, her terrible journey across the moors suggests the essential homelessness – the nameless, placeless, and contingent status – of women in a patriarchal society. Yet because Jane, unlike Hetty, has an inner strength which her pilgrimage seeks to develop, 'kind angels' finally do bring her to what is in a sense her true home, the house significantly called *Marsh End* (or Moor House) which is to represent the end of her march toward selfhood. Here she encounters Diana, Mary, and St John Rivers, the 'good' relatives who will help free her from her angry memories of that wicked stepfamily the Reeds. And that the Rivers prove to be literally her relatives is not, in psychological terms, the strained coincidence some readers have suggested. For having left

Rochester, having torn off the crown of thorns he offered and repudiated the unequal charade of marriage he proposed, Jane has now gained the strength to begin to discover her real place in the world. St John helps her find a job in a school, and once again she reviews the choices she has had: 'Is it better, I ask, to be a slave in a fool's paradise at Marseilles . . . or to be a village schoolmistress, free and honest, in a breezy mountain nook in the healthy heart of England?' (ch. 31). Her unequivocal conclusion that 'I was right when I adhered to principle and law' is one toward which the whole novel seems to have tended.

The qualifying word *seems* is, however, a necessary one. For though in one sense Jane's discovery of her family at Marsh End does represent the end of her pilgrimage, her progress toward selfhood will not be complete until she learns that 'principle and law' in the abstract do not always coincide with the deepest principles and laws of her own being. Her early sense that Miss Temple's teachings had merely been superimposed on her native vitality had already begun to suggest this to her. But it is through her encounter with St John Rivers that she assimilates this lesson most thoroughly. As a number of critics have noticed, all three members of the Rivers family have resonant, almost allegorical names. The names of Jane's true 'sisters' Diana and Mary, notes Adrienne Rich, recall the Great Mother in her dual aspects of Diana the huntress and Mary the virgin mother;[15] in this way as well as through their independent, learned, benevolent personalities, they suggest the ideal of female strength for which Jane has been searching. St John, on the other hand, has an almost blatantly patriarchal name, one which recalls both the masculine abstraction of the gospel according to St John ('in the beginning was the *Word*') and the disguised misogyny of St John the Baptist, whose patristic and evangelical contempt for the flesh manifested itself most powerfully in a profound contempt for the *female*. Like Salome, whose rebellion against such misogyny Oscar Wilde was later also to associate with the rising moon of female power, Jane must symbolically, if not literally, behead the abstract principles of this man before she can finally achieve her true independence.

At first, however, it seems that St John is offering Jane a viable alternative to the way of life proposed by Rochester. For where Rochester, like his dissolute namesake, ended up appearing to offer a life of pleasure, a path of roses (albeit with concealed thorns), and a marriage of passion, St John seems to propose a life of principle, a path of thorns (with no concealed roses), and a marriage of spirituality. His self-abnegating rejection of the worldly beauty Rosamund Oliver – another character with a strikingly resonant name – is disconcerting to the passionate and Byronic part of Jane, but at least it shows that, unlike hypocritical Brocklehurst, he practices what he preaches. And what he preaches is the Carlylean sermon of self-actualization through work: 'Work while it is called today, for the night cometh wherein no man can work.'[16] If she follows him, Jane realizes, she will substitute a divine Master for the master she served at Thornfield, and replace love with labor – for 'you are formed for labour, not for love,' St John tells her. Yet when, long ago at Lowood, she asked for 'a new servitude' was not some such solution half in her mind? When, pacing the battlements at Thornfield she insisted that 'women [need] a field for their efforts as much as their brothers do' (ch. 12), did she not long for some such practical 'exercise'? 'Still will my Father with promise and blessing / Take to his bosom the poor orphaned child,' Bessie's song had predicted. Is not Marsh End, then, the promised end, and St John's way the way to His bosom?

Jane's early repudiation of the spiritual harmonies offered by Helen Burns and Miss Temple is the first hint that, while St John's way will tempt her, she must resist it. That, like Rochester, he is 'akin' to her is clear. But where Rochester represents the fire of her nature, her cousin represents the ice. And while for some women ice may 'suffice,' for Jane, who has struggled all her life, like a sane version of Bertha, against the polar cold of a loveless world, it clearly will not. As she falls more deeply under St John's 'freezing spell,' she realizes increasingly that to please him 'I must disown half my nature.' And 'as his wife,' she reflects, she would be 'always restrained . . . forced to keep the fire of my nature continually low, . . . though the imprisoned flame consumed vital after vital' (ch. 34). [. . .]

* * *

Though in many ways St John's attempt to 'imprison' Jane may seem the most irresistible of all, coming as it does at a time when she is congratu-lating herself on just that adherence to 'principle and law' which he recommends, she escapes from his fetters more easily than she had escaped from either Brocklehurst or Rochester. Figuratively speaking, this is a measure of how far she has traveled in her pilgrimage toward maturity. Literally, however, her escape is facilitated by two events. First, having found what is, despite all its ambiguities, her true family, Jane has at last come into her inheritance. Jane Eyre is now the heir of that uncle in Madeira whose first intervention in her life had been, appropriately, to define the legal impediment to her marriage with Rochester, now literally as well as figuratively an independent woman, free to go her own way and follow her own will. But her freedom is also signaled by a second event: the death of Bertha. [. . .]

* * *

Jane's return to Thornfield, her discovery of Bertha's death and of the ruin her dream had predicted, her reunion at Ferndean with the maimed and blinded Rochester, and their subsequent marriage form an essential epilogue to that pilgrimage toward selfhood which had in other ways concluded at Marsh End, with Jane's realization that she could not marry St John. At that moment, 'the wondrous shock of feeling had come like the earthquake which shook the foundations of Paul and Silas' prison; it had opened the doors of the soul's cell, and loosed its bands – it had wakened it out of its sleep' (ch. 36). For at that moment she had been irrevocably freed from the burden of her past, freed both from the raging specter of Bertha (which had already fallen in fact from the ruined wall of Thornfield) and from the self-pitying specter of the orphan child (which had symbolically, as in her dream, rolled from her knee). And at that moment, again as in her dream, she had *wakened* to her own self, her own needs. Similarly, Rochester, 'caged eagle' that he seems (ch. 37), has been freed from what was for him the burden of Thornfield, though at the same time he appears to have been fettered by the injuries he received in attempting to rescue Jane's mad double from the flames devouring his house. That his 'fetters' pose no impediment to a new marriage, that he and Jane are now, in reality, equals, is the thesis of the Ferndean section. [. . .]

Nevertheless, despite the optimistic portrait of an egalitarian relationship that Brontë seems to be drawing here, there is 'a quiet autumnal quality' about the scenes at Ferndean, as Robert Bernard Martin points out.[17] The house itself, set deep in a dark forest, is old and decaying: Rochester had not even thought it suitable for the loathsome Bertha, and its valley-of-the-shadow quality makes it seem rather like a Lowood, a school of life where Rochester must learn those lessons Jane herself absorbed so early. As a dramatic setting, moreover, Ferndean is notably stripped and asocial, so that the physical isolation of the lovers suggests their spiritual isolation in a world where such egalitarian marriages as theirs are rare, if not impossible. True minds, Charlotte Brontë seems to be saying, must withdraw into a remote forest, a wilderness even, in order to circumvent the strictures of a hierarchal society. [. . .]

What Brontë could not logically define, however, she could embody in tenuous but suggestive imagery and in her last, perhaps most significant redefinitions of Bunyan. Nature in the largest sense seems now to be on the side of Jane and Rochester. *Ferndean*, as its name implies, is without artifice – 'no flowers, no garden-beds' – but it is green as Jane tells Rochester he will be, green and ferny and fertilized by soft rains. Here, isolated from society but flourishing in a natural order of their own making, Jane and Rochester will become physically 'bone of [each other's] bone, flesh of [each other's] flesh' (ch. 38), and here the healing powers of nature will eventually restore the sight of one of Rochester's eyes. Here, in other words, nature, unleashed from social restrictions, will do 'no miracle – but her best' (ch. 35). For not the Celestial City but a natural paradise, the country of Beulah 'upon the borders of heaven,' where 'the contract between bride and bridegroom [is] renewed,' has all along been, we now realize, the goal of Jane's pilgrimage.[18]

As for the Celestial City itself, Charlotte Brontë implies here (though she will later have second thoughts) that such a goal is the dream of those who accept inequities on earth, one of the many tools used by patriarchal society to keep, say, governesses in their 'place.' Because she believes this so deeply, she quite consciously concludes *Jane Eyre* with an allusion to *Pilgrim's Progress* and with a half-ironic apostrophe to that apostle of celestial transcendence, that shadow of 'the warrior Greatheart,' St John Rivers. 'His,' she tells us, 'is the exaction of the apostle, who speaks but for Christ when he says – "Whosoever will come after me, let him deny himself and take up his cross and follow me" ' (ch. 38). For it was, finally, to repudiate such a crucifying denial of the self that Brontë's 'hunger, rebellion, and rage' led her to write *Jane Eyre* in the first place and to make it an 'irreligious' redefinition, almost a parody, of John Bunyan's vision.[19] And the astounding progress toward equality of plain Jane Eyre, whom Miss Rigby correctly saw as 'the personification of an unregenerate and undisciplined spirit,' answers by its outcome the bitter question Emily Dickinson was to ask fifteen years later: ' "My husband" – women say – / Stroking the Melody – / Is *this* – the way?" '[20] No, Jane declares in her flight from Thornfield, *that* is not the way. *This*, she says – this marriage of true minds at Ferndean – this is the way. Qualified and isolated as her way may be, it is at least an emblem of hope. Certainly Charlotte Brontë was never again to indulge in quite such an optimistic imagining.

NOTES

1. All references to *Jane Eyre* are to the Norton Critical Edition, ed. Richard J. Dunn (New York: Norton, 1971).

2. See, for instance, David Lodge, 'Fire and Eyre: Charlotte Brontë's War of Earthly Elements,' in *The Brontës*, ed. Ian Gregor, pp. 110–36.

3. Cf. *The Pilgrim's Progress*: 'behold I saw a man clothed with rags . . . he brake out with a lamentable cry, saying, "What shall I do?" ' Charlotte Brontë made even more extensive references to *Pilgrim's Progress* in *Villette*, and in her use of Bunyan she was typical of many nineteenth-century novelists, who – from Thackeray to Louisa May Alcott – relied on his allegory to structure their own fiction. For comments

on Charlotte Brontë's allusions to *Pilgrim's Progress* in *Villette*, see Q.D. Leavis, 'Introduction' to *Villette* (New York: Harper & Row, 1972), pp. vii–xli.

4. In *The Poetics of Space* (Boston: Beacon Press, 1969) Gaston Bachelard speaks of 'the rationality of the roof' as opposed to 'the irrationality of the cellar.' In the attic, he notes, 'the day's experiences can always efface the fears of the night,' while the cellar 'becomes buried madness, walled-in tragedy' (pp. 18–20). Thornfield's attic is, however, in his sense both cellar and attic: the imprisoning lumber-room of the past and the watch-tower from which new prospects are sighted, just as in Jane's mind mad 'restlessness' coexists with 'harmonious' reason.

5. See M. Jeanne Peterson, 'The Victorian Governess: Status Incongruence in Family and Society,' in *Suffer and Be Still: Women in the Victorian Age*, ed. Martha Vicinus (Bloomington: Indiana Univ. Press, 1972), pp. 3–19.

6. See C. Willet Cunnington, *Nineteenth Century Feminine Attitudes* (London: Heinemann, 1935), p. 119.

7. Richard Chase, 'The Brontës, or Myth Domesticated,' in *Jane Eyre*, ed. Richard J. Dunn (New York: Norton, 1971), p. 464.

8. See, for instance, Mrs Oliphant, *Women Novelists of Queen Victoria's Reign* (London: Hurst & Blackett, 1897), p. 19: 'The chief thing . . . that distressed the candid and as yet unaccustomed reader in "Jane Eyre" . . . was the character of Rochester's confidences to the girl whom he loved . . . that he should have talked to a girl so evidently innocent of his amours and his mistresses.'

9. In a sense, Rochester's 'contemptible' prearranged marriage to Bertha Mason is also a consequence of patriarchy, or at least of the patriarchal custom of primogeniture. A younger son, he was encouraged by his father to marry for money and status because sure provisions for his future could be made in no other way.

10. Claire Rosenfeld, 'The Shadow Within: The Conscious and Unconscious Use of the Double,' in *Stories of the Double*, ed. Albert J. Guerard (Philadelphia: J.B. Lippincott, 1967), p. 314. Rosenfeld also notes that 'When the passionate uninhibited self is a woman, she more often than not is dark.' Bertha, of course, is a Creole – swarthy, 'livid,' etc.

11. Chase, 'The Brontës, or Myth Domesticated,' p. 467.

12. Adrienne Rich, 'Jane Eyre: The Temptations of a Motherless Woman,' *Ms* 2.4 (October 1973): 72. The question of what was 'bearable for a powerless woman in the England of the 1840s' inevitably brings to mind the real story of Isabella Thackeray, who went mad in 1840 and was often (though quite mistakenly) thought to be the original of Rochester's mad wife. Parallels are coincidental, but it is interesting that Isabella was reared by a Bertha Mason-like mother of whom it was said that 'wherever she went, "storms, whirlwinds, cataracts, tornadoes" accompanied her,' and equally interesting that Isabella's illness was signalled by mad inappropriate laughter and marked by violent suicide attempts, alternating with Jane Eyre-like docility. That at one point Thackeray tried to guard her by literally *tying* himself to her ('a riband round her waist, & to my waist, and this always woke me if she moved') seems also to recall

Rochester's terrible bondage. For more about Isabella Thackeray, see Gordon N. Ray, *Thackeray: The Uses of Adversity, 1811–1846* (New York: McGraw-Hill, 1955), esp. pp. 182–85 (on Isabella's mother) and ch. 10, 'A Year of Pain and Hope,' pp. 250–77.

13. See Emily Dickinson, *Poems*, J. 1072, 'Title divine – is mine!/The Wife – without the Sign!'

14. See Emily Dickinson, *Poems*, J. 512, 'The Soul has Bandaged Moments.'

15. Rich, 'Jane Eyre: The Temptations of a Motherless Woman,' p. 106.

16. *Sartor Resartus*, ch. 9, 'The Everlasting Yea,' eds K. McSweeney and P. Sabor (Oxford: Oxford University Press, 2000). Chase, 'The Brontës, or Myth Domesticated,' p. 467.

17. Robert Bernard Martin, *The Accents of Persuasion: Charlotte Brontë's Novels* (New York: Norton, 1966), p. 90.

18. *The Pilgrim's Progress* (New York: Airmont Library, 1969), pp. 140–41.

19. It should be noted here that Charlotte Brontë's use of *The Pilgrim's Progress* in *Villette* is much more conventional. Lucy Snowe seems to feel that she will only find true bliss after death, when she hopes to enter the Celestial City.

20. See Emily Dickinson, *Poems*, J. 1072, 'Title divine – is mine!'

CHAPTER THREE

The Sultan and the Slave: Feminist Orientalism and the Structure of *Jane Eyre*

JOYCE ZONANA

Joyce Zonana is Professor of Comparative Literature and Director of Women's Studies at the University of New Orleans. As an Egyptian Jew, she focuses on accounts of ethnicity in major nineteenth-century texts which, she claims, are passed over by early feminist critics since they are usually regarded as marginal. Her focus allows her to subject the casual treatment of Oriental women to an intensive scrutiny that reveals an attitude that is more oppressive than that taken towards Western women in the nineteenth century. She draws attention to the racism inherent in the use of imperialist metaphors to underwrite domestic ideology at home. The disparagement of the harem is shown to be used as a mechanism for urging the West to become unlike the Orient and more like itself. Zonana makes a case for such an approach having a long history in Western literature and she traces it in some detail. She sees her readings as a corrective to the feminist preoccupation with Western women and yet as a strengthening of the feminist approach which would otherwise remain blindly racist. The same kind of argument can be used in relation to the frequent use of slavery as a metaphor for class oppression in nineteenth-century writing.

O n the day following Jane Eyre's betrothal to her 'master' Rochester, Jane finds herself 'obliged' to go with him to a silk warehouse at Millcote, where she is 'ordered to choose half a dozen dresses.' Although she makes it clear that she 'hated the business,' Jane

Reprinted from *Signs: Journal of Women in Culture and Society* 18.3 (1993): 592–617.

cannot free herself from it. All she can manage, 'by dint of entreaties expressed in energetic whispers,' is a reduction in the number of dresses, though 'these . . . [Rochester] vowed he would select himself.' Anxiously, Jane protests and 'with infinite difficulty' secures Rochester's grudging acceptance of her choice: a 'sober black satin and pearl-gray silk.' The ordeal is not over; after the silk warehouse, Rochester takes Jane to a jeweller's, where 'the more he bought me,' she reports, 'the more my cheek burned with a sense of annoyance and degradation' (Brontë [1847] 1985: 296–97).[1]

The shopping trip to Millcote gently figures Rochester as a domestic despot: he commands and Jane is 'obliged' to obey, though she feels degraded by that obedience. At this point in the narrative, Jane is not yet aware that in planning to marry her Rochester is consciously choosing to become a bigamist. Yet the image she uses to portray her experience of his mastery as he tries to dress her 'like a doll' (p. 297) signals that not only despotism but bigamy and the oriental trade in women are on Jane's mind. Riding with Rochester back to Thornfield, she notes: 'He smiled; and I thought his smile was such as a sultan might, in a blissful and fond moment, bestow on a slave his gold and gems had enriched' (p. 297). The image is startling in its extremity: surely Jane seems to overreact to Rochester's desire to see his bride beautifully dressed.

Yet by calling Rochester a 'sultan' and herself a 'slave,' Jane provides herself and the reader with a culturally acceptable simile by which to understand and combat the patriarchal 'despotism' (p. 302) central to Rochester's character. Part of a large system of what I term feminist orientalist discourse that permeates *Jane Eyre*, Charlotte Brontë's sultan/slave simile displaces the source of patriarchal oppression onto an 'Oriental,' 'Mahometan' society, enabling British readers to contemplate local problems without questioning their own self-definition as Westerners and Christians.[2] As I will demonstrate, in developing her simile throughout her narrative, Jane does not so much criticize (in the words of Mary Ellis Gibson) 'domestic arrangements and British Christianity from the point of view of the "pagan" woman' (1987: 2) as define herself as a Western missionary seeking to redeem not the 'enslaved' woman outside the fold of Christianity and Western ideology but the despotic man who has been led astray within it.[3]

Brontë's use of feminist orientalism is both embedded in and brings into focus a long tradition of Western feminist writing. Beginning early in the eighteenth century, when European travelers' tales about visits to the Middle East became a popular genre, images of despotic sultans and desperate slave girls became a central part of an emerging liberal feminist discourse about the condition of women not in the East but in the West. From Mary Wollstonecraft to Elizabeth Barrett Browning to Margaret

Fuller and Florence Nightingale, one discovers writer after writer turning to images of oriental life – and specifically the 'Mahometan' or 'Arabian' harem – in order to articulate their critiques of the life of women in the West. Part of the larger orientalism that Edward Said has shown to inform Western self-representation, the function of these images is not primarily to secure Western domination over the East, though certainly they assume and enforce that domination.[4] Rather, by figuring objectionable aspects of life in the West as 'Eastern,' these Western feminist writers rhetorically define their project as the removal of Eastern elements from Western life.

Feminist orientalism is a special case of the literary strategy of using the Orient as a means for what one writer has called Western 'self-redemption': 'transforming the Orient and Oriental Muslims into a vehicle for . . . criticism of the West itself' (Al-Bazei 1983: 6).[5] Specifically, feminist orientalism is a rhetorical strategy (and a form of thought) by which a speaker or writer neutralizes the threat inherent in feminist demands and makes them palatable to an audience that wishes to affirm its occidental superiority. If the lives of women in England or France or the United States can be compared to the lives of women in 'Arabia,' then the Western feminist's desire to change the status quo can be represented not as a radical attempt to restructure the West but as a conservative effort to make the West more like itself. Orientalism – the belief that the East is inferior to the West, and the representation of the Orient by means of unexamined, stereotypical images – thus becomes a major premise in the formulation of numerous Western feminist arguments.

The conviction that the harem is an inherently oppressive institution functions as an a priori assumption in the writing I examine here. Even in the twentieth century, such an assumption continues to appear in Western feminist discourse, as Leila Ahmed (1982) and Chandra Mohanty (1988) demonstrate. Actual research on or observation of the conditions of the harem is rare, and what little that has been written tends toward either defensive celebration or violent condemnation. The defenses are written with an awareness of the condemnations: their authors must challenge the Western feminist imagination that unquestioningly perceives polygamy as sexual slavery and domestic confinement as imprisonment.[6] The attempt to introduce a genuinely alternate vision is fraught with the difficulties both of documenting the actualities of life in the harem and of achieving a transcultural perspective, though some writers have made the effort.[7]

This article does not claim to demonstrate any truth about the harem that would definitively contradict or even modify the Western views presented here, nor does it systematically engage in the effort to achieve an objective estimate of the harem; rather, it seeks only to show how assumptions about the East have been used to further the Western feminist project instead of either spurring research and theorizing about the actual conditions of harem life or establishing genuine alliances among women of different cultures. For what is most crucial about what I am calling feminist orientalism is that it is directed not toward the understanding or even the reform of the harem itself but toward transformation of Western society – even while preserving basic institutions and ideologies of the West. Coming to recognize the feminist orientalism in *Jane Eyre* and other formative Western feminist texts may help clear the way for a more self-critical, balanced analysis of the multiple forms both of patriarchy and of women's power, and it may also, indirectly, help free global feminism from the charge that it is a Western movement inapplicable to Eastern societies.[8]

That *Jane Eyre*, like so many nineteenth-century British texts, has a diffusely orientalist background has long been recognized and for the most part attributed to the influence of the *Arabian Nights*, a book known to have been a staple of the Brontës' childhood reading. The first simile in the novel, in the fourth paragraph of the first chapter, places Jane, 'cross-legged, like a Turk' (p. 39) in the window seat of the Gateshead breakfast room. Not much later, Jane takes down a book of 'Arabian tales' (p. 70); she reveals that she is fascinated by 'genii' (p. 82); and eventually she makes it plain that the *Arabian Nights* was one of her three favorite childhood books (p. 256). Other characters in the novel also display a loose familiarity and fascination with the Orient: the Dowager Lady Ingram dresses in a 'crimson velvet robe, and a shawl turban' (p. 201); her daughter Blanche admits that she 'dote[s] on Corsairs' (p. 208); Rochester worries when Jane assumes a 'sphinx-like expression' (p. 329). [. . .]

Among the more interesting features of the sultan/slave passage is the fact that Jane does not tell Rochester that she is mentally comparing him to a sultan. She simply asks him to stop looking at her 'in that way.' Rochester is astute enough to understand Jane's unspoken reference, suggesting that feminist orientalist discourse is so pervasive as to be accessible to the very men it seeks to change: '"Oh, it is rich to see and hear her!" he exclaimed. "Is she original? Is she piquant? I would not exchange this one little English girl for the Grand Turk's whole seraglio – gazelle-eyes, houri forms, and all!"' (p. 297). Rochester suggests that he will take Jane instead of a harem, though Jane bristles at the 'Eastern allusion': '"I'll not stand you an inch in the stead of a seraglio," I said; "so don't consider me an equivalent for one. If you have a fancy for anything in that line, away with you, sir, to the bazaars of Stamboul, without delay, and lay out in extensive slave-purchases some of that spare cash you seem at a loss to spend satisfactorily here"' (p. 297).

When Rochester jokingly asks what Jane will do while he is 'bargaining for so many tons of flesh and such an assortment of black eyes,' Jane is ready with a playful but serious response: 'I'll be preparing myself to go out as a missionary to preach liberty to them that are enslaved – your harem inmates among the rest. I'll get admitted there, and I'll stir up mutiny; and you, three-tailed bashaw as you are, sir, shall in a trice find yourself fettered amongst our hands: nor will I, for one, consent to cut your bonds till you have signed a charter, the most liberal that despot ever yet conferred!' (pp. 297–8). Although Jane promises Rochester that she will 'go out as a missionary' to 'Stamboul,' the focus of her remarks is the reform of Rochester himself within England. Her concern is that she herself not be treated as a 'harem inmate,' and her action, immediately following this conversation, succeeds in accomplishing her goal.

It is precisely Jane's experience of degrading dependency, playfully figured here as the relation of rebellious harem slave to despotic Eastern sultan, that leads her to take the step that ultimately reveals Rochester as more like a sultan than Jane had imagined. For it is at this point that Jane makes and executes the decision to write to her Uncle John in Madeira, in the hope that he will settle some money on her. 'If I had ever so small an independency,' she reasons, 'if I had but a prospect of one day bringing Mr Rochester an accession of fortune, I could better endure to be kept by him now' (p. 297). Jane's letter to John Eyre alerts Rochester's brother-in-law, Richard Mason, to Rochester's plans to become a bigamist, and Jane is freed from a marriage that would, in her own terms, have thoroughly enslaved her.

Jane's comparison of Rochester to a sultan proves to be no exaggeration. The narrative makes plain that it is because she sees him in this way that she later is able to free herself from a degrading relationship with a man who has bought women, is willing to become a bigamist, and acts like a despot. The plot thus validates the figurative language, making of it much more than a figure. This Western man is 'Eastern' in his ways, and for Jane to be happy, he must be thoroughly Westernized. To the extent that Brontë has Jane Eyre present hers as a model life – 'Reader, I married him' – she suggests that her female readers would also be well advised to identify and eliminate any such Eastern elements in their own spouses and suitors.

More than ten years ago, Peter A. Tasch observed that in having Jane call Rochester a 'three-tailed bashaw,' Brontë 'was echoing the refrain in a song by George Colman the Younger for his extravaganza *Blue Beard*.' Tasch further notes that 'the idea of an English girl in the "grand Turk's" seraglio demanding liberty forms the theme of another stage comedy, [Isaac Bickerstaffe's] *The Sultan; or, A Peep into the Seraglio'* (1982: 232). Tasch may well be correct in identifying these specific sources for Brontë's allusions; yet the image of a harem inmate demanding liberty had by 1847 become so ingrained in Western feminist discourse that Brontë need not have had any specific text in mind; her audience, whether familiar with *Blue Beard* and *The Sultan* or not, would have had a full stock of harem images by which to understand and applaud Jane's sultan/slave simile.

The stage was set for the Western use of the harem as a metaphor for aspects of Western life as early as 1721, in Baron de Montesquieu's *Persian Letters*. The letters in Montesquieu's novel, written primarily by two 'Persian' men traveling in Europe, offer dramatic images of both Eastern and Western ways of structuring domestic and political relations. Usbek and Rica, the travelers who report on the oddities of Western ways, are in constant contact with the women and eunuchs they have left behind in the harem. The Western reader moves between defamiliarized visions of Europe and 'familiar' images of Persia, eventually coming to see, in the words of one modern commentator, that in the seraglio, constructed as the heart of oriental despotism, 'It is myself, and our world, finally, that I rediscover' (Grosrichard 1979: 32–3, translation mine; for further commentary on the self-reflexive function of Western representations of the harem, see Richon 1985 and Alloula 1986). [. . .]

But it is in Wollstonecraft's 1792 *Vindication of the Rights of Woman*, the founding text of Western liberal feminism, that one finds the fullest explicit feminist orientalist perspective. Like many of the enlightenment thinkers on whom she drew – including, of course, Montesquieu – Wollstonecraft uncritically associates the East with despotism and tyranny. Her text is replete with images that link any abuse of power with 'Eastern' ways: she is not above likening women who seek to dominate their husbands with 'Turkish bashaws' ([1792] 1982: 125). Yet she reserves her fullest scorn for the gendered despotism that she sees as a defining feature of Eastern life and a perverse corruption of Western values.

Any aspect of the European treatment of women that Wollstonecraft finds objectionable she labels as Eastern. Thus, she finds that European women's 'limbs and faculties' are 'cramped with worse than Chinese bands' (Wollstonecraft [1792] 1982: 128); Western women are educated in 'worse than Egyptian bondage' (p. 221); their masters are 'worse than Egyptian task-masters' (p. 319). Upper-class women, 'dissolved in luxury,' have become weak and depraved 'like the Sybarites' (p. 130); if women do not 'grow more perfect when emancipated,' Wollstonecraft advises that Europe should 'open a fresh trade with Russia for whips' (p. 319).

Yet it is 'Mahometanism' – and the 'Mahometan' institution of the seraglio or harem – that Wollstonecraft singles out as the grand type for all oppression of women. Any Western writer who treats women 'as a kind of subordinate beings, and not as a part of the human species' is accused of writing 'in the true style of Mahometanism' ([1792] 1982: 80). This is because what she believes about 'Mahometanism' embodies for Wollstonecraft the antithesis of her own central claim: that women, like men, have souls. Although Ahmed asserts that she can find 'no record . . . in the body of orthodox Muslim literature of the notion that women are animals or have no souls,' she notes that views such as Wollstonecraft's are a staple of Western writing about Islam (1982: 526). Ahmed attributes the creation of this purported fact about Islamic culture to the same Western men who have insisted on the 'inferiority of Western women' (p. 523). Yet in *Vindication of the Rights of Woman*, a founder of modern feminism reproduces and intensifies the spurious 'fact' about 'Mahometanism,' indeed, using it as a cornerstone of her argument for women's rights in the West. [. . .]

Though the Western emphasis on the marriageability of girls makes 'mere animals' of them, 'weak beings' who 'are only fit for a seraglio' (Wollstonecraft [1792] 1982: 83), it is only 'Mahometan' women who can accept such bondage: 'If women are to be made virtuous by authority, which is a contradiction in terms, let them be immured in seraglios and watched with a jealous eye. Fear not that the iron will enter their souls – for the souls that can bear such treatment are made of yielding materials, just animated enough to give life to the body' (p. 311). [. . .]

Among the elements that feminist writers return to again and again are three aspects of the Eastern treatment of women that Wollstonecraft had emphasized: (1) the central belief that women do not have souls, which justifies and explains the other practices; (2) the excessive sexuality of the harem, embodied partly in polygamy but also in luxury, indolence, and the trade in women; and (3) the enforced confinement, undereducation, and inactivity of women in the harem that reduces them to animals or children. A few more examples may help to establish the full context of the discourse that allowed Brontë to structure her novel as the drama of a Western woman oppressed by Eastern beliefs and practices. [. . .]

When Elizabeth Barrett Browning justifies her discussion of prostitution in *Aurora Leigh*, she explains she is working to rid England of oriental prejudice: 'I am deeply convinced that the corruption of our society requires not shut doors and windows, but light and air: and that is exactly because pure and prosperous women choose to *ignore* vice, that miserable women suffer wrong by it everywhere. Has paterfamilias, with his Oriental traditions and veiled female faces, very successfully dealt with a certain class of evil? What if materfamilias, with her quick sure instincts and honest innocent eyes, do more towards their expulsion by simply looking at them and calling them by their names?' (1897: 2: 445) When Barrett Browning writes of 'shut doors and windows' and 'veiled female faces,' she also indirectly hints at another central aspect of the life of Eastern women in the imaginations of Western feminists: the confinement of the harem. This is the aspect emphasized when Walter Besant, in 1897, comments on the 'Oriental prejudice' that keeps British women out of certain professions and that earlier in the century resulted in their 'seclusion . . . in the home, and their exclusion from active and practical life' ([1897] 1989: 2: 1653, 2: 1652).

And it is this aspect that emerges most tellingly in the writing of Florence Nightingale. 'If heaven and hell exist on this earth, it is in the two worlds I saw that morning – the Dispensary and the Hareem,' she writes at the conclusion of her 1849 tour of Egypt ([1849–50] 1988: 208). Nightingale's may be the most dramatic nineteenth-century feminist condemnation of the harem: it is for her literally hell on earth. What makes it so for Nightingale is not (at least not explicitly) its sensuality, nor its domination by a male despot, nor even the slavery of its women. Rather, what Nightingale finds horrifying about the harem are its all too familiar boredom and confinement: 'A little more of such a place would have killed us . . . Oh, the *ennui* of that magnificent palace, it will stand in my memory as a circle of hell! Not one thing was there laying about, to be done or to be looked at' (p. 208). [. . .]

It is the image of domestic immurement that most obviously haunts *Jane Eyre* and shapes its very structure. Examining this narrative structure, one sees that each household in which Jane finds herself is constructed to resemble a harem; each of her oppressors is characterized as a Mahometan despot; and each of her rebellions or escapes bears the accents of Roxanna, the harem inmate declaring her existence as a free soul. At Gateshead, at Lowood, at Thornfield, and at Moor House, one discovers a series of communities of dependent women, all subject to the whim of a single master who rules in his absence as much as his presence and who subjects the imprisoned women to the searching power of his gaze.[9] In each of these households, Jane finds her own power of movement and of vision limited; even when she is most in love with Rochester at Thornfield, she recognizes that he stands in her way, 'as an eclipse intervenes between man and the broad sun' (Brontë [1847] 1985: 302).

The pattern of home as harem is established at Gateshead, where the household consists of John Reed, Mrs Reed, Eliza and Georgiana Reed,

Jane, and the two female servants, Bessie and Abbott. There are also a male 'butler and footman' (p. 60), though these are shadowy presences, nameless men inconsequential in the dynamics and management of the household. The 'master' is young John Reed, a boy of fourteen who demands that Jane call him 'Master Reed' (p. 41) and against whose arbitrary rule Jane has no appeal: 'the servants did not like to offend their young master by taking my part against him, and Mrs Reed was blind and deaf on the subject: she never saw him strike or heard him abuse me, though he did both now and then in her very presence' (p. 42).

Like the sultans described by Montesquieu and the eighteenth-century travelers, John considers the privileges of seeing and knowing to be his. What enrages him in the novel's opening scene is that Jane is out of his sight. Hidden behind the curtain of the window seat, reading and looking out the window, she has usurped his role as the 'Turk.' 'Where the dickens is she?' John asks his sisters, and when Eliza finds Jane for him, John castigates his cousin not only for 'getting behind curtains' but also for reading: 'You have no business to take our books' (p. 42). In the course of his tirade, John calls Jane a 'bad animal' (p. 41) and a 'rat' (p. 42); later she will become a 'wild cat' (p. 59). John's descriptions of Jane as beast and his wish to keep her from educating herself through books may recall Wollstonecraft's definition of the 'true style' of Mahometanism: the view of women as 'domestic brutes' ([1792] 1982: 101), 'not as a part of the human species' (p. 80).

The sexuality of the harem is absent from the Reed home, but the indolent, pampered sensuality that so offends Wollstonecraft is not. In the opening scene, Mrs Reed lies 'reclined on a sofa by the fireside . . . with her darlings about her' (p. 39). John is constantly plied with 'cakes and sweetmeats,' even though he 'gorged himself habitually at table, which made him bilious, and gave him a dim and bleared eye with flabby cheeks' (p. 41). John is the effete, attenuated tyrant made weak by his abuse of power, familiar from Wollstonecraft's characterizations of 'bashaws.' The Reed sisters are 'universally indulged' (p. 46) and 'elaborately ringleted' (p. 60); their mother dresses regularly in silks. The luxury of Gateshead, associated as it is with the degeneracy and despotism of the harem, is something Jane learns to abhor, and this abhorrence informs her later attempts to resist Rochester's desire to see her 'glittering like a parterre' (p. 296). [. . .]

Jane's outburst leads to her departure from Gateshead, though she soon finds herself in another institution that even more closely resembles the harem that haunts the Western feminist imagination. Lowood, 'a large and irregular building' through which on her arrival Jane is led 'from compartment to compartment, from passage to passage' (p. 76), perfectly embodies the confinement of the harem. The building is oppressive, dark, and gloomy, and the garden is no better: 'a wide enclosure,' it is 'surrounded with walls so high as to exclude every glimpse of prospect' (p. 80). These walls not only limit the vision of the institution's 'inmates' but they are 'spike-guarded' (p. 107) to prohibit freedom of movement.

Within the confines of this dwelling, Jane discovers 'a congregation of girls of every age . . . Their number to me appeared countless' (p. 76). Over this community of women rules the redoubtable Mr Brocklehurst, 'the black marble clergyman' (p. 98) whom Jane perceives as a 'black column,' a 'piece of architecture' (p. 94). Like John Reed, Brocklehurst's characteristic gesture is to gaze searchingly upon his assembled dependents. When he makes his first appearance at Lowood, he 'majestically surveyed the whole school' (p. 95); a few moments later he 'scrutinize[s]' the hair of the terrified girls. As with John Reed, Jane seeks to hide from this master's eyes: 'I had sat well back on the form, and while seeming to be busy with my sum, had held my slate in such a manner as to conceal my face' (p. 97). Jane does not escape Brocklehurst's look, however, and is forced to suffer the humiliation of his description of her as a liar. Jane is freed by the good offices of Miss Temple, and later, when the scandal of Brocklehurst's despotic rule is revealed (significantly, it takes the death of a number of the inmates to cause this revelation) he is stripped of some of his power. Lowood becomes a fairly happy home for Jane, though a 'prison-ground' nonetheless (p. 117).

It may be objected that the ascetic aspects of Lowood accord ill with the suggestion that it is figured as a harem. Certainly Lowood harbors neither the sensuality nor the overt sexuality associated with the harem. Yet its structure, with one man controlling an indefinite number of dependent women, mimics that of the seraglio. Further, Brocklehurst's wish to strip the girls of all adornment, of all possibilities of sensual gratification, has its parallel in the sultan's wish to keep the women of the harem restrained from any sexuality not under his control. That Brocklehurst is figured in plainly phallic terms only underscores his identification as a sultan whose perverse pleasure here consists in denying pleasure to the women he rules. For his wife and daughters, however – women over whom presumably he can exert even greater control – Brocklehurst allows a greater sensuality: these women are 'splendidly attired in velvet, silk, and furs' (p. 97).

When Jane leaves Lowood for her 'new servitude' at Thornfield (p. 117), she happily anticipates entering the domain of Mrs Fairfax, an 'elderly lady' (p. 120) whom she believes to be the mistress of a 'safe haven' (p. 129), a 'snug' and secure realm of feminine 'domestic comfort'

(p. 127). To her initial dismay, Jane discovers that this new household of women also has a 'master,' the absent yet omnipotent Mr Rochester. Jane first meets Rochester on the moonlit lane connecting Thornfield to the town of Hay, unaware he is her master. She perceives this stranger to have a 'dark face, with stern features and a heavy brow' (p. 145); later she will call his skin 'swarthy,' his features 'Paynim' (p. 212). The man has fallen from his horse, and Jane offers to assist him. Before accepting her help, however, he subjects her to intense 'scrutiny' in order to determine her identity (p. 146).

Jane reveals that she is the governess at Thornfield; Rochester offers no information about himself, except to say, when Jane fails in her effort to lead his horse to him: 'I see . . . the mountain will never be brought to Mahomet, so all you can do is to aid Mahomet to go to the mountain' (p. 146). Though uttered in jest, these words do not bode well for Jane's relationship with her master. Rochester gives himself the one name that, to a nineteenth-century audience, would unambiguously identify him as a polygamous, blasphemous despot – a sultan. After such an introduction, it comes as no surprise when Rochester chooses to dress 'in shawls, with a turban on his head' for a game of charades, nor that Jane should see him as 'the very model of an Eastern emir' (p. 212).

The most striking identification of Rochester as an oriental despot – again a characterization that comes from his own lips – occurs when he begins to contemplate marriage with Jane. The intimacy between master and dependent has begun to develop and, in the course of guardedly discussing his past with the governess, Rochester admits that he 'degenerated' when wronged by fate (p. 167). As Jane and the reader will later learn, he is referring to his marriage with Bertha Mason, and his subsequent indulgence in 'lust for a passion – vice for an occupation' (p. 343). With no knowledge of the details of Rochester's 'degeneration,' Jane nevertheless encourages him to repent, though Rochester insists that only pleasure, 'sweet, fresh pleasure' (p. 167), can help him. Jane suggests that such pleasure 'will taste bitter' (p. 167) and warns Rochester against 'error.' Rochester, apparently referring to his wish to love Jane, replies that the 'notion that flitted across my brain' is not error or temptation but 'inspiration': 'I am laying down good intentions, which I believe durable as flint. Certainly, my associates and pursuits shall be other than they have been . . . You seem to doubt me; I don't doubt myself: I know what my aim is, what my motives are; and at this moment I pass a law, unalterable as that of the Medes and Persians, that both are right' (pp. 168–9).

Rochester's aim is to find happiness with Jane; his motives are to redeem himself from his association with Bertha; the unalterable law that he makes his own has its antecedent in the one decreed by King Ahasuerus – 'written among the laws of the Persians and the Medes, that it not be altered' – when he banishes his Queen Vashti and vows to 'give her royal estate unto another that is better than she' (Esther 1:19). Ahasuerus, to whom Jane will later compare Rochester (in the same chapter in which she compares him to a sultan [Brontë (1847) 1985: 290]), had been angered by Vashti's refusal to come at his command. His counselors point out that the queen's refusal to be commanded might 'come abroad unto all women' (Esther 1:17), and the Persian king passes his law so that 'every man should bear rule in his own house' (Esther 1:22). Rochester's decision to banish Bertha and marry Jane is dangerously like Ahasuerus's replacement of Vashti by Esther; Jane's resistance signals her engagement in both the reform of her master and the liberation of her people.

The conversation between Jane and Rochester about Rochester's 'Persian' law offers readers clear signals about how they should perceive Rochester's relationship to Jane. Expressed as a conflict between Judeo-Christian law and Persian arrogance, the conflict can also be understood as Jane's struggle to retain possession of her soul, to claim her rights as a Western, Christian woman. Thus, when Rochester begins his actual proposal to her, Jane insists, 'I have as much soul as you' (Brontë [1847] 1985: 281). Later, when she resists his wish to take her to a 'white-washed villa on the shores of the Mediterranean,' where, as his mistress, she would live a 'guarded' life (p. 331), she expresses her triumph in precisely the same terms: 'I still possessed my soul' (p. 344).[10]

It is at Thornfield, of course, that the confinement and sexuality of the seraglio/harem are most fully represented. Rochester has a wife whom he keeps literally caged in a 'wild beast's den' (p. 336), 'a room without a window' (p. 321). In her first explicit view of Bertha Mason, Jane depicts her in the ambiguous, nonhuman terms Wollstonecraft had applied to harem inmates: 'What it was, whether beast or human being, one could not, at first sight tell: it grovelled, seemingly, on all fours; it snatched and growled like some strange wild animal: but it was covered with clothing, and a quantity of dark, grizzled hair, wild as a mane, hid its head and face' (p. 321). Referred to by Jane as a 'clothed hyena' (p. 321), Bertha incarnates a brute sensuality that apparently justifies her imprisonment. Rochester calls her his 'bad, mad, and embruted partner' (p. 320), whom he married without being 'sure of the existence of one virtue in her nature' (p. 333).

When Rochester takes his first wife, he is himself acting purely on the basis of his own 'excited' senses (p. 332), not seeking a rational companion. He discovers in Bertha a 'nature wholly alien' to his own, a 'cast of mind common, low, narrow, and singularly incapable of being led to anything higher, expanded to anything larger' (p. 333). Bertha is characterized here as a woman without a soul. This Western man has married a figuratively Eastern woman, an 'embruted' creature who, through the marriage bond, becomes a 'part of' him (p. 334). When Rochester, responding to the 'sweet wind from Europe,' decides to leave Jamaica and 'go home to God' (p. 335), his behavior continues to be governed by the 'most gross, impure, depraved' nature that is permanently 'associated' with his own (p. 334). Instead of remaining faithful to his wife, he roams Europe seeking 'a good and intelligent woman, whom I could love' (p. 337). Of course he finds only the 'unprincipled and violent,' 'mindless,' and faithless mistresses his money buys him (p. 338). Rochester knows that 'hiring a mistress is the next worse thing to buying a slave' (p. 339), yet he persists on this course – even with Jane – because, the narrative suggests, his association with Bertha has deformed him into a polygamous, sensual sultan.

Thus Brontë appears to displace the blame for Rochester's Eastern tendencies on the intrusion of this 'Eastern' woman into his Western life. Though Jane protests in Bertha's behalf – 'you are inexorable for that unfortunate lady' (p. 328) – Rochester's account of his first marriage serves as the narrative explanation of his own oriental tendencies. The fact that he does not reform until Bertha dies suggests how powerful her oriental hold on him has been.[11]

Bertha, of course, is West Indian, not 'Mahometan,' and she scarcely resembles the conventional image of an alluring harem inmate – no 'gazelle eyes' or 'houri forms' here. Indeed, as Susan L. Meyer convincingly shows, she is consistently figured as a 'nightmare' vision with 'savage,' 'lurid,' and 'swelled' black features (1989: 253–4) and associated with the oppressed races subject to British colonialism. Yet, as Grosrichard points out, 'The West Indies can end by rejoining, in the imagination, the East Indies' (1979: 32, translation mine). Bertha's characterization in other significant ways recalls the terms used by Wollstonecraft to depict the fate of 'Mahometan' women: she is soulless, regarded as 'not . . . a part of the human species,' and her all-too-real imprisonment at Thornfield invokes the root meaning of *seraglio*: a place where wild beasts are kept. One might say that Bertha's characterization as a 'clothed hyena' manifests the Western view of the underlying reality of the harem inmate, the philosophical view of women that underpins both their confinement within the harem and their more conventional adornment.[12]

Thus, to note Bertha's 'blackness' and her birth in Jamaica need not preclude seeing that she is also, simultaneously, figured as an 'Eastern' woman. Indeed, in Bertha's characterization a number of parallel discourses converge: she is the 'black woman who signifies both the oppressed and the oppressor' (Meyer 1989: 266); she is Jane's 'dark double' who enacts both Jane's and Brontë's repressed rage at patriarchal oppression (Gilbert and Gubar 1979: 360); she is the Indian woman consumed in sati (Perera 1991); she is Vashti, King Ahasuerus's uncontrollable queen; and she is a harem inmate whose purported soullessness justifies and enforces her own oppression. Bertha is overdetermined; as the 'central locus of Brontë's anxieties about oppression' (Meyer 1989: 252) and as the spark for the redemptive fire that clears the way for Jane's fulfillment, she serves to focus a number of different systems of figuration that structure the novel.

Indeed, Brontë equivocates still further in her presentation of Bertha, never fully indicating whether she is inherently soulless or only made so by Rochester's treatment of her. In a few significant passages, Brontë allows her narrative to suggest that Bertha, like Jane, is consciously aware of and legitimately enraged by her enslavement. On the eve of the doomed wedding, Bertha enters Jane's room, not to harm her as Rochester fears but to rend the veil, which Rochester in his 'princely extravagance' had insisted upon buying (Brontë [1847] 1985: 308). Jane sees in the veil an image of Rochester's 'pride' (p. 309). When Bertha rends it 'in two parts' and 'trample[s] on them' (p. 311), her action may be explained as emanating from her resentment of and jealousy toward Jane. Or, it may be viewed as a warning to Jane about the 'veiled' existence she would have to lead as Rochester's harem slave.

That Bertha kills herself in her attempt to burn down the house of her master can also be linked to Roxanna's ultimately self-destructive rebellion in *Persian Letters*. Defying the master who has enslaved her, she asserts her freedom only to find death as its inevitable price. As long as the despotic system is in place, no woman can truly be free, yet the suicide of a rebellious woman serves as a powerful condemnation – and potential transformation – of that system.[13] Thus it is no accident that Rochester is blinded in the conflagration caused by Bertha's rebellion. Stripped of his despotic privilege to see, he can no longer function as a sultan. Despite her earlier promises to 'stir up mutiny' in the harem (p. 298), Jane owes her freedom not to her own rebellion but to that of the actual 'harem-inmate,' the 'dark double' who acts as her proxy.

After Bertha's death, Rochester is free to reform, and this reform is significantly figured as a conversion: 'Jane! you think me, I dare say, an irreligious dog: but my heart swells with gratitude to the beneficent God of this earth just now . . . I did wrong . . . Of late, Jane – only – only of late – I began to see and acknowledge the hand of God in my doom. I began to experience remorse, repentance, the wish for reconcilement with my Maker. I began sometimes to pray' (p. 471). The man who had passed a 'Persian' law to justify his own behavior here acknowledges the authority of the Christian God who mandates monogamy and respect for the souls of women. Despite the many critiques of Christian ideology and practice that abound in *Jane Eyre*, Brontë's feminist orientalism here takes priority, as she obscures the patriarchal oppression that is also a part of Christianity.

And by ending her novel with the words of the Christian missionary St John Rivers, himself one of the domestic despots Jane has had to defy, Brontë leaves the reader with an idealized vision of Christianity as the only satisfactory alternative to Eastern, 'Mahometan' – and even Hindu – despotism. While this reversal in the characterization of St John and the expressed attitude toward Christianity has struck many readers as a self-contradictory shift in Brontë's focus, it in fact confirms and seals the pattern begun with Jane's promise to 'go out as a missionary to preach liberty to them that are enslaved' (p. 297).

The novel's concluding paean to St John and to Christian values takes place against the backdrop not of a vaguely conceived Middle East but of the Far East, India. The groundwork establishing India as another locale for gendered oriental despotism had been laid early in the novel, in the same chapter that features the 'sultan/slave' simile. Back at Thornfield after the trip to Millcote, Jane objects to a 'pagan' tendency in Rochester (p. 301). Her master has just sung a song to her in which a woman swears 'to live – to die' with her beloved (p. 301). Jane seizes on the seemingly innocent phrase and asserts that she 'had no intention of dying' with Rochester: 'I had as good a right to die when my time came as he had: but I should bide that time, and not be hurried away in a suttee' (p. 301).

Though this identification of India as another Eastern site for the oppression of women is not in my view extensively developed throughout the text, it returns in the novel's conclusion, as well as in the penultimate section of the novel, when Jane faces the threat of being 'grilled alive in Calcutta' (p. 441) if she chooses to accompany St John to India. For during her stay at Moor House, Jane once again encounters a man with a 'despotic nature' (p. 434) who rules over a household of dependent women and who threatens not only to immure but also to immolate her (p. 430).

At first Jane finds Moor House less oppressive than her earlier homes. Yet when Jane consents to give up her study of German in order to help St John learn Hindustani, she discovers another form of 'servitude' (p. 423) and she experiences the kiss that St John gives her as a 'seal affixed to my fetters' (p. 424). Jane's subjection to St John is in fact stronger than any she has felt before. 'I could not resist him,' she uncharacteristically admits (p. 425). Part of Jane's difficulty in resisting St John's wishes is that they come cloaked in Christian doctrine. Jane recognizes the despotism in St John, knowing that to accede to his wishes would be 'almost equivalent to committing suicide' (p. 439). Yet because St John is a 'sincere Christian' (p. 434), not an 'irreligious dog,' she has a harder time extricating herself from the seductions of his proposal that she marry him and accompany him to India: 'Religion called – Angels beckoned – God commanded' (p. 444).

Brontë here reveals the motive behind feminist orientalism as a mode of cultural analysis as well as a rhetorical strategy. Jane finds it possible to resist Rochester because he calls himself and acts in ways that clearly echo the Western conception of 'Mahomet,' not Christ. But a man who assumes the language and posture of Christ is harder to combat. Jane ultimately does find the strength to resist St John, however, when he unwittingly sets her a challenge that obviously mimics the behavior of a Western feminist's notion of a sultan.

What St John asks of Jane is that she abandon her already established love for Rochester. With this demand, he manifests what was, to Western feminists, perhaps the most threatening feature of 'Mahometan' practice: interference with a woman's free choice of love object. Indeed, what had motivated Roxanna's rebellion in *Persian Letters* was not her desire to escape confinement nor her position as one of many wives. Rather, it was her desire to be free to love another man, coupled with her abhorrence of her sexual 'master.' In denying Jane her freedom to love (and in promising to impose the forms of sexual love upon her), St John becomes the most brutal (and literal) of her harem masters and thus the one who evokes from her the greatest effort of rebellion.[14]

Yet in the concluding paragraphs of the novel, St John – the archetypal Christian man – is redeemed from the flaw in his own nature. By her resistance to his desire to enslave her, Jane frees him from his own oriental tendencies. If she is not a slave, he cannot be a master. Brontë makes explicit the implication behind Wollstonecraft's assertion that the women of the harem have souls 'just animated enough to give life to the body.' A woman of soul, as Jane has by now firmly established herself to be, has the power not only to resist the harem but to transform it: as Jane had once promised Rochester, 'you, three-tailed bashaw as you are, sir, shall in a trice find yourself fettered amongst our hands' (p. 298).

St John, like Rochester, becomes a true Christian after his encounter with Jane and thus is free to pursue her orientalist project. For St John, as a Christian missionary in India, 'labours for his race' with the same impulses as do Jane and her author: 'Firm, faithful, and devoted, full of

energy and zeal, and truth . . . he clears their painful way to improvement; he hews down like a giant the prejudices of creed and caste that
encumber it' (p. 477). Jane Eyre ends her story with St John's words –
'Amen; even so, come, Lord Jesus!' (p. 477) – because they externalize and
make global what has been her own internal and local project all along:
the purging of oriental elements from her society, the replacement of
'Mahometan' law by Christian doctrine. In voicing these words, St John
is recommitting himself to the specifically Christian project of combating
alien religious forms. Thus, although the novel's primary focus is the
occidentalization of the Occident, it ends with the vision of the occidentalization of the Orient that simultaneously underlies and expands that
focus. Readers, both male and female, are encouraged to follow both St
John and Jane in the task of clearing the thicket of oriental 'prejudices'
abroad, at home, and within their own souls. It remains for readers in
the twentieth century to clear yet another thicket, the tangle of feminist
orientalist prejudice that continues to encumber Western feminist
discourse.

NOTES

1. Hereafter, unidentified page numbers in text refer to the Penguin edition of *Jane Eyre*.
2. Although the feminist orientalism I discern in the novel is parallel to the 'figurative use
   of blackness' earlier identified by Susan L. Meyer (1989: 250), it also has significant
   differences. Whereas Meyer focuses on the opposition 'white/black,' I examine the
   opposition 'West/East.' The two forms of opposition are related but not identical: the
   one privileges skin color or 'race,' and the other 'culture,' a phenomenon that may
   be associated with but that is not necessarily reducible to 'race.' Meyer's essay
   admirably demonstrates how *Jane Eyre* uses racial oppression as a metaphor for
   class and gender oppression. However, in systematically linking gender oppression
   to oriental despotism, *Jane Eyre* focuses on a form of oppression that is, from the
   first, conceived by Westerners in terms of gender.
3. Gibson, one of the few critics to note how the sultan image pervades *Jane Eyre*,
   makes the sanguine assumption that Brontë's critique of Eastern despotism 'extends
   to British imperialist impulses themselves,' leading Gibson, like many critics, to find
   the novel's conclusion 'strange' (1987: 1, 7). As I shall show, however, Jane's concluding paean to her missionary cousin in India is thoroughly grounded in the novel's
   figurative structure. Gayatri Spivak, for her part, argues that Brontë's novel reproduces the 'axiomatics of imperialism' (1985: 247) and that its 'imperialist project'
   remains inaccessible to the 'nascent "feminist" scenario' (p. 249). My argument
   emphasizes less the acts of political domination that constitute imperialism than how
   its ideology (and specifically its orientalism) infects the analysis of domestic relations

'at home' and posits that orientalism is in fact put to the service of feminism. See also Suvendrini Perera's discussion of how 'the vocabulary of oriental misogyny' became 'an invisible component in feminist representations' in the nineteenth century (1991: 79). Perera's chapter on *Jane Eyre*, published after the research for this article had been completed, focuses on sati as the text's 'central image' (p. 93), while my reading emphasizes the use of the harem as the central image of gender oppression. Western feminist uses of both sati and the harem function equally, as Perera points out, to objectify the 'colonized or imagined "oriental" female subject' (p. 82).

4. See Said 1979 for the definitive exposition of orientalism as a 'Western style for dominating, restructuring, and having authority over the Orient' (p. 71).

5. Al-Bazei's excellent study does not consider the specifically feminist adaptation of this strategy. Interestingly, however, Al-Bazei identifies Byron's Turkish Tales as a crucial locus for the development of 'self-redemption' as the dominant mode of nineteenth-century literary orientalism. Byron's influence on Brontë has been well documented, and further study might establish a link between his Turkish Tales and Brontë's feminist orientalism.

6. For a recent defense of polygamy in the context of Western Mormonism, see Joseph 1991. Earlier in this century, Demetra Vaka argued that women living in harems were 'healthy and happy,' possessing a 'sublimity of soul . . . lacking in our European civilization' (1909: 29, 127–8). Ahmed 1982 argues that the harem can be construed as an inviolable and empowering 'women's space' that enables Islamic women to have 'frequent and easy access to other women in their community, vertically, across class lines, as well as horizontally' (p. 524).

7. See, e.g., Makhlouf-Obermeyer 1979; Gordon (1865) 1983; Delplato 1988; Croutier 1989; Gendron 1991; Leonowens (1872) 1991.

8. See Ahmed 1982 for a pointed analysis of how fundamentalist Islamic movements 'target' feminism as '"Western" and as particularly repugnant and evil' (p. 533). Similarly, Hatem 1989 shows how in the late nineteenth and early twentieth centuries 'European and Egyptian women were influenced by modern national ideologies and rivalries . . . prevent[ing] them from using each other's experience to push for a more radical critique of their own societies' (p. 183).

9. Grosrichard convincingly demonstrates that, in the Western construction of the seraglio, 'To be the master . . . is to see. In the despotic state, where one always obeys "blindly," the blind man is the emblematic figure of the subject' (73, translation mine). See also Bellis 1987 for an exploration of the politics of vision in *Jane Eyre*.

10. The other Old Testament reference to a 'law of the Medes and Persians, which altereth not' occurs in chapter 6 of the book of Daniel. Here the Persian king Darius orders that anyone who petitions 'any God or Man' other than the king 'shall be cast into the den of lions' (Dan. 6:7). Daniel prays to the God of the Hebrews; the king casts him in the lion's den; Daniel's miraculous deliverance converts Darius to an acknowledgment of the 'living God' (Dan. 6:26). Jane Eyre names Daniel as one of her favorite books in the Bible early in the novel (Brontë [1847] 1985: 65); Daniel's

ordeal, as well as Esther's, serves as a model for her own resistance to her master's desire to strip her of 'soul.' I am indebted to Jimmy Griffin for bringing to my attention the relevant biblical passages.

11. See Meyer 1989 for fuller discussion of how contact with the Other serves to besmirch the Englishman in *Jane Eyre*.

12. The reader may be reminded of Horace Walpole's comment that Mary Wollstonecraft was a 'hyena in petticoats' (Wollstonecraft [1792] 1982: 17).

13. See Donaldson 1988 for a similar argument about the self-assertion implicit in Bertha's suicide; Perera 1991, on the contrary, sees Bertha's death as a denial of her subjectivity.

14. See Leonowens (1872) 1991 for a fuller elaboration of this idea: the greatest horror of the harem, for Leonowens, is not polygamy, not confinement, not enforced sexual submission, but denial of the freedom to love.

REFERENCES

Ahmed, Leila. 1982. 'Western Ethnocentrism and Perceptions of the Harem,' *Feminist Studies* 8(3): 521–34.

Al-Bazei, Saad Abdulrahman. 1983. 'Literary Orientalism in Nineteenth-century Anglo-American Literature: Its Formation and Continuity.' PhD dissertation, Purdue University.

Alloula, Malek. 1986. *The Colonial Harem*, trans. Myrna Godzich and Wlad Godzich. Theory and History of Literature, vol. 21 (Minneapolis: University of Minnesota Press).

Barrett Browning, Elizabeth. 1897. *The Letters of Elizabeth Barrett Browning*, ed. Frederic G. Kenyon (New York: Macmillan).

Bellis, Peter J. 1987. 'In the Window-seat: Vision and Power in *Jane Eyre*,' *ELH* 54(3): 639–52.

Besant, Walter. [1897] 1989. *The Queen's Reign*. In *Norton Anthology of English Literature*, 5th edn, ed. M.H. Abrams (New York: Norton).

Brontë, Charlotte. [1847] 1985. *Jane Eyre* (New York: Penguin).

Caracciolo, Peter L., ed. 1988. *'The Arabian Nights' in English Literature: Studies in the Reception of 'The Thousand and One Nights' into British Culture* (New York: St Martin's).

Croutier, Alev Lytle. 1989. *Harem: The World behind the Veil* (New York: Abbeville).

Delplato, Joan. 1988. 'An English "Feminist" in the Turkish Harem: A Portrait of Lady Mary Wortley Montagu,' in *Eighteenth-century Women and the Arts*, eds Frederick M. Keener and Susan E. Lorsch (Westport, NY: Greenwood).

Donaldson, Laura E. 1988. 'The Miranda Complex: Colonialism and the Question of Feminist Reading,' *Diacritics* 18(3): 65–77.

Gaskell, Elizabeth. [1853] 1985. *Ruth* (New York: Oxford).

Gendron, Charisse. 1991. 'Images of Middle-Eastern Women in Victorian Travel Books,' *Victorian Newsletter*, no. 79, 18–23.

Gibson, Mary Ellis. 1987. 'The Seraglio or Suttee: Brontë's *Jane Eyre*,' *Postscript* 4: 1–8.

Gilbert, Sandra and Susan Gubar. 1979. *The Madwoman in the Attic: The Woman Writer and the Nineteenth-century Literary Imagination* (New Haven, Conn.: Yale Univ. Press).

Gordon, Lucie Duff. [1865] 1983. *Letters from Egypt* (London: Virago).

Grosrichard, Alain. 1979. *Structure du Serail: La Fiction du Despotisme Asiatique dans L'Occident Classique* (Paris: Editions Seuil).

Hatem, Mervat. 1989. 'Through Each Other's Eyes: Egyptian, Levantine Egyptian, and European Women's Images of Themselves and of Each Other,' *Women's Studies International Forum* 12(2): 183–98.

Joseph, Elizabeth. 1991. 'My Husband's Nine Wives,' *New York Times*, May 23.

Leonowens, Anna. [1872] 1991. *The Romance of the Harem*, ed. Susan Morgan (Charlottesville: Univ. Press of Virginia).

Makhlouf-Obermeyer, Carla. 1979. *Changing Veils: A Study of Women in South Arabia* (Austin: Univ. of Texas Press).

Marmontel, Jean François. 1764. *Moral Tales by M. Marmontel Translated from the French*, 3 vols (London).

Meyer, Susan L. 1989. 'Colonialism and the Figurative Strategy of *Jane Eyre*,' *Victorian Studies* 33(2): 247–68.

Montesquieu, Charles de Secondat Baron de. [1721] 1923. *Persian Letters*, trans. John Davidson (London: Routledge).

Nightingale, Florence. [1852] 1980. *Cassandra* (New York: Feminist Press).

Nightingale, Florence. [1849–50] 1988. *Letters from Egypt: A Journey on the Nile, 1849–1850* (New York: Weidenfeld & Nicolson).

Perera, Suvendrini. 1991. *Reaches of Empire: The English Novel from Edgeworth to Dickens* (New York: Columbia Univ. Press).

Poovey, Mary. 1984. *The Proper Lady and the Woman Writer: Ideology as Style in the Works of Mary Wollstonecraft, Mary Shelley, and Jane Austen* (Chicago: Univ. of Chicago Press).

Richon, Olivier. 1985. 'Representation, the Despot and the Harem: Some Questions around an Academic Orientalist Painting by Lecomte-du-Nouy (1885).' In *Europe and Its Others*, eds Francis Barker, Peter Hulme, Margaret Iverson, and Diana Loxley. Vol. 1 (Colchester: Univ. of Essex).

Said, Edward. 1979. *Orientalism* (New York: Vintage Books).

Shelley, Mary Wollstonecraft. [1818] 1974. *Frankenstein or the Modern Prometheus: The 1818 Text*, ed. James Rieger (New York: Bobbs-Merrill).

Spivak, Gayatri Chakravorty. 1985. 'Three Women's Texts and a Critique of Imperialism,' *Critical Inquiry* 12(1): 243–61.

Vaka, Demetra (Mrs Kenneth Brown). 1909. *Haremlik: Some Pages from the Life of Turkish Women* (Boston and New York: Houghton Mifflin).

Wollstonecraft, Mary. [1798] 1975. *Maria, or the Wrongs of Woman* (New York: Norton).

Wollstonecraft, Mary. [1792] 1982. *Vindication of the Rights of Woman* (London: Penguin).

Zonana, Joyce. 1991. '"They Will Prove the Truth of My Tale": Safie's Letters as the Feminist Core of Mary Shelley's *Frankenstein*,' *Journal of Narrative Technique* 21(2): 170–84.

CHAPTER FOUR

Shirley

PENNY BOUMELHA

Penny Boumelha is Jury Professor of English at the University of Adelaide where she is currently serving as Deputy Vice-Chancellor for Education. Her earliest publication, *Thomas Hardy: Sexual Ideology and Narrative Form* (1982), was a work far in advance of its time in terms of its approach. It has become a seminal text not only in Hardy studies, but also in feminist criticism generally. She has also written many chapters and articles of a significant kind on other nineteenth-century texts involving gender, class and nationality. The extract here is from her book *Charlotte Brontë* (1990) which indicates the direction that feminist criticism is taking towards combining the attention paid to gender with that paid to class and race. The chapter is characterised by its subtlety in capturing the interplay of multiple cultural meanings in Brontë's text. Boumelha does not read *Shirley* as a flawlessly feminist text but one which, having raised the class issue, compromises it by its paternalistic ending. The chapter also focuses to an unusual extent on the language of the text: both its textuality and its intertextuality.

'THE TOAD IN THE BLOCK OF MARBLE'[1]

Shirley has often been described, accurately enough, as Brontë's Thacker-ayan novel, as an attempt at a social panorama. Despite this panoramic

Reprinted from *Charlotte Brontë* (Hemel Hempstead: Harvester Wheatsheaf, 1990), pp. 78–99.

impulse, however, the character who provides the novel with its central female consciousness, Caroline Helstone, seems more cramped and confined than any other of Brontë's heroines. Her world is restricted physically and limited socially, as theirs are, but also attenuated emotionally; she has none of the fire-raising, tempest-inducing passion of Jane Eyre or Lucy Snowe. The wider focus of the novel serves only to bring into clearer focus the restraints upon Caroline's health and well-being, denied meaningful employment as she is and, for much of the novel, also denied love, in what is clearly always for Brontë the greatest deprivation imaginable. Whereas all the other main characters of the novel are linked with the possibility of some form of emigration (the fantasied Americas of Louis Moore and Shirley, the southern hemisphere of the Yorke sisters, the exile of bankruptcy in the case of Robert Moore), Caroline has only one connection with the wider world beyond Yorkshire. That link is her sewing for the 'Jew-basket', the proceeds of which are to be 'applied to the conversion of the Jews, the seeking up of the ten missing tribes, or to the regeneration of the interesting coloured populations of the globe' (p. 112). The sneering tone of this illustrates, not only a fairly commonplace Victorian racism, but also what has happened to the heroic missionary narrative of *Jane Eyre*, one in which it was conceivable for a woman to take an active part; here, by contrast, the 'Jew-basket' at each occurrence serves as the very emblem of futility and of the trivialisation of women's talents. All the usual avocations of the Victorian middle-class lady – running the home, charitable work, sewing – are seen in the course of the novel as comical or pointless or stultifying. Caroline pleads for the chance to work at something more, though in such timorous terms that Brontë's more adventurously feminist friend Mary Taylor wrote from New Zealand to comment upon them:

I have seen some extracts from *Shirley*, in which you talk of women working. And this first duty, this great necessity, you seem to think that some women may indulge in – if they give up marriage and don't make themselves too disagreeable to the other sex. You are a coward and a traitor.[2]

This work is never a fully realised project, however; what seems most important to Caroline is perhaps rather the chance simply to move: ' "I should be well if I went from home" ' (p. 189).[3] To be well is to be able to move, to leave home, as the child Jessie Yorke stresses in one of those catechistic dialogues in which the novel abounds:

'Should I be happier wandering alone in strange countries, as you wish to do?'
    'Much happier, even if you did nothing but wander . . . if you only went on and on, like some enchanted lady in a fairy tale, you might be happier than now.'
(p. 399)

To set against the obtrusive regional chauvinism of *Shirley* is this sense that to stay still is to risk misery and illness.

It is surely significant here that, where the names of Eyre and Snowe invoke elemental movement and fluidity, Caroline's name links her with stone, with what is by contrast fixed and immovable. Caroline's life, according to Jessie Yorke, is '"a black trance like the toad's, buried in marble"' (p. 399): the hell within the stone. And if Caroline is to follow the exhortations of the narrator, to 'endure without a sob' the scorpion's sting or the stone given where bread is asked (p. 105), then she risks only a future of imprisonment like that of the silent and neglected Mary Cave,[4] 'a girl of living marble' (p. 52) whose endurance without a sob has concealed both pain and need:

He thought, so long as a woman was silent, nothing ailed her, and she wanted nothing. If she did not complain of solitude, solitude, however continued, would not be irksome to her. If she did not talk and put herself forward, express a partiality for this, an aversion to that, she had no partialities or aversions, and it was useless to consult her tastes. (p. 53)

Shirley is itself caught, in its representations of both class and gender oppressions, in a radical divide between the drives toward silent stoicism and toward loud revolt, toward resigned stillness and vigorous movement. Stoicism can bring the fate of Mary Cave, revolt the fate of the transported workers. Shirley, tamed by love for Louis, nevertheless fears that she incubates within her the rage of the dog Phoebe, biting the hand that charitably feeds her. And revolt can be imaged in the 'half-crazed' Antinomian weaver and 'mad leveller' Mike Hartley (p. 635), the spectre of madness and moral anarchism who (in a structural parallel with the dog attack that says much about the novel's depiction of working-class action) shoots the newly paternalistic Robert. Movement holds its dangers, too. 'Abroad', in this novel, can be both a lure and a threat, at once the home of the true poetry (Chenier and Rousseau) and the home of the 'poisoned exhalations of the East' (p. 421) that enfever Caroline. Movement brings her Robert, from France; movement threatens to take him away from her again, to Canada. Shirley fantasises a life as '"the slave-wife of the Indian chief"' in North America (p. 468) as a way of escaping social duty; Louis imagines a life with Liberty as his bride in the '"virgin woods"' (p. 614) of the '"wild West"' (p. 613). Both settle for Yorkshire and a comfortable income instead. Robert plans to go to Canada and start again, until restored to solvency by the repeal of the Orders in Council. But there are two groups within the novel that do make their voyages: the labour leaders, transported to Australia, and the Yorke sisters, in revolt against the '"long, slow death"' of the womanly life (p. 399), whom the 'magic mirror' of prospective narration shows us 'in some region of the southern hemisphere' (p. 150). The novel's Yorkshire expels its dissidents. It is a sign at once of great pessimism and of great conservatism that the stories of social reordering and transformation will be confided to a future invisible to the novel, to a southern hemisphere apparently annexed as both unpeopled and ideologically 'empty'.

'CAPSIZED BY THE PATRIARCH BULL' (P. 245)

Shirley is structured around polarised masculine and feminine worlds, as Pauline Nestor has shown.[5] The mill versus the home, industry versus nature, head versus heart: all of these are familiar enough ideological oppositions. But a less obviously gendered polarity of no less importance to the novel is that variously presented as plain narrative versus poetry, the real world versus utopia, common sense versus fantasy: what might be called, in brief, realism versus rhapsody. The central female characters are consistently associated with the second, in differing degrees: one of the ways in which Caroline is a 'pencil-sketch' (p. 249) to Shirley's 'vivid painting' (p. 250) is their differential relation to this realism/rhapsody opposition. Caroline may on occasion be a ' "bookish, romancing chit of a girl" ' (p. 404), but it is primarily Shirley who bears the novel's linguistic theme. Both women offer passionate defences of poetry, and both, indeed, are silent, unwritten poets. Caroline hears words in the wind:

'Why, it suggested to me words one night: it poured a strain which I could have written down, only I was appalled, and dared not rise to seek pencil and paper by the dim watch-light.' (p. 427)

Characteristically, it is Caroline's timorousness that prevents her turning her inspirations into poetry, while Shirley is held back by indolence and a kind of innocent self-undervaluing: 'She does not know, has never known, and will die without knowing, the full value of that spring whose bright fresh bubbling in her heart keeps it green' (p. 388). The novel's only male 'poet', on the other hand, is Sir Philip Nunnely, who is mocked for his inability to write anything more than verse.

Nor is this a schematically applied opposition at the level of theme alone; *Shirley*, a novel whose disunity cannot but strike even the most organicist of readers, gives this impression partly because it operates two distinct strains of writing. There is the plain narrative, 'unromantic as Monday morning' (p. 5), that sets out to detail industrial conflict in West Yorkshire and abuses within the Anglican church, and then there are the set-pieces of vision, incantation and allegory that enter the novel with

Shirley herself. Tess Cosslett has drawn attention to the way in which, in the nineteenth-century novel, relationships between women tend to fall outside the events of the novel; they are often, she suggests, perceived as static, whereas male figures are 'thought to be needed to create tensions and initiate significant action'.[6] Certainly, here, it is evident that the male characters carry forward the plot, fighting and labouring and proposing and conspiring, while the female characters, in Patricia Parker's term, dilate, delaying and expanding 'plain narrative' by their very presence.[7] Caroline's is a woman's story that abuts plain narrative in its attention to social determinations, while Shirley's, in a sense the 'same' story, draws upon allegory and utopia. It is Shirley who can indulge fantasies of transcendence of social determination, in her cross-gender versions of herself as 'Captain Keeldar' and her cross-race imagining of a Rousseauesque noble savagery in the Wild West.[8] She is, Gilbert and Gubar contend, 'Caroline's double, a projection of all her repressed desire',[9] in a sense Caroline's romantic fiction of her own life. Nevertheless, Brontë never allows us to forget that Shirley's fantasies of transcendence are enabled by privileges of class position and wealth; the level of rhapsody of which she is the main vehicle is itself continually grounded in realism.

These 'masculine' and 'feminine' modes of writing connect with the insistence, here, on the images of mutually incomprehensible languages and of translation. ' "I know I speak an unknown tongue," ' says Shirley to her Uncle Sympson, ' "but I feel indifferent whether I am comprehended or not" ' (p. 473). For Sympson, her expression is 'inscrutable . . . as the writing on the wall to Belshazzar' (p. 547), but Louis, to whom he looks for assistance, has 'his own private difficulties connected with that baffling bit of translation' (p. 547). Robert may have difficulties, Caroline thinks, with his mother-in-law: ' "Be sure to let me interpret for her, whenever she puzzles you: always believe my account of the matter, Robert" ' (p. 642). Especially when speaking to men, the women do not, as it were, speak straight: they resort to silence, like Mary Cave, or else they become oracles, sphinxes:

'About each birthday, the spirit moves me to deliver one oracle respecting my own instruction and management: I utter it and leave it; it is for you mother, to listen or not.' (p. 401)

Men and women may need a little simultaneous translation in order to communicate at all, although ' "women read men more truly than men read women" ' (p. 352). Hence, at least in part, the foreignness to one another of each pair of lovers. Both Robert and Louis are shown teaching their lovers to speak their language, and Shirley finds 'lively excitement in the pleasure of making his language her own' (p. 494).[10] By the end of the novel, too, Shirley has ' "inspired romance" ' into the ' "prosaic composition" ' of Louis (p. 522), and Caroline has helped Robert to find the silent poet in himself: ' "Your heart is a lyre, Robert; but the lot of your life has not been a minstrel to sweep it, and it is often silent" ' (p. 89). Again, the image of incomprehensible language is also reflected in the activities of the narration, which translates the powerless speakers for its presumedly middle-class and often male readers; the Luddites' message to Robert must be 'translate[d] . . . into legible English' (p. 33), and Shirley's *devoir* is also translated 'on pain of being unintelligible to some readers' (p. 485). The 'Old Maids' are never permitted to speak; the narrator interposes between them and the reader. And most significantly and remarkably, in the latter stages of the novel, Shirley herself, the main speaker of the 'women's language', loses her right to direct speech; her rejection of Robert and her acceptance of Louis are given to us through the words of the men, in indirect speech, as a character in their stories. But *Shirley* as a whole, of course, never fully effects that suppression of the women's discourse of myth and rhapsody that could re-establish as its dominant form the linear plot of the historical novel. The novel does not surrender poetry and fantasy; its form enacts their disruption of the industrial narrative, and its narrative voice (ungendered for the only time in Brontë's fiction) embodies an uneasy integration of the two.[11]

These literary compositions of Louis and Shirley take their place among a range of other texts extensively referred to in the novel. Its fictionality is overtly recognised in a number of Thackerayan direct addresses to the reader, commenting on its 'unromantic' opening, its unmoralised ending, its differences from other industrial novels, for instance. There are a number of sly self-ironies: Mrs Pryor disapproves of the younger women's discussion of the mermaid they have envisioned: ' "We are aware that mermaids do not exist . . . How can you find interest in speaking of a non-entity?" ' (p. 246). The novel opens, too, with some of Brontë's favourite images, the weather and food, used somewhat humorously, and there is surely an element of self-mockery in Mrs Gale's response to the all-consuming curates: ' "c'en est trop," she would say, if she could speak French' (p. 8). There is in general an explicit interdependence of the fictional real life of the novel and its real-life fictions: Caroline's life, near the beginning of the novel, is a 'narrative of life . . . yet to be commenced' (p. 97), while Bunyan's *The Pilgrim's Progress* is invoked (p. 56) in parallel to historical events. There are, too, the usual acidulous comments on the relation of images of women in men's art and her own heroines; the most interesting of these, I think, is Shirley's account of the ' "Temptress-terror! monstrous likeness of ourselves!" ' (p. 246), the mermaid with her mirror whose glance leads men to destruction. Caroline objects:

'But, Shirley, she is not like us: we are neither temptresses, nor terrors, nor monsters.'

'Some of our kind, it is said, are all three. There are men who ascribe to "woman", in general, such attributes.' (p. 246)

This is surely Brontë's response to her own admired Thackeray, whose *Vanity Fair* (often cited as a model for the panoramic world, social comedy, double heroines, and narratorial addresses of *Shirley*) includes the following comment on his Becky:

In describing this siren, singing and smiling, coaxing and cajoling, the author, with modest pride, asks his readers all round, has he once forgotten the laws of politeness, and showed the monster's hideous tail above water? . . . They look pretty enough when they sit upon a rock, twangling their harps and combing their hair, and sing, and beckon to you to come and hold the looking-glass; but when they sink into their native element, depend upon it those mermaids are about no good, and we had best not examine the fiendish marine cannibals, revelling and feasting on their wretched pickled victims.[12]

From this kind of dialogue with other texts there emerges a stress upon the possibility of alternative readings, for particular social and political ends. Yorke and Helstone, for example, agree upon the biblical story of Moses crossing the Red Sea as an apt comparison for the hostilities between France and Britain, and yet they apply it differently: ' "You are all right, only you forget the true parallel. France is Israel, and Napoleon is Moses" ' (p. 39). More commonly, a 'man's' and a 'woman's' reading are proposed. Shirley's onslaught on Milton's Eve is probably the most famous example, but there are also discussions of the biblical Eve, Solomon's virtuous woman, Lucretia, and the parable of the talents which draw out from these texts feminist, or at least woman-centred, interpretations. The matter is raised explicitly when Joe Scott invokes St Paul's words, 'Let the woman learn in silence, with all subjection.' It is in this instance Caroline who argues in favour of appropriative reading:

'It would be possible, I doubt not, with a little ingenuity, to give the passage quite a contrary turn; to make it say, "Let the woman speak out whenever she sees fit to make an objection;" – "it is permitted to a woman to teach and exercise authority as much as may be. Man, meantime, cannot do better than hold his peace," and so on.' (pp. 329–30)

The novel's registering of its own fictionality goes beyond a simple self-reflexivity to pose a certain challenge to the reader. Not merely the tale of *Shirley. A Tale*, but the historical relations of class and gender of which it is a representation, are recognised as matters of contention;

struggle for meaning and struggle for power are shown to be thoroughly interconnected. The relations between history and story, text and interpretation, are so problematised that the novel's closing comments are a good deal more than a humorous disclaimer:

The story is told. I think I now see the judicious reader putting on his spectacles to look for the moral. It would be an insult to his sagacity to offer directions. I only say, God speed him in the quest! (p. 646)

These examples of reading otherwise that I have mentioned above form part of the novel's adumbration of a female religion, centred upon the figure of Eve as mother of humanity. Shirley and Caroline, declining to enter the church at whose gate they stand, enter instead into the vision of the natural world as the primordial mother's body: ' "I will stay out here with my mother Eve, in these days called Nature" ' (p. 321). Eve, as mother, predated ' "the first men of the earth" ' and ' "the first woman's breast that heaved with life on this world" ' gave suck to the generations that were to bring forth the Messiah (p. 320). (The role of Caroline's literal mother should not be forgotten here: her name is, precisely, Pryor.) Adam recedes into the background for much of this vision, but when he does appear, it is in a relation to Eve of parity rather than priority: ' "Eve is Jehovah's daughter, as Adam was his son" ' (p. 321). The central vision – it occurs almost exactly halfway through the novel – joins with the evident anti-clericalism and the valuing of intuitional knowledge over rationality to suggest an alternative, a path not taken, that is not wholly undermined by the women's willing enlistment in the ranks of the Anglicans in their semi-comic Whitsuntide battle against the Dissenters. This religious feminism is reinforced by a strain of diabolic imagery focused upon the male characters: Robert Moore is addressed by the Luddites as ' "the Divil of Hollow's-miln" ' (p. 33), and Mr Yorke is 'haughty as Beelzebub' (p. 47). Robert Moore, proposing to Shirley for her money, repeats the expulsion of Lucifer: ' "Lucifer – Star of the Morning! . . . thou art fallen" ' (p. 536). By contrast Shirley, who doodles 'broken crosses' while discussing her early *devoir* (p. 490), and Mrs Pryor both sing in voices angelic or even 'almost divine' (p. 431). Of course, Brontë's more orthodox (and sectarian) Protestant piety is also present throughout the novel, but it has here less power to console, reconcile or justify than anywhere else in her adult fiction.

The paganised Eve, mother of Titans, and the community of women hinted at in the women's attraction toward the conventual Nunnwood, constitute their own commentary upon the male-centred church in the world. They posit heroically feminine values under threat in the industrialising world of the novel, values associated with the vanishing 'fairishes' of the end (p. 646). For the oppressed (here, women), myth can appear as a disruption of and an alternative to that history whose terms and course have been set by the powerful. It is true that the feminist myth of a power that resides *within* the feminine sphere of personal relationship, family and nurturance unsettles what Rabine calls the 'official masculine historicity'[13] that gives industrial and political struggle primacy. But this alternative is constituted as such only within a system of polarities – female versus male, personal versus political, family versus employment – that registers and preserves the exclusion of women from the historicity of class and workplace. The ideological value of the myth offers a strategy for consolation, not for change. In this respect, the shadowy feminist religion of *Shirley* is a fantasied way of bringing together the urges towards social transformation and stoic acceptance in the novel, implying an overturning of the relative valuations of masculine and feminine spheres while leaving untouched, more or less, the delineation of the polarity and, with it, the existing distribution of power. Feminist protest is recuperated into retrospective fantasy, power in the world ceded in return for a spiritual superiority. The circular chain binding together nature/instinct/motherhood/woman is an ideological tripwire over which feminism has more than once fallen.[14]

Although these mythological forms of female power are stated in a retrospective narrative of fall and loss, there is also a forward chronological movement by which a generational change among the women characters is implicitly proposed. The older women in the book – the counterposed characters of Hortense and Mrs Yorke, for example – are truculently concerned only with their roles in relation to homes and men, or else (like Miss Ainsley), lacking the good fortune to have men in their homes, with those charitable works that are the mainstay of genteel femininity in the period. The novel's youngest women, Rose and Jessie Yorke, by contrast, while not undervaluing the skills of domestic labour (' "I should be sorry not to learn to sew: you do right to teach me, and to make me work" ' (p. 401)) are able also to envisage another life for themselves (' "Am I to do nothing but that? I will do that, and then I will do more" ' (p. 401)), even if that 'more' requires exile from the known community. Poised uneasily between the two groups stand Caroline and Shirley, able to envisage new relationships and interdependences beyond the conjugal, but still unable to find the strength or the society to practise them. Marriage, it is clear, comes to be validated only at the end of *Shirley*; otherwise it has been presented in a strongly negative light, both in principle and in practice, and especially so for women:

'[Marriage] is never wholly happy. Two people can never literally be as one: there is, perhaps, a possibility of content under peculiar circumstances, such as are seldom combined; but it is as well not to run the risk: you may make fatal mistakes. Be satisfied, my dear; let all the single be satisfied with their freedom.' (p. 379)[15]

In the course of the novel, a number of other possibilities of relationship are examined. There are the 'old maids', for example, who, however patronisingly presented, are nevertheless found ultimately to have stories and worth of their own. Miss Ainsley, indeed, is an explicitly Christ-like figure of celibacy. Even if Miss Mann is a 'Medusa' (p. 178) in Robert Moore's imaginings, it is not she who turns the women to stone; it is rather the ' "long, black trance" ' (p. 399) of femininity, of waiting for life to begin with a husband, that does that. Then, too, *Shirley* presents an unusually large number of non-marital households, uncles and nieces or brothers and sisters, in which male power is nonetheless still at issue. Relations of friendship or community among women are suggested in the imagery of nuns and Amazons, and tested out in Caroline and Shirley, who relish their first excursion together partly because it is to be without men: ' "the presence of gentlemen dispels the last charm" ' (p. 214). Their visit is to the very female landscape of the dell, ' "a deep hollow cup" ' (p. 213) wherein they find the ruined convent.

But undoubtedly the chief relationship among women which the novel considers is that of mother and daughter, a relationship explored at the levels of mythology (Eve as first mother, Mother Nature) and of individuals (Mrs Yorke, Mrs Pryor). What Nestor calls 'mother want'[16] is vividly present throughout. It is partly a search for predecessors that will bestow and confirm identity and worth. It also brings about a love powerful enough to bring Caroline back from the brink of death, from an illness triggered by Robert's apparent failure to love her; this inter-changeability of maternal and sexual love will be imaged in reverse in Shirley's composition 'The First Blue-Stocking', where the apparently unmothered, unloved Eva ' "should die" ' (p. 486) but is restored by the erotic commingling of Genius and Humanity. But, as this allegory suggests, if 'mother want' in part fuels the novel's feminist impulse through-out, it comes also to undo its anti-marriage theme. The ideological centrality of motherhood in the novel's urging of the claims of the 'feminine sphere' requires, if it is to be translated into the social climate of the 1840s, a revalidation of marriage: the middle-class woman has, you might say, to be a 'Mrs' prior to being a mother, even if the relationship leaves her ' "galled, crushed, paralyzed, dying" ' (p. 437). So it is that the ' "ordinary destiny" ' of wifedom (p. 174) is reinstated as the ground and end of being for Shirley and Caroline. If it is Nature that bestows upon women alone together ' "peaceful joy" ', then it is equally Nature that makes of relations with ' "the right sort" ' of young men ' "elation and . . . anxiety" ', ' "excitement . . . and trouble" ' (p. 214). The problem here is not, I think, the affirmation of heterosexual relationship in itself, but the unspoken assumption that this entails an acceptance of the whole train of consequences of conventional marriage, those very dependencies, exclusivities, masteries and submissions that the novel has opened to question in its portrayal of marital relationships. It is because of the novel's wavering commitments to revolt and resignation that the critiques of marriage and of male dominance that it has offered come to be undermined by the fear of 'unwomanliness', of becoming a Captain Keeldar or a Miss Mann. A certain anxiety creeps into the reassurance that Shirley is ' "girlish: not a man-like woman at all – not an Amazon" ' (p. 503), that there is ' "nothing masculine" ' about Caroline (p. 362). To pick up on Brontë's splendidly mixed metaphor, it is perhaps because *Shirley* is concentrating so hard on not rocking the boat that it comes, in the end, to be ' "capsized by the patriarch bull" ' (p. 245).

'THE FAMISHED AND FURIOUS MASS' (P. 344)

Shirley, as has often been remarked, sets up a number of parallels between working-class men and middle-class women; for example, ' "Old maids, like the houseless and unemployed poor, should not ask for a place and an occupation in the world" ' (p. 391). The implicit parallels take in the full range of images of dissatisfaction and deprivation (hunger and starvation, under- and unemployment), as well as emerging through the more analytic account of dependence upon paternalism and patriarchal power. The link between plots of romance centring upon middle-class heroines, and industrial plots of the 'social problem' kind, is not peculiar to Brontë, of course, but is shared with a number of other women writers of the period. As Bodenheimer puts it:

[T]he newly ornamental lives of genteel women and the newly threatened employment patterns of the industrial working class raise overlapping clusters of fear. Because of that (often submerged) linkage, these novels raise with a special intensity the frequently fictionalized problem of what a heroine is to do with her life.[17]

For Brontë the contradictory urges toward resignation and revolt are there in both plots, and both find a kind of spurious ideological resolu-tion in the paradoxical idea of a free (marital or quasi-feudal) subjection to one who will be master but no tyrant. The representation of revolt is weighted by a kind of social organicism that makes of conflict an image of disease and self-destruction. Shirley argues this point by positing man and woman as interdependent parts of the body:

'Shall my left hand dispute for precedence with my right? – shall my heart quarrel with my pulse? – shall my veins be jealous of the blood which fills them?' (p. 219)

When it comes to class, the organicism is less explicitly pronounced, but it is there in, for example, the odd opening metonymies of 'hands' and 'arms' for labour and ruling-class power, and also (tellingly enough in ideological terms) in the opposition of body and soul that appears during the otherwise strikingly disembodied allegorical account of the attack on the mill:

[A]nd the indignant, wronged *spirit* of the middle Rank bears down in zeal and scorn on the famished and furious *mass* of the Operative Class. (p. 344, my italics)

Characteristically, Brontë uses the reading material of her protagonists to reinforce obliquely her own imagery. The supposedly organic nature of the state is, after all, a central presupposition of *Coriolanus*, which Caroline and Robert read together; it is there that we find, in the opening scene, the allegory of the mutiny of 'all the body's members . . . against the belly' on the grounds that it consumes idly and inactively while they must labour.[18] Add to this the somatic determinations of Yorke's political views – being, phrenologically speaking, without the organ of veneration, he is 'intolerant to those above him' and 'very friendly to his workpeople, very good to all who were beneath him' (p. 47) – and the disease imagery of, for example, 'moral scrofula' (p. 132), and there emerges a powerful, if inexplicit, idea of revolt as bodily imbalance or sickness. Since all four of the novel's main characters pass through a period of illness as a marker of the adjustment of their own feelings and perspectives, it can be further supposed that, in this novel, Luddism (and probably, therefore, the Chartism of the book's actual time of writing[19]) is no more than the 'poisoned exhalations' (p. 421) from abroad or the bite of maddened dogs upon the body politic: revolution as social disease.

Shirley offers no resolution, at the level of argument, of the class conflict it represents, but it nevertheless has rhetorical and narrative means at its disposal to empty that conflict of its political and historical significance: the continual appeal to a shared quality of 'Yorkshireness' as a cohesive force overriding difference, the organic imagery that serves to bind together in metaphorical interdependence the contending forces it displays, and the introduction of the repeal of the Orders in Council to abolish in fiction the oppositions it merely realigned in history. The novel closes with unities (marriages, a hint of revived feudal communities) but the sense of strain is, I think, quite apparent in the virtual transformation of the industrial theme into a moral testing and growth for Robert Moore, in the late coming to prominence of the safely non-industrial dependence of his brother Louis, and in the chastened tone of the conclusion. Class conflict, like Shirley, seems tamed for the present; but just as she is not turned thereby into a domestic cat, but only into a pantheress gnawing at her chain (p. 629), so there remains, in contradiction to the novel's narrative drive, a sense of subduing by force rather than of voluntary subjection.

The parallels between working-class men and middle-class women provoke their own intractable problems, too. These are related not only to Brontë's own class position but also to the acceptance, here, of masculine and feminine polarities. The working class comes, in effect, to be subsumed into that 'masculine' sphere of industry and conflict which the novel's use of two central female consciousnesses serves to render strange and threatening. Joe Scott is a key figure here, as a worker and a staunch opponent of '"petticoat government"' (p. 327). Joe is throughout the novel identified with the interests of his employer, and he also urges strongly Pauline doctrines on that '"kittle and . . . froward generation"', women (p. 328). He contradicts flatly the novel's feminist mysticism with his insistence that '"Adam was first formed, then Eve"' (p. 329). He may be a kind husband (p. 330) but, unredeemed by the romantic aura of foreignness (and class privilege) that hangs over Robert Moore, it is chiefly he who binds together the industrial strain of the novel and male dominance into its masculine sphere. To set against Joe's worker misogyny, there is the feminisation of William Farren, the novel's representative of the 'good' working-class man. Turned away by unemployment from the industrial sphere, William comes to be progressively identified with nature, which, as I have argued above, is identified as the realm of the feminine.[20] William becomes a gardener, and in so doing he takes on something of the 'language' of women as it is represented by Caroline:

William and she found plenty to talk about: they had a dozen topics in common; interesting to them, unimportant to the rest of the world. They took a similar interest in animals, birds, insects, and plants; they held similar doctrines about humanity to the lower creation; and had a similar turn for minute observation on points of natural history. (p. 445)

This relationship, though it continues to be one of servant to employer (at the time of these discussions, he is pushing her in her wheelchair around the garden), is shown to evade class, and hence the implication that class (and so class conflict) belongs to the realm of industry that displaces the feminine nature. It is William Farren, incidentally, who foretells the novel's pseudo-resolution in exile; he suggests to Shirley that ' "if ye could transport your tenant, Mr Moore, to Botany Bay, ye'd happen to do better" ' (p. 325). Expulsion will, of course, prove to be the major gesture towards social transformation, but it will be not the employers but the agitators who set off on the long trip to Australia.

In a sense, then, *Shirley* accords its gender schema, the collision of masculine and feminine spheres, priority over its representation of the interests of class: indeed, in the more or less classic fashion of nineteenth-century industrial novels, it will slide class difference beneath gender in order that marriage may effect a reconciliation of sorts at the close. Eagleton has pointed out the novel's narrative disenfranchisement of the working class in the raid on the mill:

[T]he event is at once structurally central and curiously empty – empty because the major protagonist, the working class, is distinguished primarily by its absence . . . At the point of its most significant presence in the novel, the working class is wholly invisible.[21]

Helen Taylor, in answer, has pointed out that the scene also dwells upon the marginality and powerlessness of the two women; that there is a stress upon the invisibility to one another of the two groups, of working-class men and of middle-class women.[22] The parallel of the two comes up against the intractability of their different interests, too; the interests, sentimental and financial, of Shirley and Caroline, lie finally with the defence of the machinery. But, true and important as these points are, it seems to me, further, that the overlaying of a particular ideology of gender – one that serves to distance women from the site of work – upon the structures of class has resulted in a significant blind spot. I am thinking here of such as Joe Scott's wife, spoken for by him (' "My wife is a hard-working, plain woman: time and trouble have ta'en all the conceit out of her" ' (p. 330)), and as Mrs Gale, who would have said ' "c'en est trop" ' . . . if she could speak French' (p. 8) but instead is given nothing to say. The truly invisible, the truly silenced, in *Shirley* are working-class women. That is to say, for most of its length. I could wish to find a political point, and not merely a distancing effect of narration, in the fact that the novel does not end with Robert's paternalistic reformism, or with Louis's diary: it gives the last word to Martha, to a female servant.

NOTES

1. Charlotte Brontë, 'To W.S. Williams', 26 July 1849, in *The Brontës: Their Lives, Friendships and Correspondence*, eds T.J. Wise and J.A. Symington, 4 vols (1933; Oxford: Basil Blackwell, 1980), III, p. 9; cf. Charlotte Brontë, *Shirley*, eds Herbert Rosengarten and Margaret Smith, World's Classics (Oxford: Oxford Univ. Press, 1981), p. 399. Further references to the novel are to this edition and will be given in the text.

2. Mary Taylor, 'To Charlotte Brontë', 25 April 1850, Wise and Symington, III, p. 104.

3. See also p. 241.

4. Cf. Sandra M. Gilbert and Susan Gubar, *The Madwoman in the Attic: The Woman Writer and the Nineteenth-century Literary Imagination* (New Haven, Conn.: Yale Univ. Press, 1979), pp. 372–98.

5. Pauline Nestor, *Female Friendships and Communities: Charlotte Brontë, George Eliot, Elizabeth Gaskell* (Oxford: Clarendon Press, 1985), pp. 112–24.

6. Tess Cosslett, *Woman to Woman: Female Friendship in Victorian Fiction* (Brighton: Harvester Press, 1988), p. 11.

7. Patricia Parker, *Literary Fat Ladies: Rhetoric, Gender, Property* (New York: Methuen, 1987), *passim*. Parker does not discuss *Shirley*.

8. Margaret Kirkham has discussed *Shirley* in relation to Rousseau in 'Reading "The Brontës"', *Women Reading Women's Writing*, ed. Sue Roe (Brighton: Harvester Press, 1987), pp. 66–75.

9. Gilbert and Gubar, *Madwoman in the Attic*, p. 382.

10. Cf. Joseph Kestner, *Protest and Reform: The British Social Narrative by Women, 1827–1867* (London: Methuen, 1985), p. 132.

11. Cf. Nestor, *Female Friendships*, p. 124. Nestor seems, however, to have changed her mind on this point, since she later writes of the novel's 'swaggering satiric manner', ' "masculine" by default': Pauline Nestor, *Charlotte Brontë*, Women Writers (London: Macmillan Education, 1987), p. 69.

12. William Thackeray, *Vanity Fair*, ed. J.I.M. Stewart (1968; Harmondsworth: Penguin, 1983), p. 738.

13. Leslie W. Rabine, *Reading the Romantic Heroine: Text, History, Ideology* (Ann Arbor: Univ. of Michigan Press, 1985), p. 112.

14. I have discussed this point in relation to some women writers of the 1890s in *Thomas Hardy and Women: Sexual Ideology and Narrative Form* (Brighton: Harvester Press, 1982), pp. 63–97.

15. See also pp. 101, 153, 164, 435.

16. Nestor, *Female Friendships*, p. 104. Nestor takes this phrase from Elizabeth Barrett Browning, *Aurora Leigh*, I, 40.

17. Rosemarie Bodenheimer, *The Politics of Story in Victorian Social Fiction* (Ithaca: Cornell Univ. Press, 1988), p. 19. For a discussion of women's writing in the sub-genre of the industrial novel, see Kestner, *Protest and Reform*.

18. *Coriolanus*, I, i.

19. Terry Eagleton, *Myths of Power: A Marxist Study of the Brontës* (London: Macmillan, 1975), pp. 45–60, argues convincingly that 'Chartism is the unspoken subject of *Shirley*' (p. 45). His discussion of class issues in *Shirley* is surely definitive. Nevertheless, since, for the Eagleton of this book, gender and sexual relations are finally always metaphorical, always a displacement (and, as such, to some extent at least a guilty evasion) of the determining reality of class relations, there remains, I think, something for feminists to say even in this area.

20. Cf. Hélène Moglen, *Charlotte Brontë: The Self Conceived* (New York: Norton, 1976), p. 163.

21. Eagleton, *Myths of Power*, pp. 47, 49.

22. Helen Taylor, 'Class and gender in Charlotte Brontë's *Shirley*', *Feminist Review*, no. 1 (1979), 83–93.

CHAPTER FIVE

Villette: 'The Surveillance of a Sleepless Eye'

SALLY SHUTTLEWORTH

Sally Shuttleworth is Professor of English at Sheffield University and also Co-Director of the Leeds projects on the History and Philosophy of Science in the nineteenth century. She is one of the most distinguished and astute critics of nineteenth-century fiction writing today. Much of her published work draws on a detailed knowledge of nineteenth-century science to demonstrate its presence in nineteenth-century texts often as a central element. The best known of her numerous publications are *George Eliot and Nineteenth-Century Science: The Make-believe of a Beginning* (1986); *Nature Transfigured: Science and Literature 1700–1900* (1989, co-edited with John Christie); and *Charlotte Brontë and Victorian Psychology* (1996). The article reprinted here was in a later form to provide a chapter in the last of these books. In it, Shuttleworth first demonstrates the ubiquity of the terminology and concepts of Victorian psychological theory in *Villette*. She goes on to show how Lucy Snowe struggles with the ideas of the feminine self that such theory offers as she tries to reach self-definition. Shuttleworth reveals her as finally confronting the limits of that theory to achieve a degree of stable selfhood that masculine constructions of femininity denied her.

Brontë's final novel, *Villette*, represents her most explicit engagement with Victorian psychological theory and medical practice. The narrator, Lucy Snowe, is subject, seemingly, to hallucinations,

Reprinted from *Charlotte Brontë and Victorian Psychology* (Cambridge: Cambridge University Press, 1996), pp. 219–42.

undergoes a total nervous collapse, and discusses her symptoms at great length with her doctor. Whereas Brontë had distanced Jane Eyre from the mania of her 'darkest double',[1] Bertha, and preserved Caroline Helstone from the unbecoming display of 'weariness ferment[ing] . . . to phrenzy' she creates in Lucy Snowe a figure whose psychological stability is permanently in question. In probing the inner processes of mind of a subject who defines herself as 'constitutionally nervous' (p. 531), Brontë has chosen to focus not on the flamboyant extreme of 'mania', but on the more subtle area of neurosis. The reader, entering the world of *Villette*, is forced to relinquish cherished assumptions of rational order. Lucy as narrator teases and bewilders her audience, contradicting herself, withholding vital information, and confounding, as in the notorious open ending, biographical fact with readerly desire. Her commitment to evasion and displacement is articulated in the very title of her book, which gives precedence not to selfhood but to place. Through the autobiographical account of 'shadow-like' Lucy, Brontë both explores and interrogates contemporary theories of mental alienation.

In *Shirley*, Brontë had examined how social and political issues could impinge directly on the life of the body and mind. *Villette* takes further this exploration of the interaction between the social and psychological economies, focusing this time on the personal and institutional operations of surveillance. In this, her seemingly most inward text, Brontë brings to the fore the social framework which had remained implicit in her earlier dramas of psychological penetration.

The text of *Villette* is dominated by the practice of surveillance. The constant self-surveillance and concealment which marks Lucy's own narrative account, is figured socially in the institutional practices of those who surround her. All characters spy on others, attempting, covertly, to read and interpret the external signs of faces, minds and actions. Madame Beck runs her school according to the watchwords, ' "Surveillance", "espionage" ' (p. 99); M. Paul reads Lucy's countenance on her arrival in Villette, and later studies her through his 'magic lattice'; and Père Silas focuses on her 'the surveillance of a sleepless eye' – the Roman Catholic confessional (p. 592). Lucy is subjected to educational, professional and religious surveillance. Each observer tries to read her inner self through the interpretation of outer signs. This practice takes its most authoritative form in the narrative in the medical judgments of Dr John.

After Lucy's first encounter with the nun, as she is attempting to read Dr John's letter, he in turn tries to 'read' her: ' "I look on you now from a professional point of view, and I read, perhaps, all you would conceal – in your eye, which is curiously vivid and restless, in your cheek, which the blood has forsaken; in your hand, which you cannot steady" ' (p. 355).

Dr John directs onto Lucy the gaze of medical authority, calmly confident of his ability to define inner experience from outer signs. His verdict is distinguished by his insistence on his professional status, and by his unshakeable belief that, no matter how hard Lucy might try to hide from his gaze, he would penetrate through to her innermost secrets. The rhetoric of unveiling and penetrating the truth, so prevalent in nineteenth-century science, is here located as a discourse of gendered, social power: male science unveils female nature. All those who subject Lucy to surveillance present her with interpretations of her mind and character, but only Dr John claims the authority of science for his interpretation (though M. Paul, to a lesser extent, also assumes this power when he offers a phrenological reading of her skull). Against the descriptive labels offered by Madame Beck and Père Silas, Dr John actually presents a whole language of analysis and a theory of psychological functioning. His diagnosis on this occasion is that it is 'a matter of the nerves', a 'case of spectral illusion . . . following on and resulting from long-continued mental conflict' (pp. 357, 358). The terms of his analysis are drawn directly from contemporary medical science where the subject of 'spectral illusion' proved a constant source of debate.[2] Against more visionary explanations of the nun, who functions as a site of crucial interpretative conflict in the text, he offers a materialist explanation based on the functioning of the nervous system. On one level, the text falsifies Dr John's materialist explanation by presenting an even more material cause – the physical presence of the Count de Hamal masquerading as a nun. The authority of science is not, however, thereby erased from the text. The very inadequacy of the 'literal' explanation, indeed, feeds further speculation into the question of the relationship between body and mind which functions as a sub-text in the novel. As readers, interpreting the signs of Lucy's discourse, we are constantly tempted by the text into re-enacting the role of Dr John, as we attempt to pierce through the external linguistic signs of the narrative to a concealed unity lying below. The text, however, frustrates all such quests for a hidden unitary meaning, deliberately undermining the social and psychological presuppositions which underlie such a quest.

In focusing interpretative attention in the novel on Lucy's 'sightings' of the nun, Brontë is deliberately raising the issue of Lucy's psychological stability. Hallucinations, as Brontë was clearly aware, were classically regarded as signs of madness. Lucy herself invokes this mode of explanation on her first glimpse of the nun, challenging the reader to say 'I was nervous, or mad' (p. 351). Despite Lucy's stated resistance to Dr John's system of analysis, she herself constantly employs contemporary scientific language to describe her own psychological functioning. The term 'nervous system', which she distances herself from as alien and technical when used by Dr John, has already figured largely in her narrative (p. 261). Other terms from contemporary scientific discourse, such as 'monomania', 'hypochondria' and 'hysteria' are also employed with precision in her analysis. Scientific language in the novel is not confined to Dr John's specific diagnoses – the imposition of 'male reason' on a largely Gothic text – it permeates Lucy's narrative construction of her self.

The nun who becomes subject to Dr John's medical gaze is of a very different species from that which had haunted the Gothic novel. The intervening years had witnessed the rise of psychiatric medicine: doctors from henceforth claimed exclusive right to define and treat aberrations of the mind. Under the principles of moral management, the insane were no longer to be sharply distinguished from the sane, but, correlatively, no one could now rest assured of their own sanity. All had to remain vigilant against the momentary slippage of the social mask. As in the economic philosophy of the period, self-control was the watchword of the moral managers. In the medical and popular press of the period, however, one can trace increasing numbers of articles and stories devoted to explorations of dreams, apparitions, and the operations of the unconscious mind, which seem to defy control. The emphasis on an individual's necessary responsibility for action was coupled with an overwhelming sense that control was at every moment liable to be overthrown.

Social fears of an unstoppable rise in nervous disease were at their height in the mid-century. The medical and popular press were full of alarmist reports of an exponential rise in cases of insanity, and the question of how to draw the subtle dividing line between sanity and insanity received frequent press attention.[3] Such social fears and anxieties were condensed in heightened form in the Brontë household where the Reverend Brontë anxiously annotated his medical Bible, Thomas John Graham's *Domestic Medicine*, with his fears regarding his family's nervous diseases and potential insanity. In naming Dr John Graham Bretton after her father's treasured medical tome, Brontë was giving embodiment to the system of medical surveillance which had governed her own life.

Although Brontë claimed that '*Villette* touches on no matter of public interest' her actions on completing the novel suggest another story.[4] She went down to London, resolved to see 'the *real* rather than the *decorative* side of Life'. In a letter to Ellen Nussey she records that 'I have been over two prisons ancient and modern – Newgate and Pentonville – also the Bank, the Exchange, the Foundling Hospital, – and today if all be well – I go with Dr Forbes to see Bethlehem Hospital.'[5] Her definition of the 'real' is highly significant. It encompasses the centres of financial control, together with the institutional structures designed to control the marginalized groups within society: the criminal, the poor and the insane. Such a visiting list reveals a marked preoccupation with the mechanisms and operation of institutional power. *Villette*, indeed, with its obsessional concern with surveillance, fits almost too perfectly into the paradigm of nineteenth-century social control outlined by Foucault in *Discipline and Punish*. The ideal of Bentham's Panopticon, where inmates are trapped, isolated in their cells, subject always to the gaze of authority, without themselves being able to see, might describe the underlying nightmare of *Villette* from which Lucy is for ever trying to escape. If Brontë did indeed visit Bethlehem hospital with her illustrious medical guide, she would have found a microcosm of Victorian society: social and psychological ordering was achieved through constant surveillance, and its psychological reflex, the internalization of social controls.

As Lucy constructs her narrative, it is she, in the initial stages of her history, who is the principal surveillant, subjecting the passionate excesses of her alter ego, Polly, to the scrutiny of what, she insists, is her calm, and hence decorous, gaze (although her claims to possess a 'cooler temperament' are immediately undermined by her vision of Polly 'haunting' a room, and by the pressure of her emotional identification: 'I wished she would utter some hysterical cry, so that *I* might get relief and be at ease' p. 18, my emphasis). On her entry into Villette, however, it is the inner passions of Lucy herself that become subject to the calm gaze of institutional authority. Her employment at the pensionnat is based on M. Paul's reading of her head. To Lucy, reading *his* brow, (a reading she is not allowed to articulate), it 'seemed to say that he meant to see through me, and that a veil would be no veil for him' (p. 90). Like Dr John, in his later medical diagnosis, M. Paul tries to look beyond the surface sign to all that Lucy would conceal below. His reading is significant in its indeterminacy: he leaves it as an open question whether good or evil predominate in her nature. This is not a physiognomical reading, but a phrenological diagnosis of latent potential which reinforces economic ideologies of self-help. M. Paul's reading inaugurates the system of surveillance into which Lucy has entered, and reinforces its underlying central code: if Lucy is to succeed, it must be by a process of *self*-control, subduing her 'evil' propensities, and encouraging the good.

The 'system of management' employed by Madame Beck in running her school is linked by Lucy to the practices of political and industrial control (and Madame Beck herself to masculine figures of authority). Lucy observes that Madame Beck, 'ought to have swayed a nation . . . In her own single person, she could have comprised the duties of a first minister and a superintendent of police' (p. 102). The industrial parallel is suggested by her reference to Madame Beck's 'system of managing and regulating this mass of machinery' (p. 99). Like Dr John in his 'materialist' diagnosis of Lucy's experience, Madame Beck reduces her pupils to material elements, cogs within a machine. Her motives, in Lucy's eyes, are in keeping with industrial practice: 'interest was the master-key of madame's nature – the mainspring of her motives – the alpha and omega of her life' (p. 101).

Throughout her surveillance, Madame Beck herself remains totally inscrutable and impervious; she constructs a machine which seems to function independently of any personal intervention, operating rather on the participants' internalization of the mechanisms of control. Lucy, inscribing in herself these institutional constraints, allows all her actions to be dictated by the sense that she might be overlooked. Thus at one stage she even invests inanimate nature with the qualities of a spy: 'the eyes of the flowers had gained vision, and the knots in the tree-boles listened like secret ears' (p. 161). The internalization of the principles of surveillance breeds a paranoia verging on neurosis. Lucy's relationship to surveillance is not only passive, however, she actively supports its operation. On coming across Madame Beck searching her clothes, she refuses to confront her. Having invested herself in a system based on concealment and disguise, she, like Madame Beck, can ill afford exposure.

The third form of surveillance to which Lucy is subject is that of the Roman Catholic church. Her impulse to confession – the voluntary revelation of the secrets of the inner self – represents for Lucy the nadir of her mental state. Worn out by suffering, product of her internalization of the social contradictions of the female role, she sacrifices the last vestiges of her autonomy, thus opening herself up to the continued intervention of both medical and religious authorities in her life (and precipitating her entry into the 'very safe asylum' offered by the Brettons) (p. 244). Père Silas proves even more assiduous in his 'treatment' than Dr John. From that moment on, as he later informs her, he had not 'for a day lost sight of you, nor for an hour failed to take in you a rooted interest' (p. 571). He envisages her 'passed under the discipline of Rome, moulded by her high training, inoculated with her salutary doctrines' (the manuscript originally read 'sane doctrines') (p. 571). With its aim of total dominion over the mind through the discipline of its sane or salutary doctrines, Lucy's Roman Catholic church replicates precisely the alienists' system of moral management of the insane.

The perceived threat of the church to Lucy does not end with her confession. As her relationship with Dr John is subject always to the scrutiny of Madame Beck 'glid[ing] ghost-like through the house, watching and spying everywhere' (p. 100), so her relationship with M. Paul is attended by that 'ghostly troubler' (p. 600), Père Silas, and the threat of the confessional: 'We were under the surveillance of a sleepless eye: Rome watched jealously her son through that mystic lattice at which I had knelt once, and to which M. Emmanuel drew nigh month by month – the sliding panel of the confessional' (p. 592). Lucy's use of the term 'magic lattice' echoes, significantly, M. Paul's description of his 'post of observation', his window overlooking the garden, where he sits and 'reads' 'female human nature': ' "Ah, magic lattice! what miracles of discovery hast thou wrought!" ' (pp. 526, 528). The 'magic lattice' forms another medium for the male gaze to penetrate through to the recesses of the female psyche, furnishing information which is then appropriated to judge and censor, in accordance with male definitions of female decorum (M. Paul rejects Zelie St Pierre on the basis of his observations). Lucy herself, M. Paul observes, wants 'checking, regulating, and keeping down'. She needs 'watching, and watching over' (p. 526). Lucy vehemently repudiates M. Paul's methods: ' "To study the human heart thus, is to banquet secretly and sacrilegiously on Eve's apples. I wish you were a Protestant" ' (p. 530). The phrase 'Eve's apples', used in connection with the voyeuristic practice of spying on women, takes on a decisive sexual charge. The implicit connection, made throughout the book, between Roman Catholicism and the threatened exposure, and suppression, of female sexuality is here brought to the surface.

The anti-Catholicism of Brontë's earlier texts is explicitly foregrounded in this novel which was written at the time of extreme anti-Catholic agitation.[6] The local newpapers in Leeds were full of tales of 'papal aggression', and fears that 'Romish encroachments are approaching stealthily' and will soon reimpose 'an intolerable civil and spiritual bondage upon us'.[7] The case of the heiress, Miss Augusta Talbot, who after being placed in a convent, then decided to leave all her money to the Roman Catholic Church, offered further cause for outcry against the intrigues of a Church whose aims, it was asserted, were to mould and subdue the soul into 'perpetual subjection'.[8] All this agitation had a peculiar force in Leeds where the 'Perverts of Saint Saviours' were reintroducing Catholic ritual and confession, under the guidance of John Newman. The *Leeds Intelligencer* went overboard on its reporting of the libel trial in which the Protestant turned Catholic, John Newman, was called upon to defend his accusation of gross immorality and debauchery against the ex-Catholic priest, turned Protestant, Dr Achilli. The paper, only too willing, normally, to trumpet any allegation of sexual misconduct in the Roman Catholic Church, reserves its horror this time for the activities of the Church in persuading women to confess to such 'ineffaceable infamy', and for pursuing Dr Achilli with 'the unsleeping eye of Romish jealousy and vengeance'. In Brontë's text, this 'unsleeping eye' is manifest both in the workings of the confessional, and also in the malign pursuit of Lucy and M. Paul by Père Silas and the aptly named Malevola. Just as in *The Professor*, where the move to Belgium helped Crimsworth resolve, by displacement, his problems of gender and class identity, so in *Villette* Lucy's worst fears can be projected outwards onto an alien culture, against which she can then assert her own fierce Protestantism. Her real enemy, however, remains not these extreme projections of Catholic surveillance and intrigue, which modulate into fairy tale form, but the equivalent forces of surveillance offered by the attractive, seemingly benign, Dr John.

The force of anti-Catholic sentiment in *Villette* is clearly tied, as in the local newspaper agitation, to a nexus of sexual fear. The school legend of the nun 'buried alive, for some sin against her vow' (p. 148) establishes a chain of association between nuns, ghosts, and sexuality which reverberates throughout the novel. Lucy, burying her precious letters from Dr John above the nun's grave, is clearly associating the unspecified 'sin' with sexual transgression. Her 'sightings' of the nun occur, significantly, at moments of heightened sexual tension, whilst the ghostly pursuit to which she is subject seems to embody externally her own activities of self-suppression. Lucy's violent antagonism to Roman Catholicism, treated so often by critics as an intrusion of Brontë's personal prejudice, not germane to the narrative, stems from this associative sexual charge. The intensity of her response is signalled initially by her seemingly excessive reactions to the 'lecture pieuse': 'it made me so burning hot, and my temples and my heart and my wrist throbbed so fast, and my sleep afterwards was so broken with excitement, that I could sit no longer' (p. 163). The description of the content of the tales helps explain Lucy's extreme response: they contain 'the dread boasts of confessors, who had wickedly abused their office, trampling to deep degradation high-born ladies, making of countesses and princesses the most tormented slaves under the sun' (p. 163). It is this 'abuse of office' which Lucy most fears: the subjection of the self to a male authority consequent on the revelation of the inner self. The tales, 'nightmares of oppression, privation, and agony', offer an analogue of her own narrative, as she strives to keep herself hidden from the prying eyes of those who surround her.

The explicitly sexual nature of this revelation and subjection is suggested by the one tale specifically named, that of 'Conrad and Elizabeth of Hungary'. Brontë's source for this tale was Charles Kingsley's verse drama, *The Saint's Tragedy; or, The True Story of Elizabeth of Hungary* (1848). In a letter to Elizabeth Gaskell in 1851, Brontë records that her 'eyes rained' as she read this tale which offered, she believed, 'Deep truths . . . truths that stir a peculiar pity, a compassion hot with wrath and bitter with pain. This is no poet's dream: we know that such things *have* been done; that minds *have* been thus subjected, and lives thus laid waste'.[9] The process of subjection described arises directly from Elizabeth's internalization of the 'Manichean contempt' for sexuality embodied, for Kingsley, in Roman Catholicism. Elizabeth is found lying on the floor on her wedding night, covered with self-inflicted lacerations, unable to reconcile her sexual love for her husband with the teachings of the church. Burdened by these social contradictions, she later turns to the priest Conrad 'to save this little heart – The burden of self-rule', thus sacrificing the self-control prized by the Victorians as the index of sanity.[10] Conrad's responses to her are shown to be an unsavoury mixture of sexual lust, worldly ambition, and crude love of power: 'She calls herself my slave, with such an air / As speaks her queen, not slave: that shall be looked to – / She must be pinioned'.[11] The shadowy fears which lie behind Lucy's attempts to render herself illegible to male authoritative eyes are given explicit form in this work.

The parallels between *The Saint's Tragedy* and *Villette* are reinforced by comments in Brontë's letters in which she speaks of Elizabeth and Lucy in remarkably similar terms. Of Elizabeth she observes:

We see throughout (I *think*) that Elizabeth has not, and never had, a mind perfectly sane. From the time that she was what she herself, in the exaggeration of her humility, calls 'an idiot girl', to the hour when she lay moaning in visions on her dying bed, a slight craze runs through her whole existence. This is good: this is true. A sound mind, a healthy intellect, would have dashed the priest power to the wall . . . Only a mind weak with some fatal flaw *could* have been influenced as was this poor saint's. But what anguish – what struggles![12]

Her comments on Lucy, written whilst she was still in the midst of producing *Villette*, occur in response to observations made by W.S. Williams:

You say that she may be thought morbid and weak, unless the history of her life be more fully given. I consider that she *is* both morbid and weak at times; her character sets up no pretensions to unmixed strength, and anybody living her life would necessarily become morbid. It was no impetus of healthy feeling which urged her to the confessional, for instance; it was the semi-delirium of solitary grief and sickness.[13]

In both cases the weakness or morbidity (a term which in the nineteenth century designated specific mental disease) of the protagonist's mind is demonstrated by her subjection to the mind of a priest. There is a crucial difference, however: whereas Elizabeth's morbidity is assigned to an inherent mental flaw, Lucy's is attributed to the pressures of social circumstances. Insanity, Brontë here suggests, can be socially created.

The threat of confession for Lucy lay in the enforced articulation of that which should be kept hidden even from her own consciousness. In her excessive commitment to concealment, from her self, her readers and the external world, Lucy has fallen victim to the Victorian social code which stressed that women retained their necessary 'innocence' only if they remained ignorant of sexual desire. Thus, against all seeming evidence to the contrary, Lucy insists at one stage in her narrative that she never held 'warmer feelings' towards Dr John. Lucy has imbibed, and now admirably reproduces, the social code which decrees that women violate their femininity if they exhibit, or even experience, feelings which suggest a capacity to initiate desire. In keeping with this code, Lucy attempts to create for her readers a heroine who is calm and impervious, but as the narrative progresses, and the question of 'Who are you, Lucy Snowe?' becomes a focus of near-explicit attention, she acknowledges the constructed nature of this social persona.[14] After she has fled, pulse throbbing, from the 'lecture pieuse', only to discover Madame Beck searching her drawers for a love-letter which, to her sorrow and triumph, is non-existent, she undergoes a 'strange and contradictory . . . inward tumult . . . Complicated, disquieting thoughts broke up the whole of my nature. However, that turmoil subsided: next day I was again Lucy Snowe' (p. 166). This precarious division between the rigidly-defined social self, and the inner impulses which can never be articulated or even acknowledged, is to precipitate her breakdown.

In constructing Lucy's self-contradictory narrative, with its displacements, evasions and ghostly sightings which clearly signal to the modern reader the presence of sexual repression, Brontë was not thereby unconsciously articulating patterns in the human psyche which were to remain unrecognized, or even untheorized, until the advent of Freud. As I have argued, the belief that sexuality was a primary cause of nervous disorder and insanity in women was common currency in mid-Victorian England. Medical texts of the nineteenth century emphasized repeatedly that hysteria occurred mainly in young, unmarried women.[15] By mid-century one also finds the repeated suggestion that the social constrictions imposed on the unmarried, respectable female intensify the pressures of sexual repression until fire breaks out (a process which is literally embodied by Brontë in the burning of Thornfield by the demonic Mrs Rochester, and in the outbreak of fire in the theatre as the 'fallen angel' Vashti is acting).[16]

In Caroline's reflections in *Shirley*, the life of the old maid was linked to that of nuns who 'having violated nature . . . grow altogether morbid' (pp. 440–1). Although Caroline might become 'nervous' and even look 'as one who had seen a ghost', after her veins have been kindled by the 'apparition' of her lover, she is saved from the extremes of morbidity by the textual device of brain fever. In *Villette*, by contrast, Brontë explores the mental effects of repression, exposing, through the twists and turns of her narrative, the morbid processes of mind of her designedly uncongenial 'Miss Frost', who, unlike pretty, sweet-natured Caroline Helstone, is permitted to retain none of the characteristics of a traditional heroine.[17]

The question of Lucy's actual instability must remain unanswered if we, as readers, are to avoid falling into the error of Dr John in assuming unproblematic access to a realm of hidden truth. It is possible, however, to trace the degree to which Lucy, in analysis of her own history, draws on the constructions of appropriate and 'insane' feminine behaviour to be found in mid-nineteenth-century psychological science. In her explicit use of contemporary scientific terms, Lucy draws attention to the explanatory complexes which underpin the often unconscious associations that direct her interpretation of behaviour. Her first noticeable use of scientific terminology occurs in her judgment on what she perceives to be the emotional excesses of Polly's behaviour with regard to her father: 'This, I perceived, was a one-idead nature; betraying that monomaniac tendency I have ever thought the most unfortunate with which man or woman can be cursed' (p. 16). The idea of monomania, displaced here onto Polly, is later appropriated by Lucy for herself to describe her distress at losing Dr John's letter: ' "Oh! they have taken my letter!" cried the grovelling, groping, monomaniac' (p. 353).[18] Monomania, as first defined by Esquirol, and later popularized in England by James Prichard, was a form of partial insanity, unmarked by mania, which could possibly exist within the compass of normal daily life.

Esquirol's formulation of his categories of insanity was firmly founded on assumptions of 'female vulnerability'. Women, he believed, were more susceptible, both physiologically and psychologically, to religious and erotic melancholy, and hence to the 'hallucinations the most strange and frequent' of religious and erotic monomania (a conjunction of religion and sexuality which clearly lies behind the figure of the nun).[19] The unleashing of religious or erotic passion, which for Esquirol marked incipient insanity, is figured in *Villette* in the young 'monomaniac', Polly, whom Lucy catches sight of 'praying like some Catholic or Methodist enthusiast – some precocious fanatic or untimely saint'. Lucy's thoughts on this occasion, she remarks, 'ran risk of being hardly more rational and healthy than that child's mind must have been' (p. 15). The correlation of 'rational' and 'healthy' suggests that Lucy endorses Esquirol's association of mental health with socially-prescribed forms of rationality. Whilst her own moderate Protestantism represents for her the requisite model of mental balance and control, Catholicism, and extreme Methodism, suggest a frightening addiction to passionate excess, and hence a sacrifice of the mind's autonomy and control.

Lucy's own monomania clearly follows the course of Esquirol's erotic monomania which he defines as a literal disease, a 'chronic cerebral affection . . . characterized by an excessive passion'.[20] In a formulation which reflects cultural attitudes of the era, Esquirol divides sexual afflictions into chaste erotomania, whose origins lie in the imagination, and 'obscene', 'shameful and humiliating' nymphomania and satyriasis which originate in the organs of reproduction. Erotomaniacs differ from the latter class in that their affections are 'chaste and honourable', they 'never pass the limits of propriety'. Instead, these subjects tend to 'forget themselves; vow a pure, and often secret devotion to the object of their love; make themselves slaves to it; execute its orders with a fidelity often puerile; and obey also the caprices that are connected with it'.[21] The description offers an outline of Lucy's 'chaste', obsessional behaviour; her devotion to Dr John, like that of the erotomaniac, is secret: 'I liked entering his presence covered with a cloud he had not seen through, while he stood before me under a ray of special illumination, which shone all partial over his head, trembled about his feet, and cast light no farther' (p. 250). In this passage which describes Lucy's 'system of feeling', her determined refusal to reveal her identity to Dr John, knowledge and sexuality are clearly assimilated: whilst Lucy wishes not to be 'seen through', the projection of her ray of illumination, which trembles about Dr John's feet, clearly functions as a displaced enactment of her own sexual desire, her longed-for self-abasement. Lucy's first concern, like that of Esquirol's erotomaniacs, is to reduce self so as to glorify the chosen object of her passion.

Esquirol's formulation of erotomania, like his other categories of insanity, dresses recognized social stereotypes in the authority of science. In his hands, the disease becomes socially respectable. Erotomaniacs, he insists, do not, even in fantasy, seek fulfilment of their desires: 'The erotomaniac neither desires, nor dreams even, of the favors to which he might aspire from the object of his insane tenderness.'[22] The social repression, so evident in Lucy's narrative, which forbade women the articulation, or even conscious acknowledgement, of their desires, is encoded in his very definition of the disease. Esquirol's theory of erotomania, however, does not merely reinforce accepted social wisdom: chaste, hopeless passion is transformed into a cerebral disease, and must henceforth be treated as a possible symptom of insanity. The fear of mental illness signalled by Lucy's references to monomania underpins all her narrative: insanity is no longer limited to the recognizably disruptive forces of sexual desire, which may be locked away in the attic, but lurks as an incipient threat even in the 'chaste' repressed imaginings of the 'respectable' woman.

Lucy's imposition of the label 'monomaniac' on her 'double', Polly, is clearly expressive of a self-revelatory fear.[23] Polly's function as Lucy's alter ego is made explicit in Lucy's later confession that:

'As a child I feared for you; nothing that has life was ever more susceptible than your nature in infancy: under harshness, or neglect, neither your outward nor your inward self would have ripened to what they now are. Much pain, much fear, much struggle would have troubled the very lines of your features, broken their regularity, would have harassed your nerves into the fever of habitual irritation: you would have lost in health and cheerfulness, in grace and sweetness.' (p. 545)

Beneath the anguish of self-portrait that directs these lines, there lies the disturbing suggestion that mental health is not a norm, from which only an unfortunate, physiologically determined, minority deviate, but rather an ideal which few are lucky enough to attain. To encounter pain or struggle is to develop nerves 'harassed' into 'habitual irritation'. Mental disease, Lucy suggests, is incipient in us all.

Polly's successful capture of that golden prize, Graham Bretton (a figure distinct from the Dr John of Lucy's acquaintance) is attended by both material conditions denied to Lucy, and superior psychological powers of self-control. The child who had demonstrated a 'sensibility which bends of its own will, a giant slave under the sway of good sense' (p. 17), which proved so 'burdensome' to Lucy, displays in adolescence a perfect mastery of the socially requisite powers of repression. Lucy writes two letters to Dr John, one dictated by Feeling and the other by Reason, but Polly writes 'three times – chastening and subduing the phrases at every rescript' until her letter resembled 'a morsel of ice' (p. 544). Despite her attempts to live up to her name, Lucy fails to attain this icy level of control. Yet, notwithstanding Lucy's envy of her ideal counterpart, *Villette* does not fundamentally endorse the doctrine of control which had been so central to *Jane Eyre*. Jane's history had seemed to vindicate the mid-Victorian belief that successful regulation of the mental economy would lead to material social success. Bertha is sent to her death so that Jane can achieve the bourgeois dream. *Villette*, a more radical work, politically, than *Jane Eyre*, refuses this compromise. The limited form of success allotted to Lucy, who dwells outside the realm of the ideal inhabited by Graham and Polly, actually stems from her allowing her passion to break bounds as she finally defies Madame Beck. Although Lucy achieves economic competency at the end, the dominant final note in the novel is not one of triumph or content, but rather overwhelming loss (though marriage to M. Paul might, as Brontë hints in a letter, have been an even worse fate).[24]

In calling into question in *Villette* the doctrine of control, Brontë is thereby implicitly challenging the economic model of healthy regulation which underpinned mid-Victorian theories of social, psychological and physiological functioning. The mind, like the body, or the social economy, was to be treated as a system to be guided, regulated and controlled. As John Elliotson observed, 'the laws of the mind are precisely those of the functions of all other organs, – a certain degree of excitement strengthens it; too much exhausts it'.[25] In the mental, as in the social economy, the aim must be to obtain maximum efficiency, neither over-stretching, nor under-deploying the natural resources. Theories of insanity drew on this model. Whether the cause were seen to be physical or moral, menstrual irregularities or the exclusive direction of the efforts of the mind into one channel, the net effect was seen to be the unbalancing of the body's natural economy which was founded on the free flow of 'secretions' and a hierarchical regulation of the mental forces.[26] Such theories of the bodily economy were based, however, on normative, gender-specific, codes of social behaviour. The social construction of insanity went hand in hand with that of femininity.

Lucy, in her vocabulary, seems initially to endorse enthusiastically the phrenological world view, believing that cultivation of the correct faculties and suppression of the troublesome lower propensities would lead directly to social advancement. In London she feels a surge of confident energy: 'Who but a coward would pass his whole life in hamlets, and for ever abandon his faculties to the eating rust of obscurity?' (p. 64). Later, once launched in her teaching career, she feels satisfied 'I was getting on; not lying the stagnant prey of mould and rust, but polishing my faculties and whetting them to a keen edge with constant use' (p. 113).[27] Such confidence soon dissolves, however, to be replaced by a rather different theory of social and psychological life. Brontë still uses the vocabulary of regulation and control, but to rather different effect. Lucy's efforts at regulation are no longer seen to be healthful. She strives for a literal form of live burial, recapitulating the experience of the nun: 'in catalepsy and a dead trance, I studiously held the quick of my nature' (p. 152). In a world where inner energies, when duly regulated, can find no external outlet, it is better, Lucy argues, that they be suppressed, if they are not to become self-consuming. Alternatively, they should be allowed to range in the world of fantasy. In this, her last novel, Brontë finally, tentatively, asserts the claims of the realm of imagination, in opposition to the reason and control of the masculine world, with all its spurious offers of healing aid. Lucy deliberately rejects her envenomed stepmother, Hag Reason, for the saving spirit of the imagination (pp. 327–9), while the 'Real' – that realm to which the moral managers sought so assiduously to return their patients – is figured for her in the iconography of the fallen woman: 'Presently the rude Real burst coarsely in – all evil, grovelling, and repellent as she too often is' (p. 153). The description, which prefigures the emergence of that 'grovelling, groping, monomaniac', Lucy, suggests the consequences for women of living according to male-defined reality (the 'Real' here is the casket containing the love letter which simultaneously dismisses Lucy as a sexual possibility and condemns her as a monster). Lucy's narrative, which dissolves the real into the imaginary, challenges male constructions of the social and psychological world.

This is not to suggest, however, that Lucy thereby steps entirely outside the formulations of psychological experience to be found in contemporary science. Her descriptions of her sufferings during the Long Vacation follow medical wisdom in assigning both physical and moral causes for this 'strange fever of the nerves and blood' (p. 222). Her fantasies concerning Ginevra (who functions as rival, alter ego and object of desire) and Dr John, and her nightmares of rejection, are underpinned by the responsiveness of her physical frame to the winds and storms outside, held by contemporary alienists to occasion and exacerbate insanity (pp. 219–20).[28] In projecting herself as a physical system, at the mercy of external physical changes, Lucy is able to deny her responsibility for her mental disorder: it is her 'nervous system' which cannot stand the strain; the controlling rational ego is dissolved into the body. The figure of the cretin, however, with its 'propensity . . . to evil' (p. 220), stands as a warning projection of a model of mind where the physical is dominant, and the passions and propensities are not subject to any mental restraint.

Lucy seems to shift in and out of physiological explanation of the self as it suits her convenience. In opposition to Dr John, who clearly regards her in the same professional light as the 'singularly interesting' disease whose symptoms had detained him in the old town, she denies understanding of his diagnosis: ' "I am not quite sure what my nervous system is, but I was dreadfully low-spirited" ' (p. 261). Her attempt to define why she went to confession is marked by a similar resistance: ' "I suppose you will think me mad for taking such a step, but I could not help it: I suppose it was all the fault of what you call my 'nervous system' " ' (p. 264). Rejecting this materialist mode of interpretation, she admits to the difficulty of finding language to describe her state, concluding that ' "a cruel sense of desolation pained my mind: a feeling that would make its way, rush out, or kill me – like (and this you will understand, Dr John) the current which passes through the heart, and which, if aneurism or any other morbid cause obstructs its natural channels, impetuously seeks abnormal outlet"' (p. 264). Although Lucy distances herself from Dr John's technical explanation, her description of her own mental state actually draws even more decisively on current theories of physiological psychology. Her interpretation is founded on a metaphorical transposition of the medical explanation of insanity as a morbid obstruction of the channels of the mind.

Lucy's resistance to Dr John stems less from the actual content of his medical verdicts, than from his reduction of her to a bundle of symptoms, open to his professional definition and control. Her first preoccupation after her collapse, occasion of her double exposure to the eyes of religious and medical authority, was to re-establish her private domain, subduing feeling so as to be 'better regulated, more equable, quieter on the surface' where the 'common gaze' will fall. The turbulent realm below was to be left to God: 'Man, your equal, weak as you, and not fit to be your judge, may be shut out thence' (p. 255). Dr John, however, attempts just that act of judgment, but in diagnosing her case as one of hypochondria, he is forced to acknowledge limitations in his medical art which 'looks in and sees a chamber of torture, but can neither say nor do much' (p. 261). He is restricted to recommending the cheerful society and exercise listed by Graham as the means by which 'moral management' should attempt to cure hypochondriasis.[29] Even Dr John's more limited claim to an authoritative power of diagnosis is undermined, however, by his failure to remark, as Lucy does, that the King of Labassecour is a sufferer from 'constitutional melancholy' (p. 304). Medical knowledge is matched against experiential understanding and found wanting.

Lucy claims for herself the sole power of deciphering the 'hieroglyphics' of the king's countenance which suggest to her that, 'Those eyes had looked on the visits of a certain ghost – had long waited the comings and goings of that strangest spectre, Hypochondria' (p. 303). The conflation of medical and Gothic terminology in this passage echoes Brontë's description of her own experience of hypochondria in a letter written several years earlier. Brontë speaks initially of the suffering of a friend who 'has felt the tyranny of Hypochondria – a most dreadful doom, far worse than that of a man of healthy nerves buried for the same length of time in a subterranean dungeon'. Of her own experience she remarks that she had endured 'preternatural horror which seemed to clothe existence and Nature – and which made life a continual waking Nightmare – Under such circumstances the morbid nerves can know neither peace nor enjoyment – whatever touches – pierces them – sensation for them is all suffering'. Considering her effect upon Margaret Wooler, she concludes she must have been 'no better company for you than a stalking ghost'.[30] The letter, like the novel, suggests a sense of powerlessness in the face of physiological tyranny. The terms of the description offer a similar mixture of metaphorical and physiological language: the idea of being buried alive, literally embodied in *Villette*, is linked to the notion of 'morbid nerves', which are themselves then personified, endowed with the capacity to suffer and experience. The ghostly qualities, attributed to hypochondria in the novel, are here appropriated by Brontë for herself, in a transposition which mirrors the novel's dissolution of the boundaries of the self. Lucy not only dwells in a realm where furniture becomes 'spectral', but also attributes that quality to herself in others' eyes: she feels, at one stage, she must look to Dr John 'like some ghost' (p. 157). Perception, in Lucy's spectral world, is integrally related to the social construction of identity.

Lucy's final discussion of hypochondria returns once more to the question of the relationship between physiology and mental suffering. She contrasts the world's ready acceptance of the idea of physical illness with its reluctant understanding of an equivalent mental disease:

> The world can understand well enough the process of perishing for want of food: perhaps few persons can enter into or follow out that of going mad from solitary confinement. They see the long-buried prisoner disinterred, a maniac or an idiot! – how his sense left him – how his nerves first inflamed, underwent nameless agony, and then sunk to palsy – is a subject too intricate for examination, too abstract for popular comprehension. Speak of it! you might almost as well stand up in an European market-place, and propound dark sayings in that language and mood wherein Nebuchadnezzar, the imperial hypochondriac, communed with his baffled Chaldeans. (p. 392)

The idea of psychological deprivation, dramatized throughout the novel in the motif of live burial, is here grounded in the physiological experience of the nerves which undergo inflammation and then 'nameless agony'. As soon as Lucy moves away from available technical vocabulary she reaches the limits of the expressible: the agony must remain 'nameless'. Unlike her Biblical counterpart, Lucy knows better than to try and describe to others a form of experience that has never received social recognition or articulation. The passage represents an implicit rebuke to the medical establishment who believe that in naming the 'symptoms' of hypochondria, they have somehow mastered the experience. Lucy is both asserting her own belief in the material basis of psychological suffering, and denying Dr John's claim to authoritative knowledge.

Lucy's battle for control over self-definition and interpretation of the processes of her own mind is not conducted solely with Dr John; the fiery M. Paul also enters the lists. On encountering Lucy in the art gallery after her illness, M. Paul berates her for her unfeminine behaviour in not being able to look after the cretin: '"Women who are worthy the name,"' he proclaims, '"ought infinitely to surpass our coarse, fallible, self-indulgent sex, in the power to perform such duties"' (p. 290). The covert subject of this conversation is clearly the model of the female mind which suggested that women are more 'naturally' able than men to suppress their 'evil propensities'. Lucy, in self-defence, resorts to another male model of the female mind, asserting a physical illness: '"I had a nervous fever: my mind was ill"' (p. 290). Diminished responsibility, which figured so largely in mid-Victorian trials of female criminals, becomes the basis of her excuse for 'unwomanly' conduct. Unlike Dr John, M. Paul refuses to accept this model of the mind and so draws attention back again to his own image of the constitution of the feminine. Dismissing the idea of nervous fever, he points instead to Lucy's 'temerity' in gazing at the picture of Cleopatra. The portrait of the fleshy Cleopatra, and the four pictures of 'La vie d'une femme', 'cold and vapid as ghosts', which M. Paul prefers for Lucy's instruction in the arts of femininity, take on iconographic significance in the narrative, representing the two alternative models for womanhood created by men.[31] Lucy's challenge to these models, implicit throughout her narrative, takes decisive form in the Vashti section.

The narrative sequence which culminates in the performance of Vashti actually starts, not in the theatre, but on Lucy's apparent sighting, that evening, of the nun. Dr John, refusing to respect her reticence, invokes once more his professional authority to diagnose the symptoms of her 'raised look', thus provoking Lucy's angry dismissal of his explanation: 'Of course with him, it was held to be another effect of the same cause: it was all optical illusion – nervous malady, and so on. Not one bit did I believe him; but I dared not contradict: doctors are so self-opinionated, so immovable in their dry, materialist views' (p. 368). Lucy rejects the 'doctor's' opinion on principle, although his physiological explanation appears perhaps surprisingly close to views she herself has expressed elsewhere. The grounds of her objection to Dr John's 'dry' materialism are made explicit, however, in her analysis of their mutual responses to the performance of Vashti.

For Lucy, Vashti on stage transcends socially imposed sex-roles; she is neither woman nor man, but a devil, a literal embodiment of inner passion: 'Hate and Murder and Madness incarnate, she stood' (p. 369). Lucy's response is to invoke the male author of a rather different image of womanhood: 'Where was the artist of the Cleopatra? Let him come and sit down and study this different vision. Let him seek here the mighty brawn, the muscle, the abounding blood, the full-fed flesh he worshipped: let all materialists draw nigh and look on' (p. 370). In a significant elision, Lucy has drawn together the materialism of doctors who seek to explain the processes of the mind with reference only to the physiological behaviour of the nerves, and the materialism of men who construct their images of women with reference only to the physical attributes of the flesh. The creation of the feminine in male-executed art is directly allied to the medical construction of women.

Lucy perceives, in Vashti, a force which could re-enact the miracle of the Red Sea, drowning Paul Peter Rubens [sic] and 'all the army of his fat women', but Dr John remains unresponsive to her challenge. He replicates, in the 'intense curiosity' with which he watches her performance, the professional gaze he has recently imposed on Lucy. His verdict underscores, for Lucy, his indifference to the inner movements of female experience: 'he judged her as a woman, not an artist: it was a branding judgment' (p. 373). Dr John's response is determined entirely by pre-defined categories of suitable female behaviour. As in his medical practice, he is insulated from any attempt to understand the causes or experiential detail of the cases he is examining through his possession of a socially validated system of classification which allows him to speak with unreflecting authority. Like his counterparts in the Book of Esther (from where the name Vashti is drawn) he trusts to the codification of male power to protect him from the 'demonic' challenge of female energy. (Queen Vashti's refusal to show her beauty at the king's command had provoked, from a worried male oligarchy, a proclamation 'to every people after their language, that every man should bear rule in his own house'.)[32]

In choosing to equate medical and artistic constructions of the female identity through the notion of 'materialism,' Brontë was drawing on the terms of contemporary debate. As an artistic term, implying the 'tendency to lay stress on the material aspects of the objects represented' the first use of materialism seems to date only from the 1850s (OED). Although the philosophical usage of materialism dates back to the eighteenth century, it had, at the time of Brontë's writing, become the focus of a virulent social and theological debate concerning the development of psychological theories which stressed that the brain was the organ of mind. Phrenology and mesmerism were located, in the popular press, at the centre of this controversy, as evidenced by the 1851 *Blackwood's* article which inveighed against the phreno-mesmerism of authors who believed that 'upon the materialism of life rest the great phenomena of what we were wont to call mind'.[33] Clearly, as Brontë's use of phrenological terms and concepts reveals, she was not stirred into opposition by this controversy. Lucy's objections to materialism are not based on the religious grounds of contemporary debate; nor, as her own use of physiological vocabulary demonstrates, are they founded on an opposition to the use of a physiological explanation of the mind *per se*. Her rejection of medical and artistic materialism stems rather from the rigid and incomplete nature of their conception; she objects less to the idea of an interrelationship between body and mind, than to their rather partial vision of this union. Under the medical and artistic gaze, woman is *reduced* to flesh and the material functioning of nerves.

In describing the impact of Vashti, Lucy herself employs the vocabulary of contemporary physiological psychology; Vashti's acting,

instead of merely irritating imagination with the thought of what *might* be done, at the same time fevering the nerves because it was *not* done, disclosed power like a deep, swollen, winter river, thundering in cataract, and bearing the soul, like a leaf, on the steep and steely sweep of its descent. (p. 371)

The term 'irritating' here is a technical one as used, for example, in Graham's observation that 'The nervous headache generally occurs in persons with a peculiar irritability of the nervous system.'[34] Coupled with the idea of 'fevering the nerves' it suggests two different levels of response within the nervous system, whilst the concluding imagery of the thundering river draws on physiological ideas of channelled energy within the brain. The power disclosed is both internal and external: it describes the force of Vashti's own inner energy, and the impact on the observer Lucy. What Brontë has done, in this metaphorical usage of contemporary physiological theory, is to dramatize an even closer integration of body and mind than physiology envisaged, while simultaneously breaking down the traditional boundaries of the self. Mind is not reduced to body, it becomes literally 'embodied', as Lucy earlier observed: 'To her, what hurts becomes immediately embodied: she looks on it as a thing that can be attacked, worried down, torn in shreds. Scarcely a substance herself, she grapples to conflict with abstractions. Before calamity she is a tigress; she rends her woes, shivers them in convulsed abhorrence' (p. 370). Whilst the artist reduces woman to a material expanse of flesh, and the doctor to a mere encasement of nerves, Vashti reveals a true union between the worlds of mind and body: abstractions, the experiential details of mental life which physiology cannot describe, are given material form. In her treatment of Vashti, as throughout the novel, Brontë actually employs contemporary physiological theory to break through the narrow definition of the self it proposes.

The description of Vashti tearing hurt into shreds anticipates Lucy's later destruction of the figure of the nun:

All the movement was mine, so was all the life, the reality, the substance, the force; as my instinct felt. I tore her up – the incubus! I held her on high – the goblin! I shook her loose – the mystery! And down she fell – down all round me – down in shreds and fragments – and I trode upon her. (p. 681)

Like Vashti, Lucy undertakes a material destruction of an inner hurt: the force and *substance* are Lucy's own.[35] The term 'incubus', with its associations of sexuality and mental disturbance, draws together the arenas of physical and mental life. In nineteenth-century psychological usage, incubus had become synonymous with nightmare. In a passage noted by Patrick Brontë, Robert Macnish observed in *The Philosophy of Sleep* that it was possible to suffer nightmare whilst awake and in 'perfect possession of [the] faculties'. Macnish records that he had 'undergone the greatest tortures, being haunted by spectres, hags, and every sort of phantom – having, at the same time, a full consciousness that I was labouring under incubus, and that all the terrifying objects around me were the creations of my own brain.'[36] Brontë takes this idea of waking nightmare or incubus one stage further, giving it a literal embodiment in her fiction which defies attempts to demarcate the boundaries between 'creations of the brain' and external forms.

*   *   *

Brontë offers, in *Villette*, a thorough materialization of the self. The construct 'Lucy' is not a unified mental entity, located within a physiological frame, but rather a continuous process which extends beyond the confines of the flesh. Lucy's entire mode of self-articulation breaks down the hierarchy of outer and inner life upon which definitions of the 'Real' (and sanity) depend. Her description of the death of Hope, for instance, parallels that of the literal burial of the letters: 'In the end I closed the eyes of my dead, covered its face, and composed its limbs with great calm' (p. 421). The burial itself is the wrapping of grief in a 'winding-sheet'. Later, as Lucy pauses beside the grave, she recalls 'the passage of feeling therein buried' (p. 524). Metaphor has become inoperable: it functions, as Lucy's text makes clear, only if the speaker endorses normative social demarcations between different states. Thus the classrooms which initially only 'seem' to Lucy to be like jails quickly become 'filled with spectral and intolerable memories, laid miserable amongst their straw and their manacles' (p. 652). The controlling distance of 'seems' is collapsed, as 'memories', normally restricted to the realm of the mind, take on vivid physical form.

Lucy's intricate dramatizations of her feelings undermine traditional divisions between external social process and inner mental life, revealing their fictional status.[37] Her tale of Jael, Sisera and Heber, for example, simultaneously portrays physiological pain, psychological conflict, and the social drama of repression. Speaking of her desire to be drawn out of her present existence, Lucy observes:

This longing, and all of a similar kind, it was necessary to knock on the head; which I did, figuratively, after the manner of Jael to Sisera, driving a nail through their temples. Unlike Sisera, they did not die: they were but transiently stunned, and at intervals would turn on the nail with a rebellious wrench; then did the temples bleed, and the brain thrill to its core. (p. 152)

The distinction between figural and literal quickly fades, as the inner psychic drama develops, and the rebellious desires themselves perpetuate their torture, in a description which captures the physiological and psychological experience of socially inflicted repression (the term 'thrill' carried the medically precise meaning, in the mid-nineteenth century, of 'vibratory movement, resonance, or murmur'). The narrative evocation of inner life does not, however, end there. Lucy develops the story, envisaging, with a precision of detail unmatched in the descriptions of the external scenes of her life, the physical landscape of the action under the soothing light of imagination. Jael, the controlling self responsible for maiming the desires to whom she had promised shelter, begins to relent, but such thoughts are soon outweighed by the expectation of her husband, Heber's, commendation of her deed: female self-repression is accorded patriarchal endorsement. This drama of internal pain and division, with its precise enactment of the social processes of control, reveals the falsity of normative divisions between inner and outer experience.

The famous account of Lucy's opiate-induced wanderings into the night landscape of Villette also dissolves the divisions between inner and outer realms, as social experience now takes on the qualities of mental life, defying the normal boundaries of time and space. Amidst the physical forms of Cleopatra's Egypt, Lucy witnesses all the figures of her inner thoughts parade before her eyes (only Ginevra and De Hamal are excluded, but, as Lucy later insists, it was her own excursion which released them into sexual freedom).[38] Even here, however, where she seems most free from external social controls, she is still subject to fears of surveillance: she feels Dr John's gaze 'oppressing' her, seeming ready to grasp 'my identity . . . between his never tyrannous, but always powerful hands' (p. 661). As dominant male, and doctor, empowered by society to diagnose the inner movements of mind, and legislate on mental disease, Dr John threatens Lucy's carefully-nurtured sense of self.

Identity, as Brontë has shown throughout *Villette*, is not a given, but rather a tenuous process of negotiation between the subject and surrounding social forces.

The opposition to male materialism, voiced by Lucy in her confrontation with medical authority, gives dramatic expression to the interrogation of male constructions of the female psyche which underpins the narrative form of *Villette*. In seeking to avoid the surveillance of religious, educational and medical figures, trying to render herself illegible, Lucy attempts to assume control over the processes of her own self-definition. Yet her narrative, as I have argued, reveals a clear internalization of the categories and terms of contemporary medical psychology. Lucy employs physiological explanations of mental life and appropriates to herself theories of a female predisposition to neurosis and monomania. In creating the autobiography of her troubled heroine, Brontë explores both the social implications of contemporary psychological theory, and its inner consequences. The form of her account, with its dissolution of divisions between inner psychological life and the material social world, suggests an alternative vision – one that challenges the normative psychological vision implicit in male definitions of the 'Real'.

NOTES

1. Sandra Gilbert and Susan Gubar, *The Madwoman in the Attic: The Woman Writer and the Nineteenth-century Literary Imagination* (New Haven: Yale Univ. Press, 1979), p. 360.

2. The Leeds Philosophical and Literary Society, for example, had a public lecture on 'The Philosophy of Apparitions' in 1850–1 (E.K. Clark, *The History of 100 Years of Life of the Leeds Philosophical and Literary Society*, Leeds: Jowett and Sowry, 1924). Two works held in the Keighley Mechanics' Institute library offer extensive discussions of the relationship between 'spectral illusion' and insanity: John Abercrombie, *Inquiries Concerning the Intellectual Powers* (Edinburgh: Waugh & Innes, 1832) and Robert Macnish, *The Philosophy of Sleep* (Glasgow: W.R. M'Phun, 1830), a work the Reverend Brontë quotes in his medical annotations.

3. See, for example, the article in the *Times*, July 1853, quoted ch. 3, n. 1.

4. T.J. Wise and J.A. Symington, *The Brontës: Their Lives, Friendships and Correspondence*, 4 vols (Oxford: Basil Blackwell, 1933), IV, p. 14. Hereafter cited as *Letters*. Letter to George Smith, 30 October 1852.

5. Ibid., IV, p. 35. 19 January 1853.

6. For a helpful account of the ways in which *Villette* relates to contemporary anti-Catholic literature see Rosemary Clark-Beattie, 'Fables of Rebellion:

Anti-Catholicism and the Structure of *Villette*', *English Literary History*, 53 (1986), pp. 821–47.

7. *Leeds Intelligencer*, 5 April 1851. The concern about 'papal aggression' had arisen in 1850 when the Pope had proclaimed a Catholic hierarchy in England, which was seen to exert territorial claims. Combined with all the fears about the influence of the Tractarians, this papal move resulted in the passing, in July 1851, of the Ecclesiastical Titles Act, the last measure of discrimination against religious denominations to be passed by a British Government. See G.I.T. Machin, *Politics and the Churches in Great Britain, 1832–1868* (Oxford: Clarendon Press, 1977), pp. 218–28. Leeds was a particularly vociferous centre of anti-Catholic feeling at this time, holding public meetings and setting up petitions on 'papal aggression' (see reports in the *Leeds Intelligencer* for March and April 1851).

8. *Leeds Intelligencer*, 22 March 1851. The paper not only ran extensive reports on the case, but also devoted several editorials to what it revealed about Catholic ambitions for subjecting the British soul.

9. *Letters*, III, p. 269. To Mrs Gaskell, 6 August 1851.

10. Charles Kingsley, *Poems* (London: Macmillan, 1884), p. 46.

11. Ibid., p. 51.

12. *Letters*, III, pp. 268–9. To Mrs Gaskell, 6 August 1851.

13. *Letters*, IV, p. 18. To W.S. Williams, 6 November 1852.

14. Lucy's question of the nun, 'Who are you?' (p. 426) is echoed by Ginevra 'Who *are* you, Miss Snowe?' (p. 440).

15. See George Man Burrows, *Commentaries on the Causes, Forms, Symptoms, and Treatment, Moral and Medical, of Insanity* (London: 1828; repr. New York: Arno Press, 1976), p. 191, and for unmarried women's susceptibility to nightmare see Macnish, *Philosophy of Sleep*, pp. 139, 143.

16. See J.G. Millingen, *The Passions; or Mind and Matter* (London: J. & D. Darling, 1848), p. 158, and Robert Brudenell Carter, *On the Pathology and Treatment of Hysteria* (London: John Churchill, 1853), p. 34.

17. Brontë's original name for Lucy was 'Frost'. As she observes in a letter to W.S. Williams, 'A *cold* name she must have . . . for she has about her an external coldness'. *Letters*, IV, p. 18. 6 November 1852.

18. The edition here actually reads 'monamaniac'. I assume, however, that this is a printing error.

19. J.E.D. Esquirol, *Mental Maladies: A Treatise on Insanity*, trans. E.K. Hunt (1845; New York: Hafner, 1965), p. 109. In a passage which reveals all the nineteenth-century preconceptions about 'female vulnerability', Esquirol observes: 'Are not women under the control of influences to which men are strangers: such as menstruation, pregnancy, confinement, and nursing? The amorous passions, which among them are so active; religion which is a veritable passion with many, when love does not exclusively occupy their heart and mind, jealousy, fear, do not these act more energetically upon the minds of women than men?' (p. 211).

20. Ibid., p. 335.

21. Ibid., p. 336.

22. Ibid.

23. Lucy, meeting Polly again in Villette, views her as her own 'double' (p. 398).

24. See *Letters*, IV, pp. 55–6. To George Smith, 26 March 1853.

25. Elliotson, *Human Philosophy*, 5th edn (London: Longmans, 1840), p. 37.

26. These were two of the causes of insanity cited by Thomas John Graham in *Modern Domestic Medicine* (London: Simpkin & Marshall *et al.*, 1826), p. 392.

27. Her vocabulary is precisely that employed in the Annual Report of the Keighley Mechanics' Institute in 1832: 'The faculties of the mind can only be preserved in a sound and healthful state by constant exercise . . . as the metallic instrument corrodes and wastes with indolence and sloth, so with continued use, an edge is produced capable of cutting down every obstacle'.

28. See T.J. Graham, *Modern Domestic Medicine*, p. 392, Esquirol, *Mental Maladies*, p. 31, and *Villette*, p. 388.

29. Ibid., p. 346.

30. *Letters*, II, 116–17. To Margaret Wooler, approx. November–December 1846.

31. For an analysis of the functions of these paintings, see Gilbert and Gubar, *Madwoman*, p. 420.

32. Esther, I, 22.

33. 'What is Mesmerism?' *Blackwood's Edinburgh Magazine*, 70 (1851), p. 84.

34. Graham, *Modern Domestic Medicine*, p. 332.

35. Mary Jacobus, in her excellent article on *Villette*, offers a slightly different reading of this passage: 'The Buried Letter: Feminism and Romanticism in *Villette*', in *Women Writing and Writing about Women*, ed. M. Jacobus (London: Croom Helm, 1979), p. 54.

36. Macnish, *Philosophy of Sleep*, p. 136. The Reverend Brontë records under 'nightmare' in his copy of Graham, 'Dr McNish, who has written very ably on the philosophy of sleep – has justly described, the sensations of Night mare, under some modifications – as being amongst the most horrible that oppress human nature – an inability to move, during the paroxysm – dreadful visions of ghosts etc. . . . . He was, himself – often distressed by this calamity, and justly said, that it was worst, towards the morning, 1838 B.' (Graham, *Modern Domestic Medicine*, pp. 425–6).

37. As Inga-Stina Ewbank has observed in *Their Proper Sphere: A Study of the Brontë Sisters as Early Victorian Female Novelists* (London: Edward Arnold, 1966), the personifications, lengthened into allegories of Lucy's emotional crises 'do not arrest the action of *Villette*, for in a sense they *are* the action: even more than in *Jane Eyre* the imagery of *Villette* tends to act out an inner drama which superimposes itself on, or even substitutes for, external action' (p. 189).

38. The sequence of events is rather unclear since Lucy herself walks easily out of the pensionnat, but in the ensuing debate as to how Ginevra could have escaped, Lucy cannot forget how she, 'to facilitate a certain enterprise', had neither bolted nor secured the door (pp. 684–5).

CHAPTER SIX

Words on 'Great Vulgar Sheets': Writing and Social Resistance in Anne Brontë's *Agnes Grey* (1847)

SUSAN MEYER

Susan Meyer teaches English at Wellesley College, Massachusetts, and focuses primarily on literature and imperialism in the nineteenth-century novel. In her book *Imperialism at Home: Race in Victorian Women's Fiction* (1996) she examines metaphors of race in Charlotte Brontë's novel in order to explore the relationship between domestic fiction and imperialism. This article on *Agnes Grey* is taken from *The New Nineteenth Century* (1996), a collection of feminist readings of lesser-known Victorian novels which she co-edited with Barbara Harman. Like her work on imperialism, it brings to light areas of the text which have been treated as marginal. She reads this apparently conventional and unexciting novel as a vehement protest against the silencing and devaluing of both women and the working class.

Anne Brontë is usually remembered only as the younger sister of Emily and Charlotte, but she was a talented novelist in her own right who, in the course of her short life (1820–49), published two novels, *Agnes Grey* (1847) and *The Tenant of Wildfell Hall* (1848), as well as contributing a selection of her poetry to a collection of the poems of the three sisters, published pseudonymously as *Poems by Currer, Ellis and Acton Bell* (1846). Anne Brontë's first novel was somewhat overshadowed by the fiction of her sisters, partly because it appeared as part of a three-volume set, along with *Wuthering Heights*, which occupied the other

Reprinted from *The New Nineteenth Century: Feminist Readings of Underread Victorian Fiction*, eds B.L. Harman and S. Meyer (New York and London: Garland, 1996), pp. 3–16.

two volumes, and partly because critics speculated that the sisters' three pseudonyms belonged to the same writer. But *Agnes Grey* has since received its own more limited acclaim, including an accolade from the novelist George Moore (quoted by virtually everyone who writes on Anne Brontë), who termed *Agnes Grey* 'the most perfect prose narrative in English literature.' *The Tenant of Wildfell Hall*, Anne Brontë's second novel, was both controversial and an immediate success: it was in such demand that within a month of its publication the publishers brought out a second edition. Both of Anne Brontë's novels are available in print, in various paperback editions (Oxford, Penguin, Banquo, Everyman's Classic); a selection of her poems (as well as Emily's and Charlotte's) appears in an Everyman's Classic paperback.

* * *

Late in Anne Brontë's first novel, the cultivated and diligent governess-heroine, Agnes Grey, is taken to task by her employer concerning the behavior of her hoydenish student, Matilda. 'If you will only think of these things and try to exert yourself a *little* more . . . then, I am convinced, you would *soon* acquire that delicate tact which alone is wanting to give you a proper influence over the mind of your pupil,' Mrs Murray tells Agnes. It seems for a moment as if the long-suffering and much-criticized Agnes is finally going to respond to one of the many unjust attacks to which she has been subjected in the course of her employment. But Agnes is never able, throughout the events the novel narrates, to 'talk back' to her employers. 'I was about to give the lady some idea of the fallacy of her expectations,' Agnes writes, 'but she sailed away as soon as she had concluded her speech. Having said what she wished, it was no part of her plan to await my answer: it was my business to hear, and not to speak' (p. 207).

In this novel about a heroine who is, at crucial moments, nearly speechless, Anne Brontë explores the nature of a society that makes it quite literally the 'business' of some of its members 'not to speak': that requires silence and acquiescence of some due to the conditions of their employment or of their social position. But *Agnes Grey* is written in the form of a first-person autobiography by this silenced heroine: in the form of the novel itself Agnes 'talks back,' and in the course of the novel Anne Brontë both subtly criticizes and resists the unjust silencing and disempowerment of the poorer classes by an autocratic and immoral British ruling class. At the same time, however, the novel hints that some of the same problems that characterize the relationship between classes characterize the relationships between men and women, and these problems remain more irresolvable at the novel's close.[1]

Anne Brontë's fiction is frequently dismissed in a cursory fashion as less passionate and original than the fiction of her two better-known sisters; when her fiction *is* discussed, the second, and more obviously complex of her two novels, *The Tenant of Wildfell Hall*, receives most of the attention, while *Agnes Grey* is often described as slight and emotionally flat.[2] The novel tells the story of a young woman, the daughter of a clergyman, whose family loses its patrimony due to ill-advised speculation on the part of the father. To help the family finances, Agnes, the younger of two daughters, goes out as a governess to two wealthy families, first the Bloomfields, a prosperous family whose money was earned in trade, and then to the Murrays, 'thorough-bred gentry' (p. 113). In both families Agnes is ill-treated – in the first she is required to keep several headstrong young children in check, and yet is deprived of any means of offering reward or punishment, while in the second family she deals with older but equally spoiled young ladies. The Murray daughters are frivolous and thoughtless and have lax moral standards. They treat Agnes as a personal servant, and, on a whim, the flirtatious elder daughter, Rosalie, decides to interpose herself between Agnes and the man she is coming to love, the local curate, Mr Weston. At the death of her father, Agnes leaves her painful position with the Murrays and sets up a school with her mother in a seaside town, fearing that, in part due to Rosalie's interference, she will never see Mr Weston again. But Mr Weston has taken a living in a nearby village, and, after a brief courtship, he asks Agnes to be his wife. The novel comes to a close with Agnes's report that the pair has had three children and are able to subsist happily on their modest income.

Agnes Grey is, as critics have noted, characterized by a quiet, emotionally restrained tone. But the coolness and restraint are both deliberate on Anne Brontë's part and important to the novel's aims, because in *Agnes Grey* Anne Brontë offers the chronicle of a life of emotional and verbal repression. And if the plot of *Agnes Grey* is simple, the social criticism it offers, through this chronicle of repression, is complex.

As a condition of her employment, self-repression and the suppression of speech are continually required of Agnes. As soon as Agnes arrives at her first place of employment, for example, and is instructed in how she is to proceed, Mrs Bloomfield warns her that she is to tell no one but herself of the children's defects. As Agnes's mother has already warned her to mention them 'as little as possible to *her*, for people did not like to be told of their children's faults,' Agnes rightly concludes that she is 'to keep silence on them altogether' (p. 79). Later the Bloomfield parents indirectly reprove Agnes by discussing in her presence what they see as their children's recent deterioration, and this method of criticism makes it impossible for Agnes to respond:

All similar innuendoes affected me far more deeply than any open accusations would have done; for against the latter I should have been roused to speak in my own defence: now, I judged it my wisest plan to subdue every resentful impulse, suppress every sensitive shrinking, and go on perseveringly doing my best. (p. 91)

Although Agnes suggests here that against direct accusations she would find a voice, this supposition is not borne out by the novel: even when Mrs Bloomfield fires Agnes, although she wishes to speak in her own justification, she feels her 'voice falter,' and 'rather than testify any emotion,' she writes, 'I chose to keep silence, and bear all' (p. 107). And Agnes is not only prevented from using her voice toward her employers in her own defense, she is also prevented from using it forcefully toward her young charges as she works. When Agnes needs to raise her voice in an attempt to enforce order among little Tom, Mary Ann, and Fanny Bloomfield, their father chastises her for 'using undue violence, and setting the girls a bad example by such ungentleness of tone and language' (p. 98). All this stifling of Agnes's voice, in her position as governess, makes it virtually impossible, paradoxically, for her to succeed in her task of instruction.

The same situation continues in Agnes's next position, with the Murrays, when Mrs Murray tells Agnes never to engage in forceful remonstrance with her children, but instead to 'come and tell me; for *I* can speak to them more plainly than it would be proper for you to do' (p. 120). Agnes also finds that she is expected not to speak to the Murray girls' friends, or to anyone in their social circle: instead she is required to comport herself 'like one deaf and dumb, who could neither speak nor be spoken to' (p. 184). Both sets of Agnes's charges prevent her from engaging in communication with others: the Bloomfield children interrupt her letter-writing on her first evening with them, Rosalie Murray prevents her from *reading* a letter in one episode, and Fanny Bloomfield, at her brother's command, nearly throws Agnes's writing desk out of the window. The novel clearly demonstrates that the 'business' of being a governess is one completely at odds with all healthful self-expression.

But the story of Agnes's silencing also has a larger resonance: it is about more than the problems with this particular mode of women's labor. What happens to Agnes, the novel suggests, is representative of the kind of verbal suppression to which girls and women in this era are disproportionately subjected. Although as a working woman Agnes is particularly subjected to verbal suppression, girls and women at home also experience it. Agnes is silenced, although in a gentler and more loving fashion, in her own family, long before she ever goes out to work.

When she proposes seeking employment, she is told to 'hold [her] tongue' and termed a 'naughty girl' (p. 69). Even among the upper classes, the girls are subjected to some linguistic control. Matilda Murray is constantly chastised by her parents for speaking as freely as the grooms do: she is not even supposed to term her 'horse' a 'mare' (p. 134). Mr Bloomfield's complaint about Agnes's raised voice is that she is setting a bad example to his daughters, not to his son. And from the first evening of Agnes's arrival at the Bloomfields', it is clear that the son's voice is permitted more freedom, and accorded more authority, than those of the daughters. Tom stands 'bolt upright . . . with his hands behind his back, talking away like an orator, occasionally interrupting his discourse with a sharp reproof to his sisters when they made too much noise' (p. 76). Tom's verbal authority is linked to the ownership of property: he claims possession of the schoolroom and the books. Despite Mary Ann's protests (p. 76) that 'they're mine too,' Tom decisively asserts the prerogative of the first-born son (like John Reed in Charlotte Brontë's *Jane Eyre*) and claims ownership of these instruments of language.

Yet if male claims to authoritative speech are boosted by men's easier access to the ownership of property, the possession of property by those of either sex is shown to be linked to linguistic authority. *Agnes Grey* demonstrates that neither gender nor social class alone is explanatory: both class and gender are significant factors in determining who wields the power of language, the power to silence others. The young ladies whom Agnes instructs in her second position, Rosalie and Matilda Murray, make charitable visits to the cottagers on their father's estate, believing themselves to be revered there as ministering angels, and they certainly use their voices freely in this context:

They would watch the poor creatures at their meals, making uncivil remarks about their food, and their manner of eating; they would laugh at their simple notions and provincial expressions, till some of them scarcely durst venture to speak; they would call the grave, elderly men and women old fools and silly blockheads to their faces; and all this without meaning to offend.

I could see that the people were often hurt and annoyed by such conduct, though their fear of the 'grand ladies' prevented them from testifying any resentment; but *they* never perceived it. They thought that, as these cottagers were poor and untaught, they must be stupid and brutish; and as long as they, their superiors, condescended to talk to them, and to give them shillings and half-crowns, or articles of clothing, they had a right to amuse themselves, even at their expense. (p. 144)

Toward the very end of the novel, despite all of Agnes's attempts at moral instruction, Rosalie Murray more explicitly articulates her mother's position, expressed at an earlier point to Agnes, that it is the social 'business' of some to speak as freely as they please, and of others never to speak, or even to formulate an internal perspective critical of those of higher rank. Agnes points out to Rosalie that she has just said, in front of her footman, that she finds her mother-in-law detestable, to which Rosalie responds:

I never care about the footmen; they're mere automatons – it's nothing to them what their superiors say or do; they won't dare to repeat it; and as to what they think – if they presume to think at all – of course, nobody cares for that. It would be a pretty thing indeed, if we were to be tongue-tied by our servants! (p. 233)

In telling the story of the travails of Agnes Grey, of one woman obliged to work in the homes of the wealthy, Brontë obliquely comments on the larger problem of the unjust distribution of the power of language by gender and by class.

In answer to the problem of verbal repression, Anne Brontë posits the act of novel-writing itself. In *Agnes Grey*, Brontë narrates a tale from the perspective of a woman who works in the house but nonetheless presumes to think for herself, who refuses, at least in written form, to be tongue-tied by the social order, and who offers a scathing account of what her self-styled social superiors say and do in the privacy of their own homes. Agnes shows the people from wealthy families with whom she lives to be vain, frivolous, and unprincipled, prone to drinking and gluttony, quarrelsome, and self-centered. She recounts domestic altercations between husband and wife that have taken place in her presence, as if she were an automaton, shows a mother determined to marry her daughter to the wealthiest possible man, and displays the mutual hatred that substitutes for love in upper-class marriages. And while the novel describes what *really* goes on in upper-class homes, it takes issue, subtly, with some of the central ideas of that class, the ideas by which they justify the class hierarchy to themselves.

Both the Murrays and the Bloomfields make clear that, like other members of their class, they believe their social rank to be natural: they consider those of lower rank to be innately inferior to them, to be, in fact, like animals. The Murray daughters believe the cottagers whom they insult to their faces to be incapable of understanding their humiliation because they are 'stupid and brutish,' and indeed Rosalie Murray's favorite epithet for those without money is the term 'vulgar brute' (p. 154). Mr Bloomfield describes Agnes's hygienic standards as bestial: he condemns Agnes for the mess his children have made, exclaiming, 'No wonder your room is not fit for a pigsty – no wonder your pupils are worse than a litter of pigs!' (p. 99). Little Tom Bloomfield shows that he has assimilated this idea that his social inferiors are to be treated like animals when he sees his uncle kicking a dog, and vows that he will make him kick Agnes instead. It seems that to be treated like an animal by the ruling classes is to be treated as insentient, to be treated as an expendable commodity. Mrs Bloomfield voices this attitude when she defends Tom's practice of torturing fledgling birds to death in various diabolical ways by telling Agnes, with an eerie calm, that she seems to have forgotten 'that the creatures were all created for our convenience' (p. 105).

But in *Agnes Grey*, Anne Brontë slyly reverses the ruling-class conceit that the lower classes are like beasts whom they may burden at will. She repeatedly compares the young Bloomfields to animals – they behave like 'wild, unbroken colt[s]' (p. 84), or quarrel over their food 'like a set of tiger's cubs' (p. 98). The Murrays are also animal-like: John Murray is as rough 'as a young bear' (p. 124). Even the young ladies are likened to beasts. As Agnes says of Matilda, damning her with faint praise, 'As an animal, [she] was all right, full of life, vigour, and activity' (p. 124). Of Rosalie, who prides herself on her delicacy and her ladylike behavior, Agnes comments, bitingly: 'Dogs are not the only creatures which, when gorged to the throat, will yet gloat over what they cannot devour, and grudge the slightest morsel to a starving brother' (p. 196). Unable to reason with her unreasoning charges, Agnes has to resort to the ploys of animal trainers – she deprives the little Bloomfields of their food until they cooperate, and to assert dominance over Tom, she uses what is in fact a technique from dog training, 'throw[ing] him on his back, and hold[ing] his hands and feet till the frenzy was somewhat abated' (p. 85). Perhaps the novel's most sarcastic equation of the ruling class with animals comes from Mr Weston, the curate. Matilda Murray comes 'panting' up to him and Agnes, after running with her dog, as he captures a hare out of season, asking them whether it was not a fine chase. 'Very!' Mr Weston replies, 'for a young lady after a leveret' (p. 209).

Those of high social rank in *Agnes Grey* also acquire a sense of superiority by envisioning themselves as civilized and Christian in relation to the ignorant 'savages' beneath them. This colonial metaphor is conceptually linked to their sense of themselves as human and others as bestial. In the same passage in which Mr Bloomfield compares Agnes's schoolroom to a pigsty and defends his standards of decency against her low influence, he goes on to tell her that there was never anything like her room 'in a Christian house before' (p. 99). And when Mr Bloomfield complains about the way the servants have cut the meat, he reviles them as 'savages' (p. 83).

But the novel is concerned, throughout, to reveal the un-Christian, uncivilized behavior of these professed Christians. The two Murray girls go to church twice on Sundays, not out of devout spirituality, but to flirt with anyone available. When Rosalie describes her husband-to-be, Sir Thomas Ashby, a womanizing, gambling rake whom she imagines marriage will reform, as the 'greatest scamp in Christendom' (p. 172), Anne Brontë wryly suggests that those who think like Rosalie have very little idea of in what true Christianity consists – or who lives within a moral space that might truly be termed 'Christendom.' The elitist, wealthy rector of the church they attend similarly has a self-serving idea of Christianity: he preaches sermons about the duty of the poor to obey the rich with deference. He dismisses a poor, elderly parishioner, who comes to him in spiritual distress, by sneering at her and telling her not to read the Bible on her own but to hobble to church to hear him speak, despite her debilitating rheumatism. In following his advice old Nancy Brown contracts a telling ailment: she catches a cold in her eyes and is no longer able to read the Bible. The self-styled, superior Christianity of the ruling class, the novel indicates, simply serves to support the class structure, and to impede the poor from direct access to the egalitarian Word.

Not only are the rich not civilizing Christians, Brontë suggests, they themselves are the barbarians they imagine the lower classes to be. The novel directly reverses this authorizing metaphor by representing Agnes, in the homes of the wealthy, as a civilized person among colonial savages. It does not seem to occur to Anne Brontë to question British colonialism or to criticize the concept of a racial hierarchy as she does so; she simply uses the supposed racial hierarchy as a metaphor to question the class hierarchy rather than to support it. When Agnes arrives at the Murray household, she compares her feelings to those of a colonist who awakes one morning to find himself 'at Port Nelson, in New Zealand, with a world of waters between himself and all that knew him' (p. 118). Indeed, in her various positions, Agnes finds an uncle of the Bloomfields who engages in and encourages the children in 'barbarities,' while Matilda Murray is 'barbarously ignorant' (pp. 103, 124). In the course of her civilizing mission among the barbarous upper class, Agnes begins to fear at one point, as British colonists sometimes feared, that she will 'degenerate' until she is like those around her, that she will, as it were, 'go native.' 'Those whose actions are ever before our eyes,' she comments:

whose words are ever in our ears, will naturally lead us, albeit against our will – slowly – gradually – imperceptibly, perhaps, to act and speak as they do. I will not presume to say how far this irresistible power of assimilation extends; but if one civilized man were doomed to pass a dozen years amid a race of intractable savages, unless he had power to improve them, I greatly question whether, at the close of that period, he would not have become, at least, a barbarian himself. And I, as I could not make my young companions better, feared exceedingly that they would make me worse. (p. 155)

In an article on Victorian images of Africa, Patrick Brantlinger describes the pervasive anxiety, on the part of the nineteenth-century British in the colonies, that they would 'degenerate' or 'go native'; he points out that missionaries were particularly subject to the fear that they would regress to the state of the 'heathens' around them. He quotes one, J.S. Moffat, who writes that a missionary must be 'deeply imbued with God's spirit in order to have strength to stand against the deadening and corrupting influence around him . . . I am like a man looking forward to getting back to sweet air and bright sunshine after being in a coal-mine' (Brantlinger 194). In an absolute reversal of the self-authorizing metaphors of the upper class, Anne Brontë has Agnes imagine herself, among them, as one living, as it were, on a 'dark continent' among 'savages.' Only the presence of Mr Weston appears like the 'morning star in my horizon,' Agnes writes, 'to save me from the fear of utter darkness' (p. 155).[3]

In an attempt to escape the darkness created by the upper class, and to keep their words *out* of our ears, Anne Brontë's novel calls into question not only their metaphors, but also their more direct wielding of the power of language, their mode of assigning names to things. Agnes's first encounter with the father of the Bloomfield children is one in which he uses the power of naming to put her in her social place. The little Bloomfield children are disobeying Agnes's fruitless commands and dabbling in the water when Mr Bloomfield rides up and rebukes her, never introducing himself, but simply exclaiming, 'Don't you see how Miss Bloomfield has soiled her frock? – and that Master Bloomfield's socks are quite wet?' (p. 82). Agnes is surprised that 'he should nominate his children [at the ages of seven and five] Master and Miss Bloomfield, and still more so, that he should speak so uncivilly to me – their governess, and a perfect stranger to himself' (p. 82). Agnes continues to feel that the formal naming of children is 'chilling and unnatural,' but she finds, while with the Bloomfields, that if she calls the children by their simple names, it is regarded as 'an offensive liberty' (p. 118). Having learned this lesson, she determines, when she arrives at the Murrays, to begin 'with as much form and ceremony as any member of the family would be likely to require . . . though the little words Miss and Master seemed to have a surprising effect in repressing all familiar, open-hearted kindness, and extinguishing every gleam of cordiality that might arise between us' (p. 118).

The terms 'Miss' and 'Master' repress cordiality, of course, because they emphasize the children's superior rank, and in her own writing about them Agnes resists this convention, using the terms only ironically, to emphasize the children's offensive training in the behavior of domin- ance. She describes one of her pupils, for example, as 'John, *alias* Master Murray' (p. 124), and she notes at one point that seven-year-old 'Master Tom, not content with refusing to be ruled, must needs set up as a ruler' (p. 84). The novel also brings to our attention the way in which class rank is imposed through the dehumanizing naming of servants: Agnes notes that on her arrival at the Murrays, Matilda Murray says that she will 'tell "Brown"' that Agnes is in need of a cup of tea (p. 116). As we later meet a poor woman with the same surname, the cottager Nancy Brown, and are given a more full and humanizing portrait of her, the novel suggests what it is that the elite are preventing themselves from seeing about other human beings by their system of appellation.

Agnes Grey's narrative was compiled, she notes, from the diary she kept during her years as a governess. The diary and subsequent narrative are her quiet act of resistance to the words of those around her, her resist- ance to the way that they dominate through language and metaphor, to the way that they silence those of lesser means. At one point in the novel, Agnes is reading an eagerly awaited letter from her sister at home, when Rosalie Murray interrupts her, and tells her she should bid her friends to write 'on proper note-paper, and not on those great vulgar sheets!' Her own mother, she tells Agnes, writes 'charming little lady-like notes' (p. 130). Although Agnes does reluctantly fold up her letter at Rosalie's command, she also quietly tells her that she would be very disappointed to receive a 'charming little lady-like note' from her family. Rosalie may be surprised and disconcerted by this, but Agnes is happy only when she is able to write, speak, and communicate at length with those like herself. In *Agnes Grey*, Brontë enables her protagonist to respond to the verbal suppression that she and others experience by answering it in her own words, the words of her own class, indited on the 'great vulgar sheets' of the novel itself.

The novel comes to an end with Agnes's marriage to Mr Weston: she notes, after recounting his proposal, that the diary, 'from which [she has] compiled these pages, goes but little further' (p. 250). By this point, it would seem, she has made her critique of the oppressive forces to which she has been subject, pointed out the moral failings of the upper class, and thus come to the end of the need for resistant speech. The end of the novel holds up as an alternative the middle-class domestic sanctity of the marriage between Agnes and Mr Weston, one in which a mother educates the children herself, and in which the family is able to subsist happily on their modest income.

The novel's ending, which is, like those of many novels, more conservative than the rest of the novel, does not fully resolve the problems of social class it has brought to the reader's attention. By returning Agnes to a modest middle-class home, the novel does restore her to a more secure status, and continues its critique of the misplaced values of the wealthy. And it is also true that, unlike many nineteenth-century novels, *Agnes Grey* does not hint that class status is innate by returning all protagonists to the class position from which their families have fallen: although Agnes's mother was the daughter of a squire, who disinherited her when she chose to marry a man beneath her in rank, the novel ends with Agnes and her sister happily married to modest clergymen, and their mother presiding over a school for girls. The novel even evokes the possibility of such a restoration of originary class status and has the protagonists reject it. On the death of her father, Agnes's maternal grandfather writes to Agnes's mother and the girls offering to make her a 'lady' again 'if that be possible after [her] long degradation' as long as she is willing to repent of her 'unfortunate marriage' (p. 214). The novel has both mother and daughters refuse this proposal with scorn. The money they decline on such terms goes, at the grandfather's death, to some already wealthy, remote cousins.

But, nonetheless, when it comes to its close, the novel does not reject the system of inherited wealth, nor does it evoke a vision of significant changes in the class structure. The Nancy Browns of the world, to whom the solution of a middle-class marriage is not available, are left largely outside the space of the reader's vision in the novel's last pages. Through strenuous exertions, we are told, Edward Weston has worked 'surprising reforms' in his parish, though we are not told in what exactly those reforms consist. The novel's attention turns at the last to Agnes and Edward Weston themselves, who, by practicing 'the economy . . . learnt in harder times,' manage each year to have, Agnes reports in the novel's penultimate sentence, 'something to lay by for our children, and something to give to those who need it' (p. 251). A system of inherited wealth, tempered by a true Christian charity, is the only solution the novel finally poses to the problems of class inequality detailed in its pages.

The novel ends with the sentence 'And now I think I have said sufficient,' as if to imply that now that the novel has come to something of a solution to the problem of the unjust class hierarchy, there is no need for further resistant speech. But the cessation of speech has been shown in the novel to be ambiguous. We have learned, as readers, to be wary about what the absence of words signifies. And if the novel seems to have come to a solution, satisfactory in middle-class terms, to the problem of class, the problem of gender remains, at the novel's close, more submerged and unresolved.

Immediately after the account of Mr Weston's proposal to her, Agnes's narrative comes to a pause, and she notes: 'My diary, from which I have compiled these pages, goes but little further' (p. 250). Only one page of the novel remains, in which Agnes sums up the events of the subsequent years. But it is disconcerting for the reader to see Agnes once again falling silent, and at such a crucial moment: the period of Agnes's resistant use of language comes to a close with the proposal of marriage. What is more, the title given the novel, this space of free expression, is Agnes's name in her maidenhood, not her married name, as if, with her marriage, her capacity for resistant speech comes to an end.

These two disquieting facts might be explained away as common conventions in nineteenth-century fiction were it not that other subtleties in the novel's conclusion draw our attention to the way Agnes's marriage has a silencing effect. During Weston's preliminary visits to her and her mother, Agnes regresses into the state of near speechlessness she has seemed to be coming out of – so much so that even her mother asks her, after one visit, 'But why did you sit back there, Agnes, . . . and talk so little?' (p. 247). When Weston does propose, her assent is almost wordless, monosyllabic. Weston explains that, knowing what Agnes would like, he has already asked her mother to live with them, and continues:

'And so now I have overruled your objections on her account. Have you any other?'
'No – none.'
'You love me then?' said he, fervently pressing my hand.
'Yes.' (p. 250)

With this monosyllable of assent, Agnes moves back into a period of virtual wordlessness.

It is disconcerting also to notice that the animal/human metaphor, through which the novel has expressed and resisted an oppressive class hierarchy, comes back at the end of *Agnes Grey*. As the next to last chapter of the novel comes to a close, Mr Weston and Agnes have a conversation about his dog, Snap, whom he has rescued from the rat-catcher because he once belonged to Agnes. 'Now that he has a good master, I'm quite satisfied,' Agnes says. 'You take it for granted that I *am* a good one, then?' Mr Weston rejoins (p. 245). The question remains resonant and unanswered, but it prepares us for the next chapter, in which Weston will ask Agnes to be his wife – and in which she will, implicitly, answer the question with which the previous chapter ends. 'Master Tom' will no longer be around to assert dominance over Agnes, the novel very discreetly suggests in this exchange, but Agnes may have found herself another, far more subtle 'master.'

If there is a problem even with Agnes's marriage to the good and gentle Mr Weston, the novel quietly suggests, it is because the relationship between men and women unfortunately mimics the relationship between the wealthy and the poor. The novel has taught us to attend carefully to the system of names, to the way they establish hierarchies and set up barriers. It can hardly be accidental, then, that the novel, in its final pages, draws our attention also to the change in the system of appellation that takes place between Agnes and Weston during his courtship of her. Up until this point in the novel, he has, in accordance with the conventions of politeness, addressed her as 'Miss Grey,' precisely as she has addressed him as 'Mr Weston.' But during his series of visits to Agnes and her mother, he begins to use her Christian name. Agnes records that she is glad of the change, and, given her earlier comments on the way little words like 'Miss' and 'Master' repress cordiality, the change would seem to be a sign of their growing intimacy and equality, were it not that she continues to address him as 'Mr Weston.' Trained by the novel to attend to such nuances, we can hardly be completely easy with the inequality thus established.

The return of the subtle cues of a problematic hierarchy in the marriage with which *Agnes Grey* draws to a close suggests Anne Brontë's consciousness that, while she may have brought the issue of an unjust class hierarchy to a solution satisfactory to herself, she has not yet done so with the problem of gender inequality. It remains an issue that she will continue to pursue in her next novel, *The Tenant of Wildfell Hall*. And so when Agnes Grey ends her narrative with the sentence 'And now I think I have said sufficient,' it remains ambiguous what degree of completion or satisfaction her cessation of speech indicates. Has Agnes now 'said sufficient' because Anne Brontë has made her critique of the British upper class in the words indited on the 'great vulgar sheets' of the novel? Or has Agnes 'said sufficient' because the solution to the problem of hierarchy, insidiously entering the relationship between loving men and women, remains, for now, inconceivable, for now beyond the scope of Anne Brontë's resistant words?

NOTES

1. Janet Freeman discusses the issues of speech and silence in Agnes Grey, but in her reading the novel disqualifies all words as worldly, and turns instead to a silence that Brontë expects few to understand, and in which the highly moral commune. Terry

Eagleton briefly describes the novel as a critique of the moral failings of the aristocracy in favor of values with 'petty-bourgeois roots', Priscilla Costello similarly sees the novel as a critique of a materialism located particularly in the upper class. My argument builds on these readings by attending to the patterns of imagery through which this critique is made, and by discussing the way this imagery links the issues of class and gender in the novel. See Langland for another reading of the novel attentive to issues of gender: she argues that the novel emphasizes the acquisition of female independence. I agree that this is quite true, until the novel comes to its close.

2. See for example George Saintsbury, who dismisses Anne Brontë as 'a pale reflection of her elders' (p. 243). Eagleton agrees that 'the orthodox critical judgement that Anne Brontë's work is slighter than her sisters' is just' (p. 134).

3. The presence of these metaphors in Anne Brontë's fiction shows the influence of the childhood games with which she and her brother and sisters invented themselves as writers. All four children collaborated in creating an intricate imaginary world set in a fictitious British colony in Africa. See my ' "Black" Rage and White Women: Ideological Self-formation in Charlotte Brontë's African Tales.'

WORKS CITED

Brantlinger, Patrick. 'Victorians and Africans: The Genealogy of the Myth of the Dark Continent,' *Critical Inquiry* 12 (1985): 166–203.

Brontë, Anne. *Agnes Grey*, ed. Angeline Goreau (New York: Penguin, 1988).

Costello, Priscilla. 'A New Reading of Anne Brontë's *Agnes Grey*,' *Brontë Society Transactions* 19 (1986): 113–18.

Eagleton, Terry. *Myths of Power: A Marxist Study of the Brontës* (New York: Harper & Row, 1975), pp. 123–38.

Freeman, Janet H. 'Telling over *Agnes Grey*,' *Cahiers Victoriens et Edouardiens* 34 (1991): 109–26.

Langiand, Elizabeth. *Anne Brontë: The Other One* (London: Macmillan, 1989).

Meyer, Susan. ' "Black" Rage and White Women: Ideological Self-formation in Charlotte Brontë's African Tales,' *South Central Review* 8.4 (1991): 28–40.

Saintsbury, George. *The English Novel* (London: J.M. Dent, 1913).

CHAPTER SEVEN

The Profession of the Author: Abstraction, Advertising, and *Jane Eyre*

SHARON MARCUS

Sharon Marcus is a member of the English department in the University of California at Berkeley. Her research centres on the nineteenth-century novel, and on the relationship between literature, urban culture and domestic architecture in nineteenth-century Paris and London. This interdisciplinary interest is represented by her book *Apartment Stories: City and Home in Nineteenth-century Paris and London* (1999). The article reprinted here similarly draws on a knowledge of the material conditions of publishing in the early nineteenth century to throw light on Charlotte Brontë's ability to use them to her advantage. She argues that Charlotte deploys the distancing effect of mass circulation to conceal her physical person and explore areas otherwise open only to men in the economic market. This splitting of the self, Marcus argues, is the only way for a woman to take this role in a capitalist society.

S ince its publication in 1847, *Jane Eyre* has been read by its detractors and admirers as the portrayal of a willful female subject who claims her own identity. Readers have failed to note, however, that the most basic and encompassing marker of that identity, her name, tends to emerge when her will is most in abeyance. A key instance of Jane's involuntary self-promotion occurs toward the end of the novel, during her stay with the Rivers family, when St John Rivers identifies Jane as the relative for whom 'advertisements have been put in all the papers'

Reprinted from *PMLA* 110. 2 (1995): 206–19.

(p. 406). St John recognizes her as the rightful heir of a fortune before Jane herself does. His proof of her identity consists of a signature in 'the ravished margin of [a] portrait-cover,' which Jane confronts as if it belonged to another: 'He got up, held it close to my eyes: and I read, traced in Indian ink, in my own handwriting, the words "JANE EYRE"' (p. 407). Jane has failed to answer the advertisements of others, but her unwitting self-advertisement has found its ideal reader.

Jane construes her signature as 'the work doubtless of some moment of abstraction' (p. 407) and thus disowns it as the product of her own volition, even as it fulfills the conditions of her uncle's will and her own desires to be financially independent and to belong to a family. Although Jane has consistently refused to speak her personal story to St John Rivers or his sisters, her unintentional signature publicizes it for her. Through the use of typographical conventions for designating titles – capitalization and quotation marks – the words 'JANE EYRE' also emblematize the text itself, suggesting that *Jane Eyre* the novel, as well as Jane Eyre the character, is the 'work . . . of some moment of abstraction.'

In this essay, I analyze abstraction through close readings of scenes of speech, writing, and advertising in *Jane Eyre* and through a consideration of Charlotte Brontë's dealings in the Victorian literary market. The concept of abstraction is crucial to understanding the relation of writing to female subjectivity in *Jane Eyre* and in Brontë's literary career because it mediates between apparently contradictory categories: embodiment and invisibility, self-effacement and self-advertisement, femininity and professional identity, fragmentation and wholeness, and profit and loss. *Abstraction* takes on four meanings in *Jane Eyre*, each instantiated by different aspects of the text and all related as ways in which Jane becomes a particular kind of female subject. First, Jane uses the term to mean an absence of will, mind, and attention, as she describes the semiconscious state in which she distractedly signs her real name on her sketch. Second, abstraction becomes a sublation and 'separat[ion] from matter, from material embodiment' ('Abstraction,' *OED*), which *Jane Eyre* represents as the displacement of an embodied self into writing and visual representation. Third, abstraction involves the externalization or objectification of the self into a partial image, sign, or object, which occurs in the novel as the splitting and alienation of Jane's self into portraits, truncated names, and instrumentalized body parts. Finally, abstraction is the synthesis of the particular into a more general concept or system based on resemblance rather than difference, a concept the novel exemplifies as Jane's rhetorical membership in a professional body of governesses.

The importance of abstraction in *Jane Eyre* is due in part to the text's contemporaneity with the height of British capitalism and imperialism, historical phenomena that moved spatial and human relations in the direction of greater and greater abstraction through developments in areas such as statistics, cartography, a bureaucratic civil service, and a manufacturing system that increasingly organized workers' space and time (Marx: 88, 92, 96; Thompson; Poovey, *Social Body*). The capitalist ideology of political economy defined human relations and economic value in terms of abstractions – money, markets, and generalized exchange – while imperialism sought to extend the reach of those abstractions and often justified the domination of other peoples by claiming that Europeans had a greater capacity for abstract reasoning.

Capitalism's tendency toward abstraction necessarily transformed authorship and publishing during the first half of the nineteenth century. The replacement of patronage with a middle-class market rendered authorship and the sale of books more rationalized, generalized, and generalizing (Heyck: 24–28). Advertising rapidly developed as a means of regulating relations among publishers, authors, and consumers. Improved communications and the spread of railway transportation during the 1840s helped create an abstract space, based on imagined proximity rather than face-to-face contact, in which authors and publishers could locate, solicit, and supply a mass market (see Collins: 19–20, 191; Sutherland: 64). At the same time, a growing number of incipient professionals in fields other than writing sought to convince the public to purchase various types of expertise defined as abstract by uniform standards and credentials and by distinction from the more material skills and goods of artisans and tradespeople.

How did these tendencies toward abstraction affect middle-class women who worked either as writers or as governesses? In the final section of this paper I examine how Brontë negotiated the conflict between the embodiment attributed to women and the increasing abstraction of the publishing, advertising, and professional identities she sought to assume. Brontë's career as Currer Bell, like Jane Eyre's as Jane Elliott, transformed pseudonymity into a form of veiled self-advertisement, into a strategy for disowning the difficulties of female embodiment by exploiting the powers of abstraction.

My argument that Jane's and Brontë's subjectivities emerge most strongly during moments of abstraction and alienation is informed by both Lacanian and Marxist understandings of subjectivity. *Alienation* and *abstraction* are linked terms since alienation, in the structural sense of separation, is the process by which abstraction from the material or the particular occurs. For both Lacan and Marx, alienation is not the absolute loss of the thing alienated but a means of elaborating a relation to that thing. In the Lacanian notion of the mirror stage, subjects attain an illusory but powerful sense of coherence and selfhood only by alienating themselves into such nebulous objects as mirror images (Lacan: 1–7). The mirror stage thus anticipates the symbolic stage, in which the subject is alienated into language, into abstract signifying systems and social exchanges, and into such idealizations as the phallus, which represents lack and 'can play its role only when veiled' (288). Lacan's choice of the phallus as the sign of abstraction suggests that men and women have asymmetrical positions within the symbolic and that women, by lacking or being the phallus, may lack lack itself. The reading of *Jane Eyre* that follows shows how a female protagonist and female author might instead productively attain lack.

Abstraction and alienation are also key concepts in Marx's readings of labor and of capitalist political economy. In translations of Marx's writings, *alienation* can mean capitalists' exclusive appropriation of wealth or the pain experienced by proletarianized workers. My use of the term combines Marx's positive definition of human labor as a person's ability to conceive of material products abstractly and to 'contemplate . . . himself in a world that he has created' (p. 77) with his critique of capitalism as an increasingly abstract system that subordinates labor, use value, and human relations to commodification and exchange value. Nineteenth-century capitalism worked to link these disparate views by making it possible for workers to perform productive labor (positive abstraction) only through alienation into the structures of political economy (negative abstraction). The subject of capitalism becomes the possessive individual, 'human *qua* proprietor of his own person,' who belongs to a society that 'is essentially a series of market relations between . . . free individuals' (Macpherson: 158). The possessive individual exists by virtue of his ownership of self, labor, land, and objects, but this ownership is constituted less by appropriation than by the ability to alienate possessions through sale to others, which translates the self into money and exchange value. Only through alienation into such abstractions does the subject of political economy come into being.

Convention and law defined the alienated and possessive individual as male, but *Jane Eyre*'s representation of Jane's abstraction extends to its heroine the imbricated gains and losses attendant on subjection to political economy. When Jane advertises for governess work, she alienates her embodied existence into abstractions (printed texts, truncated names) and thus arrogates to herself the normatively masculine conditions of agency in a capitalist political economy, which simultaneously limit and enable agency by subordinating it to the abstract laws of the marketplace.

I

My reading of Brontë's novel and of her strategies as a professional writer questions the critical school that has evaluated *Jane Eyre* as the story of its heroine's successful attainment of 'full person-hood' and her transcend-ence of self-division and alienation. Interpreters of *Jane Eyre* have reacted to a tradition of condemning the heroine as an indecorously outspoken and desiring female subject, a tradition represented most famously by Elizabeth Rigby's 1848 article in the conservative *Quarterly Review* chastis-ing 'a mere heathen mind which is a law unto itself' (p. 173) and by Virginia Woolf's disapproval of Jane's and Brontë's rage in *A Room of One's Own* (pp. 71–3). The feminist critical turn of the 1970s and 1980s, which reclaimed the novel as a parable of female development, praised the 'rebellious feminism' that earlier critics had denounced (Gilbert and Gubar: 338). In reinterpreting Jane as moving toward 'mature freedom' (p. 339) and 'a complete female identity' (Showalter: 112), critics under-stood the novel as a cautionary tale about the perils of the split self and interpreted Bertha Mason as a symbol of the disruptive sexuality that Jane must either incorporate or expel.

In turn, however, feminists including Gayatri Spivak, Firdous Azin, and Joyce Zonana have criticized *Jane Eyre* for representing Bertha Mason, India, and 'the East' as othered entities that the plot destroys or appro-priates in order to make Jane a unified subject. Spivak criticizes the 'whole-ness' (pp. 244–5) that earlier feminist critics embraced; Azin contends that Jane is a 'unified Enlightenment subject . . . [produced] by the invoca-tion and subsequent obliteration of the Other subject, differentiated by class, race and gender' (p. 88); and Zonana shows that Jane uses 'feminist orientalism' to 'secure more rights for herself,' the rights of the unified democratic subject (p. 596). These critics persuasively explicate *Jane Eyre*'s imperialism, but they continue to claim that it consists in the creation of a subject free of internal contradictions; none considers how Jane Eyre's transformation of herself into an other suggests that the split subject and the imperialist-capitalist subject may be equivalent.

Yet scenes of writing in the novel depict Jane as being most success-fully herself when she suppresses, evacuates, or commodifies her material being. Jane becomes an economic actor and the apparent author of her fate only when she alienates herself into writing, into advertisements, and into an abstract professional body. Writing and the written adver-tisement in *Jane Eyre* mediate between the embodied and the metaphys-ical, between the self and objects external to it, between the individual and the social. Writing, which always bears the traces of its own materi-ality, provides Jane with a medium for the successful transfer of her own embodiment, and alienation into an anonymous advertisement enables 'J.E.' to cash in on her self even as she masks it.

Studies of nineteenth-century sexuality and gender ideology have shown that women were characterized by overidentification with their bodies (or were substituted for the very idea of the body) and that many discourses represented female bodies as glaringly visible, material spectacles (Foucault; Poovey, *Uneven Development*, pp. 24–50; Bruno: 58–76; Shuttleworth). Although *Jane Eyre* begins with that version of female identity, the novel proposes abstraction as a technique for displacing the heroine's potentially troublesome embodiment and sexualization onto the medium of writing (in the form of a printed newspaper advertisement) and thus for gaining the heroine a place in an economic market. Throughout the novel, Jane realizes her desires for liberty and mobility most successfully through advertising copy and the reproducibility of textuality and print. At crisis points in her narrative, she comforts herself with the knowledge that 'let the worst come to the worst I can advertise again' (p. 126); when Rochester's unexplained absence from Thornfield distresses her, she responds by 'involuntarily framing advertisements' (p. 192). Jane uses the medium of the written advertisement to negotiate between absolute self-effacement, represented by Helen Burns, and spectacular, Byronic embodiment, personified by Rochester.

Jane first appears not as a writer, however, but as a speaker, one whose words are identified with her body and are vitiated by that material incarnation. The novel's second paragraph evokes Jane's 'consciousness of . . . physical inferiority' (p. 39), and the novel's first chapters establish Jane as a vocal child who cries out to her repressive Aunt Reed, '*Speak* I must' (p. 68). Jane's 'fierce speaking' makes an impression on her auditors but garners her few concrete benefits, and indeed in those opening chapters Jane experiences attacks on her body that often stem from her verbal outbursts or from an insufficiently abstract relation to reading and writing (p. 70). Jane is concerned with equating pictures and words and with making each sign system embody the meaning of the other; when she reads Bewick's *History of British Birds* she focuses on how '[t]he words in these introductory pages [connect] themselves with the succeeding vignettes' and how '[e]ach picture [tells] a story' (p. 40). That very text becomes a catastrophically material object when her cousin John uses the book to make her bleed. After ordering Jane to '[s]how the book,' John throws it at her, causing her to fall, cut herself, and become a mass of painful sensation: 'every nerve I had feared him, and every morsel of flesh on my bones shrank when he came near . . . I felt a drop or two of blood from my head trickle down my neck, and was sensible of somewhat pungent suffering: these sensations for the time predominated over fear' (pp. 42–3). If those emotions enable Jane to speak up and fight back, her resistance leads only to more violent punishment.

At Lowood School, writing continues to serve as an instrument or weapon that makes girls' bodies into the objects of sadistic visual attention. Jane attempts to hide her face from Mr Brocklehurst behind her school slate, but, she reports, '[M]y treacherous slate somehow happened to slip from my hand, and falling with an obtrusive crash, directly [drew] every eye upon me' (p. 97). As in the episode with John Reed, the visibility and the materiality of a written text or a writing instrument highlights and wounds an embodied self, for Jane becomes more conscious of her body after dropping her writing tablet: Miss Temple's whispered words of comfort go 'to my heart like a dagger,' and the other students' 'eyes [are] directed like burning-glasses against my scorched skin' (pp. 97–8). Later, Jane reacts with fury and horror when Helen Burns also endures a corporal punishment that involves writing and must stand with 'the word "Slattern"' written 'in conspicuous characters' and 'bound . . . like a phylactery round [her] forehead' (p. 105).

In each of these instances, writing impresses itself on the girls in ways that make them public spectacles. When writing marks the body in *Jane Eyre*, it negates self-authorization. Helen's willingness to have punishment written on her body culminates in her death by consumption. As Robert Keefe has suggested, Helen poses a seductive threat to Jane, '[f]or Helen Burns is a creature in love with death,' and 'death holds a strong attraction for Jane' (pp. 98, 100). But Jane appears to take Helen as a countermodel: 'the spectacle of [Helen's] sad resignation gave me an intolerable pain at the heart' (p. 106). At Gateshead, Jane contemplates 'never eating or drinking more, and letting myself die' (p. 47), but at Lowood she learns to adopt a more nuanced stance toward death that entails neither complete rejection nor utter embrace.[1] She begins to construct her subjectivity on the basis of an alien grammar and a system of representation without referents or material grounds: in the paragraphs that follow her account of Helen's punishment, she writes, 'I learned the first two tenses of the verb *Etre* . . . That night, on going to bed, I forgot to prepare in imagination the Barmecide supper . . . with which I was wont to amuse my inward cravings. I feasted instead on the spectacle of ideal drawings, which I saw in the dark' (p. 106). As Jane articulates her being (*être*) in an alien language and shifts from material imaginings to more abstract, 'ideal' representations, she also accepts Lowood for the liberty its negativity offers: she declares, 'I would not now have exchanged Lowood for all its privations for Gateshead and its daily luxuries' (p. 106).

Jane orchestrates her departure from Lowood to seek work as a governess by reducing her ambitions to become a subject in her own right:

'I want [a position as governess] because it is of no use to want anything better. . . . A new servitude! There is something in that,' I soliloquized (mentally, be it understood; I did not talk aloud). 'I know there is, because it does not sound too sweet. It is not like such words as Liberty, Excitement, Enjoyment: . . . now all I want is to serve elsewhere. Can I not get so much of my own will!' (pp. 117–18)

Jane thus aims to achieve liberty through constraint and settles for a subjectivity of diminished expectations. In the context of her social dis-advantages, this approach offers her a way to expand her field of action. Concurrently, her speech becomes less embodied as it takes the form of a silent inner monologue that she explicitly qualifies as mental. Jane's rhetoric also becomes more abstract as she rejects the personifications of 'Liberty, Excitement, Enjoyment' for the abstraction of an abbreviated signature drawn from the corpus of the letters of her name.

Jane's shift from internal speech to a printed advertisement also entails the mental abstraction that produces her involuntary signature at the Riverses'. She represents the advertisement as originating outside herself, during a suspension of conscious thought and deliberate effort. Strictly speaking, she does not decide to advertise at all: after 'feverish' but 'vain labour,' a 'kind fairy in my absence had surely dropped the required suggestion on my pillow.' Jane's will is thus carried out through a splitting of the self, first into an absent self and the fairy, then into two rhetorical interlocutors – a questioning 'I' who lacks knowledge of advertising and a savvy respondent who addresses this 'I' as 'you':

[A]s I lay down, [the suggestion] came quietly and naturally to my mind: 'Those who want situations must advertise . . .'
   'How? I know nothing about advertising.'
   Replies rose smooth and prompt now –
   'You must enclose the advertisement and the money to pay for it under a cover directed to the editor of the *Herald*.' (p. 118)

The momentary absence of Jane's self and her subsequent splitting into the first and the second person constitute profitable forms of self-alienation because they condense her self into a text, 'a clear, practical form' (p. 118).

Jane recounts her advertisement as follows:

'A young lady accustomed to tuition' (had I not been a teacher two years?) 'is desirous of meeting with a situation in a private family where the children are under fourteen.' (I thought that as I was barely eighteen, it would not do to undertake the guidance of pupils nearer my own age.) 'She is qualified to teach the usual branches of a good English education, together with French, Drawing, and Music' (in those days, reader, this now narrow catalogue of accomplishments would have been held tolerably comprehensive). 'Address J.E., Post Office, Lowton,——Shire.' (pp. 118–19)

The juxtaposition of the advertisement's text, which is isolated within quotation marks, and the parenthetical asides that pose rhetorical questions, qualify the advertisement's statements, and directly address the reader, highlights the advertisement's nonreferential status: Jane's advertisement does not reflect her person; it constructs her as a third-person object, a 'young lady,' and alienates her name into mere initials. Yet the near anonymity of 'J.E.' enables Jane to make a name for herself: *je* spells 'I' in French, the foreign language that she later speaks with her pupil and that she is studying when she learns 'the first two tenses of the verb *Etre*.'[2] And when Jane arrives at Millcote Inn on her way to Thornfield, the waiter who 'answer[s] her summons' asks, 'Is your name Eyre, miss?' (p. 125). As a result of her quasi-anonymous advertisement, Jane's name becomes a question to which she can affirmatively respond. Just before she is inspired to advertise, Jane sits in her room at Lowood School and hears 'a bell . . . [that] called me downstairs' (p. 117); after she has framed her ad, however, it is Jane who 'ring[s] the bell' at Millcote Inn, Jane who summons both a prospective consumer and her self.[3] While her advertisement expresses her desire to serve, it solicits and produces a buyer to pay for her services; by invoking that buyer, Jane also invokes her self as a worker with services to sell.

The advertisement's involuntary appearance and abbreviated, semi-anonymous signature neutralize the danger and unsuitability of female self-promotion. Jane commodifies herself while avoiding the stigma of prostitution often attached to governesses (Poovey, *Uneven Development*, pp. 129–31), indeed to all working women and to all professionals who put prices on personal services. Alienation into the third and second persons and into written signs does not disable or degrade Jane. Instead, she profits from this opportunity to differ from her embodied, particular self and others' views of her by entering what she represents as a professional body of governesses.

Jane Eyre's implied arguments for female professionalization reside in the form and content of the notorious pronouncement Jane utters when she mounts the rooftop of Thornfield: 'Anybody may blame me who likes' (p. 140).[4] After invoking an audience whose members' individuality has been generalized into 'anybody,' Jane outlines her desire to participate in a social space that exceeds the bounds of her body by imagining 'a power of vision which might overpass that limit; which might reach the busy world, towns, regions full of life I had heard of but never seen' and 'more of intercourse with my kind' (pp. 140–1).

Although Jane's language of romantic plentitude at first implies that she seeks an emotional outlet for feeling, for 'exultant movement, . . . trouble, . . . [and] life,' her concluding arguments present feeling as an abstract index of humanity that serves as the basis for demanding equal opportunity in the realm of work: 'women feel just as men feel; they need exercise for their faculties, and a field for their efforts as much as their brothers do . . . It is thoughtless to condemn them, or laugh at them, if they seek to do more or learn more than custom has pronounced necessary for their sex.' Addressing a generalized 'anyone,' Jane invokes the 'millions' of women who resemble her and the 'masses' of people with whom these women share their discontent (p. 141). As critics have noted, Jane's use of the terms *millions* and *masses* aligns women with workers (Kaplan: 172), but it also rhetorically connects women to the 'wave of association' that in England was often the first sign of formal professionalization (Larson: 5). Jane's generalization of her listeners and of herself as a speaker shifts attention from her individual situation to the shared condition of a collective body, a nascent professional entity.

When *Jane Eyre* was written, real professional opportunities did not exist for governesses, but the rhetorical force the novel confers on this professional body is reflected in Rigby's review, which uses the novel as an occasion to insist that middle-class women confine themselves to unpaid domestic labor. Rigby understands Jane's objection to the gap between existing female capacities and nonexistent professional opportunities as advocacy of the professionalization of governesses. After criticizing Jane as 'not precisely the mouthpiece one would select to plead the cause of governesses' (p. 176) and denouncing the novel's implied arguments for the professionalization of governess work, Rigby's review rejects the Queen's College proposal to license governesses:

What we . . . require and seek for our children is not a learned machine stamped and ticketed with credentials like a piece of patent goods, but rather a woman endowed with that sound principle, refinement, and sense, which no committee of education in the world could ascertain or certify . . . [N]o governess can teach an art or accomplishment like a regular professor.[5] (pp. 184–5)

Rigby praises governesses for qualities 'far too precious . . . to have any stated market value,' but her compliment takes a fundamentally negative form: 'no governess can teach . . . like a regular professor.' She argues against any institutionalized form of credentialization and approves governesses' inability to form professional or trade associations: 'the governess [has] no means of resistance. Workmen may rebel, and tradesmen may combine . . . but the governess has no refuge – no escape; she is a needy *lady*' (p. 179).

In disapproving of the automatization and commodification of women as 'patent goods,' Rigby opposed other aspects of professionalization for women. Although professionals did not deal in commodities, they commodified themselves. The term *professionalism*, as opposed to *amateurism*, signified payment for and standardization of services, the abstraction of work into the universal equivalent of money, and the subjection of work to systematic criteria, those 'homogeneous and universalistic principles' used to assess and compare different members of the same profession (Larson: 13). The generalization inherent in professionalism thus exemplified Locke's sense of abstraction in *An Essay concerning Human Understanding*: 'This is called abstraction, whereby ideas, taken from particular beings, become general representatives of all of the same kind' ('Abstraction,' *Century Dictionary*). Professionals also generated and solicited an abstract market of 'wide and anonymous publics,' a process made possible by the development of railways, telegraph systems, a modernized postal service, and improved roads (Larson: 10). In scorning the equation of women and 'patent goods,' Rigby placed women above the abstractions of exchange value, standardization, and rationalization deemed necessary for professionalization. However, by equating women with the unmeasurable qualities of 'sound principle, refinement, and sense,' Rigby unwittingly suggested that women already *were* professionals, since in contrast to tradespeople, who trafficked in material goods and 'the external wants or occasions of men,' professionals dealt in intangible knowledge such as medical theory or the principles of architectural design ('Profession'). In this sense a profession entailed a greater degree of abstraction than the physical labor of a surgeon or builder did (Perkin: 258; Kaye), and professionals claimed to have expertise in 'an abstract system of knowledge,' which for Andrew Abbott 'best identifies the professions' (p. 8).

Whereas Rigby's review warned that professionalizing governesses would mechanize women and make governesses too powerfully abstract, other writers justified their opposition to professionalization by identifying governesses with the excessive embodiment of 'unregulated female sexuality' (Poovey, *Uneven Development*, p. 131). Although not sexualized to the degree that working-class nannies and nursemaids were, governesses often received 'dishonourable proposals [and] insulting attentions' and figured in pornographic writings (Adburgham: 87; see also Blessington: 41, 184; Peterson: 15; Renton: 191). Advertisements in the London *Times* stipulated that in addition to being well-versed in academic subjects, a candidate 'must . . . be lady-like in manners and appearance,' 'her person and manners lady-like,' and must supply 'the fullest and most explicit communications as to age, health, &c' (Advertisement, 6 Jan. 1840;

Advertisement, 24 July 1840; Advertisement, 12 Apr. 1841). By placing the governess's physical characteristics alongside her pedagogical accomplishments as if the two belonged to the same register, such advertisements suggested that the governess exemplified her lessons in her person as much as she transmitted knowledge contained in books.

Jane Eyre thus gains professional status not only because she addresses a generalized group of peers but also because she eludes physical scrutiny, advertising her accomplishments in print without reference to her appearance. Throughout her narrative, most famously during her brief engagement to Edward Rochester, she resists identification with femininity as an embodied spectacle. In her conflicts and triumphs after her departure from Lowood, Jane draws not on what Rigby calls her merely 'moderate capital of good looks' but on what an *Athenaeum* reviewer describes as her 'capital of principle' (Rev. of *Jane Eyre*). The metaphor of 'capital' indicates an abstract quantity separable from the self; the attribute of 'principle,' a spiritual quality distinct from the body.

Jane Eyre culminates with a final instance of abstraction: Jane's instrumentalization through marriage to the blind and crippled Edward Rochester. Although Rochester eventually regains his sight, his right hand cannot be restored. As Jane concludes her tale, she reports, 'I was then his vision, as I am still his right hand' (p. 476). Critics have often interpreted Rochester's blinding and mutilation as a form of symbolic castration, but Jane appears to adopt – rather than to triumph over – her husband's bodily fragmentation by transforming herself into a prosthetic part.[6] Her insistence on the continuity and permanence of her position as a writing instrument and on her absorption into her husband's body ('I am *still his* right hand') and the homophony of *right* with *write* ('I am still his *write* hand') highlight the place of writing in Jane's progress. By using writing to abstract her body into a mechanized body part, Jane accedes to sovereignty through service and becomes the scribe of both her own and her husband's stories.

II

Jane's strategies for abstracting herself into texts and writing instruments parallel Brontë's strategies for advertising herself as the author of *Jane Eyre*. Even though Brontë wrote fiction as a professional author and Jane only advertises herself as a governess, both author and character represent themselves through abstractions in order to bypass the scrutiny to which women were subject as writers or governesses.

As Jennifer Wicke's work on Charles Dickens has shown, authorship without advertising was impossible during the 1840s, a period that witnessed 'the confluence of advertising and literature' (p. 21). During the first half of the nineteenth century, '[a]uctioneers and booksellers were among the heaviest advertisers in terms of the number of advertisements taken' (Nevett: 29). Indeed, an 1831 *Edinburgh Review* article about the taxes on literature surmised that '[a] third part of the advertisement duty is . . . derived from announcements of books' ('Observations': 434), and an 1843 article on advertising noted that although 'no trade, profession, or condition in life is entirely free from [puffery] . . . we are by no means sure that [authors] would not take precedence of even quackdoctors and auctioneers' (Rev. of *César Birotteau*: 4, 13) in terms of money and effort expended on advertising. As Charles Mitchell stated in an 1846 article titled 'The Philosophy of Advertising,' 'It may now be laid down as an established axiom, that no trade or profession can be followed advantageously without some species of advertising' (Linton: 29).

When the authors of the works advertised were women, however, the necessary self-promotion of advertising collided with the self-effacement demanded of them. The unpleasant glare of publicity often hampered female writers, even those who exercised their skills circumspectly in private, and the frequent equation of female writers with the sexualized, embodied figures of the prostitute and the fallen woman belied the increased rationalization of publishing (Mermin: xiv–xvii, 17, 21, 39).[7]

Brontë's own career illustrates the double standard used to evaluate men's and women's writing. When critics assumed that Currer Bell was a man, they rarely speculated on his experiences or physicality. When they assumed that Currer Bell was a woman, however, they imagined an autobiographical identity between the author and her heroines and remarked on the traces her embodied experience supposedly left in the text. In a review of *Jane Eyre* for *Fraser's Magazine*, G.H. Lewes wrote that 'the writer is evidently a woman' and concluded that the work was 'an autobiography . . . in the actual suffering and experience' (Allott: 84). Reviews of *Shirley* (1849) trumpeted the appearance of what the *Daily News* reviewer called 'a female pen' and rhetorically stripped the author down to her female attributes: 'that Currer Bell is petticoated will be . . . little doubted by the readers of her work' (Allott: 118). The *Atlas* remarked that 'there is woman stamped on every page of the present fiction,' and the *Standard of Freedom* wrote that '[t]he hand of a woman is unmistakably impressed on the present brilliant production' (Allott: 120, 133), while the *Critic* highlighted the notion that a woman's text did not abstract from experience but directly embodied it:

[W]e have come to the conclusion . . . that Currer Bell is a lady. The female heart is here anatomized with a minuteness of knowledge of its most delicate fibres, which could only be obtained by one who had her own heart under inspection. The emotions so wondrously described were never *imagined*: they must have been *felt*. (Allott: 141, emphasis mine)

Critics have argued that the tendency to see the woman in the work fostered the use of pseudonyms as shields from personal remarks, but few have asked how nineteenth-century women writers simultaneously publicized their works. Similarly, while scholars have shown that it was difficult for women to think of themselves as professional writers, less attention has been paid to how women nevertheless established professional relationships with publishers and reviewers. According to Mary Poovey, male writers of the 1840s resisted the alienation inherent in the professionalization of writing by modeling their work on an idealized version of women's domestic labor; the entry of women into the literary field was thus particularly problematic, for it threatened to evacuate the category of nonalienated female labor (*Uneven Development*, pp. 124–5).[8] In Poovey's analysis, alienation signifies a painful self-estrangement and psychological affliction (pp. 121, 125). That notion of alienation, stemming from Marx's concept of *Entfremdung* (Axelos: xxxi–xxxii), points to the emotional and physical state either of a sensationalized body in pain or of a body painfully severed from consciousness (Cvetkovich: 174, 179). In this sense, alienation describes both the proletarian worker's condition under capitalism and Jane's suffering in the first chapters of *Jane Eyre*; it posits an identification with the body rather than an abstraction from it.

In *Modes of Production of Victorian Novels*, N.N. Feltes applies the notion of alienation as *Entfremdung* to Victorian publishing history and to women's use of masculine pseudonyms. He describes a transition from a petty-commodity model of production, in which authors maintained some direct control over their product, to an alienated capitalist mode of production, which proletarianized authors, gave capitalist publishers a monopoly over the means of production and distribution, and transformed books into 'commodity-texts' characterized by alienability (pp. 6, 8). Feltes's discussion of George Eliot, however, replaces the general alienation of all writers with the specific suffering and alienation of female writers. Feltes maintains that Marian Evans took on the masculine pseudonym George Eliot as her 'professional name' because of 'her particular woman's material need'; her writing name 'specifies the effect of social coercion enforcing feminine subordination on the level of production' and signifies her exclusion from any 'professional title' (pp. 38, 40, 43). Although Feltes acknowledges the extent to which George Eliot attained professional status and profits, he sees Marian Evans and George Eliot as representatives of a femaleness and a professionalism radically opposed to each other. Feltes's argument that the masculine pseudonym referred to the alienation-as-suffering of the female writer's body helps explain how advertising could hamper women's attempts to exploit publishing's opportunities for profitable alienation-as-abstraction. A woman writer could not promote her work as Dickens did when he gave widely publicized readings of his book (Wicke: 51), and publicity from reviews often reduced women to a sensationalized femininity that militated against claims to professional status. Distressed by reviewers' insistence on the feminine garb, hand, and heart of *Shirley*'s author, Brontë was driven to exclaim, 'Why can they not be content to take Currer Bell for a man?' (Allott: 117).

However, Feltes's interpretation of the masculine pseudonym as a form of negative alienation occludes the extent to which a woman writer could circumvent the pitfalls of publicity by using a masculine or ambiguous pseudonym. The name Currer Bell enabled Brontë to materialize her professional self in abstract form, to put herself forward while simultaneously receding from view, a paradoxical strategy of self-promotion through self-effacement that is exemplified in an incident from Brontë's juvenile writing career. In 1837, the young Brontë wrote to the poet laureate Robert Southey and received a discouraging reply that included a piece of advice she apparently acted on throughout her career: 'the less you aim at celebrity, the more likely you will be to deserve and finally to obtain it' (Spark: 64). Southey presumed that his correspondent had used a pseudonym, although she had in fact signed her given name. In replying to Southey, Brontë accepted his censure but also followed a golden rule of advertising expounded (sarcastically) in an 1843 *Edinburgh Review* article: 'never . . . omit an opportunity of placing your name in printed characters before the world' (Rev. of *César Birotteau*: 2). Ostensibly an apology for her ambition, Brontë's reply multiplied the very signature whose authenticity and value Southey had placed in doubt: 'The signature which you suspected of being fictitious is my real name,' she wrote. 'Again, therefore, I must sign myself, "C. Brontë." ' That proclamation of her name was followed by a postscript in which she apologized for writing at all – and then signed her initials yet again (Spark: 68).

By the time Brontë published her novels, she had chosen to efface her given name completely in order to further the success of her writing name. 'If I could,' she wrote in 1841, 'I would always work in silence and obscurity, and let my efforts be known by their results' (Gaskell: 221); after publishing *Jane Eyre*, Brontë exclaimed in correspondence with a reader for the firm of Smith, Elder, 'What author would be without the advantage of being able to walk invisible?' (Symington and Wise 2: 174). Indeed, Brontë split herself into Charlotte Brontë and Currer Bell. Charlotte

Brontë, the real author, masqueraded in business letters as an intermediary who brokered the Bells' poems. In that guise, she implied to publishers 'that she was not acting on her own behalf' yet suggested a nominal rather than a corporeal status for the Bells 'by signing her correspondence "In the name of C., E., and A. Bell"' (Gaskell: 292).

To the extent that her pseudonym enabled her to produce herself as a published writer, as a brand name, Brontë engaged in a process of self-construction deemed a crucial aspect of professionalism (Larson: 14). Professional writers depended on the commodification of their names and on the alienation of their books into a network of advertisements through which the names and the books mutually promoted each other. Advertising thus abstracted the author's body into a series of texts, and the written advertisements could even be 'decorporealizing' (Wicke: 53) because of their distance from the icons, gestures, and speech of earlier advertising modes (Sampson: 19–22). Advertisements were also abstract by virtue of their emphasis on form and effect over content (Elliott: 117–19), their focus on exchange and sale rather than use, and their generalized address to an anonymous and global public (Linton: 30).

Brontë's pseudonym inserted her into and alluded to the literary marketplace and its advertising system. Although pseudonyms seem to mask authors' identities, an overtly artificial one like Currer Bell, which advertises its own fictiveness, constituted a common nineteenth-century ploy known as the 'puff mysterious,' which aroused readers' curiosity and interest by making reference to an anonymous, 'unknown' author (Hindley and Hindley: 92–93).[9] The name Bell itself also signified advertising and publishing to the mid-Victorian public. *Bell's Universal Advertiser* was the foremost advertising newspaper of Brontë's time, and the name Bell was attached to several popular weekly and penny newspapers in the 1830s, including *Bell's Weekly Messenger*, which was 'chiefly read in the country' and which carried many book reviews (Grant: 133).[10] Stuart and John Bell, the founders of the Bell newspapers, were successful publicists at the end of the eighteenth century; John Bell launched the *Morning Post* 'as a Daily Advertising Pamphlet' and also issued *The Universal Catalogue* (a catalog of books that was subsequently called *The British Library*) in 1772 (Elliott: 149). Bell was also the name attached to a series of cheap nineteenth-century reprints of poetry and drama. And an 1875 *History of Advertising* gave *bellmen* as the name for town criers, who advertised news and goods well into the nineteenth century (Sampson: 59).

Brontë's choice of the sexually ambiguous first name Currer enabled her to generalize her authorial power in a way that she believed a feminine name could not. To be sure, as Gaye Tuchman suggests, female authorship had a certain market value until the 1870s, and male writers often assumed feminine pseudonyms (pp. 48–55). However, that value was limited to the specifically feminine sensibility implied by a feminine name; it rarely translated into the universal currency of genius. Brontë advertised an authorship without reference to a sexed body in order to avoid the invidious standards used to evaluate women's writings, as she indicates in describing her and her sisters' decision to adopt pen names:

Averse to personal publicity, we veiled our own names under those of Currer, Ellis, and Acton Bell; the ambiguous choice being dictated by a sort of conscientious scruple at assuming Christian names, positively masculine, while we did not like to declare ourselves women, because . . . we had a vague impression that authoresses are liable to be looked on with prejudice. (Gaskell: 286)

By choosing 'ambiguous' names, the Brontës prevented attention from fixing on the bodies suggested by feminine or masculine names; indeed, Brontë notes that the pseudonyms Currer, Ellis, and Acton 'veiled [her and her sisters'] own *names*,' thus emphasizing the nominal and figurative rather than the material and personified existence of the Brontë sisters.

Although 'averse to personal publicity' and anxious to avoid any 'personal interview' with prospective publishers (Symington and Wise 2: 87), Brontë avidly sought the impersonal publicity provided by writing and encouraged advertisements of Currer Bell's work. She was familiar with advertising rhetoric from her earliest days as a reader and writer; her and her siblings' juvenilia 'frequently imitate[d] the format of . . . [news]papers and their specific advertising copy' (Shuttleworth: 48–49), and Brontë used that knowledge in her tenacious correspondence with Aylott and Jones, the firm that printed the Bells' poetry. Written under the cover of Currer Bell, her letters determined the volume's price, its advertising costs, the periodicals to which copies were to be sent for review, and the extracts of reviews to be used in subsequent advertisements (Symington and Wise 2: 89–135). After *Jane Eyre*'s publication, Brontë also wrote at length to her publisher George Smith about advertising strategies and sought recognition for the name Currer Bell (2: 147–52). Her suggestions to her publishers resembled those of successful entrepreneurs, who counseled that advertisements helped create the objects they advertised. For example, Josiah Wedgwood, a pioneer in the use of advertising, noted that objects 'want a name – a name has a wonderful effect I assure you – . . . it will be absolutely necessary for us to mark them, and advertise that mark' (McKendrick: 112, 124).[11] Although Brontë told her publishers that she thought reviews were more valuable than advertisements, most reviews differed little from advertisements in purpose, since both sought to affect sales and circulation (Collins: 191).

The *Edinburgh Review* called favorable reviews 'indorsements' (Rev. of *César Birotteau*: 14–15) and accused them of being veiled advertisements; indeed, until 1853 favorable book reviews were taxed as though they were advertisements (Turner: 82).

Brontë produced names for both herself and her works and used those names to advertise each other; all Currer Bell's books published after 1847 were labeled 'by the author of *Jane Eyre*.' Brontë suggested to Smith, Elder that publication of *The Professor* would give the name Currer Bell a recognition value that would help to sell subsequent works by that author. She viewed her works as mutual advertisements for one another: *The Professor* 'might be published without serious risk' because the 'more striking and exciting' *Jane Eyre* would follow; the success of the second work might increase if its author's name were circulated through the publication of the first; the first novel would retrospectively ride on the second's success, and 'thus the interest of the public (if any interest was aroused) might not be suffered to cool' (Gaskell: 317). Brontë's self-contained and self-sustaining advertising system was designed to have bodily effects on an abstract public, 'arousing' and heating its interest. Writing from behind a disembodied name, Brontë could then relish the materiality of her books, describing them as if they had bodies. On receiving the first copies of *Jane Eyre* she thus wrote to her publishers, 'You have given the work every advantage which good paper, clean type, and a *seemly outside* can supply . . .' (Gaskell: 321, emphasis mine).

Although advertisements for *Jane Eyre* named Currer Bell as the author of the novel, the title page of the first edition designated Currer Bell as the editor of *Jane Eyre: An Autobiography*. The editorial device came from earlier forms of the novel in which authors posed as editors to lend veracity to their tales and to authorize the public circulation of autobiographical confessions, whose content required privacy and anonymity. *Jane Eyre*'s editor, however, never appears within the work's frame. Currer Bell thus takes on an invisible, phantom existence as an abstract convention that saves Jane from being the author of the text: without the words 'Edited by Currer Bell,' the reader would assume that Jane Eyre herself had written the eponymous text subtitled *An Autobiography*. Jane Eyre and Currer Bell cover for each other: Jane's story can be published only under the protection of a nonfeminine name, while Currer Bell attains the invisibility that Brontë sought for that name by disappearing within the text that Jane Eyre writes. Charlotte Brontë, Jane Eyre, and Currer Bell all publish under cover of a veiled visibility that exploits print's erasure of the author's body to authorize women's professional participation in a market. This abstraction into market value is both a cause and an effect of capitalism's political economy, and in exploiting that economy and allowing it to exploit them, Currer Bell, Jane Eyre, and Charlotte Brontë share the limitations that Jane avows when she states, 'I was not heroic enough to purchase liberty at the price of caste' (p. 57). If *Jane Eyre* and Charlotte Brontë retain a place in a posthumanist and postcolonial feminist canon, it is because they reveal the lures as well as the limits, the profits as well as the costs to themselves and to others, of a woman's alienation into the capitalist marketplace and its advertisements.

NOTES

1. For a detailed discussion of Jane's attitude toward death and of death's imbrication with acts of writing and with texts, see Susan Derwin: 98–108.
2. Mark W. Hennelly, Jr, also notes that 'J.E.' suggests *je* and calls this 'text-self equation' one of the novel's many 'reflexive signatures of self-hood' (p. 703).
3. London *Times* advertisements from the early 1840s show that governesses and employers advertised in roughly equal numbers; Jane's decision to advertise for an employer rather than to answer a preexisting advertisement thus represents a deliberate effort to call her future employer into existence – the desire Jane serves is an alienated version of her own.
4. Virginia Woolf viewed this passage as the disfigurement of the novel by an excessively personal rage (pp. 71–3), while subsequent critics have been drawn to the scene's cathartic release of anger.
5. Although established in 1841, the Governesses' Benevolent Institution was less a professional entity than an employment agency and charitable resource until 1848, when its head, F.D. Maurice, founded Queen's College in London to train governesses. In an 1846 essay 'On the Relative Social Position of Mothers and Governesses,' Anna Jameson emphasized that governesses did not belong to a profession (pp. 156, 159). Although Rigby's review nominally referred to the governess 'profession' (pp. 177, 180), governess work was not professionalized in the 1840s, as architecture was (Kaye), nor did it conform to what Magali Larson identifies as the sociological-ideological definition of professionalism: there was no qualifying exam, standardized course of study, mechanism for exclusion or for recruitment of members, control over fees, autonomy, or prestige (pp. xi, x).
6. Derwin interprets Rochester's mutilation as a displacement and literalization of the 'symbolic embodiment' and 'symbolic violence' Jane undergoes in the course of her 'achievement of selfhood' (pp. 97–98).
7. For an interpretation of the author-prostitute equation that links prostitution not to embodiment but to the abstraction and alienation of exchange, see Catherine Gallagher, 'George Eliot,' 41–42; 'Masked Woman,' 27–28.
8. Women as well as men, however, often modeled their authorial efforts on familial labor, service, and self-sacrifice and resolved the conflict between alienated market

production and nonalienated domestic service by assimilating one form of work to the other. Brontë, for example, reconciled her displays of talent with a self-effacing desire to serve, acknowledging Elizabeth Gaskell's dictum that the woman writer must 'not hide her gift in a napkin; it was meant for the use and service of others' (Gaskell: 334; see also Mermin: 18).

9. Writing about the pseudonym George Eliot, Alexander Welsh notes that '[p]seudonymity . . . cannot be regarded as solely a defensive maneuver . . . since it immediately fuels speculation and publicity for a successful book' (Mermin: 155 n. 11).

10. An 1843 journal article reported that of 616 families who read newspapers in a London parish inhabited by domestic servants and laborers, 283 read *Bell's Weekly Dispatch*, and 23 read *Bell's Life in London* (Altick: 342–43); *Bell's Life in London* had an average weekly circulation between 17,700 and 21,000, and the name Bell was also attached to a penny weekly, *Bell's Penny Dispatch*, and, as already noted, to *Bell's Weekly Messenger*, which Altick calls the 'Tory farmer's old standby' (pp. 343, 349). These figures may not be accurate, and I have found no direct evidence that the Brontë family received a Bell paper, but beyond any doubt, the name Bell was overdetermined and easily available as a signifier of newspapers, advertising, and literary editions.

11. Daniel Stuart, the proprietor of the *Morning Post*, stated that '[a]dvertisements act and react. They attract readers [and] promote circulation, and circulation attracts advertisements' (Wood: 81).

WORKS CITED

Abbott, Andrew. *The System of Professions: An Essay on the Division of Expert Labor* (Chicago: Univ. of Chicago Press, 1988).

'Abstraction,' *Century Dictionary and Cyclopedia*, vol. 1 (New York: Century, 1911).

'Abstraction,' *Oxford English Dictionary*, 2nd edn. 1989.

Adburgham, Alison. A Punch *History of Manners and Modes, 1841–1940* (London: Hutchinson, 1961).

Advertisement. *Times* [London]. 6 Jan. 1840: 1.

Advertisement. *Times* [London]. 24 July 1840: 1.

Advertisement. *Times* [London]. 12 Apr. 1841: 1.

Allott, Miriam, ed. *The Brontës: The Critical Heritage* (London: Routledge, 1974).

Altick, Richard D. *The English Common Reader: A Social History of the Mass Reading Public, 1800–1900* (Chicago: Univ. of Chicago Press, 1957).

Axelos, Kostas. *Alienation, Praxis, and Techné in the Thought of Karl Marx*, trans. Ronald Bruzina (Austin: Univ. of Texas Press, 1976).

Azin, Firdous. *The Colonial Rise of the Novel* (London: Routledge, 1993).

Blessington, Marguerite. *The Governess* (Paris: Baudry's European Library, 1840).

Brontë, Charlotte. *Jane Eyre* (Harmondsworth: Penguin, 1986).

Bruno, Giuliana. *Streetwalking on a Ruined Map: Cultural Theory and the City Films of Elvira Notari* (Princeton: Princeton Univ. Press, 1993).

'Rev. of *César Birotteau* and *Histoire de M. Jobard*,' *Edinburgh Review* 65 (1843): 1–43.

Collins, A.S. *The Profession of Letters: A Study of the Relation of Author to Patron, Publisher, and Public, 1780–1832* (New York: Dutton, 1929).

Cvetkovich, Ann. *Mixed Feelings: Feminism, Mass Culture, and Victorian Sensationalism* (New Brunswick: Rutgers Univ. Press, 1992).

Derwin, Susan. *The Ambivalence of Form: Lukács, Freud, and the Novel* (Baltimore: Johns Hopkins Univ. Press, 1992).

Elliott, Blanche B. *A History of English Advertising* (London: Business Publications, 1962).

Feltes, N.N. *Modes of Production of Victorian Novels* (Chicago: Univ. of Chicago Press, 1986).

Foucault, Michel. *An Introduction*, trans. Robert Hurley (New York: Pantheon, 1978), vol. 1 of *The History of Sexuality*.

Gallagher, Catherine. 'George Eliot and *Daniel Deronda*: The Prostitute and the Jewish Question,' in *Sex, Politics, and Science in the Nineteenth Century*, ed. Ruth Bernard Yeazell (Baltimore: Johns Hopkins Univ. Press, 1986), pp. 39–62.

Gallagher, Catherine. 'Who Was That Masked Woman? The Prostitute and the Playwright in the Comedies of Aphra Behn,' *Women's Studies* 15 (1988): 23–42.

Gaskell, Elizabeth. *The Life of Charlotte Brontë* (London: Penguin, 1985).

Gilbert, Sandra, and Susan Gubar. *The Madwoman in the Attic: The Woman Writer and the Nineteenth-century Literary Imagination* (New Haven: Yale Univ. Press, 1979).

Grant, James. *The Great Metropolis*, 1st ser., vol. 2 (London: Saunders, 1836).

Hennelly, Mark W., Jr. '*Jane Eyre*'s Reading Lesson,' *ELH* 51 (1984): 693–717.

Heyck, T.W. *The Transformation of Intellectual Life in Victorian England* (London: Croom, 1982).

Hindley, Diana, and Geoffrey Hindley. *Advertising in Victorian England, 1837–1901* (London: Wayland, 1972).

Jameson, Anna. *Memoirs and Essays Illustrative of Art, Literature, and Social Morals* (New York: Wiley, 1846).

Rev. of *Jane Eyre*. *Athenaeum*, 23 Oct. 1847: 1101.

Kaplan, Cora. 'Pandora's Box: Subjectivity, Class and Sexuality in Socialist Feminist Criticism,' *Sea Changes: Essays on Culture and Feminism* (London: Verso, 1986), pp. 147–76.

Kaye, Barrington. *The Development of the Architectural Profession in Britain* (London: Allen, 1960).

Keefe, Robert. *Charlotte Brontë's World of Death* (Austin: Univ. of Texas Press, 1979).

Lacan, Jacques. *Ecrits: A Selection*, trans. Alan Sheridan (New York: Norton, 1977).

Larson, Magali Sarfatti. *The Rise of Professionalism: A Sociological Analysis* (Berkeley: Univ. of California Press, 1977).

Linton, David. 'Mr Mitchell's "National Work,"' *Journal of Advertising History* (Jan. 1979): 29–31.

McKendrick, Neil. 'Josiah Wedgwood and the Commercialization of the Potteries,' *The Birth of a Consumer Society: The Commercialization of Eighteenth-century England*, eds McKendrick, John Brewer, and J.H. Plumb (Bloomington: Indiana Univ. Press, 1982), pp. 99–144.

Macpherson, C.B. *Democratic Theory: Essays in Retrieval* (Oxford: Clarendon, 1973).

Marx, Karl. *Economic and Philosophic Manuscripts of 1844*, trans. Martin Milligan (Buffalo: Prometheus, 1988).

Mermin, Dorothy. *Godiva's Ride: Women of Letters in England 1830–1880* (Bloomington: Indiana Univ. Press, 1993).

Nevett, T.R. *Advertising in Britain: A History* (London: Heinemann, 1982).

'Observations on the Paper Duties,' *Edinburgh Review* (1831): 427–37.

Perkin, Harold. *The Origins of Modern English Society* (London: Ark, 1969).

Peterson, M. Jeanne. 'The Victorian Governess: Status Incongruence in Family and Society,' *Suffer and Be Still: Women in the Victorian Age*, ed. Martha Vicinus (Bloomington: Indiana Univ. Press, 1972), pp. 3–19.

Poovey, Mary. *Making A Social Body: British Cultural Formation, 1830–1864* (Chicago: Univ. of Chicago Press, forthcoming).

Poovey, Mary. *Uneven Development: The Ideological Work of Gender in Mid-Victorian England* (Chicago: Univ. of Chicago Press, 1988).

'Profession,' *Oxford English Dictionary*, 2nd edn. 1989.

Renton, Alice. *Tyrant or Victim? A History of the British Governess* (London: Weidenfeld, 1991).

Rigby, Elizabeth. '*Vanity Fair, Jane Eyre*, and *Governesses' Benevolent Institution Report for 1847*,' *Quarterly Review* 84 (1848): 153–83.

Sampson, Henry. *A History of Advertising from the Earliest Times* (London: Chatto, 1875).

Showalter, Elaine. *A Literature of Their Own: British Women Novelists from Brontë to Lessing* (Princeton: Princeton Univ. Press, 1977).

Shuttleworth, Sally. 'Female Circulation: Medical Discourse and Popular Advertising in the Mid-Victorian Novel,' *Body/Politics: Women and the Discourses of Science*, eds Mary Jacobus, Evelyn Fox Keller, and Shuttleworth (New York: Routledge, 1990), pp. 47–68.

Spark, Muriel, ed. *The Letters of the Brontës: A Selection* (Norman: Univ. of Oklahoma Press, 1954).

Spivak, Gayatri Chakravorty. 'Three Women's Texts and a Critique of Imperialism,' *Critical Inquiry* 12 (1985): 243–61.

Sutherland, J.A. *Victorian Novelists and Publishers* (Chicago: Univ. of Chicago Press, 1976).

Symington, John Alexander, and Thomas James Wise. *The Brontës: Their Lives, Friendships and Correspondence in Four Volumes*, 4 vols (Oxford: Blackwell, 1932).

Thompson, E.P. 'Time, Work-Discipline and Industrial Capitalism,' *Customs in Common* (London: Merlin, 1991), pp. 352–403.

Tuchman, Gaye, with Nina E. Fortin. *Edging Women Out: Victorian Novelists, Publishers, and Social Change* (New Haven: Yale Univ. Press, 1989).

Turner, E.S. *The Shocking History of Advertising!* (London: Joseph, 1952).

Wicke, Jennifer. *Advertising Fictions: Literature, Advertisement, and Social Reading* (New York: Columbia Univ. Press, 1988).

Wood, Josiah P. *The Story of Advertising* (New York: Donald, 1958).

Woolf, Virginia. *A Room of One's Own* (New York: Harcourt, 1929).

Zonana, Joyce. 'The Sultan and the Slave: Feminist Orientalism and the Structure of *Jane Eyre*,' *Signs* 18 (1991): 592–617.

CHAPTER EIGHT

Gothic Desire in Charlotte Brontë's
Villette

TONI WEIN

Toni Wein teaches on the Writing Programme at Princeton University. The article reprinted here focuses on intertextual connections between *Villette* and 'Monk' Lewis's *The Monk*, drawing on the language of deconstruction to do so. She reads Charlotte's novel as a calculated rewriting of both *The Monk* and – as then unpublished – *The Professor*. In rewriting Lewis's novel, Wein argues that Brontë turns a text which articulates sexuality as constructed by men into one which replaces that with sexuality as construed by a woman. She pushes the argument further by asserting that this usurpation of a 'masculine' text represents Charlotte's own claim to the supposedly masculine career of authorship.

A letter of 16 June 1854 reads as follows: 'My dear Ellen, Can you come next Wednesday or Thursday? I am afraid circumstances will compel me to agree to an earlier day than I wished. I sadly wished to defer it till the 2nd week in July, but I fear it must be sooner, the 1st week in July, possibly the last week in June . . . This gives rise to much trouble and many difficulties as you may imagine, and papa's whole anxiety now is to get the business over. Mr Nicholls with his usual trustworthiness takes all the trouble of providing substitutes on his own shoulders.'[1]

Despite the language of reluctance and regret, Charlotte Brontë was facing neither surgery nor the firing squad. Rather, the 'it' she refers to in

Reprinted from *Studies in English Literature* 39.4 (1999): 733–46.

this letter to her friend, Ellen Nussey, is her long-deferred marriage. Admittedly, this letter carries biographical and psychological interest. But I am more interested in the way her characterization of Arthur Nicholls as 'providing substitutes' announces a theme and dominant trope crucial to understanding Brontë's literary maneuverings.[2] Like her future husband, Brontë works a series of substitutions in her novels.

Much light has been shed by critics who have focused on these doublings, displacements, repressions, and subversions.[3] Despite their varying theoretical backgrounds, consensus that Brontë employed these strategies as a critique of Victorian culture has gradually coalesced. To that end, identities, bodies, gender, and genre have all been said to migrate; and, indeed, all of these emigrants wash up on the shores of Belgium's Villette. Yet less attention has been paid to an even more significant aspect of Brontë's work: her reterritorialization of migratory texts. Pondering Brontë's substitutions for possible relocations yields insights about her professionalism as well as her literary products.

After all, *Villette* is Brontë's reworking of her first novel, *The Professor*. Her initial efforts to publish it had provoked continual rebuffs from publishers; after the encouragement of George Smith had produced the success of *Jane Eyre*, Brontë's repeated suggestions that he next publish *The Professor* prompted gentle rebukes. Part of the objection to *The Professor* was its size, two volumes, a distinctly anomalous commodity.[4] Charlotte wrote Smith on 5 February 1851, withdrawing her offer of her 'martyrized M.S.' to one 'who might "use it to light an occasional cigar."' In her letter, Charlotte ironically suggests that she should be locked up in prison for twelve months, at the end of which time she would come out either 'with a 3 vol. M.S. in my hand, or else with a condition of intellect that would exempt me ever after from literary efforts and expectations.'[5] In September, Smith placed additional pressure on her by repeating the firm's post-*Jane Eyre* suggestion that she write a novel in serial form. Charlotte refused.[6]

Although little credit is given to Charlotte as a business-woman, we can see her awareness of literary marketing from the very beginnings of her career as a novelist, a transition motivated by financial pragmatics after the failure of the sisters' volume of poems, for whose publication they had been forced to pay.[7] When she finally revised *The Professor*, her remodeling entailed more than a narrative elaboration and a narratorial shift from the third into the first person. Brontë also carved emphatically Gothic features onto what had been principally a double *bildungsroman*. Those Gothic features bear a canny resemblance to one of the most scandalous Gothic texts of the previous century, Matthew Lewis's *The Monk* (1796).

A tale of substitutions and possession, *The Monk*'s relics in *Villette* speak to Brontë's struggle to gain possession of herself as a woman, as an author, and as an heir to literary conventions. As Luce Irigaray imagines the dilemma: 'How find a voice, make a choice, strong enough to cut through these layers of ornamental style, that decorative sepulchre, where even her breath is lost. Stifled under all those airs.'[8] But the voice that Charlotte Brontë finds by tunneling out from within the tomb of the Gothic novel does more than keen a 'female Gothic' or lament the 'feminine carceral' of domestic space.[9] In *Villette*, that voice cries out against institutional forces of education, of art, and of religion, a message also contained in *The Monk*.[10] She thereby sounds a second alarm: that possession can be barred as effectively by business conventions of literature as by literary conventions of style or voice. At the same time that the word possession points to ownership, it also means a haunting. To form the self, whether as a private individual or as a professional author, one must strive to ensure that the self one possesses is not formed or possessed by others.

Brontë's possession by Gothic in general may have provided her with models to substitute a different structural logic of desire from that fostered by serialization,[11] as Linda K. Hughes and Michael Lund have described it: '[its] intrinsic form more closely approximates female than male models of pleasure. Rather than inviting sustained arousal of attention until the narrative climax is reached, spending the driving energy of narrative and sundering the readers from the textual experience, the installment novel offers itself as a site of pleasure that is taken up and discharged only to be taken up again (some days or weeks later), and again, and again.'[12] Yet I do not thereby mean to imply that Brontë resorts to a male structure of desire. Instead, in true Gothic tradition, she hybridizes: she encloses her structurally deferred climaxes in a three-volume tomb, at the same time that she thwarts the serial's (and autobiography's) construction of intimacy between readers and characters through her (and Lucy's) refusal to provide closure.

Brontë's structural Gothicizing reads as evidence that she consciously engaged in rewriting gender codes.[13] But by limiting our attention to examples of so-called 'female Gothic,' and by seeing Ann Radcliffe as the only precursor for Brontë, we miss seeing how her reworking of gender codes also serves her professionalism.[14] Narratively and thematically, Brontë redefines desire. In mapping the traces of *The Monk* in *Villette*, then, I will contend that Brontë draws on *The Monk* because in that novel she finds an analysis of substitution's dangers and delights. For Lewis, both dangers and delights lie in substitution's resemblance to a pornographic economy of exchange. Lewis sees women as counters in that system of barter. Forced to enter into an economy of exchange that demanded she relinquish autonomy while it promised her some range of mobility beyond the confines of the home, Brontë responds by making the nun the figure through which erotic desire becomes buoyantly disembodied and endlessly deferred, the possession of the self through substitution.[15]

Even more than *Jane Eyre*, with its 'madwoman in the attic,' *Villette* is a haunted text. Brontë possesses her literary heritage by creating a surrogate Gothic. Critics usually point to the haunting figure of the nun as the key Gothic element, although they seldom agree about its significance. To Sandra Gilbert and Susan Gubar, the nun is a projection of Lucy's need for nullity;[16] for Eve Sedgwick, the nun dramatizes Lucy's constitutive need for doubleness. Christina Crosby detects the nun as mirroring the narcissistic Lacanian Imaginary Other.[17] To some, the nun represents Brontë's anticlericalism;[18] while Q.D. Leavis, who saw the nun as nothing more than a plot device for maintaining suspense and for generating sales, is not far removed from Brontë's contemporary, the reviewer of the *Literary Gazette*, who recognized a Byronic prototype when identifying the nun as 'a phantom of the Fitz-fulke kind.'[19] But a covey of nuns broods over more characters than Lucy. Paul's history with Justine-Marie forms the most obvious analogue. The prehistory of the pensionnat also suggests whole generations subject to ecclesiastic visitations whose terror – diurnal or nocturnal – may have been equal. These nuns form a sisterhood that extends beyond the borders of Villette, back to the Gothic novels half a century old.

Of all the possible precursors, Lewis's *The Monk* looms the largest in Brontë's text. Our first introduction to the legend of Brontë's nun reveals its close bonds with the story of Lewis's Agnes. Like the pensionnat's nun, Agnes is immured alive in the vaults of her convent 'for some sin against her vow.'[20] Agnes's sin is fecund concupiscence; we never learn what the Belgian nun had done, although a sexual aura attaches to her by association, both because wanton nuns and monks were a cliché by that time, and because Ginevra confiscates the nun's identity to cover her own escapades.[21] Confiscation of identity lies at the core of Lewis's tale as well: Agnes lands in the convent only after she has attempted to elope with her lover, Don Raymond, by assuming the guise of a bleeding nun, said to haunt the castle of her aunt.

If any figure can be said to haunt the pages of *Villette*, it is this last unwilling nun, Beatrice de las Cisternas. Raymond and Agnes's concerted plan fails when the real ghostly nun appears in Agnes's stead. Raymond cannot tell the difference; instead, he rapturously clasps the phantom to his breast and exclaims: 'Agnes! Agnes! Thou art mine / Agnes! Agnes! I am thine! / In my veins while blood shall roll, / Thou art mine! / I am thine! / thine my body! thine my soul!' (p. 166). This jubilant crowing of patriarchal possession soon sticks in Raymond's craw, however. The Bleeding Nun nightly visits Raymond's bedchamber, not to glut him with the pleasures of the flesh, since she has none, but to rewrite his poetic will by reversing the possessive pronouns: 'Mine thy body! Mine thy soul' (p. 170). Beatrice's haunting of Raymond's bedchamber, at the precise moment when his desire was to be realised, resembles the nun's appearances to Lucy at moments when she, too, seems poised to find happiness beyond the walls of her confinement, especially through her growing intimacy with Dr John. Given the resemblance, it is doubly surprising that critics of Brontë read the scene as revealing Lucy's psychological inability to cathect with another human being or her anxieties about sex, or that critics of Lewis fail to so read his scene. Rather than evenly distribute a unilinear reading of this nature to either scene, however, we should recognize the similarity of their underlying logic. Like Lucy, Raymond has his desire stimulated by the encounter, setting off a chain reaction through which he will learn to love precisely the same kind of emaciated nun, as though the nun carries a contagion which purges the fleshly from both Raymond and Agnes.

Raymond escapes the nun's possession when the Wandering Jew miraculously arrives to shrieve her soul. Raymond, too, is enjoined to penitence: he must lay Beatrice's bones to rest in her ancestral grave, much as Lucy can only free herself from her obsession with Dr John by burying his letters to her. In fact, Lucy creates a second tomb, sealing her letters under a slab of slate and mortar right beside that of the Belgian nun. And she acquires the casket in which those letters will rest by journeying into the 'old historical quarter of the town,' and purchasing a used glass jar from the 'old Jew broker' who owns the pawn shop, as though *Villette*, the book, had metaphorically domesticated and domiciled the Wandering Jew in Villette, the town.[22]

This scene does not exhaust the presence of resemblances between *The Monk* and *Villette*.[23] Nevertheless, the burial in the garden marks an apotheosis. Raymond's scene of burial may stage his penitence, but that repentance permits him to substitute new objects of desire. The same interpretation applies to Brontë's reenactment of Lewis's scenes. Like Lucy and Raymond, Brontë has her desire pointed by her Gothic encounters. Like theirs, this desire substitutes a new outlet for its original source. We can read these resemblances as a metanarrative about Brontë's authoring of her own literary self, for, while she exhumes ancestral texts, she also buries the spirit of their letters.

Brontë rejects and rewrites the perverted representations of women and/or of values that rustle through these earlier Gothic letters. It is not so much the logic of substitution to which she objects. This logic governs male Gothic from the time of Horace Walpole's *The Castle of Otranto*, where Theodore is rewarded with another bride to replace the innocent female destroyed by Gothic ambition.[24] Brontë targets the locus of this substitution in Lewis. With the exception of Beatrice, women are either bartered brides, functioning to consolidate wealth and status, or battered virgins, servicing a similar passion for power now figured as sexual dominance.

At first glance, Lewis may seem to critique such an instrumental attitude toward sexuality by revealing the pornographic outlook underlying it through his portrait of Ambrosio. Ambrosio, 'drunk with desire,' consummates his apostasy and his ecstasy in Matilda's arms, muttering 'Thine, ever thine' (Lewis, p. 109). But just as Ambrosio's reference to his liaison as his 'commerce with Matilda' reveals the economics of desire, so his swift revulsion betrays the tendency of consummation to consume the consumer, making any such lasting fidelity impossible (pp. 230, 236–7). Both Matilda and Ambrosio are victims of a gendered double bind. The more time Matilda spends with Ambrosio, the more she wants him; the more she wants him, the less he wants her. But Lewis here seems to want to have it both ways: he first blames Matilda for having caused Ambrosio's disgust, then delineates how such generosity inaugurates an increasingly selfish reaction.

The ambiguity of Lewis's position could arise from his attempt to analyze the way Ambrosio's entrapment in this situation, like his incarceration in the monastery, teaches him progressively to devalue other lives. Lewis shows how such induration causes Ambrosio to split Matilda in two. When Ambrosio mentally divorces Matilda from her body, emotionally discarding all but her physical shell which he refers to as 'it,' Lewis brilliantly conveys the magnitude of such objectification of the feminine (p. 241). Offended, Lewis's censors made him substitute the conventional pronoun 'she' in the fourth and fifth editions for the blatant disregard suggested by the indefinite pronoun. But their tiny sentimentalizing gesture seems impotent against the onslaught of Ambrosio's dehumanization of Antonia. Ambrosio may at first *think* that he loves Antonia chastely, but appreciation of her beauty rapidly transforms itself into appetite (p. 243): 'Grown used to her modesty, it no longer commanded the same respect and awe: he still admired it, but it only made him more anxious to deprive her of that quality which formed her principal charm' (p. 255). When Ambrosio finally captures Antonia in the charnel vaults of the monastery, even his gaze can no longer hold her in a fixed image. Instead, her identity migrates, mingling first with the corrupt bodies surrounding her, then dissolving into that of her dead mother, killed by Ambrosio (p. 364).

However, Lewis's delight in describing these scenes supplements and cancels the analysis of danger. Although Ambrosio's desire for Antonia vanishes with her rape, he still cannot let her go free; he imagines keeping her a prisoner of his new desire for an endless succession of penitent nights (p. 371). Only Matilda's arrival, and the warning that they are surrounded by archers come to rescue Antonia, breaks the spell of irresolution in which Ambrosio seeks to hold Antonia. He takes her in the same position in which he had earlier raped her, both times prostrate with supplicating prayers, now using his poniard as the weapon of penetration.

Beyond the pornographic violence of the scene lies a still more pernicious implication, one that mitigates his seeming sympathy with Matilda and Antonia's plight. Women are trapped in a double bind. As vestal females, they are vulnerable to appropriation. But Lewis also implies that sexual desire in women unleashes in them a potential masculinity that provokes Ambrosio's distaste: 'Now [Matilda] assumed a sort of courage and manliness in her manners and discourse, but ill calculated to please him. She spoke no longer to insinuate, but command . . . *Pity is a sentiment so natural, so appropriate to the female character, that it is scarcely a merit for a woman to possess it, but to be without it is a grievous crime'* (pp. 233–4, my emphasis). The final words of the passage collapse the values of the omniscient narrator with those of Ambrosio. So, too, does the portrait of Beatrice, who like Matilda momentarily rises above her gendered fate and receives in consequence a narrative punishment all the more severe.

Only women who mask their masculine intelligence with feminine modesty receive approbation. The reward to women for such complicitous compliance is to become commodified and hence substitutable. With Antonia conveniently dead, it does not take Lorenzo long to substitute Virginia. Once again, the narrator foreshadows his approval of Lorenzo's decision, placing 'not unwisely' into the mouth of Lorenzo's uncle the maxim that ' "men have died, and worms have ate them, but not for love!" ' – a proverb that failed to disturb the censors (p. 381). This unacknowledged quotation from William Shakespeare's *As You Like It* also disguises the potential feminism of its original utterance. Rosalind speaks those words to Orlando while playing Ganymede playing Rosalind, in order to cure Orlando of his idealism and to incite his appreciation for her self, rather than for some Petrarchan fiction. By surreptitiously relocating those words into the mouth of the duke, Lewis makes the maxim part of the 'old boy' network of truth, which is further validated by the authority of the omniscient narrator who boldly declares his status as M.P. in the third edition. In contrast to the protean authority of the men, the women are unidimensional clichés, fixated in their affections and transfixed accordingly by their circumstances.

If Lewis's novel collapses the authorial and characterological perspectives, its message also merges with that articulated by Brontë's father and Robert Southey. They warned her that women had no right to possess a literary career. Later in life, Charlotte wrote that her father had always instilled in her the view of writing and literary desires as a rebellion from her female duties.[25] She heard the same strictures from Southey, whom she wrote for advice about how to become a professional poet. Despite his protestation of impropriety, Southey must certainly have known how many women had successfully made literature the 'business' of their lives at that juncture.

Brontë's novel, then, is 'new Gothic' insofar as it makes women's authorization of substitution, demonic in Lewis, heroic.[26] Each of the women in *Villette* – Madames Beck and Walravens, Mrs. Bretton, Ginevra, Lucy, and Polly – survives by a strategy of substitution. Ginevra stands as the most obvious entry here. Madame Beck fails to obtain a youthful lover, but she gains voyeuristic satisfaction from her role as *surveillante*. Mrs. Bretton lives in John (Brontë, p. 267); Madame Walravens becomes a death-like ringer for her granddaughter, stealing in the process the house, affection, and jewels that might otherwise have been Justine-Marie's.[27]

Perhaps the most astute pupil of substitution is little Polly, who early learns to corral her desire precisely by displacing it. The first example of her mastery of this technique, which she will employ to such great effect with John, occurs when she is merely seven. Knowing she is about to leave the household and return to her papa, Polly longs to rush to Graham and tell him the news, hoping that his despair will match her own. Instead, she fondles Lucy Snowe: 'In the evening, at the moment Graham's entrance was heard below, I found her at my side. She began to arrange a locket-ribbon around my neck, she displaced and replaced the comb in my hair; while thus busied, Graham entered' (p. 40). Polly then gets Lucy to deliver the news, freeing herself to observe Graham's reaction.

In fact, alone of all the women in *Villette*, Lucy at first seems to be innately passive. Peter Brooks may see desire as the very spark necessary for all narrative, but Lucy seems curiously devoid of passion or need at the start of hers.[28] But, of course, the novel reveals that calm to be fictive, the result of a momentary translation, a fact that the mature Lucy knows and signals to the reader by prefacing her momentary poise in language that underscores its artificiality: 'In the autumn of the year ——, I was staying at Bretton; my godmother having come in person to claim me of the kinsfolk with whom was at that time fixed my permanent residence'

(p. 6). The unnamed 'kinsfolk' from whom Lucy so strenuously distances herself can be none other than the parents she loses. Although we never learn what happens, the shadow of those events and the subsequent vagrancy of Lucy's life cast doubt on the 'fixity' and 'permanence' of all existence, as does the passive construction of her temporary placement there. What Lucy learns in the course of her life is to seize control of her translations. Without that lesson, her fate would have resembled that of Miss Marchmont, frozen into place by events. And it is through Polly that Lucy will first learn to activate her desires.

Lucy feels compelled to intervene in Polly's actions, to exercise vicarious restraint over the child's emotions (p. 13); Polly's emotions, however, seem to exercise more power over Lucy than the reverse. Stoic Lucy, 'guiltless' of the 'curse' of 'an overheated and discursive imagination,' nonetheless imagines rooms to be 'haunted' by Polly's presence (p. 15). Polly's proposed absence causes Lucy to break through her normal reserve. She invites Polly into her bed 'wishing, yet scarcely hoping, she would comply'; when Polly comes, 'gliding like a small ghost over the carpet,' she is 'warmed . . . soothed . . . tranquillized and cherished' in Lucy's arms (p. 44).

Moreover, as far as we know, Polly is the only person ever to share Lucy's bed. Gilbert and Gubar are right to follow Leavis in seeing Polly as Lucy's other self. But they miss the fact that, from the beginning, Polly is described in imagery that connects her to the full-grown nuns Lucy will later encounter. If Polly is a 'demure little person in a mourning frock and white chemisette,' a frock that Lucy pointedly tells us is black three pages earlier, her costume merges with her actions to turn her into a type of the bleeding nun (p. 20): doggedly hemming a handkerchief for her father, the needle 'almost a skewer, pricking herself ever and anon, marking the cambric with a track of minute red dots; occasionally starting when the perverse weapon – swerving from her control – inflicted a deeper stab than usual; but still silent, diligent, womanly, absorbed' (p. 20). Far from representing a type that must be feared or renounced, the nun in *Villette* represents Lucy Snowe's embrace of her provisional status.[29] The nun blends into Lucy's persona so that she, too, becomes a 'silence artist,' defying mystery by adopting it (pp. 680–2).[30] How fitting, then, that Ginevra bequeaths the costume of the nun to Lucy.

Once so metaphorically habited, the swelled presence of desire takes on a religious cast.[31] For both Lucy and Polly, the handwritten word of John supplants the word of God and becomes a physical revelation (pp. 254, 326–7, 342–3). Each performs a similar ritual of dilation, going so far as to pray before she revels in the letter. But Paul's letters do more than refresh or sustain (p. 713); they enable Lucy to incorporate her lover, so that his absence marks the summit of their love: 'I thought I loved him when he went away; I love him now in another degree; he is more my own' (p. 714). Paul's fate when clasped to Lucy's heart must mirror Lucy's when cradled in the 'bosom of my kindred': both types of love can be safely possessed only in the reflection of memory, while the actual bodies must endure the clammy embrace of the engulfing sea. Immured in the convent of knowledge Paul had created for her, Lucy's life becomes one of singular, not serial, devotion. Her conventual existence appears most strongly in the collapse of her narrative into the histories of the three Catholics who had seemed her nemeses, in a final act of substitution (p. 715). She may not count her beads in a Carmelite convent, but she does tell her story, her metaphorical habit of black and white a fitting emblem of the printed page.

The unspoken fact of Paul's fate signals how heretical Brontë's narrator and narrative truly are.[32] Charlotte had originally planned to end the book with a clear announcement of Paul's death. Her father objected strenuously, declaring his dislike for books that 'left a melancholy impression on the mind.'[33] Unable or unwilling to defer completely to his wish for a 'happy ending,' Charlotte left her story open, thus resigning it to the pornographic imagination that her father, Patrick Brontë, had always identified with the novelistic. In his book, *The Cottage in the Wood*, he had written: 'The sensual novelist and his admirer, are beings of depraved appetites and sickly imaginations, who having learnt the art of *self-tormenting*, are diligently and zealously employed in creating an imaginary world, which they can never inhabit, only to make the real world, with which they must necessarily be conversant, gloomy and insupportable.'[34] Literary endeavor becomes masturbation in Patrick's barely-coded epithet of 'self-tormenting'; the hothouse secrecy surrounding such employment accounts for its resultant depravity and sickliness.

Southey had warned her of such danger: 'The day dreams in which you habitually indulge are likely to induce a distempered state of mind; and, in proportion as all the ordinary uses of the world seem to you flat and unprofitable, you will be unfitted for them without becoming fitted for anything else. Literature cannot be the business of a woman's life, and it ought not to be.'[35] Southey's reference to Charlotte's 'habitual indulgence' also characterizes her ambition as a 'distempered,' diseased fixation for which the only prescription is healthy, self-abnegating work. The patronizing chauvinism of his attitude resonates through the uncredited allusion to Shakespeare. Here Southey, a male poet wielding masculine privilege through the words of another male poet, simultaneously implies that Charlotte has fallen into Hamlet's state, and invokes Hamlet's injunctions to Ophelia to 'get thee [to] a nunn'ry.'[36] *Villette* demonstrates Brontë's acceptance of Southey's implicit advice, as well as the perverse spin she put on it.

While the pseudonymical 'Currer Bell' occupied a high niche in literary opinion, her reviews harp on her 'depravities' even as they praise her 'Passion and Power.'[37] The *Christian Remembrancer* admits that Brontë has tempered 'the outrages on decorum, the moral perversity, the toleration of, nay, indifference to vice' which had 'deform[ed]' her *Jane Eyre*, but it joins numerous other critics of Lucy who decry her for her willingness to fall in love and her ability to be in love with two men at the same time or for her 'masculine' style.[38] Even reviewers who found *Villette* 'pleasant' criticized Lucy Snowe's morbidity and her 'tormenting self-regard.'[39] While all uniformly praised the abundance of well-drawn characters, they nonetheless bemoaned the lack of 'breathless suspense, more thrilling incidents, and a more moving story.'[40] Conversely, the story is said to move too much: the narrative jumps and the focus wavers.[41] Reviewers' desires seem to be piqued and frustrated at the same time.[42] Their complaints ironically vindicate the triumph with which Charlotte Brontë pursued her anomalous path. Eschewing simultaneously the need for closure and for the embodiment of desire in a female body, a containment that in Lewis enforces female powerlessness, Brontë frees the hallmark of the pornographic, the desire *for* desire,[43] into the space of literary contingency, as generations of readers and critics who have been teased by Lucy Snowe can testify.

NOTES

1. Clement Shorter, *The Brontës: Life and Letters*, 2 vols (New York: Haskell House Publishers, 1969), vol. 2, p. 362.

2. Nicholls had to find a substitute curate for Patrick Brontë's congregation and a priest to preside at the wedding. On the marriage day, Patrick Brontë suddenly refused to attend, and Nicholls had to find a substitute to give Charlotte away. Her friend, Miss Wooler, performed that function. On Charlotte Brontë's arrogation of fact to fancy in *Villette*, see Juliet Barker, *The Brontës* (New York: St Martin's Press, 1995), pp. 668, 704–5, 708, 713, 715. Cf. Claudia Klaver, 'Homely Aesthetics: *Villette*'s Canny Narrator,' *Genre* 26.4 (Winter 1993): 409–29.

3. A brief listing would include Robyn R. Warhol, 'Double Gender, Double Genre in *Jane Eyre* and *Villette*,' *SEL* 36.4 (Autumn 1996): 857–75; Patricia E. Johnson, ' "This Heretic Narrative": The Strategy of the Split Narrative in Charlotte Brontë's *Villette*,' *SEL* 30.4 (Autumn 1990): 617–31; John Kucich, *Repression in Victorian Fiction: Charlotte Brontë, George Eliot, and Charles Dickens* (Berkeley, Los Angeles, and London: Univ. of California Press, 1987); Nina Auerbach, *Woman and the Demon:*

The Life of a Victorian Myth (Cambridge MA and London: Harvard Univ. Press, 1982), pp. 127–8; Sandra Gilbert and Susan Gubar, *The Madwoman in the Attic: The Woman Writer and the Nineteenth-century Literary Imagination* (New Haven and London: Yale Univ. Press, 1979); Eve Sedgwick, *The Coherence of Gothic Conventions* (New York: Arno Press, 1980), especially ch. 3, 'Immediacy, Doubleness, and the Unspeakable: *Wuthering Heights* and *Villette*,' pp. 104–53.

4. On the importance of length, see Shorter, vol. 1, p. 382, and Herbert Rosengarten and Margaret Smith, introduction to *Villette* by Brontë, eds Rosengarten and Smith (Oxford: Clarendon Press, 1984), pp. xi–xlix, xv.

5. Quoted in Rosengarten and Smith, p. xv.

6. Rosengarten and Smith, p. xviii. Brontë's claim that 'she was unwilling to release her work for publication before it had been completed' flies in the face of other evidence. According to Elizabeth Gaskell, Brontë contemplated 'tales which might be published in numbers' (*The Life of Charlotte Brontë*, ed. Alan Shelstone (New York: Penguin, 1975), p. 293). I owe this information to Catherine A. Judd's 'Male Pseudonyms and Female Authority in Victorian England,' in *Literature in the Marketplace: Nineteenth-century British Publishing and Reading Practices*, eds John O. Jordan and Robert L. Patten (Cambridge: Cambridge Univ. Press, 1995), pp. 250–68, 264–5 n. 20. Barker records in *The Brontës* that Brontë had originally planned 'three distinct and unconnected tales which may be published either together as a work of three volumes of the ordinary novel-size, or separately as single volumes' (p. 499).

7. Judd forms one recent exception, drawing on the healthy precedent of Gaskell's treatment of Charlotte Brontë in *The Life*.

8. Luce Irigaray, 'Any Theory of the "Subject" Has Always Been Appropriated by the "Masculine,"' in *Speculum of the Other Woman*, trans. Gillian C. Gill (Ithaca: Cornell Univ. Press, 1985), pp. 133–46, 143.

9. See Ellen Moers, *Literary Women* (New York: Doubleday, 1976); Tamar Heller, '*Jane Eyre*, Bertha, and the Female Gothic,' in *Approaches to Teaching Brontë's 'Jane Eyre,'* eds Diane Long Hoeveler and Beth Lau (New York: Modern Language Association of America, 1993), pp. 49–55. Klaver aligns the Gothic elements, especially the nun, with 'typically Radcliffean devices to create suspense and speculation in her narrative, but then [Lucy], also like [Ann] Radcliffe, dismisses them all with the most banal of rational explanations' (p. 418). On the distinction between male and female Gothic, from which I wish to distance myself, see Robert Miles, *Gothic Writing, 1750–1820: A Genealogy* (London and New York: Routledge, 1993), especially pp. 88, 98, 103–4; and Anne Williams, *Art of Darkness: A Poetics of Gothic* (Chicago and London: Univ. of Chicago Press, 1995), pp. 18–24. She calls *The Monk* a pornographic narrative because sexuality is shown as the 'prime motive' of all action (p. 116). Yet to her, Ambrosio's carnality lines him up with the feminine.

10. By comparison, Bretton Hall and La Terrasse seem almost the only nonconfining spaces.

11. See Barker, pp. 160–1, 191, 500.

12. Linda K. Hughes and Michael Lund, 'Textual/Sexual Pleasure and Serial Publication,' in Jordan and Patten, pp. 143–64, 143.

13. A position shared by Warhol, p. 858.

14. Rather than being suffocated by the present's contradictory attitude to female authorship, Charlotte cleared space for herself by preserving the male pseudonym and simultaneously creating a very private female persona as the source for her literary output. See Judd's very persuasive discussion, especially pp. 252–3, 257–8.

15. This essay both draws on and modulates the work of Kucich. I find Kucich's discussion extremely attractive, especially his attention to the place of desire in Brontë's work, but he defines her desire as repressed (pp. 38–9); see p. 30 for his definition of repression. Cf. Steven Marcus, *The Other Victorians: A Study of Sexuality and Pornography in Mid-nineteenth-century England* (New York: Basic Books, 1964), especially p. 195. Marcus's attention to the pornographic fantasy of endless seminal fluid finds an interesting counterpart in Brontë's text, which increasingly spews out water imagery inextricably intertwined with eruptions of desire, whether frustrated or realized. For a small sample, see pp. 6, 152, 218–9, 221, 223, 258, 420–1 of *Villette*. The 'lecture pieuse' of Catholic martyrs incites the same pornographic response: 'it made me so burning hot, and my temples and my heart and my wrist throbbed so fast, and my sleep afterwards was so broken with excitement, that I could sit no longer' (p. 162).

    Obviously, *The Monk* fixed much of its pornographic gaze on the explicit sexuality of religious figures. Perhaps another telling resemblance between the two novels lies in *The Monk*'s greatest provocation to scandal: its censure of the Bible as pornographic. Though considerations of length prevent me from detailing Brontë's biblical allusions, she heretically rewrites the Bible as much as she piously cites it. Cf. Susan VanZanten Gallagher, '*Jane Eyre* and Christianity,' in Hoeveler and Lau, pp. 62–8; and Keith A. Jenkins, '*Jane Eyre*: Charlotte Brontë's New Bible,' in Hoeveler and Lau, pp. 69–75. Many of *Villette*'s citations are perverse applications of water, fountain, and thirst imagery originally found in the two books of 'Johns' – the Gospel according to John and Revelation; see John 4:13–5, 6:35, and 7:37 and Rev. 7:16, 14:7, and 22:17. I would suggest that, in this imbricated relationship, we find Brontë's greatest heresy, her incorporation of and twist on the pornographic imagination.

16. Gilbert and Gubar, p. 425.

17. Christina Crosby, 'Charlotte Brontë's Haunted Text,' *SEL* 24.4 (Autumn 1984): 701–15. LuAnn McCracken Fletcher articulates a similar position when she claims the nun emphasizes the fictionality of identity ('Manufactured Marvels, Heretic Narratives, and the Process of Interpretation in *Villette*,' *SEL* 32.4 (Autumn 1992): 723–46).

18. See Robert Heilman, 'Charlotte Brontë, Reason, and the Moon,' in *Critical Essays on Charlotte Brontë*, ed. Barbara Timm Gates (Boston: G.K. Hall, 1990), pp. 34–49, 36; and Harriet Martineau, 'Review of *Villette* by Currer Bell,' in Gates, pp. 253–6, 255. Janice Carlisle considers the nun a figure of repressed desire in 'The Face in the

Mirror: *Villette* and the Conventions of Autobiography,' in Gates, pp. 264–87, 282–3, while E.D.H. Johnson sees her as equal to the unreason Lucy must renounce (' "Daring the Dread Glance": Charlotte Brontë's Treatment of the Supernatural in *Villette*,' *NCF* 20.4 (March 1966): 325–36).

19. Q.D. Leavis, introduction to *Villette* (New York: Harper Colophon, 1972), p. xxiii, cited by Gilbert and Gubar, p. 683, n. 13. Review of *Villette* in *The Literary Gazette* (5 February 1853), repr. in *The Brontës: The Critical Heritage*, ed. Miriam Allott (London and Boston: Routledge & Kegan Paul, 1974), pp. 178–81, 180.

20. Matthew Lewis, *The Monk*, ed. Louis Peck (New York: Grove Press, 1952), p. 148. Citations will come from this edition and henceforth will be cited parenthetically.

21. See Max Byrd, 'The Madhouse, the Whorehouse, and the Convent,' *PR* 44.2 (Summer 1977): 268–78.

22. Brontë, *Villette*, eds Rosengarten and Smith, p. 423. All references to *Villette* will be to this edition and henceforth will be cited parenthetically in the text.

23. Cf. the descriptions of Baroness Lindenburg and Madame Beck in character (Brontë, pp. 95, 98, 100–2, 695–7; Lewis, pp. 123, 145); in habits of spying (Brontë, pp. 100, 421–2, 647; Lewis, p. 155); and in a taste for young men (Brontë, pp. 140–5; Lewis, pp. 147–50). Paul's history after the death of Justine-Marie reads like Raymond's fate had he not been freed from the Bleeding Nun. More importantly, when Lucy describes Paul as monitor of mores and the human heart, he suddenly resembles Satan (Brontë, pp. 486–7; Lewis, pp. 416–7).

24. As the Gothic novel reaches the end of its first phase with Charles Robert Maturin's *Melmoth the Wanderer*, the structural logic of substitution dominates the sexual logic.

25. Barker, p. 243. Thus, Carol Christ sees Brontë steeling herself to prefer a realist aesthetic, especially in *Villette*, as a means of subduing this mutinous attraction ('Imaginative Constraint, Feminine Duty, and the Form of Charlotte Brontë's Fiction,' *WS* 6.3 (1979): 287–96).

26. The phrase is Heilman's; see his 'Charlotte Brontë's "New" Gothic,' in *From Jane Austen to Joseph Conrad: Essays Collected in Memory of James T. Hillhouse*, ed. Robert Rathburn and Martin Steinmann Jr (Minneapolis: Univ. of Minnesota Press, 1958), pp. 118–32. I interpret her 'newness' very differently.

27. When the old woman emerges from the stone walls of the Rue des Mages, behind the portrait of her granddaughter, 'the portrait seemed to give way' (Brontë, p. 562).

28. Peter Brooks, *Reading for the Plot: Design and Intention in Narrative* (Oxford: Clarendon Press, 1984). Brooks's strictly male notion of desire and its accompaniments deforms his definition of women's plots as resistance and endurance: 'a waiting (and suffering) until the woman's desire can be a permitted response to the expression of male desire' (p. 330).

29. Lucy is not unique among Brontë's women in this respect: Eliza Reed in *Jane Eyre* and Sylvie in *The Professor* both enter convents. See Kucich, p. 92. Kate Millett has Lucy trying on and rejecting all of the alternative female role models (*Sexual Politics*

(New York: Doubleday, 1970), pp. 140–7, repr. in Gates, pp. 256–64). Joseph P. Boone calls the nun the 'false mirror of [Lucy's] sexuality' ('Depolicing *Villette*: Surveillance, Invisibility, and the Female Erotics of "Heretic Narrative,"' *Novel* 26.1 (Fall 1992): 20–42).

30. On Lucy as a 'silence artist,' see Sedgwick, pp. 130–1. Ultimately Sedgwick sees the nun as corresponding to the letters. Cf. Gilbert and Gubar's suggestion that 'Lucy is the nun who is *immobilized* by this internal conflict' (p. 412, my emphasis).

31. Cf. Kucich, p. 109.

32. Anne Mozley's unsigned review for the *Christian Remembrancer* (April 1853) shows that the narratorial and characterological heresy fused in the public's mind (repr. in Allott, pp. 202–8, 202).

33. Barker, p. 723.

34. Quoted in Barker, p. 243.

35. Barker, p. 262.

36. William Shakespeare, *The Tragedy of Hamlet, Prince of Denmark*, in *The Riverside Shakespeare*, 2nd edn, ed. G. Blakemore Evans (Boston and New York: Houghton Mifflin, 1997), pp. 1183–245, III.i.120.

37. G.H. Lewes in the *Leader* (12 February 1853), repr. in Allott, pp. 184–6, 184.

38. Mozley, p. 203. See esp. William Makepeace Thackeray's letters of March and April 1853, repr. in Allott, pp. 197–8.

39. Review of *Villette* in *The Spectator* (12 February 1853), repr. in Allott, pp. 181–4, 181.

40. Lewes, p. 184.

41. Mozley, p. 204; review of *Villette* in the *Athenaeum* (12 February 1853), repr. in Allott, pp. 187–90, 188; and review of *Villette* in *Revue Des Deux Mondes* (15 March 1853), repr. in Allott, pp. 199–200, 199.

42. Review of *Villette* in *Putnam's Monthly Magazine* (May 1853), repr. in Allott, pp. 212–5, 214.

43. On the link between the specularized female body and female powerlessness, see Elaine Scarry, *The Body in Pain* (Oxford: Oxford Univ. Press, 1992), pp. 207, 361 n. 20. Susan Faludie's article on the Hollywood porn industry shows male porn stars in suffering acknowledgment that the 'desire *for* desire' rules pornographic producers and consumers alike ('The Money Shot,' *New Yorker* (30 October 1995), pp. 64–87).

CHAPTER NINE

The Other Case: Gender and Narration in Charlotte Brontë's *The Professor*

ANNETTE R. FEDERICO

Annette Federico teaches English at James Madison University, Virginia. She researches the nineteenth-century novel and gender studies. Her publications include *Masculinity in Hardy and Gissing* (1991) and *Idols of Suburbia: Marie Corelli and Late-nineteenth Century Literary Culture* (2000). The article reprinted here deals with the issue of gender in Charlotte Brontë's *The Professor* by addressing the construction of masculinity in the text. Federico demonstrates that the Victorian theory of separate spheres as a necessary consequence of gender difference has adverse consequences for men as well as for women. She argues the case that Crimsworth undergoes a series of experiences leading to his recognition that supposedly feminine virtues of compassion and emotional sensibility are necessary for any whole personality.

Male novelists who use female narrators have been praised for their insights into 'feminine psychology,' yet we seldom expect women writers to represent masculinity from a male point of view. In her recent work on feminism and narratology, Susan Lanser considers 'the social properties and political implications of narrative voice,' claiming that 'female voice' – the grammatical gender of the narrator – 'is a site of ideological tension made visible in textual practice' (pp. 4–5). This tension is conspicuous in novels published in the nineteenth century: a strict literary double-standard reflects a cultural double-standard

Reprinted from *Papers on Language and Literature*, 30.4 (1994): 323–45.

that devalues feminine discourse in the public sphere. Like everything else, narrative voice corresponds to the cultural needs of Victorian society, and so an age comparatively rich in literary heroines (and in women writers) still finds the masculine voice more representative, and, supposedly, more rational, more 'objective.' Because narrative voice carries the burdens of Victorian gender polarization – in its representation of male or female language and the expectations it raises about masculine or feminine plots[1] – grammatical gender in a Victorian novel is as ideologically constructed as the gendered body inhabited by the author.

If narrative voice is a site of ideological tension, it is even more difficult to construe when a male voice is adapted self-consciously by women writers who call themselves 'Currer Bell' or 'George Eliot.' Indeed, because narrative authority conforms to rather than challenges 'hierarchical, patriarchal norms' (Cohan and Shires: 146) we can gain insight into the ways women who use male narrators understand gender relations, and how they reproduce masculinity – and with it, dominant discourse – in the choice of male language, preoccupations, and pursuits.

* * *

In her first novel, *The Professor*, Charlotte Brontë uses a first-person male narrator, and, as I will discuss, critics have tended to see this as both an artistic error and an elision of her feminist voice. But whether she takes a male or female narrator, Brontë is no less intent on examining the encoding of gender in nineteenth-century discourse. Specifically, the male voice provides an opening to confront a central issue for Brontë – power – which is different from her explorations of powerlessness in her later heroine-centered novels. In *The Professor*, she is learning what it is to have the power of authorship, and therefore it is consistent that she should go inside the system to attempt to represent the source of that power.[2]

Many psychoanalytic approaches to *The Professor* accept the 'feminization' of the male narrator as the woman writer's personal experience of subordination translated into a pseudo-male voice. Though this helps in understanding biographical issues and the so-called 'female imagination,' such readings tend to overlook how the appropriation of the male voice may challenge a tradition of androcentric narrative and Victorian patriarchal hegemony. As Terry Eagleton explains, one interpretation of feminism 'is not just that women should have equality of power and status with men; it is a questioning of all such power and status. It is not just that the world will be better off with more female participation in it; it is that without the "feminization" of human history, the world is unlikely to survive' (p. 150). Brontë engages this concern by using an intrinsically authoritative male voice to tell a story that is not about a heroine's traditional growth into power, but instead authorizes a masculine growth out of power by asserting the need to temper male authority with 'feminine' social virtues, usefully defined by Susan Morgan as 'gentleness, flexibility, openness to others, friendship, and love' (p. 19). At the same time, however, Brontë describes the practical and psychological obstacles to this 'feminization' for men who are subject to ideological constraints, particularly the insistence on sexual difference. For as Mary Poovey has persuasively argued, '[M]en were too thoroughly ensnared in the contradictions that characterized this ideology to be charged with being simple oppressors' (p. 22). William Crimsworth, the hero-narrator of *The Professor*, represents a view of masculinity that differs entirely from Brontë's later portraits of attractive and powerful men who threaten the heroine's autonomy. In her first novel, Brontë attempts to be the autobiographical male, to imagine what he imagines, even to have a male body[3] – in other words, to treat the burdens of sex from the male point of view, and thereby explore the social consequences of her culture's constructions of gender.

Critics tend to speak summarily about *The Professor*, written in 1846 and published posthumously in 1857. It is 'a rehearsal for *Villette*' (Lane: vii) or an early 'failed' attempt to create a heroine like Jane Eyre (Basch: 68–9). In *A Literature of Their Own*, Elaine Showalter mentions *The Professor* only briefly as an example of how 'women writers internalized the values of their society' (pp. 136–7). Even critics who turn their full attention to the novel, such as Helene Moglen and Sandra Gilbert and Susan Gubar, are conscious of a tendency to make excuses for its flaws. Moglen sees Brontë's choice of a male narrator as evidence that she is still 'bound to the ambivalent attitudes of adolescence,' unable to associate a female voice with authority; Crimsworth's voice is the novel's most 'crucial problem' (pp. 86–8). In *The Madwoman in the Attic*, Gilbert and Gubar concede that to discuss the novel as they have done 'in terms merely of roles and repressions is . . . to trivialize the young novelist's achievement in her first full-length book' (p. 335). Their descriptions of *The Professor* as an extension of Brontë's 'exotic "male"' Angrian tales full of 'obsessive and involuntary' characterizations (pp. 313–15), and as a 'pseudo-masculine *Bildungsroman*,' 'literary male-impersonation,' and 'male mimicry' (pp. 318–19) suggest that the novel's difficulties or flaws are linked to Brontë's handling of gender, especially the use of a male narrator. Instead of dismissing the narrator as a clumsy mistake by a young writer, Gilbert and Gubar at least try to make sense of the masculine voice, explaining that 'by pretending to be a man, [the woman writer] can see herself as the crucial and powerful Other sees her' (p. 317). To put it differently, by pretending to be male, Brontë can better analyze what really concerns her: being female.

Gilbert and Gubar make a similar argument about the male narrator in George Eliot's novella, *The Lifted Veil* (1859), a text that, like *The Professor*, has been either ignored or dismissed as an unsuccessful attempt by a relatively inexperienced writer of fiction.[4] Claiming Eliot's debt to Charlotte Brontë and Mary Shelley, Gilbert and Gubar see *The Lifted Veil* as a dramatization of Eliot's 'internalization of patriarchal culture's definition of the woman as "other"' (p. 466). The clairvoyant male narrator, Latimer, who finds women both fascinating and repulsive, is an expression of Eliot's divided consciousness and represents her attempt to survive 'in a male-dominated society by defining herself as the Other' (p. 476). 'Like Charlotte Brontë's early male persona . . . Latimer reflects his author's sense of her own peculiarity' (p. 447). In both *The Professor* and *The Lifted Veil*, then, the woman writer with the masculine pseudonym engages her own status as female Other by assuming the voice, the authority, and the privileged position of the male subject. In this interpretation, Brontë and Eliot are not concerned with the experience of the narrator as a man or the representation of masculinity; authorial voice is still tied to female 'schizophrenia,' a 'dis-ease with authority,' self-hatred, and internalization (Gilbert and Gubar: 444–5, 449).

Such readings are useful in their focus on the whole problem of 'otherness' for Victorian women writers. But to claim that a woman chooses a male voice in order to work out her ambivalence about being female narrows the ideological implications of otherness, as well as the revisionist possibilities of these texts. Indeed, the resonance of 'otherness' in these interpretations, with its suggestions of psychological oppression, indicates the problem inherent in women's writing, so that female subjectivity and feminist discourse is necessarily undermined by the constraints of man-made language.

* * *

The fact that the Brontës' books were called 'masculine' by contemporary reviewers and George Eliot's quasi-dramatized narrators arrogate masculine authority[5] suggests how well the language and voice of the male subject can serve the cause of sexual equality. 'In order to be a complete individual, on an equality with man, woman must have access to the masculine world as does the male to the feminine world, she must have access to the *other*' (de Beauvoir: 761). For Brontë and Eliot, as for many Victorian women, such access was not always possible. Brontë admitted as much in a letter to James Taylor written in 1849: 'In delineating male characters, I labour under disadvantages; intuition and theory will not adequately supply the place of observation and experience. When I write about women, I am sure of my ground – in the other case I am not so sure' (Shorter: 30). For Brontë, men occupy a world that is closed to her observation: masculine psychology and motivation are mysterious, impenetrable. He is truly 'the *other* case.' Yet if one accepts Carolyn Heilbrun's claim that 'No woman writer struggled as [Brontë] struggled against the judgments of sexual polarization' (p. 78), *The Professor* may be read as Brontë's earliest effort to confront the ideology of separate spheres. To tell a man's story is to insist on access, to insist on her complete individuality as a person and as an artist. Indeed, Brontë's interest in socialized gender roles, for boys in particular, is evident in a letter written to Miss Wooler just a year before she began *The Professor*:

You ask me if I do not think men are strange beings. I do, indeed – I have often thought so: and I think too that the mode of bringing them up is strange, they are not sufficiently guarded from temptations. Girls are protected as if they were very frail and silly indeed, while boys are turned loose on the world as if they, of all beings in existence, were the wisest and the least liable to be led astray. (Shorter: 315)

By using the voice of one of these 'strange beings' in *The Professor*, Brontë examines with a mixture of irony and compassion the moral and emotional immunity built into Victorian constructions of masculinity. As 'a tale of socialisation[,] of becoming masculine' (Boumelha: 47), *The Professor* is attentive to the costs of being indoctrinated into patriarchy, and of naturalizing characteristics Victorian society admired in men, such as fixity, dominance, exclusion, competition, and stoicism.

The voice of William Crimsworth, far from sounding 'curiously androgynous' (Gilbert and Gubar: 319), is aggressively masculine throughout his narrative, locked into a socially sanctioned tone of superiority. There is no feminine apologizing, no womanly code of docility. His voice approximates the literary qualities assigned to men, which Showalter has identified as 'power, breadth, distinctness, clarity, learning . . . shrewdness, knowledge of life, and humor,' along with 'masculine faults,' such as 'coarseness and passion' ('Double Standard': 340). In other words, Brontë, who aspires to professional status as a novelist, is writing as a professional – that is, as a man. Although Crimsworth tells the reader 'I always speak quietly,' and he is an idealistic young man, his language has a feel of license which for Brontë probably defined male discourse: 'to scout myself a privileged prig' (p. 77), or ' "Stuff! I have cut them" ' (p. 41). If the voice comes across as false machismo, it may be because Brontë felt permitted to be extreme. Crimsworth has a man's right to say what he wants, for the basis of his character is his relative power and his uneasy participation in various systems of oppression. Despite his physical weaknesses (he is near-sighted, and describes himself as thin and slight) and his temporary status as a dependent, Crimsworth's voice resonates with confidence. As it should. Simone de Beauvoir has claimed that 'One of the benefits that oppression confers upon the oppressors is that the most humble among them is made to *feel* superior . . . The most mediocre of males feels himself a demigod as compared with women' (xxviii). It is precisely this assumption of male power that Brontë seems to question. For Crimsworth *does* feel a demigod compared with women. He is not one of Brontë's feminine heroes, a man who 'must learn how it feels to be helpless and to be forced unwillingly into dependency' (Showalter, *Literature*, p. 152). For one thing, he has an Eton education.[6] He also has a choice of professions, and obtains some influential male friends – Hunsden, Brown, and Vandenhutten – who write letters of recommendation and advise him about his investments. The material conditions of his life are not unbearable, and unlike the heroine of *Villette* in a similar situation, he can at least walk down the streets without being harassed.[7] If gender in the novel is a semantic symbol denoting power, as Moglen suggests (p. 89), Crimsworth's masculinity automatically confers social and psychological advantages over, for example, Jane Eyre or Lucy Snowe. He does possess, at least to some degree, four qualities which define power in Victorian society: education, money, mobility, and autonomy (Newton: 7).

Nevertheless, Brontë begins *The Professor* with Crimsworth as a victim of male exploitation: his wealthy maternal uncles had refused to aid Crimsworth's dying mother, and for this (after accepting the ten years at Eton), Crimsworth denies any future aid. He is then pitted against the tyranny of his elder brother, Edward, who employs him as a clerk in his mill. He resents being treated as an inferior by other men ('I hate to be condescended to' [p. 19]), and loathes being his brother's 'slave' – a word Brontë applies almost obsessively to his situation in the first five chapters of the novel. Again, one is reminded of Brontë's heroines – particularly Jane and Lucy – when they suffer similar privations; although Jane longs for a new servitude, for example, the language of Brontë's heroine is nothing compared to the fierce resentment of her hero. According to Susanne Kappeler, 'The status of the slave . . . is not in itself objectionable or dehumanizing, it is only so in the context of a male being held a slave, that is to say, held like a woman' (p. 154). Crimsworth has been thoroughly emasculated, and Brontë understands this. By allowing himself to be treated as a slave, 'kept down like some desolate tutor or governess' (p. 17), he is obeying a feminine code of passivity which is mocked by his acquaintance Yorke Hunsden, who further insults his masculinity by telling him the only way he'll get ahead in the world is through a woman's agency: 'your only chance of getting a competency lies in marrying a rich widow, or running away with an heiress' (p. 31). Yet the apparent extremity of his situation does not approximate that of a governess, 'disconnected, poor, and plain' (*Jane Eyre*, p. 190), as much as it does that of any middle-class woman, who must rely on the charity of those in power for security.[8] But Crimsworth's position fails to call out the reader's sympathy because it is described in the self-satisfied tones of masculine authority; his superior attitude, as a man and an aristocrat, only invites us to objectify the desolate governess as the lowest of the low. The fact that the hero has been a victim of male oppression (his brother even whips him) does not quicken his sympathies for the oppressed; he seeks to exert his prerogative and find someone – and why not a woman? – to exploit in return. If he cannot do this materially, he will do it verbally in his narrative by, for example, privately abusing '"That slut of a servant"' who neglects to light his grate (p. 24). Crimsworth is disinherited and strange-looking, and he is brought low; obviously he is an example, along with Jane Eyre and Lucy Snowe, of Brontë's misunderstood misfits. But the voice of this novel is never really conscious of being perceived as less than fully human, which is the female experience of otherness: he always maintains the privilege of the masculine subject. Even after Brontë drops the artificial, epistolary opening with its male interlocutor, one has the feeling throughout the novel that the narratee is also male.[9] The absence of feminine consciousness contributes to this, of course, but there is also the narrator's complete failure of imagination when it comes to female experience, and his persistent distancing from and objectification of women.

For example, in the blighted industrial town where he goes to work 'with other slaves' (p. 31), Crimsworth's tendency is to view the feminine element with aloofness. He would deem it 'like a nightmare' to marry one of his six cousins, and especially abhors 'the large and well-modelled statue, Sarah.' The 'young, tall, and well-shaped' (p. 7) wife of his rich brother is dismissed as childish, and the other 'tall, well-made, full-formed, dashingly dressed' young ladies (sexually mature women clearly make him uncomfortable) are totally uninteresting: 'I considered them only as something to be glanced at from a distance; their dresses and faces were often pleasing enough to the eye: but I could not understand their conversation . . . When I caught snatches of what they said, I could never make much of it' (p. 181). Brontë did not approve of the accepted standards of female attractiveness – tall and full-figured, vain, coquettish – any more than she approved of the social ideal of masculinity. But she is even-handed enough to give the lie to Crimsworth's attitude of superiority. Yorke Hunsden tells the hero that it is his own fault if women do not find him interesting, for he is too narrow-minded to find *them* interesting: a man who only perceives otherness is deprived of the *pleasures* of equality. 'There are sensible as well as handsome women . . . women it is worth a man's while to talk with, and with whom I can talk with pleasure,' says Hunsden (p. 181). Instead, Crimsworth is drawn to the portrait of his dead mother, whom he resembles: he has her aristocratic features, such as the 'true and tender feeling' expressed in her face (p. 8). Every man Crimsworth knows, however, treats this susceptibility to emotion as a defect (even though most of the time they discover it by examining his physiognomy, rather than in any emotional words on his part), thereby applying pressure on Crimsworth to conform to a strict gender role. After ten years at Eton, it can be supposed that Crimsworth made only one friend, and this turns out to be a 'sarcastic . . . cold-blooded' man who could acceptably converse about the masters, but received Crimsworth's occasional allusions to beauty or sentiment with 'sardonic coldness' (p. 1). Hunsden judges Crimsworth's features as too like his mother's, saying 'There's too much of the sen-si-tive' (p. 19). And later, M. Pelet bluntly tells Crimsworth the 'weak point' in his character is 'the sentimental' (p. 79). These indictments of male feeling or 'weakness' work effectively to construct a masculine ideal that is stoic, shrewd, and masterful. The voice of *The Professor* is just such a man; that he is imbued with Charlotte Brontë's Romanticism does not really dilute her critique of sexual polarization. The 'bull-like,' aggressive Edward Crimsworth is a melodramatic villain, but he is also the cultural ideal of manliness, 'fine-looking,' 'well-made,' 'of athletic proportions,' a man with 'business-like habits' (p. 5). Brontë clearly calculates the emotional costs of a repressed sensibility in men: Edward mistreats his horse, is cruel to his brother, and eventually abuses his wife. But that he is thoroughly masculine is never questioned.

For his patient endurance of injustice, Crimsworth is labeled ' "a fossil," ' ' "an automaton," ' ' "an essential sap, and in no shape the man for my money" ' (p. 29) by the feminine-looking Hunsden. Brontë's loose, cynical tone describes masculine banter affecting to disguise care and compassion with sarcasm and insults. The masculine expression of emotion is couched in terms of perverse indifference – for example, Hunsden's sneering generosity and Crimsworth's constant refusal to express his gratitude. At one point, after Hunsden meets Crimsworth's future wife, Frances, the two men grapple on the street:

No sooner than we got into the street than Hunsden collared me . . . [H]e swayed me to and fro; so I grappled him round the waist. It was dark; the street lonely and lampless. We had then a tug for it; and after we had both rolled on the pavement, and with difficulty picked ourselves up, we agreed to walk on more soberly. (p. 215)

What seems like antagonism is more like a male version of an embrace, and points to the cultural prohibitions placed on expressions of affection between men.[10] The 'feminine' qualities of solicitude and compassion, which he identifies with his mother's portrait, are driven underground by other men in the novel who are equally bound by ideological constraints. The hero's 'feminization' is constantly embattled and subdued, despite his half-suppressed longing for love or the confession that, 'I am my mother's son, but not my uncles' nephew' (p. 42).

Crimsworth's voyage to Belgium initiates a psychological quest for the 'mother's son,' and, significantly, commences a conventional (feminine) love and marriage plot, as the hero seeks 'the mother who looms in each woman for the grown-up boy' (Rich: 152). In Brussels, he is forced to confront aspects of himself that both define and diminish his masculine identity. Crimsworth's tearful exclamation, 'Mother!' as he gazes on her portrait, echoes two earlier raptures: the strange 'reedy' and 'fertile' countryside draws the breathless cry, 'Belgium!' (p. 45), followed by the equally strange 'Pensionnat!' (p. 50) as Crimsworth gazes at the walls restraining the adolescent demoiselles. His maternal legacy emanates from a foreign landscape that is totally Other – Flemish, Catholic, French-speaking – for until this time, Crimsworth admits that 'feminine character' was as alien to him as Brussels. At the Pensionnat de Demoiselles, he has an opportunity to consolidate as well as to modify the *pleasure* of being a man – that is, of having personal power. But as we have already seen, in doing so he relinquishes the pleasures of sexual equality – the pleasures of shared humanity. For example, Crimsworth takes a scientific pleasure in studying the 'hundred specimens of the genus "jeune fille,"' but Brontë also makes it clear that the hero must unlearn what patriarchal, and capitalist, ideology has reinforced, and 'that unlawful pleasure, trenching on another's rights, is delusive and envenomed pleasure' (p. 166).

But the habit of privilege is difficult to surrender. Even when he arrives in Belgium – a foreigner, poor, without friends or connections – he is in the position of the masculine subject, almost immediately telling the reader about a 'picturesque,' though 'eminently stupid' Flemish housemaid, and seeking pretty faces under the bonnets of the demoiselles at the Pensionnat. Crimsworth is, in fact, virtually obsessed with knowing the mysterious female, but this may be less because Brontë is also obsessed with femaleness than with the fact that in creating a male figure she is engaged in a study of oppression from the inside. What nineteenth-century woman writer, taking a male voice, would not need to imagine how men see women? For if she doesn't know 'the other case' she does know what it is like to be the object of male scrutiny.

Along with the authority that comes with his status as professor, Crimsworth reveals an insufferable snobbishness based on his nationality, his aristocratic lineage, *and* his sexual superiority. If Brontë is using a male narrator to engage in fantasies of power, she nevertheless does not make that power attractive. This sexually fastidious man assumes almost immediately, for example, that Zoraide Reuter is 'an old duenna of a directress' (p. 55) or 'a stiff old maid' (p. 65), and totally dismisses the kind Madame Pelet as 'ugly, as only continental old women can be' (p. 59). His smug curiosity about the 'unseen paradise' of the demoiselles' garden reveals the degree of his unchallenged indoctrination into his rights as subject: 'I thought it would have been so *pleasant* to have looked upon a garden planted with flowers and trees, so *amusing* to have watched the demoiselles at their play; to have *studied* female character in a variety of phases, myself the while sheltered from view by a modest muslin curtain' (p. 54, my emphasis).

To handle male appropriation of the feminine from the center of masculine consciousness is crucial to Brontë's critique. Crimsworth's interest in the demoiselles as female 'specimens,' his sexual 'mastery' over both Zoraide Reuter and Frances Henri, his critical observations of young women's bodies and faces are precise means for developing and affirming his manliness. As Kappeler has explained, what is at stake in the objectification of women is the very basis of patriarchy and of masculine selfhood: 'His understanding of gender relations is at the very bottom of his understanding of himself, it informs his understanding and organization of society, and it informs his semantics, his symbolization of it' (p. 155). Brontë thus makes Crimsworth's masculinity and his discourse almost entirely dependent on how he relates to women. The 'sketches' of young women Crimsworth describes in close physical detail are all negatively stereotypic: viragos, coquettes, peevish brats, cool manipulators (there is one attentive student, Sylvie, who is also 'the ugliest . . . in the room' [p. 74]). The level of discomfort Crimsworth endures when confronting these womanly-looking students (p. 72) seems particularly sexual. This is adolescent female sexuality without the 'modest muslin curtain' to protect his *amour-propre*. The peep show, which would have displayed 'the angels and their Eden' (p. 64) and which protected Crimsworth from interacting with real women, has become uncomfortably confrontational. The professor who had earlier stated 'I am not easily embarrassed' (p. 66) can blush with shame when in the presence of the demoiselles.

More obvious, more prominent, shone on by the full light of the large window, were the occupants of the benches just before me, of whom some were girls of fourteen, fifteen, sixteen, some young women from eighteen (as it appeared to me) up to twenty: the most modest attire, the simplest fashion of wearing the hair, were apparent in all, and good features, ruddy, blooming complexions, large and brilliant eyes, forms full, even to solidity, seemed to abound. I did not bear the first view like a stoic: I was dazzled, my eyes fell . . . (p. 71)

Though disturbed by his sexual interest in young women, what is most troubling is their bold disregard for his privilege of objectifying them. 'If I looked at these girls with little scruple, they looked at me with still less' (p. 72). Their exhibitionism and their aggressive looks – 'An air of bold, impudent flirtation, or a loose, silly leer, was sure to answer the most ordinary glance from a masculine eye' (p. 84) – appalls Crimsworth.[11] He earlier has confessed how he deplores Pelet's free allusions to 'le beau sexe,' telling the reader, 'I abhorred, from my soul, mere licentiousness' (p. 59). Whereas these young women are abundantly female, they are not (with the exception of Frances) demurely feminine, and this is what Crimsworth both expects and requires. In fact, they are as rowdy as his male pupils: 'when it came to shrieking the girls indisputably beat the boys hollow' (p. 55). These deviants' sexual curiosity about him gives Crimsworth some relief from guilt about his voyeuristic fantasies. But finding his subjectivity challenged, he retrenches his power, he covers his emotional nakedness: 'I had buckled on a breast-plate of steely indifference, and let down a visor of impossible austerity' (p. 73). Thus psychologically armored, Crimsworth can reassert his subjective authority by repeatedly describing the now-repulsive physical features and the bold glances of his pupils (received 'with the gaze of stoicism' (p. 103)); he launches his erotic conquests over their sluggish minds instead of their bodies: 'Owing to her education or her nature books are to her a nuisance, and she opens them with aversion, yet her teacher must instil into her mind the contents of these books; that mind resists the admission of grave information, it recoils, it grows restive . . .' (p. 104). The use of the generic feminine pronoun in his discourse consolidates his subjective privilege.

This social form of power is based, of course, on the narrator's role as tutor; but it is equally based on gender (age is not much of a factor, since Crimsworth is only a few years older than his pupils) and is endowed with the eroticism that Brontë must certainly have felt simmering in the classrooms of the Pensionnat Heger, but which would have been unacceptable if described from a female point of view. Indeed, Crimsworth's insistence on his superiority to sexual temptation gives the lie to his professional disinterestedness, and only attests to the appreciable tensions of his situation. As if suspecting how impossible it is to believe a male teacher could show such self-control, he declares, 'Know, O incredulous reader! that a master stands in a somewhat different relation toward a pretty, light-headed, probably ignorant girl, to that occupied by a partner at a ball, or a gallant on the promenade' (p. 104). The incredulous (male) reader then receives privileged information about how women *really* are (or at least, how Belgian women really are). In those rare situations where prettiness and ignorance are not encouraged in order to attract male admiration, women are fully men's equals in aggressiveness and pride.

Crimsworth among the demoiselles seems an effort to correct patriarchy's appropriation and symbolization of women. At least twice Brontë deliberately calls attention to the fact that 'female character as depicted in Poetry and Fiction' (p. 76) is one-sided and sentimental. Crimsworth must discover that women are not 'earthly angels and human flowers' (p. 83). It would be a misreading to suppose that here Brontë castigates her own sex as mendacious, foolish, and sensual. On the contrary, it is to insist on women's individuality and full participation in human life. 'Give us back our suffering!' cries Florence Nightingale in *Cassandra* (p. 29), meaning give us back our faults, our humanity. It could be the motto for Brontë's entire *oeuvre*.

*   *   *

When Zoraide Rueter, a forerunner of Madame Beck in *Villette* and a woman who uses seduction and flattery to achieve her political ends, tells Crimsworth, 'men have so much more influence than women have – they argue more logically than we do; and you, Monsieur, in particular, have so paramount a power of making yourself obeyed' (p. 112), Brontë displays her awareness of two ideological assumptions. First, that to possess power of any kind is a virtue, and second, that it is intrinsically a male privilege. Zoraide's remark is intended to appeal to Crimsworth's vanity; but it also serves to remind him of his complicity in male dominance and the unearned advantages of masculinity. Later, when she is debased by his rejection of her, Crimsworth has an important revelation about his capacity for despotism:

I had ever hated a tyrant; and behold, the possession of a slave, self-given, went near to transform me into what I abhorred! There was at once a sort of low gratification in receiving this luscious incense from an attractive and still young worshipper; and an irritating sense of degradation in the very experience of the pleasure. When she stole about me with the soft step of a slave, I felt at once barbarous and sensual as a pasha. (p. 162)

Brontë makes it clear that power is sexually stimulating (it is important that Zoraide is 'attractive and still young'), and yet it is 'irritating' to
the masculine ego that he should derive pleasure from feminine submission. Nevertheless, Brontë obviously sees this intersection of power and
pleasure as a defining factor in male socialization, and she is critical of the
cultural myths that reinforce it, chiefly the doctrine of separate spheres
and women's economic dependence. When Frances insists on giving
lessons after they are married, for example, Crimsworth describes, in
chivalric terms, the egotistical pleasure of controlling women: 'There is
something flattering to a man's strength, something consonant to his
honourable pride, in the idea of becoming the providence of what
he loves – feeding and clothing it, as God does the lilies of the field'
(pp. 199–200). Here he does not feel a 'demigod' compared with women,
but God himself – 'it' becomes his creation, just as 'Woman' is an icon of
Victorian patriarchy. Brontë, though, undermines the intense pleasure of
the narrator's generosity and power: Crimsworth's God-like fantasy gives
way, and he 'permits' his wife to continue teaching. Physically, though,
during these negotiations, Crimsworth keeps Frances on his knee with
his arms tightly around her. He describes her as 'a mouse in its terror' and
says he holds her 'with restraint that was gentle enough, so long as no
opposition tightened it' (p. 199).[12]

Allowing his wife to work is not much of a concession, given the fact
that it is Frances's 'pleasure, her joy to make me still the master in all
things' (p. 223). Unlike Rochester, Crimsworth does not undergo 'the
inevitable sufferings necessary when those in power are forced to release
some of their power to those who previously had none' (Heilbrun: 57).
On the contrary, the 'feminization' of the male narrator involves very
little suffering. By the end of the narrative, Crimsworth even seems more
manly and powerful than ever: he continues to conceal his emotional
vulnerability, thinks of his love and his sexuality as a 'gift' to confer on
the 'penniless and parentless' Frances (he later refers to himself as 'a man
of peculiar discernment' for finding a plain woman sexually appealing)
and after they are married, continues to treat her as a 'docile . . . well-
trained child' (p. 219). Eventually Crimsworth and Frances open a school,
return to England, make sound investments, and retire with an independency. In this novel, to 'feminize' the hero is clearly not to symbolically
castrate him, nor have him killed during a voyage, nor have him submit
to a woman's influence. Still, despite Crimsworth's mastery over his wife
and his full participation in patriarchal hegemony, Brontë concludes *The
Professor* with an important critique of the system that produces male
privilege – produces, in effect, the disconcerting sexism of *The Professor*,
a novel written only a year before Brontë's feminist manifesto, *Jane Eyre*.

The real 'masquerade' in the novel has not been Charlotte Brontë as William Crimsworth (Gilbert and Gubar: 318), but the character of Crimsworth himself as a perfectly adjusted Victorian gentleman. Though he adopts a manly role – as master, squire, professor, husband, and, improbably, killer of rabid dogs – he finally questions the virtue of passing on a patriarchal legacy to his young son, Victor. Elaine Showalter writes, 'Victor Crimsworth will learn self-mastery in an all-male world' (*Literature*, p. 137). But Crimsworth's description of the all-male world of Eton is highly qualified, and the tone is clearly that of regret. Their neighbor, Hunsden, affirms that Victor's mother 'is making a milksop' – but, Crimsworth gives us Frances's retort: 'Better a thousand times he should be a milksop than what he, Hunsden, calls a "fine lad"' (p. 232). Despite Hunsden's praise of the boy's manly potential, Victor has the 'swelling germs of compassion, affection, fidelity' (p. 235) which threaten to undermine his development as a genuine 'good fellow.' But the suggestion that Eton will take care of these tendencies indicates that Brontë understands what an education in competition and mastery will produce, since after all, Crimsworth is a product of Eton, too. But Brontë also seems to understand that in a man's world such qualities are necessary to achieve material success – at the end of the novel we learn that Crimsworth's vicious older brother 'is getting richer than Croesus by railway speculations' (p. 237).

* * *

Descriptions of male mastery, voyeurism, or sexual suppression are not signs of Brontë's self-loathing, her disgust with the female body, or 'a characteristically female desire to comprehend the mysteries of femaleness' (Gilbert and Gubar: 321). On the contrary, the masculine voice of *The Professor* is a representation of Victorian masculinity. It is not a picture of unqualified heroism, nor is it an unqualified success as a realistic novel – I agree with those critics who find the narrator sometimes awkward, his choice of language occasionally only 'the verbal equivalents of aggressiveness' (Taylor: 7). But if we consider Brontë's limited experience, the novel is a fascinating transposition of her culture's construction of men as masters of their emotions, who are nonetheless driven by desires for power and sexual domination. Certain scenes seem remarkably insightful; for example, as a Victorian man who would have absorbed his culture's construction of the Other as virgin/whore, Crimsworth is fascinated with young women, but also ambivalent towards female sexuality. The attack of 'Hypochondria' he suffers after he has proposed to Frances has been interpreted both as his fear of sexual initiation (Moglen: 95–6), and as 'guilt for unresolved boyhood desires for his mother' (Maynard: 88). But his illness could also be provoked by the loss of his voyeuristic freedom: being sexually faithful to one woman significantly curtails his right to sexually dominate many women.

The sexual tensions of *The Professor* do reflect indirectly those felt by Victorian women; but the novel also attempts to comprehend the tensions felt by Victorian men who enjoyed the privilege of cultural subjectivity. For Brontë, such pleasure, linked to the exploitation of other human beings as 'specimens,' was morally dangerous – 'delusive and envenomed pleasure' as Crimsworth eventually concedes (p. 166). *The Professor* is a remarkable early effort to confront how Victorian ideologies of gender both form and limit personality, for in using a male voice, Brontë uncovers how the gender of her character largely makes him who he is.

In this sense, Brontë's confidently masculine, objectifying, often misogynist voice itself embodies anxieties about Victorian sexuality. And although each of Brontë's novels confronts issues of power, *The Professor* deals not with how to obtain power (the problem for Brontë's heroines), but how to outgrow the need for power. Crimsworth has the desire for power, but he also learns the terror of being powerful. It is specifically a masculine and middle-class problem, and perhaps the principal artistic inheritors of social privilege – middle-class male novelists – were unable to treat so studiously, from within a man's experience, their own complicity in Victorian society's treatment of women. Of course, it is important to acknowledge that any use of a male narrator is a reinscription of male authority and hence of male power – male narrators generally tend to be invested with authority, and this leaves the reader with the difficult question of how we evaluate a novelist's perspective on a first-person narrator. And it is certainly feasible – and probable – that Crimsworth's scorn for Belgian Catholics, for example, is an indirect expression of Brontë's feelings based on her experiences at M. Heger's pensionnat. Though these considerations are important, they do not, I think, on the whole obscure Brontë's interrogation of Victorian gender roles. The whole experience of socialized gender may have been more recognizable to women writers, who have not only felt social prejudice more acutely, but have a greater awareness of themselves as sexually defined members of society. In this sense, the mid-Victorian woman writing from the male perspective has the difficult task of reproducing a voice which trivializes her experiences, while at the same time maintaining an alternative, subtextual authority – her own – with its insider's knowledge of the conditions of women's lives. This double perspective in literature may be connected with her double consciousness as a middle-class woman living within a patriarchal, capitalist society; she is part of the dominant culture, but she occupies a place separate and inferior within it. If nothing else, because Brontë chooses in *The Professor* to negotiate, rather than ignore, this double perspective, she amplifies the importance of recognizing the gendered nature of all discourse.

NOTES

1. These segregated terms seem to undercut any critique of gendered language or narrative that Brontë might have wished to engage. But a pervasive Victorian ideology of separate spheres has led modern readers quite naturally to construct readings of these texts largely based upon sexual difference. To refer to male or female language, male/quest or female/marriage plots, male or female *Bildungsromane*, etc., is almost unavoidable. What is interesting is how some women novelists who use male narrators still produce a heroine-centered story and a female plot. George Sand's *Indiana* (1832), for example, is narrated by a man, but the book belongs to the heroine entirely, as does, to a lesser extent, Willa Cather's *My Antonia* (1918). Brontë's eponymous narrator, on the other hand, is not telling a woman's story, he is telling his own; the heroine is secondary. This is important to keep in mind in an attempt to understand Victorian attitudes towards sexual polarity, since even the title of a novel may be an attempt to raise expectations in terms of plot, literary value, and even language. George Eliot's masculine titles (*Silas Marner*, *Adam Bede*, *Daniel Deronda*) signal a male-centered story, though women are more often than not the psychological focus. Dealing with 'masculine' and 'feminine' language is difficult without falling into facile stereotypes. Brontë's narrator, however, uses language that is marked, sometimes exaggeratedly, as masculine according to Dale Spender's use of gender differences as described by linguists: men's speech is 'forceful, efficient, blunt, authoritative, serious, effective, sparing and masterful' (*Man Made Language*, p. 33). This is certainly the style of speech the narrator often adopts, usually as a way to hide certain 'feminine' propensities.

2. Charlotte Brontë sought professional advice, and she wanted to be published. More than her sisters Emily and Anne, she wished to be a professional novelist, and 'regardless of any woman writer's ambivalence toward authoritative institutions and ideologies, the act of writing a novel and seeking to publish it . . . is implicitly a quest for discursive authority: a quest to be heard, respected, believed, a hope of influence' (Lanser: 7).

3. For a woman writer, to imagine what it is like to be a man seems difficult enough even today. When recently asked in an interview if she felt able to imagine what it is like to live in a male body, American novelist Mary Gordon said, 'To be larger . . . Not to be afraid of being raped . . . No, I can't imagine it yet' (p. 25; 'Love Has Its Consequences,' *The New York Times Book Review*, August 8, 1993: 1+). This suggests that the greatest challenge for some women writers may be imagining personal

security and control of the body in a society hostile to women. As Lanser explains, 'the authorial mode has allowed women access to "male" authority by separating the narrating "I" from the female body' (p. 18). But Brontë seems yet unable to separate her male 'I' from her female body: it is significant that Crimsworth sometimes feels sexually threatened. Penny Boumelha has pointed out that in the episode where he is invited to tea with Madame Pelet and Madame Rueter 'he undergoes a fantasy of rape-seduction far more fearful and explicit than anything Brontë assigns to her female characters' (p. 43).

4. Beryl Gray's Afterword to the 1985 Virago edition briefly summarizes the novel's reception: Henry James called it a '*jeu d'esprit*,' Marghanita Lanski a 'sadly poor supernatural story,' and Christopher Ricks 'the weirdest fiction she ever wrote' (*The Lifted Veil*, pp. 69–70).

5. In the 'Biographical Notice' to the 1849 edition of *Wuthering Heights*, Brontë wrote that she and her sisters chose pseudonyms 'without at that time suspecting that our mode of writing and thinking was not what is called "feminine."' Most readers of *Scenes of Clerical Life* and *Adam Bede* did not doubt that 'George Eliot' was a man (although Dickens was convinced the author was female), and her publisher, John Blackwood, continued to address Eliot as a man even after he knew her true identity. See Redinger: 332–4.

6. However much he despised Eton, his training there is instrumental to his status as hero, and comes in handy when the boat of one of his Flemish pupils capsizes: 'I had not been brought up at Eton and boated and bathed and swam there for ten long years for nothing; it was a natural and easy act for me to leap to the rescue' (p. 174).

7. In chapter 7, when Lucy Snowe first arrives in the city, she is warned that it is too late 'for a woman to go through the park alone'; she is subsequently followed by two insolent men whom she calls 'my dreaded hunters.' They pursue her until she is 'out of breath . . . my pulses throbbing in inevitable agitation' (p. 125).

8. Brontë was severely critical of women's economic dependence within marriage. She wrote to Ellen Nussey (August 9, 1846), 'I do not wish for you a very rich husband, I should not like you to be regarded by any man ever as "a sweet object of charity."'

9. Lanser has observed that in *Jane Eyre*, the female voice is insistently and personally 'in contact with a public narratee in the manner of the "engaging" authorial narrator' (p. 185), and I think this is true partly because, for most of the story, Jane's voice represents many voices: 'Millions are condemned to a stiller doom than mine, and millions are in silent revolt against their lot . . . Women feel just as men feel . . . It is thoughtless to condemn them . . .' (p. 141). Rhetorically, personal contact with a reader who may be sceptical or complacent is crucial in *Jane Eyre*, for Brontë wants to change the reader's way of thinking about governesses, class privilege, beauty, even novel-writing. There are addresses to the reader in *The Professor*, but they do not have the same urgency for connection with an oppressed class.

10. Ruth Johnston views this episode, in the context of Lacan's theory of the production of the subject/reader, as another way of alienating the reader by withholding

knowledge and the identification necessary in realism (pp. 370–1). But the scene is accessible if we think of the pressures of Victorian manliness. Brontë may have been describing the constraints for men in expressing their affections within the polarized bounds of 'male' reason and 'female' emotion. Of course, the scene can also be read as homosocial bonding.

11. Beth Newman's ' "The Situation of the Looker-On": Gender, Narration, and Gaze in *Wuthering Heights*' uses Lacanian theory to discuss the implicit gendering of gaze, associating the female gaze with male castration anxiety.

12. Basch (pp. 165–66) and Moglen (pp. 64–77) identify a pattern in Brontë's fiction, based on her belief in romantic love, where the woman's pleasure is derived from feeling physically overpowered at the same time that she successfully asserts her autonomy.

WORKS CITED

Basch, Francoise. *Relative Creatures* (New York: Schocken, 1974).

Boumelha, Penny. *Charlotte Brontë* (New York: Harvester, 1990).

Brontë, Charlotte. *The Professor* (1857; London: Dent, 1969).

Brontë, Charlotte. *Jane Eyre* (1848; Harmondsworth: Penguin, 1988).

Brontë, Charlotte. *Villette* (1853; Harmondsworth: Penguin, 1985).

Cohan, Steven and Linda M. Shires. *Telling Stories: A Theoretical Analysis of Narrative Fiction* (New York: Routledge, 1988).

de Beauvoir, Simone. *The Second Sex*, trans. H.M. Parshley (New York: Vintage, 1952).

Eagleton, Terry. *Literary Criticism: An Introduction* (Minneapolis: Univ. of Minnesota Press, 1983).

Gilbert, Sandra, and Susan Gubar. *The Madwoman in the Attic: The Woman Writer and the Nineteenth-century Literary Imagination* (New Haven: Yale Univ. Press, 1979).

Gray, Beryl. Afterword. *The Lifted Veil*, by George Eliot (New York: Virago, 1985), pp. 69–91.

Heilbrun, Carolyn. *Towards a Recognition of Androgyny* (New York: Norton, 1973).

Johnston, Ruth D. '*The Professor*: Charlotte Brontë's Hysterical Text, or Realistic Narrative and the Ideology of the Subject from a Feminist Perspective,' *Dickens Studies Annual* 18 (1989): 353–80.

Kappeler, Susanne. *The Pornography of Representation* (Minneapolis: Univ. of Minnesota Press, 1986).

Lane, Margaret. Introduction. *The Professor*, by Charlotte Brontë (London: Dent, 1969).

Lanser, Susan Sniader. *Fictions of Authority: Women Writers and Narrative Voice* (Ithaca: Cornell Univ. Press, 1992).

Maynard, John. *Charlotte Brontë and Sexuality* (Cambridge: Cambridge Univ. Press, 1984).

Moglen, Helene. *Charlotte Brontë: The Self Conceived* (New York: Norton, 1976).

Morgan, Susan. *Sisters in Time: Imagining Gender in 19th-century British Fiction* (New York: Oxford Univ. Press, 1989).

Newman, Beth. ' "The Situation of the Looker-On": Gender, Narration, and Gaze in *Wuthering Heights*,' *PMLA* 105 (1990): 1029–42.

Newton, Judith Lowder. *Women, Power, and Subversion: Social Strategies in British Fiction, 1778–1860* (Athens: Univ. of Georgia Press, 1981).

Nightingale, Florence. *Cassandra* (1852; New York: Feminist Press, 1979).

Poovey, Mary. *Uneven Developments: The Ideological Work of Gender in Mid-Victorian England* (Chicago: Univ. of Chicago Press, 1988).

Redinger, Ruby. *George Eliot: The Emergent Self* (New York: Knopf, 1979).

Rich, Adrienne. *Of Woman Born* (New York: Norton, 1976).

Shorter, Clement. *The Brontës: Life and Letters*, 2 vols (1908; New York: Haskell, 1969).

Showalter, Elaine. *A Literature of Their Own* (Princeton: Princeton Univ. Press, 1977).

Showalter, Elaine. 'Women Writers and the Double Standard,' *Woman in Sexist Society*, eds Vivian Gornick and Barbara K. Moran (New York: Basic Books, 1971), pp. 323–43.

Spender, Dale. *Man Made Language* (London: Routledge, 1980).

Taylor, Anne Robinson. *Male Novelists and Their Female Voices: Literary Masquerades* (Troy, NY: Whitston, 1981).

CHAPTER TEN

Edward Rochester and the Margins of Masculinity in *Jane Eyre* and *Wide Sargasso Sea*

ROBERT KENDRICK

At the time when he wrote this article, Robert Kendrick taught English at the University of Southern Illinois. The essay is included as an example of the recent use of adaptations of various kinds and of sequels and prequels to provide readings of the texts. In this instance the material used is Jean Rhys's *Wide Sargasso Sea* (1966), which recounts events that supposedly happened before Rochester returned to England and imprisoned his wife in the attic at Thornfield. Using Rhys's novel Kendrick aims to reveal a new sub-text in *Jane Eyre* relating to the contemporary construction of masculinity.

Though Edward Rochester is neither the central figure of Charlotte Brontë's *Jane Eyre* nor of Jean Rhys's complement text *Wide Sargasso Sea*, he nevertheless occupies a crucial position in each text – in *Jane Eyre*, he is the desired object of Jane's romantic 'quest' (Friedman: 119), while in *Wide Sargasso Sea* he is the immediate manifestation and enforcer of the network of patriarchal codes (sexism, colonialism, the English Law, and the 'law' which demarcates and creates sanity and insanity) that imprisons Antoinette Cosway. Though the literary and political relationship between Rhys's and Brontë's texts has received increasing amounts of attention in the past decade, the emphasis on defining the relationship between Jane and Antoinette/Bertha as either antagonistic or complementary has failed to give due consideration to the changing role

Reprinted from *Papers on Language and Literature* 30.3 (1994): 235–56.

of the man who profoundly influences and irrevocably alters their lives. Though the changes that occur in the characters of Antoinette and Jane have been much noted and discussed, the efforts of feminist readings to chart Antoinette's and Jane's rearticulations of their relations to the patriarchal discourses embodied by Rochester have not explored fully the possibility that Edward himself rearticulates and redefines his position as a masculine subject, as he reexamines the ethical implications of the masculine prerogatives that he has enjoyed and abused. This question must be addressed if the depth and potential of Brontë's ethical revision of gendered subjectivity in her 'original' work, and the reaffirmation of this re-vision in Rhys's 'supplement,' are to be recognized, for the novels of Brontë and Rhys offer intriguing representations of how Victorian subjects lived at odds with the dominant cultural narratives of class and gender. [. . .]

Rhys presents the anti-*Bildungsroman* of the young Edward Rochester. He has left England as a younger son of the landed gentry (though the Rochesters are quite wealthy, the family is not titled), but without money and holdings of his own he does not fit his class's narrative of a mature male subject. Presumably, the mercenary marriage to Antoinette Cosway Mason will enable Edward to assume his 'proper' place, but as Rhys's novel illustrates, this marriage threatens some dissolution, some ultimate inability to imagine himself within the dominant ideological frame as a 'mature' or 'whole' male subject.

This frame can best be understood by the model presented by Kaja Silverman in *Male Subjectivity at the Margins*. Complementing Althusser and Lacan, Silverman argues that ideological identification is the result of the entry into the various symbolic discourses which constitute the lived relation to the world (p. 34). [. . .]

Shortly after Edward's voice begins Part Two, he attempts to contain the apprehension, and perhaps fear, that lies underneath his inability to 'make sense' out of the environment in which he finds himself. Though he wishes to impose a sense of closure and order – the first words in his voice are 'So it was all over, the advance and retreat, the doubts and hesitations' (p. 66) – it is clear that such closure will prove elusive. Indeed, the first example of his interaction with another results in his own misreading and self-misrecognition. When Amélie greets him with 'I hope you will be very happy, sir, in your sweet honeymoon house,' Edward is aware that the greeting is parodic and mocking, that 'She was laughing at me I could see' (p. 66). Though he recognizes that he is being laughed at, he cannot tell why, and as a result Amélie's laughter cannot be contained within a frame that will allow him to see himself reflected in her response as he would wish to. Her supplementary laughter is not an affirmation of his position and the power attached to it, but rather a demonstration of his own dependence upon her recognition of this power and position if it is to maintain its status as the 'real.' [. . .]

Rochester, though, introduces the possibility that he is not to be himself, ever. In the letter he imagines himself writing to his father, he thinks 'I have sold my soul or you have sold it, and after all is it such a bad bargain? The girl is thought to be beautiful, she is beautiful. And yet . . .' (p. 70). His soul/self has been sold, and the veracity of the new mirrors for his self-identification – Colonial society (the girl is thought to be beautiful) and Antoinette herself – is questioned by the taint of the 'and yet . . .' which lies behind them. When Edward first attempts to reduce Antoinette's 'otherness' by imagining her as 'any pretty English girl,' and compares the soil to that of England, Antoinette responds with the parodic echo of 'Oh England, England,' a (mis)repetition that to Rochester 'went on and on like a warning I did not chose to hear' (p. 71). By the end of Part Two's first section, it is evident that Edward has entered a space in which his discourses of ideological and subjective identification are to be deconstructed by the very 'subjects' that these discourses would create, Antoinette, the 'half-castes,' and the ex-slaves. Their refusals to recognize Rochester on his terms introduce the possibility of his own lack, and he closes the section with 'There are blanks in my mind that cannot be filled up' (p. 76).

The marriage between Edward and Antoinette is destined to fail as a result of the disjuncture between their respective imaginings of the marital bond. Antoinette developed an awareness of the 'lack' that was forced upon her at an early age. The castigation of her family as ex-slave holders by both the new colonials and the newly freed Blacks, the burning of Colibri by vengeful ex-slaves, the rock thrown at her by the ex-slave girl Tia, her 'rejection' by her mother, and her upbringing in a Catholic Convent (in an English colony) all mark her as caught within the 'blank' spaces of the ideological imaginings of race, class, and family in Colonial Jamaica. Her position is such that even the nature of her particular marginalization cannot be recognized fully by her 'peers.' 'They are safe,' she says of the girls at the Convent, 'How can they know what it can be like outside?' (p. 59). It is not possible for Antoinette to escape outside the bounds of these narratives as long as she lives in Jamaica. It is possible, however, for her to attempt to renegotiate her relation to the discourses through which she lives her relation to material culture. Though it is not of her design, the arranged marriage to Rochester allows for this possibility. Initially, she rejects the match because she perceives, quite rightly, that Rochester will not accept her unconditionally, and will not attempt to see her as a woman who does not 'lack' anything. She does not wish to marry Rochester because she is 'afraid of what may happen' – that he will force her back into the state of dereliction which has been prescribed for her. His response, that 'I'll trust you if you trust me' would seem to imply that he is willing to provide the unconditional acceptance she desires. However, he follows this promise with 'Is that a bargain,' an utterance which introduces the discourses of exchange and thereby hints at his real reasons for entering into the relationship. Though Edward promises her 'peace, happiness, and safety,' he will not accept her as an unconditionally loved equal. To the contrary, Rochester accepts her only because of the symbolic value she carries within the dominant order – her fortune and her beauty make her a prized possession for him, an easy way to acquire his status as an 'independent' gentleman.

The irony is, of course, that the very means by which Rochester would establish himself as a mature subject results in his inability to do so. By attempting to imagine Antoinette into the role of a proper English wife, he is forced to recognize her ultimate inability to conform to the discourses which constitute the normal within the frame of English upper class subjectivity. She is neither English nor a properly Anglicized Creole, and the possibility of madness and alcoholism in her family further distances her from Edward's imagined normal. In addition, Antoinette and the others in the house continue to act as his 'unreflective' mirrors. Antoinette is 'uncertain about facts' – but they are his facts, not hers. She is 'careless' with the family's money, distributing it to her cousins, brothers, and sisters, whom he does not recognize as 'legitimate.' Finally, Antoinette herself is not 'reflective' in the same manner as Edward. When she shares with him the narrative of her encounter in the mirror with the rats, she presents an image of an unresolved, unreturned gaze into the mirror that ultimately 'tells' nothing. All that she recounts is that 'I could see myself in the looking-glass the other side of the room, in my white chemise with a frill round the neck, staring at those rats and the rats quite still, staring at me' (p. 82). The act of reflection says nothing about either her or the rats – they are simply there, in suspension. When Rochester looks to her for his own legitimizing reflection, he is left in the same aporia. Lacking a proper English wife, he cannot in turn imagine himself as a proper English husband, and as the novel progresses the blank spaces threaten to eclipse the 'definite' self-image of Edward Rochester. [. . .]

He has no desire to renegotiate his position *vis à vis* the dominant narrative(s), and, if anything, he wishes for others to accommodate themselves to his imaginings, as illustrated by his attempt to figure an Anglicized Bertha out of Antoinette. This attempt represents another unsuccessful effort at covering up the threat that Antoinette's refusal to recognize Edward's 'legal' authority and subjectivity presents. Though the dominant Colonial narrative opposes English laws and customs to Christophine's obeah, Antoinette reveals that the underpinnings of English narratives are as 'false' and 'primitive' as those which lie outside the bounds of official culture. 'Bertha is not my name,' she says, 'You are trying to make me into someone else, calling me by another name. I know, that's obeah too' (p. 147). [. . .]

Antoinette's particular form of subjection, in this instance, illustrates the inability of law to insure justice. Antoinette has been 'subjected' to a position of lack by the dominant narratives, and the 'peace' (p. 79) she desires is that of an unconditional acceptance by Edward. Edward, however, desires to see himself reflected as a subject of the English Law, which will not allow for anything to be 'unconditional' precisely because it is a code of mandates and conditions. It would appear that for Antoinette, justice is impossible because it represents a moment of aporia. [. . .]

What makes the retreat back to 'England' impossible is that Rochester has seen and lived enough in the West Indies to have recognized the 'truth' of the game of legal and legitimate subjects under the Law, to know that he is not, and will never be, anything other than a subject who is haunted by the recognition that 'Edward Rochester' was always-already 'lost' before he was found in any ideological imagining. It is certainly no accident that his final passage in Part Two is marked by the presence of the same stream-of-consciousness, 'insane' narrative flow that marks Antoinette's, though their voices are still quite distinct. The calm, rational Edward Rochester recognized and imagined within the English order remains, but only as an attempt to veil the 'madness' and misrecognition which has come to the fore in the West Indies and which cannot be erased. As Friedman has suggested, Rhys's novel casts the credibility of 'Edward Rochester' in doubt, but not because he has been rewritten as '. . . his own author [who] . . . creates a narrative in which he is no longer insufficient, in which he achieves mastery' (p. 122), because he possesses the awareness that his attempts to do so ultimately lead him back to a position of insufficiency and 'slavery.' Though he will hide Antoinette/ Bertha away in an 'English' house, she will nonetheless remind him constantly of the fictive nature of this hiding, and of the identity he has created that is founded on keeping 'her' hidden. Rochester's credibility is in doubt not just in the eyes of the reader, as Friedman maintains, but in his own eyes as well. When one approaches Brontë's text after reading Rhys's, this change makes it difficult for readers of *Jane Eyre* to position Rochester as a stock representative of the patriarchy, because he cannot see himself as such, even before his supposed emasculation/maiming during the Thornfield fire. At the end of Rhys's novel Edward is at the margins of Victorian masculinity precisely because he is aware of the fictive nature of the dominant narrative, though he is unable at this point to identify securely with any other imagining of himself. [. . .]

Brontë's Edward will, however, move in this direction as *Jane Eyre* unfolds. Rhys's novel, in presenting the reader with a Rochester who has lost complete belief in the dominant narratives of male subjectivity, enables one to envision his character in a somewhat different light than one might be accustomed to, both before and after the burning of Thornfield by 'Bertha.' The Rochester that Rhys creates is not so much a wholesale revision of Brontë's existing creation as a reillumination and reemphasization of aspects that are present, though perhaps not stressed, in the Rochester of *Jane Eyre*. Reading Rhys's Rochester 'first' allows for the recognition that Brontë's Edward Rochester, far from being a man who quite unproblematically occupies the position of Victorian patriarch and who retains this position after his inconveniently mad wife and obstacle to his freedom is eliminated, represents a man who is quite at odds with the dominant narrative of being an 'English Gentleman' and who does not attempt to reenter this narrative after his position within it has been rendered untenable by Bertha/Antoinette's act of revenge.

As Sandra M. Gilbert and Susan Gubar note, Edward Rochester's first appearance in *Jane Eyre* is by way of a pratfall, while his dog comes off looking more myth-like and masterful than he (pp. 351–2). The 'spell' of the Gytrash is broken by the actual appearance of Edward, who as a 'human being, broke the spell at once' (*Jane Eyre*, p. 115). Gilbert and Gubar note that this incident indicates that 'the master's mastery is not universal' (p. 352), and indeed, it would appear that each of this Edward's attempts at playing the patriarch in England, like those of Rhys's Edward in the West Indies, ultimately demonstrates the limits of his power and his own insufficiency. The first exchange between Edward and Jane illustrates this dynamic. Though it would be easy to read their first conversation as an example of Edward's assumption of the position of the Socratic 'master' leading Jane by induction with questions that he can already answer 'correctly,' the doubts raised by Rhys's Rochester suggest another possible reading. When Edward asks 'Whose house is this,' and 'Do you know Mr Rochester,' he is asking Jane to participate in the dominant narrative which authorizes him as the master. By asking Jane to acknowledge his status, rather than simply declaring it to her (as does the young John Reed, for example) Rochester is revealing that his 'mastery' is only the result of his being recognized by a believing audience of 'servants.' When it is revealed that Jane is the Governess – neither Edward's class equal nor his inferior at Thornfield (Eagleton: 35) – her helping Edward and delivering the letter for him function not so much as affirmations but as suspensions of Rochester's desire for recognition. Aside from and in addition to her own 'spunks,' Jane's ambiguous class status as a Governess prevents her from being an adequate mirror for Edward. In addition, Jane has learned that in the game of the dominant narrative, the master's recognition as a subject must come at the expense of her own. Her experiences with John Reed and Mr Brocklehurst have shown her the stakes in the legitimacy game, and although she cannot escape England and its ideological imaginings, she can nonetheless exploit her marginal position as Governess to allow her some means of negotiation with, rather than subjection to, these narratives.

It is precisely this refusal to submit to patriarchal discourses that makes Jane the only fit match for Edward. As Parama Roy quite correctly notes,

Jane and Rochester are both victims of the conventions of the English landed class – he by virtue of being an insider, she . . . by virtue of being an outsider. It may not unreasonably be argued that Rochester's miseries and corruption stem from his subservience to the demands of his situation. (p. 719)

They are 'right for each other' because each realizes the fictive nature of the dominant ideologies of gender and class. This does not mean, however, that they can run off together to a paradise outside of ideology. Rochester's wish that 'I were in a quiet island with only you: and the trouble, and danger, and hideous recollections removed from me' (p. 205) does not represent anything like an adequate solution to the problem of his and Jane's antagonistic relation to the discursive structures in and under which they live. The attempt to escape to a place of wholeness, where there is no ideological contradiction and no lack evident in an imagined 'Edward Rochester,' is an unfulfillable fantasy. If he is to create an 'Edward Rochester' that can live with Jane Eyre, then he must attempt to embrace ideological contradiction, lack, 'hideous recollections,' and the disruptions that they bring to the gender and class fiction that he is expected to live up to.

It is for this reason that his imagined solutions to what he regards as his problem – not having a wife who will recognize him as an authoritative subject – cannot succeed. Taking Jane as his illegal wife or as his mistress is an attempt to erase Bertha and the 'problem' she represents for Rochester – the problem of his own representation *vis à vis* others within the dominant fictions. Brontë, and her heroine, will not allow for any sort of closure to occur within the dominant narratives, and this would include the closure created by Edward's attempted elimination of both Jane's and Bertha's problematic status by co-opting the former as his mistress so that he may forget the latter. Brontë's Jane, like Rhys's Antoinette, exists to sustain narrative disjunctures, rather than to cover them up.

Though she says that she will eventually forgive Edward for his attempt to trick her into revealing herself to him while he is disguised as the gypsy, she does not answer his question, 'What does that grave smile . . . signify?' (p. 205), and as a result nothing is revealed and resolved except that Edward has once again demonstrated the limits of his own power. A similar pattern occurs during their other exchanges while she is at Thornfield. During one of the most important of these, the discussion about the nature of laws, Edward proclaims that 'unheard-of combinations of circumstances demand unheard-of rules' (p. 141). This is, ironically, both his presumed justification for confining Bertha and attempting to take Jane as his illegitimate wife and the eventual justification that will underlie his future 'just' marriage to her. The difference between the two 'unheard-of' solutions is that in the first case, Rochester does not defer to any other authority. His transgressions, in the form of the mercenary marriage and subsequent abuse of Bertha, and his attempt to marry outside the codes that sanction marriage, are not so much violations of the patriarchal norm as they are exaggerations of it so that it exceeds its original boundaries. What makes his re-imaginings unethical is that they are efforts of mastery and control rather than negotiation, moves that simply exaggerate and exacerbate his previous acts of domination. It would appear that Brontë's Jane, like Rhys's Antoinette, holds a concept of justice similar to Derrida's – if, according to Jane, 'the human and fallible should not arrogate a power with which the divine and perfect alone can be safely entrusted' (p. 141), and that the limit of human judgment is '*May* it be right' (p. 141), then the just decision is impossible, always yet to come because it is the judgment of the Divine. Though Jane feels 'the uncertainty, the vague sense of insecurity, which accompanied a conviction of ignorance' (p. 141) after this exchange, her 'ignorance' proves to be her wisdom. Rochester is ignorant in that he believes he can decide for himself, and justly.

Jane's appeal to the Divine has been read by Roy as an acceptance of the dominant ideology of the church (p. 725). This is mistaken for two reasons. First, Roy critiques Brontë's novel for being unable to present a unified ideological view, a counternarrative to the dominant narratives it is obliged to rehearse (p. 724). This critique seems to assume that there is such thing as a space outside of the dominant narratives. This, as mentioned before, is an impossibility – first, because ideological narratives themselves are not unified, but overdetermined and inextricably intertwined with each other (Laclau and Mouffe: 104–5), and second, because the discourses of the dominant narratives are the means by which we articulate our relation to the imagined real (Silverman: 40). Finally, if Jane's 'may it be right' suggests that it is not within any human's power to judge, including the representatives of the Church of England, her God would appear to function as a force which always dictates that human judgment or ordering be, 'always-already,' suspended, and as such it would suggest that her Christian belief is not a force of closure but one of postponement. As such, her belief functions as a revision of the function of Christian belief within the dominant ideological narrative.

With the exception of Edward's offer of marriage at Thornfield, Jane postpones/defers each of his requests for reflection within the dominant narrative. The marriage proposal is, of course, postponed indefinitely by Richard Mason's revealing of the truth about Bertha during the ceremony. The 'outing' of Edward's secret, and Jane's subsequent departure, forces Rochester to recognize his insufficiency and his lack of a legitimate subjectivity. Without a sane English wife to recognize him as a legitimate patriarch in the home, the dominant fiction of identity is left incomplete. The position of libertine that Rochester has affected in the past, though not legitimized by moral codes, was certainly not without precedent in his class, and the role of sexual master represents a return to a position of patriarchal power. However, during the affair with Céline Varens this imagining has also demonstrated Rochester's own insufficiency, and he lives with the reminder of this (for him) embarrassing union. Likewise, his posturing as a brooding Byronic hero does not result in his successful conquest of Jane. What he is left with after her departure is the inescapable reflection of his own 'error,' as he puts it (p. 220), and with the departure of the woman whom he thought he could make into a properly reflective wife, what he 'has sought for twenty years' (p. 220), he is left with only his failure to become a mature male subject within the framework of the dominant narratives.

The last the reader sees of Edward before the scenes at Ferndean, he tells Jane '*Little* Jane's love would have been my best reward, without it, my heart is broken. But Jane will give me her love: yes – nobly, generously' (p. 321, emphasis mine). This remark shows that Brontë's Rochester, though perhaps more courteous than Rhys's, nevertheless feels compelled to belittle what he cannot have. Brontë does not present us with a narrative of Edward's forced confrontation with his own inadequacy following Jane's departure – this is, after all, Jane's story, and how could she narrate what she hasn't seen? However, the old butler's recounting of the events leading up to and including the fire provides the reader with a crucial moment in the development of Edward's character.

Rochester is said to have 'broke off all acquaintance with the gentry, and shut himself up like a hermit, at the Hall' (p. 430), and is said to become 'dangerous' after Jane's departure. In short, he begins to resemble Bertha. Rhys's Edward 'follows' Brontë's in that his inability to realize himself along the lines of the dominant narrative results in his violent withdrawal from the environment and people which make his successful reflection impossible. Though Rhys's Edward can 'escape' to England, it is in England, presumably his last refuge, where Brontë's Edward finds himself trapped, with no retreat offered other than back into the walls in which both he and his wife are imprisoned. Ironically, the woman Rochester had previously wished to negate now becomes, along with Grace Poole, the sole 'reflector' of his person, even if her role is only to show Edward what he is not, rather than what he is or might have been. As such, he cannot suffer her loss, even though he has wished to lose her for some time. The ex-butler recounts that he witnessed 'Mr Rochester ascend through the skylight on to the roof: we heard him call "Bertha." We saw him approach her; and then ma'am, she yelled, and gave a spring, and the next minute she lay smashed on the pavement' (p. 431). Rochester risks his life attempting to save her, though he has regarded her as a 'hag' (p. 303) and an impediment to his happiness in the past. If one were to ignore Rhys's text, it would be possible to see this as a final acceptance of Bertha as his wife, and a recognition of his own responsibility to defer to an authority other than his own – neglecting to attempt to save her would be tantamount to delivering a death sentence, and thus an assumption of the power to judge and 'let it be right.' In light of Rhys's text, however, it is difficult to see this episode as the moment of Rochester's turning away from the violence of his past. He does not call out 'Antoinette,' but 'Bertha,' indicating that he does not wish to save his wife, but the wife that he has created. In either case, though more strongly in the latter, it is the final and complete demonstration of his own lack of patriarchal power. Mrs Rochester does not acknowledge his hailing of her as 'Bertha' and jumps to her death. This refusal to answer is, in a sense, the final negation of the 'authoritative' Edward Rochester. She does not attack him as she has in the past, an act that partially affirms his position by virtue of its recognizing him as a representative, if not a holder, of patriarchal authority and thus a suitable target for her rage. Rather, she simply ignores the hailing, and her refusal to acknowledge him, even with mad laughter, leaves the exchange in suspension as she jumps. Even though she is dead, she is not 'finished,' because she does not die as 'Bertha Rochester.' She dies unrecognized, and unrecognizing, and her remains remain the disruptive supplement to the narrative of English normalcy in which Rochester participates.

His wounds, meanwhile, are not so much the sign of a recently passed judgment or his castration as they are the signs of his final inability to hide the guilt and insufficiency that have been present since the beginning of the narrative, the outward manifestation of a preexisting inward powerlessness that has finally broken through the layers of dissimulation that he has constructed. He now has no choice but to represent himself as a figure for insufficiency, and as a result must, like Jane, articulate a position which will allow subjectivity without mastery, a position that will allow him to embrace contradiction and lack as the conditions under which one can choose which narrative strands to appropriate and which (partially) to reject, to re-imagine his relation to the dominant discourses of male subjectivity.

Though Rochester's conversion experience is what enables him to enter into a marriage with Jane in which he does not try to regain his lost patriarchal power, it would be a mistake to read this acceptance of God as a reaffirmation of a patriarchal discourse. As indicated earlier, Jane's faith appeals to a belief which runs 'against the grain' of the Anglican structure, and though modern readers may be too quick to read the acceptance of religion in the novel as a capitulation to a dominant ideology, it should be remembered that for Jane, and for Rochester, belief becomes a means with which to create an oppositional self, not a means by which the self is 'subjected' to the dominant social order. Peter Allan Dale notes that

Rochester, his own conversion to Christianity notwithstanding, calls to her as 'the alpha and omega of his heart's wishes' (p. 572; cf. Rev. 1:8), and she responds with her own resounding echo of Revelation: 'I am coming.' As the two are reunited, the language in which Jane describes their renewed relationship is really no less blasphemous than her earlier metaphorical association of their impending sexual union with the marriage of the Lamb. (p. 125)

Their eventual marriage takes them not only away from the order of landed society, but away from traditional religious conceptions of the husband as master. Though Rochester has certainly retained some patriarchal power – Jane notes that he dictates letters to her, correspondence that may represent business dealings, and indicates that she is not carrying on all of their relations, public or private – he is at the same time her dependent. His voiced acceptance of Divine justice (p. 450) amounts to an acceptance of a suspension of his own power, and a suspension of the decision of who exactly is to be the master in their marriage. This suspension of definite positions creates a just relation by virtue of the equitable sharing of domestic power between the two, and because their final identities will not come from intersubjective reflection, but from the divine decision that is yet to come, the 'à-venir.' Dale has noted that the speculative ending of the novel implies a partial rejection of 'a particular historical structure of expectation' (p. 129), and though he is referring to narrative structure in this instance, it is not unreasonable to conclude that this statement can refer to Brontë's relation to religious and 'gendered' closure as well. The dominant imaginings of identity (of religion, class, gender, and the points at which these discourses intersect) no longer, in Dale's terms, 'command implicit assent' (p. 129), but neither can they be escaped. The result is Brontë's subjection of the subject to a 'higher' code which suspends all 'subjection' by earthly discourses. This solution is provisional at best, but it is nonetheless an attempt to articulate an identity that cannot be contained by the dominant narratives.

Brontë creates her 'ladies' man' in Edward Rochester by forcing her creation to envision himself not as the master but as an insufficient subject of God, thus revealing the ultimate powerlessness of patriarchal imaginings of male social and sexual power and making it necessary for him to imagine himself on terms which enable a just and ethical relationship between himself and Jane. Though the imperialist and racist biases of Brontë's text noted by Gayatri Spivak (*passim*) remain, there is at the same time a questioning of dominant imaginings of masculinity, and the social order which relies on these narratives for its self-legitimation. Rhys's text, by virtue of its presentation of Rochester as a man who has already lost full belief in the dominant narratives of masculinity 'before' he appears in *Jane Eyre*, restores this aspect of the text by requiring the reader's recognition of Rochester as an inadequate subject, and not as the ideal romantic patriarch, before his alleged 'castration' during the fire at Thornfield. By demanding that the reader see Rochester as an identity in flux and without a stable base, Rhys's Rochester illuminates the process of reconstruction that Edward undergoes in Brontë's text, emphasizing an important aspect of his character that might otherwise be missed by contemporary readers who might be too ready to read Edward as stock representative of patriarchal values.

WORKS CITED

Brontë, Charlotte. *Jane Eyre* (New York: Signet, 1982).

Dale, Peter Allan. 'Charlotte Brontë's "Tale Half-told": The Disruption of Narrative Structure in *Jane Eyre*,' *Modern Language Quarterly* 47.2 (1986): 108–29.

Eagleton, Terry. *Myths of Power: A Marxist Study of the Brontës* (Houndmills: Macmillan, 1988).

Friedman, Ellen G. 'Breaking the Master Narrative: Jean Rhys's *Wide Sargasso Sea*,' *Breaking the Code: Women's Experimental Fiction*, eds Ellen G. Friedman and Miriam Fuchs (Princeton: Princeton Univ. Press, 1989), pp. 117–28.

Gilbert, Sandra M., and Gubar, Susan. *The Madwoman in the Attic: The Woman Writer and the Nineteenth-century Literary Imagination* (New Haven: Yale Univ. Press, 1979).

Laclau, Ernesto, and Chantal Mouffe. *Hegemony and Socialist Strategy* (London: Verso, 1985).

Rhys, Jean. *Wide Sargasso Sea* (New York: Norton, 1982).

Roy, Parama. 'Unaccommodated Woman and the Poetics of Property in *Jane Eyre*,' *Studies in English Literature* 29.4 (1989): 713–27.

Silverman, Kaja. *Male Subjectivity at the Margins* (New York: Routledge, 1992).

Spivak, Gayatri. 'Three Women's Texts and a Critique of Imperialism,' *Critical Inquiry* 12 (1985): 243–61.

CHAPTER ELEVEN

Gender and Layered Narrative in *Wuthering Heights* and *The Tenant of Wildfell Hall*

N.M. JACOBS

Naomi Jacobs is Professor of English at the University of Maine. She works on British and American fiction and, in particular, on women writers. She has published many articles on these areas as well as a book *The Character of Truth: Historical Figures in Contemporary Fiction* (1990). The article reprinted here analyses the structure of Anne Brontë's *The Tenant of Wildfell Hall* and of Emily's *Wuthering Heights*. It demonstrates that both offer critiques of contemporary masculinity by representing starkly the brutal reality that underlies middle-class domesticity at both the Huntingdon and the Heights households. In Anne's novel, Jacobs argues, Gilbert Markham is not Helen's rescuer from her dissolute first husband but potentially a similar figure to the latter. The article offers a bleaker but more convincing reading than earlier accounts.

> What tenants haunt each mortal cell,
>
> What gloomy guests we hold within –
>
> Torments and madness, tears and sin!

EMILY BRONTË

I n thinking of the Brontës as a group – something it is difficult not to do – we have tended to see Anne and Emily at opposite ends of the clan's continuum: Emily the wild pagan, Anne the mild Christian, with

Reprinted from *The Journal of Narrative Technique* 16.3 (1986): 204–19.

Charlotte somewhere in between. But in fact, Branwell's portrait of his sisters, with Emily and Anne close together on the left and Charlotte keeping company with the ghost of Branwell's face on the right, is a true one. Though the twinship of the younger sisters faltered as Anne went into the world and tired of Gondal, a certain kinship of mind remained, which shows itself in the structures of their major works. In both *Wuthering Heights* and *The Tenant of Wildfell Hall*, we approach a horrific private reality only after passing through and then discarding the perceptual structures of a narrator – significantly, a male narrator – who represents the public world that makes possible and tacitly approves the excesses behind the closed doors of these pre-Victorian homes. This structure, appropriated and modified from the familiar gothic frame-tale, here serves several functions that are strongly gender-related: it exemplifies a process, necessary for both writer and reader, of passing through or going behind the official version of reality in order to approach a truth that the culture prefers to deny; it exemplifies the ways in which domestic reality is obscured by layers of conventional ideology; and it replicates a cultural split between male and female spheres that is shown to be at least one source of the tragedy at the center of the fictional world.

Unlike Charlotte, whose novels also critiqued the myth of domestic bliss but who eroticized the very dominance/submission dynamic from which she longed to escape, Emily and Anne seem to have moved beyond any faith in categories of gender as formulated by their culture. To them, gender is a ragged and somewhat ridiculous masquerade concealing the essential sameness of men and women. Each expressed direct opposition to the establishment of separate moral standards for men and women. According to Charlotte, nothing moved Emily 'more than any insinuation that the faithfulness and clemency, the long-suffering and loving-kindness which are esteemed virtues in the daughters of Eve, become foibles in the sons of Adam' (p. 11); and in the Preface to her novel Anne wrote, 'I am at a loss to conceive how a man should permit himself to write anything that would be really disgraceful to a woman, or why a woman should be censured for writing anything that would be proper and becoming for a man' (p. 31). Yet both sisters, in approaching subjects they must have known would be controversial, seemed to find it necessary first to become that constructed creature, a man, to appropriate and delegitimize his power, before telling their anti-patriarchal truths. Each of these books depicts an unpleasant and often violent domestic reality completely at odds with the Victorian ideal of the home as a refuge from the harshly competitive outside world. And each shows that those with social power inflict violence on the powerless, including children, women, and landless men. Any observers who might attempt to intervene are equally powerless, aware of that fact, and concomitantly fatalistic about the occurrence of violence. This reality, hidden beneath layers of narration in the two novels, was as well-hidden in mid-century English society as it often is today. As late as 1878, when Frances Power Cobbe wrote 'Wife-Torture in England,' she found it more politic to suggest that Englishmen of the middle and upper classes were unlikely to perpetrate domestic abuse of a really serious sort (Bauer and Ritt: 106).

Similarly, many early critics of both *Wuthering Heights* and *The Tenant of Wildfell Hall* preferred to attribute domestic abuse solely to yokels and ruffians.[1] The reviewer for the *Examiner* wrote, 'it is with difficulty that we can prevail upon ourselves to believe in the appearance of such a phenomenon [as Heathcliff], so near our own dwellings as the summit of a Lancashire or Yorkshire moor' (p. 221). The *Britannia* reviewer was equally determined to differentiate the world of the book from the world of its readers: 'The uncultured freedom of native character . . . knows nothing of those breakwaters to the fury of tempest which civilized training establishes to subdue the harsher workings of the soul' (p. 223). Lewes in the *Leader* granted the story a certain truth, but maintained a similar distance: 'such brutes we should all be, or the most of us, were our lives as insubordinate to law; were our affections and sympathies as little cultivated, our imaginations as undirected' (p. 292). Even Charlotte, in the Preface to the 1850 edition of *Wuthering Heights*, assured readers that they had nothing in common with its characters:

Men and women who . . . have been trained from their cradle to observe the utmost evenness of manner and guardedness of language, will hardly know what to make of the rough, strong utterance, the harshly manifested passions, the unbridled aversions, and headlong partialities of unlettered moorland hinds and rugged moorland squires.

Unable to dismiss Anne Brontë's characters as uneducated Yorkshire brutes, the reviewers attacked *The Tenant of Wildfell Hall* on the grounds not of untruthfulness but of an unpleasant excess of truth, often using terms such as 'morbid' and 'unhealthy' to imply pathological interest on the part of the author in aspects of experience which are better ignored. The *Spectator* wrote, 'there seems in the writer a morbid love for the coarse, not to say the brutal; so that his level subjects are not very attractive, and the more forcible are displeasing or repulsive, from their gross, physical, or profligate substratum' (p. 250). The *Rambler* condemned the book's 'uncalled-for and unhealthy representation of the vilest phases of human life' (p. 268). The *North American Review* complained that 'the reader of Acton Bell gains no enlarged view of mankind, giving a healthy action to his sympathies, but is confined to a narrow space of life, and held down, as it were, by main force, to witness the wolfish side of his nature literally and logically set forth' (p. 262). Strongest in its denunciations was *Sharpe's London Magazine*, which called the book 'unfit for perusal . . . we will *not* believe any woman would have written such a work,' with its 'disgustingly truthful minuteness' (pp. 263–4).[2] These reviewers sought to reassure themselves and their readers that education, cultivation, and civilization will preclude brutal behavior, and objected to powerful fictional representations contradicting this premise. Yet the novels quite pointedly locate the brutality, sometimes physical and sometimes psychological, in civilized families, the 'best' in their neighborhoods. Even Heathcliff, the Liverpool orphan, commits his worst crimes only after he has acquired the manners and resources of a gentleman.

The narrative structure of both of these novels represents an authorial strategy for dealing with the unacceptability of the subject matter, a strategy drawn but significantly modified from the familiar framing narrator of the gothic tales. According to MacAndrew, the gothic frame-tale creates a 'closed-off region within an outer world . . . The mind is turned in on itself' (p. 110). This internal or closed world approximates the hidden self within the social world, the dark side of the psyche. The framing narrator or fictional editor generally belongs to the world of the reader, and is a conventional and pragmatic sort who is shocked by the gothic evils he encounters. Anne Brontë's Markham and Emily Brontë's Lockwood serve in a somewhat analogous way to 'define the limits of propriety and to measure observed events against the official standards of morality' (Taylor: 22), but differ from their gothic predecessors in that they and the official standards they represent are shown to be in part the cause of the shocking reality they encounter. In fact, the metaphor of a framed picture implies a static two-dimensionality that is nothing like the experience of reading these novels. In looking at a picture we are only peripherally aware of the frame, which marks the limits beyond which our eyes need not stray: it is not a presence but the boundary between an artifice which deserves our attention and a surrounding mundane reality which does not. But the Brontës' framing narratives are more like competing works of art, or outer rooms in a gallery, or even the picture painted over a devalued older canvas. We cannot see or experience the buried reality of the 'framed' story without first experiencing the 'framing' narrative. There is no other way in.

In these novels, the outer reality is male and the inner reality is largely female; it is perhaps not entirely irrelevant to this conceptual structure that the laws of the Victorian age classified married women or underage unmarried women such as Helen Huntingdon, Catherine

219

Earnshaw, and Catherine Linton as 'femmes couvertes'; their legal identities were 'covered' by and subsumed into that of the husband or father. I would contend that for Emily and Anne Brontë, there was no other way into the tabooed realities at the cores of their novels than through the satirical miming and disempowering of a masculine authority which 'covered' and often profited from those realities. Notwithstanding Heathcliff's ghoulish fancies, the evil hidden at the center of these pseudo-gothic narratives is not supernatural or even particularly diabolical; it is mundane, vulgar, and grounded in the legal and economic structures of the time and the effects of those structures on the consciousness of both those in power (the 'covering' narrators) and those without power (the 'covered' narrators).

Taylor has discussed the use of a female persona as a 'literary masquerade' through which certain classic male authors have expressed vulnerabilities and emotions that the culture denies to men. Many female writers use male personae and particularly male pseudonyms in the same way. But the comic qualities of the Brontës' male personae suggest that they are using them less to enlarge themselves than to free themselves from the restrictive ideology and consciousness for which the personae speak. This mockery of conventional masculinity involves also mocking the conventional or 'male' element in the authors themselves, and thus is not so cheerful as the gaming with gender that Gilbert has described in female modernists such as Woolf and Barnes.[3] A useful, if somewhat anachronistic, analogue to this narrative practice can be found in professional 'drag,' female impersonation by male homosexuals, which simultaneously reinforces and challenges gender definitions by combining an extremely persuasive replication of traditional femininity with a final 'unmasking' in which the performer removes wig or brassiere, symbolically proclaiming that femaleness – and, by implication, maleness – is an act, a psychological uniform devised and enforced by society. Yet despite this ironic consciousness of the artificiality of gender behavior, the drag queen also expresses profound ambiguity about his own failure to fit into a traditional gender category. The performer is usually an apolitical homosexual who sees himself as unnatural, as having something wrong with him, and that something is female. By satirizing female biology and mannerism, the performer exaggerates and thus gains some control over what he perceives as the 'woman' in himself (Newton).

There are a number of intriguing similarities between Victorian male impersonation in fiction and modern female impersonation on stage, for writing, particularly that dealing with 'coarse' subject matters, was seen by the Victorians as a masculine activity, unnatural to women. Gilbert and Gubar have described the anxiety created in the nineteenth-century woman writer by participation in an art dominated by male writers and male-oriented metaphors of creation. In one sense, becoming a writer meant becoming a man, or at least something other than what the culture considered to be a woman. By contrast with the relatively innocuous masquerade of a male pseudonym – a common enough ploy, and one justified by ladylike modesty as well as economic prudence – the extended assumption of a male persona must have required a great deal of courage in a time almost obsessively concerned with defining the differences in consciousness between men and women.[4] Nevertheless, Emily and Anne Brontë seem to have found their male impersonations necessary, as a way to silence the dominant culture by stealing its voice, to exorcise the demon of conventional consciousness and male power by holding it up to ridicule. Only by first discrediting views that the readers of these novels were likely to share – and from which the writers themselves, as products of their culture, could not entirely be free – could they hope to make the reality clear to themselves and to their readers.

The Tenant of Wildfell Hall reflects the phenomenon of the silencing of the powerless and of the denial of their reality both in its structure and in its content. Gerin, who dismissed the narrative structure of this novel as the 'clumsy device of a plot within a plot' (p. 13), is certainly not alone in her dissatisfaction. The central premise – that Gilbert Markham is willing to write letters comprising several hundred pages and to copy out a journal of equal length – is of course implausible, and the two narratives do seem discontinuous. George Moore argued that Helen's diary should have been eliminated so that she could tell her story directly to Gilbert. Ewbank, on the other hand, found the epistolary framework superfluous and the journal the essential part of the story. Eagleton has objected to the fact that 'What is officially an interlude [the diary] becomes the guts of the work, displacing the framework that surrounds it' (p. 136). But that displacement is exactly the point of the novel, which subjects its readers to a shouldering-aside of familiar notions and comfortable perceptions of the world. Both narrators, both narrations, and the jarring discrepancies of tone and perspective between them, are necessary to this purpose.

Markham is presented as a product of his society's obsession with gender and reinforcement of male privilege; he is, through much of the first section of the book, a caricature of maleness something like the caricature of femaleness in drag. The narration is extremely complex, for the voice is that of a mature man only half-aware of the extent to which his younger self was ridiculous. Young Gilbert is childish, vain, competitive with other men even to the point of violence, and unable to control or manage his emotions; and he tends to evaluate women almost entirely

221

according to their willingness to flatter and conciliate him. His superficial gallantry masks an essential cynicism about any woman he believes has stepped outside the bounds of socially proper behavior. In the words of Helen, he is the 'fine gentleman and beau of the parish and its vicinity (in his own estimation, at least)' (p. 400). Though 24 years old, and manager of a sizable farm, he describes himself as 'getting to feel quite a good boy' (p. 128) at his mother's stroking and petting; he accepts her 'maternal admiration' (p. 37) for him but finds it excessive when given to his brother. He protests that his mother's attentions will make him self-indulgent and unaware of the needs of others, but he will come in late for tea and then complain about the flavor of the 'overdrawn' drink, so that his sister has to make another pot (p. 77).

His vanity and self-absorption are nowhere more evident than in his attitudes toward the women of the neighborhood. Upon first seeing Helen, he feels confident that he can make her like him, if he should 'think it worthwhile,' and he immediately evaluates her as a potential mate, thinking 'I would rather admire you from this distance, fair lady, than be the partner of your home.' His negative opinion is based on the feeling that the set of her lips indicates 'no very soft or amiable temper' (p. 41); he is repelled by her 'quiet, calm civility' (p. 81) and strong opinions. His preference is for Eliza Millward's 'gentle and childish' voice and kittenish manners (p. 42). His feeling for Eliza is largely the pleasure of gratified vanity; he leaves her, he says, 'with a heart brimful of complacency for myself, and overflowing with love for Eliza' (p. 50) after her attentiveness has soothed the ruffled feelings produced by an encounter with Helen. At a tea-party, he focuses on Eliza's 'delight in having me near her' (p. 61) and at the picnic his heart 'warms' toward Eliza, who 'exerted herself to be agreeable' (p. 86). At this point, he is also enjoying the fact that Helen is an observer to his conversation with Eliza – that is, he enjoys displaying Eliza's interest in him – for after Helen leaves he grows 'weary of amusing' Eliza (p. 87). Eliza's practical sister Mary is little disposed to please Gilbert by artifice and exaggerated attention; he therefore evaluates her as 'good for nothing else' but to amuse children (p. 88) and 'little better than a nonentity' (p. 96), though her intelligence and sensitivity far outweigh those of her sister. Eliza is, in fact, a vicious gossip and an arrant manipulator, but because she flatters Gilbert's vanity he is unable to see through her stratagems, though he understands the same behavior quite well in women like Jane Wilson who are attempting to catch another man than himself. His desire to be the focus of attention is shown by his pleasure when Lawrence, whom he sees as a rival for Helen's attention, declines to participate in the picnic; he later 'snubs' Lawrence with a 'sulky nod' when he fears his rival is succeeding (p. 106).

All of this anti-heroic behavior is presented as the logical result of Gilbert's upbringing and milieu. His mother has convinced her darling son that he is capable of 'great achievements' (p. 35), and she runs her household on the principle that 'we have only two things to consider, first, what's proper to be done, and secondly, what's most agreeable to the gentlemen of the house.' It is a husband's business to please himself, she tells Gilbert, and a wife's to please her husband. Though Gilbert says that he expects 'to find more pleasure in making my wife happy and comfortable, than in being made so by her,' his general behavior supports his mother's opinion that this is 'mere boy's talk' (pp. 78–9). Gilbert's mother says a boy should 'learn to be ashamed' of being tied to his mother (p. 52) and objects to Helen's program of training little Arthur to dislike wine: 'the poor child will be the veriest milksop that ever was sopped! Only think what a man you will make of him if you persist . . . you will treat him like a girl – you'll spoil his spirit, and make a mere Miss Nancy of him' (pp. 54–5). Helen's vigorous arguments for giving children of both sexes equal protection and equal experience are met with amused disapproval by her cheerfully conventional neighbors, who would no more approve of Arthur Huntingdon's debauchery, if they knew of it, than of his runaway wife. Yet their attitudes, which seem harmless traditionalism, are shown in Helen's diary to be essentially identical with those that produce the domestic hell at the center of the novel.

Though set in the 1830s and written in the '40s, the novel critiques an ideology of woman's sphere that would be expressed most eloquently by Ruskin in the '60s. Both Helen and Arthur are victims of a psychological fragmentation created by definitions of manhood and womanhood that leave each incomplete and neurotically dependent on the other for their sense of meaning. Helen's diary shows that like Gilbert, Arthur was indulged by his mother and raised to see himself as the rightful focus of all feminine attention. His understanding of his manhood is essentially that implied by Mrs Markham's comments; to be a man is equated with an imperious will, 'spirit,' and disdain for those qualities associated with women: piety, abstinence, selflessness, and dependence. Deciding to 'make a man' of his four-year-old son, Arthur will teach him 'to tipple wine like papa, to swear like Mr Hattersley, and to have his own way like a man, and [send] mamma to the devil when she tried to prevent him' (p. 356). This definition of manliness creates an extremely destructive dynamic in which Arthur is in fact totally dependent on Helen's disapproval – combined, paradoxically, with her complete subservience to him – for his sense of himself as a man.

Like Mrs Markham, Arthur believes that a wife is a

thing to love one devotedly and to stay at home – to wait upon her husband, and amuse him and minister to his comfort in every possible way, while he chooses to stay with her; and, when he is absent, to attend to his interests, domestic or otherwise, and patiently wait his return; no matter how he may be occupied in the meantime. (p. 257)

Helen at first accepts the ideology of woman as man's helpmate – particularly his spiritual guide and companion – because it offers her a personal importance that amounts to an almost divine power. She sees her marriage as a god-ordained mission: not merely to civilize an undisciplined boy but to rescue an immortal soul. When her aunt objects to the profligate Arthur as a prospective husband, the young Helen says, 'I shall consider my life well spent in saving him from the consequences of his early errors, and striving to recall him to the path of virtue – God grant me success' (p. 167). Arthur, only half in jest, encourages this belief, saying that he would 'never do or say a wicked thing' if he had Helen always with him (p. 166). Such transference to women of all responsibility for male behavior – echoed in Lowborough's belief that Annabella will save him, 'body and soul, from destruction' (p. 211) and in Hargraves' assertion that after the ladies leave the men 'there is no one to humanize them and keep them in check' (p. 359) – amounts to an infantilizing of the man, as Helen unwittingly expresses when she says, 'his wife shall undo what his mother did!' (p. 191).

Ultimately, this ideology is equally degrading to the woman, for in order to carry out her role of 'angel monitress' (p. 212) she must become a completely controlled and thus radically truncated human being, continually repressing (or, as Helen so often says, 'suppressing') her own legitimate emotions. The novel shows secretiveness as a necessary survival skill for women; a woman's reality must be concealed beneath a layer of conventionality. Though Helen is too proud to affect an emotion she does not feel, her circumstances force her to conceal what she does feel, for openness brings vulnerability. Very early on, her aunt warns her, 'Keep a guard over your eyes and ears as the inlets of your heart, and over your lips as the outlet, lest they betray you in a moment of unwariness' (p. 150), and experience bears out this advice. When Arthur sees Helen's sketches of him on the backs of her carefully impersonal drawings of landscapes, he openly exults in the knowledge of her infatuation and proceeds to steal a kiss. The infuriated Helen feels, 'he despises me, because he knows I love him . . . he would not have done so but for that hateful picture!' (pp. 172–3). Arthur's attempts to uncover Helen's feelings become increasingly sadistic: his 'favourite amusement' in the early days of their marriage is to recite 'stories of his former amours' in order to provoke her into an emotional outburst. Learning 'that his delight increased in proportion to [her] anger and agitation,' she endeavors 'to receive his revelations in the silence of calm contempt' (p. 221). But she is thus placed in an intolerable double bind; Arthur both complains of her 'marble heart and brutal insensibility' when she doesn't respond to his insults (p. 330) and resents her failure to preserve patient cheerfulness: 'A burst of passion is a fine, rousing thing upon occasion, Helen, and a flood of tears is marvellously affecting, but, when indulged too often, they are both deuced plaguy things for spoiling one's beauty and tiring out one's friends' (p. 271). Similarly, Arthur's friend Hattersley physically forces his wife to tell why she is crying and then curses her when he gets the answer (p. 290); he is provoked at her both for seeming to have no feeling and for crying over 'nothing' (p. 300).

This silencing process is founded, as Helen comes to realize, in the fact that she is legally nothing more than a 'slave, a prisoner' (p. 373) to her husband, whose power over her property and person is well-nigh absolute. Though Arthur never physically abuses Helen, he constantly submits her to verbal abuse and humiliation, flaunting his affairs, bringing his mistresses into the house, and 'exulting . . . in his power to control [her] fate' (p. 398). After destroying the painting materials with which she had hoped to support herself, he 'held the candle in my face and peered into my eyes with looks and laughter too insulting to be borne' (p. 371). He proceeds to 'confiscate' her money and jewels and to cut off her access to household funds, describing the whole as carrying his 'point like a man' (p. 373). Ironically, Helen would not have been so completely powerless had she not believed so implicitly in the ideal of domestic bliss; though Arthur would have been willing to arrange fairly generous 'settlements' of her own inheritance, she had preferred to devote that money to paying Arthur's gambling debts, saying, 'all I have will be his, and all he has will be mine; and what more could either of us require?' (p. 193). Her awareness that she is at least partly responsible for her situation, having married Arthur against the advice of her family, further silences her. She is reluctant to tell her aunt or her brother about her problems, both because pride will not allow her to admit having made a mistake and because she doesn't want to burden them. The result of all this is that Helen experiences her own mind as a structure within which her thoughts and feelings are confined, just as her narrative of secret misery is confined within Gilbert's less painful one in the structure of the novel.

Though Arthur had at first seemed to offer 'ease and freedom . . . repose and expansion,' in contrast to the 'constraint and formality' (p. 153) she had experienced in society, her life with him is even more constrained than before, and she laments, 'how many of my thoughts and feelings are gloomily cloistered within my own mind; how much of my higher and better self is indeed unmarried' (p. 256). She has become her own jailor, enforcing an isolation more complete than that of a cloistered nun, for she lacks even community with fellow prisoners. One might expect that she and her friend Millicent Hattersley, equally ill-married, would share their grievances, but Millicent 'either is or pretends to be quite reconciled to her lot' (p. 239), preserving the public fiction of domestic bliss. When Hattersley, in a public situation, presses Millicent to explain her tears, she pleads, 'Do let me alone, Ralph! remember we are not at home'; he attempts to 'extort the confession by shaking her and remorselessly crushing her slight arms in the gripe of his powerful fingers,' but she only murmurs, 'I'll tell you some other time . . . when we are alone' (p. 289). In another scene when he grasps her hair and twists it unmercifully, she smiles through her tears and complains that he has 'disarranged her hair a bit.' Helen, though certainly not so abjectly submissive in the face of ill-treatment, is equally careful to preserve a 'cheerful, undisturbed serenity' even when her jealousy or anger is most painful (p. 242). She becomes so alienated from her emotions that she describes any release of her feelings as a state of being 'outside of herself' or 'beside herself.' If her mind is a closed structure, then the release of emotion means that she has in fact let a part of herself 'out,' for silent self-control is her only way of retaining her self-respect and thus her sense of self. She resists 'demeaning [herself] by an uncontrollable burst of passion' (p. 357); such loss of control would represent a victory for her opponent.

Helen pours into her diary all the rage and frustration she must suppress when with other people. She mentions several times that the writing 'calms' her: 'I have found relief describing the very circumstances that have destroyed my peace' (p. 317). This is so because, in writing down her experience, she affirms its reality; by making visible the invisible, speaking her forbidden rage, she breaks out of her emotional prison. It is thus highly significant that she offers this diary to Gilbert, for in so doing, she admits him to a knowledge of her self and her experience more intimate than that of any other person in her world. As Gordon has remarked, 'Behind her gift is a repressed desire to turn the text back into speech' (p. 212). The effect on Gilbert of reading this document – of being admitted into the reality hidden within and behind the conventional consciousness in which he participates – is revolutionary, and absolutely instrumental to the partnership of equals their marriage will become. Its revelations force him outside the restricted boundaries of an ego that defines itself through its difference from and superiority to someone else. His concluding description of the mutuality of his relationship with

Helen suggests that Gilbert's consciousness now incorporates hers, just as his narrative encloses her narrative.

Wuthering Heights, though much more complex in its narrative structure than *Wildfell Hall*, follows an essentially similar process of approaching a pervasively violent private reality through a narrator who embodies an ideology that justifies the violence. From the opening scene, when Heathcliff tells Lockwood to 'walk in!' through a locked gate, this novel stresses the boundaries between public and private realities as well as the parallels between the two. Though known as a great love story, the book focuses less on the relationship between Catherine and Heathcliff than on the ways in which that relationship and others are distorted by the power structure of the characters' world. Class differences certainly are a major issue here, as Marxist analyses of Heathcliff's career have shown. But what is less often recognized is the way in which most of the violence and abuse in this fictional world is made possible by the vestiture of total power in the patriarch of the home and by the psychic fragmentation this concept of male power imposes on both men and women. To discipline the members of the household as he sees fit is both the legal and moral right of the master of the house, and in the Earnshaw family – 'a respectable house, the next best in the neighborhood' (p. 168) – this right leads to frequent abuse. Mr Earnshaw, though kind-hearted enough to take up a starving orphan, freely uses his power as master. When six-year-old Cathy spits at Heathcliff, she earns 'for her pains a sound blow from her father to teach her cleaner manners' (p. 39). Heathcliff warns that if Mr Earnshaw knows of the blows Hindley has dealt to the younger boy, he'll pay Hindley back 'with interest' (p. 41). After illness confines him to inactivity, Earnshaw becomes extremely sensitive to 'suspected slights of his authority' and trembles with rage when he cannot reach Hindley to strike him with a stick (pp. 41–2).

Thus, the Earnshaw children understand very early that social power legitimizes violence. Even as a child, Cathy likes 'to act the little mistress; using her hands freely and commanding her companions' (p. 43). Hindley beats Heathcliff several times a week, taunting him as a 'gipsy' and 'beggarly interloper' (p. 41). This abuse escalates after Hindley becomes head of the household; when Cathy and Heathcliff defy him, he says, 'You forget you have a master here . . . I'll demolish the first who puts me out of temper' (p. 26). When Hindley threatens to murder Nelly, he says, 'no law in England can hinder a man from keeping his house decent' (p. 67). As master, Hindley tends to delegate the actual infliction of punishment; when ordered to flog Heathcliff for missing church, Joseph accepts the task with relish, thrashing Heathcliff 'till his arm ached' (p. 46). Significantly, Heathcliff never returns Hindley's violence or, in fact, perpetrates violence until he himself has gained the legal and economic status of paterfamilias. But he has learned very well not only how to exercise his power but how to justify that exercise. He imagines with pleasure bruising Isabella's face 'and turning the blue eyes black, every day or two' (p. 93), for nothing more than her resemblance to her brother. Imprisoning his wife, he says, 'you're not fit to be your own guardian, Isabella, now; and I, being your legal protector, must retain you in my custody' (p. 128). He refers to his son as his 'property' and as 'it' (p. 169). When the younger Catherine defies him, he administers 'a shower of terrific slaps on both sides of the head' and says, 'I know how to chastise children, you see . . . you shall have a daily taste, if I catch such a devil of a temper in your eyes again!' (pp. 215–16). He teaches Linton to regard such 'chastisement' as a husband's prerogative, promising that the boy will be able to 'pay her back her present tyrannies, with a vigorous hand' once they are married (p. 217). Edgar Linton is certainly not a violent man, but he is equally ready to assert control over his household, both in ceasing to 'humour' Catherine by allowing her friend to enter the house and in disinheriting his sister when she marries against his wishes. Learning of Isabella's misery with Heathcliff, he says only, 'Trouble me no more about her' (p. 113), and refuses, with self-righteous mildness, to help: 'I am not *angry*, but I'm *sorry* to have lost her . . . My communication with Heathcliff's family shall be as sparing as his with mine. It shall not exist' (p. 123). Clearly, to Edgar, Isabella now belongs to Heathcliff and is no longer his concern.

Lockwood is a product and beneficiary of the social structure that justifies the oppression and abuse at the Heights. Much like the readers and reviewers of the Brontë novels in the 1840s, he is a 'civilized man,' who 'likes . . . to shut out the possibilities of darkness and violence' (Tanner: 112). He closes himself into that panelled bed hoping to secure himself 'against the vigilance of Heathcliff and everyone else' (p. 25); but by thus isolating and, as it were, concentrating his own self, he finds himself at the epicenter of the house's demonic energy. In the violence of his attempt to keep out the wailing child, he 'pulled its wrist on to the broken pane, and rubbed it to and fro till the blood ran down and soaked the bedclothes' (p. 30), showing that the 'polite, civilized gentleman, is capable, albeit in a dream, of greater cruelty than any of the savage inhabitants of Wuthering Heights' (McCarthy: 54). And just as he stops his ears 'to exclude the lamentable prayer' (p. 30) of the ghost-Cathy, he stops his eyes, in a sense, to exclude knowledge of the plight of the living Cathy. The agency of his self-blinding is the ideology of domestic harmony. His fatuous courtesies are completely inappropriate to the scene before him, but he has no other vocabulary for describing what he sees.

Observing the 'ferocious gaze' and savage tone with which Heathcliff addresses Cathy, and the universal grim silence at the tea-table, he nevertheless offers the platitudinous opinion that Heathcliff must be happy, 'surrounded by your family and with your amiable lady as the presiding genius over your home and heart' (p. 20). Learning that Cathy is not Heathcliff's 'amiable lady,' he assumes that Hareton is the 'favoured possessor of the beneficent fairy' (p. 21). The real meaning of this sentimental language is clarified by Heathcliff, who echoes sarcastically, 'We neither of us have the privilege of owning your good fairy' (p. 21). That the 'favoured possessor' of a woman owns her is a fact of the law, which Isabella learns most painfully and which Anne Brontë's Helen Huntingdon recognized when she warned a young friend, 'You might as well sell yourself into slavery at once, as marry a man you dislike' (p. 380).

Lockwood realizes, of course, that this 'pleasant family circle' (p. 21) does not live up to the ideals expressed by his own language, but his only response is repression or avoidance. When Cathy informs him that she is a prisoner, not allowed outside the garden wall, he sidesteps this fact by gallantry: 'I should be sorry to ask you to cross the threshold, for my convenience, on such a night' (p. 23). It becomes clear that she is the subject of both verbal and physical abuse, but when Lockwood sees Heathcliff lift his hand against her, he trivializes the exchange: 'Having no desire to be entertained by a cat and dog combat, I stepped forward briskly . . . Each had enough decorum to suspend further hostilities' (p. 34). Understanding that his presence merely interrupts the violence, he prefers to imagine its continuance as a mildly comic barnyard spat. He says that he hears 'not altogether disapprovingly' (p. 239) a blow she receives during a quarrel with Hareton, and he attributes her sullenness to a bad nature rather than to the treatment she receives. Fantasizing that marriage to him would be 'more romantic than a fairy tale' for Catherine, Lockwood imagines such a change primarily as a move to more glamorous surroundings and more stimulating society (p. 241). He is unable to imagine the very grim fairy tale of her life as prisoner to the monstrous Heathcliff.

As in *The Tenant of Wildfell Hall*, the opposition of male and female worlds that is reflected in the structure of the novel is shown to be one source of the brutality depicted. Cathy's transition into adulthood is a diminution of her powers, signaled by her reappearance, after a period of invalidism, in the garb of a lady and by the resultant forced change in her behavior. Her years as Mrs Linton before Heathcliff's return pass in a sort of somnolence, a most un-Cathylike acquiescence and calm, as she acts out the ideal of a flower-like woman without desires or passions. At Heathcliff's reappearance, her 'male' traits of anger, desire, and the power to harm resurface, as if evoked by the presence of her 'other half.' She feels that Heathcliff is 'more myself than I am' because he represents her lost self, the asexual 'girl . . . half savage, and hardy, and free' (p. 107). Her anger at Linton, who is probably more androgynous than any other character in the novel, is anger at him for refusing to complete her yet demanding that she remain only half herself. Similarly, we might say that Heathcliff's years away from Cathy make him into a man in the terms of the age: he has gone out into the world, has done battle and conquered, but has also been hardened. He returns violent, ruthlessly exploitive, and dangerous to those around him, particularly when Cathy is no longer there to keep him in check. Yet his egotism is only a less civilized version of Lockwood's (or of Arthur Huntingdon's), as his hatred for Isabella because she loves him is a harsher version of Lockwood's rejection of the 'goddess' who returned his interest (p. 15). After Cathy's death, Heathcliff is incapable of any 'feminine' or soft emotion, except perhaps for the affection he sometimes shows Nelly. Thus, when he describes Cathy as his soul, and her death as the death of his soul, he is describing the death of a part of himself that he had needed her to act out, because that part had been projected onto her as they stepped into the simplified roles of adulthood.

Like Helen Huntingdon, Nelly Dean serves as recorder or uncoverer of a hidden reality of the novel, and her story is also one of impotence and suppression. Despite her dependence on the families she serves, she attempts to protest or correct the injustices she sees, to soften Hindley's and Heathcliff's anger, to reconcile Edgar and Isabella, to moderate Catherine's outbursts, and later to protect the second Catherine from Heathcliff's schemes. But none of her white lies, manipulations, or even mistakes is successful in changing the structure of her world, and by the time that Lockwood encounters her she has been co-opted to the extent that she is working for the tyrant Heathcliff and only sighing a bit over his mistreatment of Cathy and his deception of Hareton, quite aware that nothing she says or does can make a difference. Only the death of Heathcliff can free those in his 'family' from their degradation and semi-slavery, for Cathy is restrained by fear and Hareton by love from taking steps to escape. But Cathy and Hareton promise to escape the destructive dynamic of the previous generation, for they each possess strength and tenderness, light and dark, all the qualities polarized in their parents and in the novel. The slap that Cathy gives Hareton for not attending to his lessons is a love-tap, a playful remnant of the blows he has given her in the past, and that diminution of force suggests the waning of the violence that had inhabited the house they will soon abandon. The novel's concluding image of fluttering moths and soft winds around the graves of those who had perpetrated the violence of the past, then, underlines the resolution of that violence, which occurs with the reunion of Catherine and Heathcliff and the new union of the younger lovers. Lockwood seeks the graves, seeks the knowledge that those sufferers are indeed at rest – and whether or not they do walk the moors, it is clear that they are at peace. As in *The Tenant of Wildfell Hall*, we return to the world of normality, as Hareton and Cathy will return to Thrushcross Grange and some version of the domestic bliss that was the Victorian ideal. But we have seen an under-world or other-world that is still latent in the structures of the comfortable reality.

Charlotte Brontë described both of her sisters' characters as consisting of layers much like those of their novels. Emily was a person whose mind and feelings had 'recesses' on which not 'even those nearest and dearest to her could, with impunity, intrude unlicensed,' a person who concealed under an 'unpretending outside . . . a secret power and fire' (pp. 4, 8). Anne had a reserve that 'covered her mind, and especially her feelings, with a sort of nunlike veil, which was rarely lifted' (p. 8). But in their novels, they projected a process of removing those veils, revealing those secrets. In her Preface to the so-called 'Second Edition' of *Wildfell Hall*, Anne Brontë describes 'that precious gem,' the truth, as something one must 'dive' for, sometimes becoming rather muddy in the process. And certainly the devotion to unsavory truths brought upon her and her sister 'misconstruction and some abuse' (Charlotte Brontë: 6). Neither could have been unaware of the likelihood that their truths would not be welcomed by polite society, which could more comfortably deny them. But they were nevertheless compelled to make that deep dive into themselves, beneath their own layers of conventional consciousness, to see, as Adrienne Rich would write a century later, 'the damage that was done / and the treasures that prevail,' to seek 'the wreck and not the story of the wreck / the thing itself and not the myth.' The structures of their novels reflect that intrepid search.

NOTES

1. Unless otherwise noted, all citations of contemporary reviews are to the most widely available source: Miriam Allott, ed., *The Brontës: The Critical Heritage* (London and Boston: Routledge & Kegan Paul, 1974).

2. Except for one writer who described Arthur's associates as 'a set of drunken savages, such as we do not remember to have heard of as having been tolerated for many years, within the pale of civilized society' (p. 256), few denied that the book was realistic. But even Charles Kingsley, who applauded the exposure of 'foul and accursed

undercurrents in plenty, in this same smug, respectable, whitewashed English society' and criticized 'the world' for resenting the truth, found 'unnecessary coarseness' in the book: 'what greater mistake, to use the mildest term, can there be than to fill such a diary with written oaths and curses, with details of drunken scenes which no wife, such as poor Helen is represented, would have the heart, not to say the common decency, to write down as they occurred? Dramatic probability and good feeling are equally outraged by such a method' (p. 271). One must wonder why good feeling should have been more outraged by the recording of such scenes than by their occurrence.

3. The Brontës' use of male pseudonyms can be seen as a masquerade of the merry variety, freeing them to write and to gain a fair hearing. Charlotte Brontë wrote to Hartley Coleridge, 'I am pleased that you cannot quite decide whether I am an attorney's clerk or a novel-reading dressmaker' (Gaskell: 201), and Mrs Gaskell thought that 'her sense of humor was tickled by the perplexity which her correspondent felt' (p. 202). Though Charlotte wrote that she and her sisters felt 'a sort of conscientious scruple at assuming Christian names positively masculine' (p. 4), she quite positively directed Smith and Elder to address 'Mr Currer Bell' and referred to 'Mr Bell' by the male pronoun when acting as 'his' agent. This use of male pseudonyms generally resembles the comfortable 'male impersonation' of George Sand, who loved to stroll Paris in the freedom and safety of her male trousers and cigar; it provides a certain degree of protection without much affecting the narrative voice. The emphatic maleness of George Eliot's early narrator, on the other hand, became progressively more ironic and self-parodic as readers learned that 'George Eliot' was really a woman, and a woman known to some as 'Madonna'!

4. Some of the responses to Charlotte Brontë's Shirley showed the dangers facing a female writer willing to impersonate or intimately examine male characters. G.B. Lewes wrote that literary women have too often 'written from the man's point of view . . . women have too often thought but of rivalling men. It is their boast to be mistaken for men, – instead of speaking sincerely and energetically as women.' He went on to apply to Brontë, whose work he generally admired, Schiller's criticism of Madame de Staël: 'She steps out of her sex – without elevating herself above it' (pp. 162, 163, 169). Another reviewer wrote of Shirley, 'Not one of its men are genuine. There are no such men . . . Let Currer Bell get some one else to paint men, and herself do none but the female figures, or dissect at least none save female hearts' (p. 118).

WORKS CITED

Allott, Miriam, ed. The Brontës: The Critical Heritage (London and Boston: Routledge & Kegan Paul, 1974).

Bauer, Carol and Lawrence Ritt. ' "A Husband Is a Beating Animal": Frances Power Cobbe Confronts the Wife-Abuse Problem in Victorian England,' International Journal of Women's Studies 6.2 (1983): 99–108.

Brontë, Anne. *The Tenant of Wildfell Hall* [1848], ed. G.D. Hargreaves, Introduction by Winifred Gerin (Middlesex, England: Penguin, 1979).

Brontë, Charlotte. 'Biographical Notice of Ellis and Acton Bell' and 'Editor's Preface to the New Edition of *Wuthering Heights*,' by Emily Brontë [1847], ed. William M. Sale, Jr (New York: Norton, 1972), pp. 3–12.

Brontë, Emily. *The Complete Poems of Emily Jean Brontë*, ed. C.W. Hatfield (New York: Columbia Univ. Press, 1941).

Brontë, Emily. *Wuthering Heights* [1847], ed. William M. Sale, Jr (New York: Norton, 1972).

Eagleton, Terry. *Myths of Power: A Marxist Study of the Brontës* (London and Basingstoke: Macmillan, 1975).

Ewbank, Inga-Stina. *Their Proper Sphere: The Brontë Sisters as Victorian Woman Novelists* (London: Edward Arnold, 1966).

Gaskell, Elizabeth. *The Life of Charlotte Brontë* [1857], ed. Alan Shelstone (Harmondsworth: Penguin, 1975).

Gilbert, Sandra M. 'Costumes of the Mind: Transvestism as Metaphor in Modern Literature,' *Writing and Sexual Difference*, ed. Elizabeth Abel (Chicago: Univ. of Chicago Press, 1982).

Gilbert, Sandra M. and Susan Gubar. *The Madwoman in the Attic* (New Haven, Conn.: Yale Univ. Press, 1979).

Gordon, Jan B. 'Narrative Enclosure as Textual Ruin: An Archaeology of Gothic Consciousness,' *Dickens Studies Annual* II (1983): 209–38.

MacAndrew, Elizabeth. *The Gothic Tradition in Fiction* (New York: Columbia Univ. Press, 1979).

McCarthy, Terence. 'The Incompetent Narrator of *Wuthering Heights*,' *Modern Language Quarterly* 42.1 (1981): 48–64.

Moore, George. *Conversations in Ebury Street* (London: Chatto & Windus, 1930).

Newton, Esther. *Mother Camp: Female Impersonators in America*. Anthropology of Modern Societies Series (Englewood Cliffs, NJ: Prentice-Hall, 1972).

Rich, Adrienne. 'Diving Into the Wreck.' *Adrienne Rich's Poetry*, ed. Barbara Charlesworth Gelpi and Albert Gelpi (New York: Norton, 1975), pp. 65–8.

Tanner, Tony. 'Passion, Narrative, and Identity in *Wuthering Heights* and *Jane Eyre*.' *Teaching the Text*, eds Susanne Kappeler and Norman Bryson (London: Routledge, 1983), pp. 109–25.

Taylor, Anne Robinson. *Male Novelists and Their Female Voices: Literary Masquerades* (Troy, NY: Whitston, 1981).

CHAPTER TWELVE

Siblings and Suitors in the Narrative Architecture of *The Tenant of Wildfell Hall*

TESS O'TOOLE

Tess O'Toole teaches English at McGill University, Quebec. Her research interests lie in Victorian fiction and narrative theory. She has published several articles in these areas, as well as *Genealogy and Fiction in Hardy: Family Lineage
and Narrative Lines* (1997). Her current research is on adoption in Victorian culture and literature. The article reprinted here follows up her interest in family relationships by analysing those that are found in *The Tenant of Wildfell Hall*. She
draws attention to the asymmetry of Helen Huntingdon's relationships with her
first and second husbands and that with her brother. This brings to light the
prominence that Brontë gives to the siblings' relationship which is lacking in the
drawbacks of those Helen shares with her two suitors. O'Toole does not see it
as offering a practical alternative to sexual relationships but rather as offering a
comprehensive critique of them.

Anne Brontë's *The Tenant of Wildfell Hall* has been singled out most
frequently for two elements: (1) its unusually complicated framing
device (Gilbert Markham's epistolary account of his relationship
with Helen Huntingdon surrounds her much lengthier diary account of
her first marriage and flight from her husband) and (2) its strikingly frank
and detailed description of a woman's experience in an abusive marriage.
These two features of the text, one formal and one thematic, are intertwined in the experience of reading the novel. For, in proceeding through

Reprinted from *Studies in English Literature* 39.4 (1999): 715–31.

the multilayered narrative and remaining for a surprisingly protracted time in Helen's painful account of her nightmarish marriage, the reader experiences a sensation that might be labeled narrative claustrophobia. The text thus produces an effect on the reader that mimics the entrapment Helen experiences in her marriage.

'The book is painful,' Charles Kingsley declared in his unsigned review in *Fraser's Magazine*, sounding a note that would be echoed by many contemporary critics. A notice in the *North American Review* complained that the reader 'is confined to a narrow space of life, and held down, as it were, by main force, to witness the wolfish side of [Huntingdon's] nature literally and logically set forth.'[1] This language invokes the claustrophobic sensation that I have suggested is exacerbated by the narrative form. The reader's discomfort is likely to extend beyond Helen's diary account of her hellish first marriage, however. The events recounted in the framing narrative – Helen's courtship by and eventual marriage to Gilbert Markham – purportedly provide a happy ending for Helen, released from her disastrous first marriage and free to choose a better mate. But Gilbert is an oddly unsuitable partner for Helen. Though it may be tempting to read the events in the framing narrative as representing a recovery from the events recounted in the embedded one, such a meliorist view is challenged by the fact that the framing narrative finds Helen remarried to a man who, while not the rake that Arthur Huntingdon was, is capable, like Arthur, of violence and cowardice (as evidenced by his vicious attack on Frederick Lawrence, which he does not publicly acknowledge). Gilbert, like Arthur, has been spoiled by his mother and has an inflated ego, and he subscribes to all the standard Victorian stereotypes about female nature and female merit (as evidenced by his behavior toward and descriptions of both the 'demon' Eliza Millward, his first flame, and the 'angel' Helen).

Gilbert's shortcomings become less critical, however, when attention is shifted from the relationship he describes in his letters to Halford to the one whose forging Helen narrates in her diary – the relationship with her brother Frederick, whom Gilbert perceives as his antagonist and who is his opposite in character. The formal displacement that occurs when Helen's narrative undermines Gilbert's, exceeding it in both length and power, is thus echoed in a displacement of the exogamous romantic plot articulated in his account by the endogamous brother-sister plot contained within hers. The architecture of Brontë's narrative calls attention to alternate forms of domestic containment, one deriving from courtship and marriage, the other from the natal family. Rather than representing these two forms of domesticity as continuous or overlapping, as nineteenth-century novels of family life commonly do, *The Tenant of*

Wildfell Hall stresses their disjunctions, an approach that is complemented by the narrative format.

I

Treatments of *Tenant* as domestic fiction have tended to focus on marital relationships, and hence, when examining the relationship of the framing to the framed narrative, to focus on the differences between Gilbert and Arthur as spouses. The critics I will discuss below, for instance, have suggested that the agenda Helen pursues unsuccessfully in her first marriage, an agenda consistent with prevailing domestic ideology, is realized in her second. It must be acknowledged, however, that the novel's relationship to domestic ideology is an unusually vexed one. In presenting Helen's attraction to her first husband, Brontë daringly implies that her heroine's culturally sanctioned role as the would-be reformer of a sinful man serves as a cover for her sexual attraction to him, but a hellish marriage punishes Helen for succumbing to her desire for Arthur. The novel makes a heroine out of a woman who runs away from her husband; but this transgressive act is sanctioned by a conservative motive: Helen wants to save her son from his father's corrupting influence. The more subversive kind of rebellion enacted by Arthur's mistress, Annabella – a rebellion that does not have a selfless motivation – is severely punished by her society and by the text: 'she [sinks], at length, in difficulty and debt, disgrace and misery; and die[s] at last . . . in penury, neglect and utter wretchedness.'[2] But if Annabella's fate suggests that the novel's critique of domestic ideology has its limits, her role in Brontë's treatment of domestic reform also indicates the limited efficacy of that ideology.

Helen displays the ironic naïveté of a young woman who, subscribing to the ideas about woman's moral influence articulated by Sarah Ellis and others, ardently believes that as her husband's 'angel monitress' she can redeem him. While Helen's surveillance of her home and husband accords with the function of the domestic woman posited by Nancy Armstrong in *Desire and Domestic Fiction*, Helen is not nearly so effective as that powerful creature. The futility of her efforts is underscored by Annabella; while Arthur finds his wife's moralizing tedious, he can be kept in line by his mistress's strategy, which depends on his physical desire for her. Annabella's brand of sexual management, ironically, has more pragmatic reach than domestic authority. In this way, Brontë's novel exposes rather than reproduces the myth of power embedded in cultural constructions of the domestic woman.[3] Helen's friend Millicent may be criticized for failing to provide the sort of moral management her husband needs, but the example of Helen and Arthur suggests that there is a problem with the entire notion of the wife as agent of reform.

The authorial preface to the second edition reiterates on a figural level Helen's frustrated efforts at domestic purification. Just before asserting, 'if I can gain the public ear at all, I would rather whisper a few wholesome truths therein than much soft nonsense,' Brontë compares herself to a cleaning woman who, 'undertak[ing] the cleansing of a careless bachelor's apartment will be liable to more abuse for the dust she raises, than commendation for the clearance she effects' (p. 3). If her commitment to acknowledging unpleasant truths links her to Helen, so too does this indication of the limits of her own success, since Helen's wifely attempts at cleaning up Arthur's act are met with obdurate resistance.

This essay stresses the novel's ambivalent relationship to domestic ideology because some of the best readings of this novel become entwined with it when treating the relationship between Helen's and Gilbert's narratives. Inspired by Brontë's eloquent and compelling defense of a wronged woman, and her invention of a heroine who heroically fights back, N.M. Jacobs, Linda Shires, and Elizabeth Langland have all provided insightful readings of *Tenant* as a protofeminist text. Each of these critics, however, credits Brontë's heroine with the successful moral education of her second husband, maintaining that Gilbert is reformed by his exposure to Helen's text and that their union redeems Helen's disastrous first marriage; in so doing, they risk reinscribing the domestic ideology that it is a part of the novel's accomplishment to problematize.[4] Moreover, each has at some point to ignore, minimize, or recast elements in Gilbert's narrative that qualify a positive account of Helen's second marriage. It is my contention that these elements are linked to a narrative strategy that contrasts Gilbert the suitor, would-be hero of the framing narrative, and Frederick the brother, hero of the framed narrative. The strategy behind the narrative layering is not to show Gilbert's reform and to celebrate a restored conjugal ideal, but to juxtapose siblings and suitors, to poise natal domesticity against nuptial domesticity.

In 'Gender and Layered Narrative in *Wuthering Heights* and *The Tenant of Wildfell Hall*,' Jacobs initially seems set to view Gilbert's framing narrative as part of a continuing critique of the domestic, rather than as the site of its recuperation. She notes that the enclosure of Helen's diary narrative within Gilbert's epistolary one mimics not just the division of male and female into separate spheres but also the law of couverture. The fact that Helen's diary has become her husband's possession and that he has the power to bargain with it in a bid to recover his friend's favor reinforces this point, but Jacobs does not pursue that tack. Instead, she sees the relationship between Helen's story and Gilbert's as one that works not to contain *her* but to educate *him*. According to Jacobs, the 'effect on Gilbert of reading this document – of being admitted into the reality hidden within and behind the conventional consciousness in which he participates – is revolutionary, and absolutely instrumental to the partnership of equals their marriage will become. Its revelations force him outside the restricted boundaries of an ego that defines itself through its difference from and superiority to someone else.'[5]

If this were the case, however, then the access to Helen's consciousness which Gilbert's reading of her diary gives him should have altered his behavior and assumptions. Jacobs, however, provides no evidence in support of Gilbert's moral growth. And far from demonstrating any such alteration, Brontë's novel shows us that in the events following upon his reading of the diary, Gilbert is as egotistical and as sexist as he appears in the opening chapters. His immediate response when he has concluded the account of Helen's harrowing domestic drama is pique that the pages detailing her initial impressions of him have been ripped out. While the diary might have restored Helen to his good graces, rendering her once again *'all I wished to think her . . .* her character shone bright, and clear, and stainless as that sun I could not bear to look on' (p. 382, my emphasis), it has not touched his tendency to demonize all attractive women who are not the exalted Helen, as his continued shabby treatment and vilification of Eliza make clear. His unreasonable resentment of Frederick continues, and his egotism is still intact; his pride almost leads him to lose Helen, as he refuses to make himself vulnerable to learn whether she still loves him. Most disturbing, the violence he exhibited in his attack on Frederick is still manifest in his behavior toward Eliza, the former object of his sexual interest; when she says something that angers him, he responds: 'I seized her arm and gave it, I think, a pretty severe squeeze, for she shrank into herself with a faint cry of pain or terror' (p. 444). Thus, there does not seem to be any significant revision in Gilbert's character that would encourage us to disagree with Helen's aunt when she says, 'Could [Helen] have been contented to remain single, I own I should have been better satisfied' (p. 470). The absence of growth on Gilbert's part was commented upon by Kingsley, who questioned Brontë's agenda: 'If the author had intended to work the noble old Cymon and Iphigenia myths, she ought to have let us see the gradual growth of the clown's mind under the influence of the accomplished woman, and this is just what she has not done.'[6] Precisely. We can only assume that Brontë knew what she was about when she chose to include details suggesting Gilbert's persistent limitations.

While Shires concedes those limitations, she maintains that Gilbert and his correspondent Jack Halford are both educated by their reading of

Helen's diary: '[The novel] counsels an inscribed male friend that what he may perceive as overly independent female behavior is a strong woman's only way to maintain integrity in a world where aristocratic male domin-ance can easily slip into abusiveness. It is important that the text addresses a man, for the counterhegemonic project of the text is not merely to expose a bad marriage but to teach patriarchy the value of female rebel-lion.'[7] Like Shires, Langland views the framing male narrative as one that serves a feminist agenda, though in different terms. Writing in part in response to Jacobs's description of the relationship between Gilbert's narrative and Helen's as one of enclosure, Langland argues in 'The Voicing of Female Desire in . . . *The Tenant of Wildfell Hall*' that '[a] tradi-tional analysis that speaks of nested narratives is already contaminated by the patriarchal ideology of prior and latter and so cannot effectively question what I wish to question . . . the transgressive nature of narrative exchange.' Thus she proposes viewing the 'narrative within a narrative not as hierarchical or detachable parts, but as interacting functions within a transgressive economy that allows for the paradoxic voicing of feminine desire.'[8] Central to her argument is the fact that the text as a whole is structured around an exchange of letters, and that the epistolary exchange is the prelude for an exchange of visits (Halford and Rose to Gilbert and Helen). She argues that an exchange structure is inherently destabilizing and thus can serve a feminist agenda. She does not allow the gender implications built into this particular exchange to give her pause.[9] However, it is surely not irrelevant that the exchange of letters is an exchange between two men, nor that the material exchanged is a woman's story, though this is a point Langland's reading must ignore. It strikes the reader as curious at best that Gilbert would transcribe for another man the contents of his wife's intimate diary, and disturbing at worst that Helen's hellish experience is used for a homosocial end.

The transaction between Gilbert and Halford accords with the model outlined by Eve Kosofsky Sedgwick in *Between Men*, which describes how women are used as instruments with which those economic and affective bonds between men that structure society are forged.[10] Gilbert's revela-tion of Helen's story to Halford is an act of debt paying. He has fallen out of Halford's favor because he did not respond to his friend's sharing of confidences with equal candor; the story he is telling him now, which is actually his wife's story, will acquit his debt. He instructs Halford: 'If the coin suits you, tell me so, and I'll send you the rest at my leisure: if you would rather remain my creditor than stuff your purse with such ungainly heavy pieces, – tell me still, and I'll pardon your bad taste, and willingly keep the treasure to myself' (p. 18). The exchange between Gilbert and Halford is not only an economic one, it is also an emotional one, geared toward a restoration of affection. It is clear that Halford has replaced the women in Gilbert's life for the top spot in his affections. Halford is Gilbert's brother-in-law, and he has taken his sister's place in his affections. When in Gilbert's account he first refers to his sister Rose, he pauses to comment: 'Nothing told me then, that she, a few years hence, would be the wife of one – entirely unknown to me as yet, but destined hereafter to become a closer friend than even herself' (p. 10). More intriguingly, Markham refers to his marriage to Helen Huntingdon as 'the most important event of my life – previous to my acquaintance with Jack Halford at least' (p. 8). The story wins Gilbert his friend's love again, renewing the affective bond between the two men that was in danger of dissolving: 'I perceive, with joy, my most valued friend, that the cloud of your displeasure has past away; the light of your countenance blesses me once more' (p. 19).

At one point Gilbert contrasts his warm friendship with Halford to his inability to feel that same kind of bond with Frederick Lawrence, Helen's brother: '[U]pon the whole, our intimacy was rather a mutual predilection than a deep and solid friendship, such as since has arisen between myself and you, Halford' (p. 36). His jealousy of Frederick, whom he mistakenly assumes to be Helen's lover, leads to Gilbert's resentment of him and to his violent attack on him. But even after he learns of Frederick's kinship with Helen and of how instrumental he has been in Helen's escape from Huntingdon, Gilbert is unable to forge a connection with him or even to appreciate his merit. The antipathy between the two, much more virulent on Gilbert's side, is significant, for Frederick is a man who will not engage in the sort of transactions over women that Gilbert wishes him to conduct. Frederick, while placing no impediments between Gilbert and his sister, is not willing to play the active role of go-between that Gilbert expects him to play. Gilbert resents Frederick and even considers him morally culpable for not intervening with his sister on his behalf: '[H]e *had* wronged us . . . He had not attempted to check the course of our love by actually damming up the streams in their passage, but he had passively watched the two currents wandering through life's arid wilderness, declining to clear away the obstructions that divided them, and secretly hoping that both would lose themselves in the sand before they could be joined in one' (p. 450). Though Helen sees her relationship to her brother as an end in itself, Gilbert wants the brother to serve as their mediator, to channel the passion whose object and destination is himself.

Such a structure of channeling and mediation is embodied in the novel by gossip, whose central and suspect role in this novel has been elucidated by Jan Gordon: '[G]ossip always appears as a threat to value:

it either "speculates" or exaggerates by "inflating" ... In short gossip devalues because it has nothing standing behind it. Lacking the authenticity of a definable source, it is simultaneously financially, theologically, and narratively unredeemable.'[11] (It is in fact gossip, with Frederick as its unwitting subject, that brings Gilbert and Helen together; gossip's misconstrual of Frederick's wedding as Helen's causes Gilbert to rush to the scene, a trip which ends in his engagement to Helen.) Gilbert implicitly links Frederick's refusal to play go-between with his refusal to gossip when he complains to Halford that '[h]e provoked me at times ... by his evident reluctance to talk to me about his sister' (p. 397). When Helen, on the verge of rejoining her husband, had suggested to Gilbert that he might know of her through her brother, she had specified: 'I did not mean that Frederick should be the means of transmitting messages between us, only that each might know, through him, of the other's welfare' (p. 386). In her formulation of the triangle, Frederick is less a mediating term than an apex. Gilbert's contrasting expectation that Frederick will serve as an intermediary is thwarted by the literalism and lack of expansiveness with which Frederick imparts news of Helen: 'I would still pursue my habitual enquiries after his sister – if he had lately heard from her, and how she was, but nothing more. I did so, and the answers I received were always provokingly limited to the letter of the enquiry' (p. 436). Significantly, Frederick is a character who resists transmitting gossip. He does not, for example, let the community know it was Gilbert who attacked him. He is most reluctant to gossip about women, a reluctance that baffles and aggravates Gilbert.

Gilbert's conversation with Frederick about Jane Wilson is especially revealing in this regard. His narrative has painted Jane as a social climber who wished to ensnare Frederick. Gilbert takes it upon himself to warn Frederick of the danger Gilbert believes he faces from this predatory woman. Frederick checks Gilbert's desire to gossip about the woman and to slander her: '"I never told you, Markham, that I intended to marry Miss Wilson" ... "No, but whether you do or not, she intends to marry you." "Did she tell you so?" "No, but –" "Then you have no right to make such an assertion respecting her"' (p. 401). As Gilbert continues to press his point, Frederick, who is not interested in Jane, responds with gentle sarcasm to Gilbert's diatribe. While Gilbert is miffed by Frederick's refusal to join him in maligning Jane's character, to engage in this particular kind of male bonding, he comforts himself by reflecting: 'I believe ... that he soon learned to contemplate with secret amazement his former predilection, and to congratulate himself on the lucky escape he had made; but he never confessed it to me ... As for Jane Wilson ... [h]ad I done wrong to blight her cherished hopes? I think not; and certainly my conscience has never accused me, from that day to this' (p. 402). The assumption of his own correct insight into Frederick's attitude, steadfastly maintained in the face of a lack of evidence, and the callous indifference toward the unhappy Jane Wilson are both powerful indicators of Gilbert's self-satisfied nature and the limits of his imagination and his empathy. Significantly, this smug reflection is made by the older Gilbert who has been married to Helen for many years; it thus cautions us not to assume too much about Gilbert's improvement under Helen's tutelage.

Frederick's refusal to gossip about women is in contrast not only to Gilbert's eagerness to gossip about Jane Wilson, but also to Gilbert's sharing of his wife's intimate diary with his male friend. As we have seen, attempts to read Helen's second marriage as an event which redeems the domestic ideal compromised by her first marriage must ignore evidence about Gilbert's shortcomings and the troubling implications of his transfer of the contents of her diary to his friend. It is significant that many of Gilbert's flaws are made visible through interactions with Helen's brother Frederick; this fact should encourage us to think further about the latter's role. For all the famous violence of the domestic scenes in this novel, the most violent moment in the novel is the one in which Gilbert attacks Frederick:

I had seized my whip by the small end, and – swift and sudden as a flash of lightning – brought the other down upon his head. It was not without a feeling of strange satisfaction that I beheld the instant, deadly pallor that overspread his face, and the few red drops that trickled down his forehead, while he reeled a moment in his saddle, and then fell backward to the ground . . . Had I killed him? . . . [N]o; he moved his eyelids and uttered a slight groan. I breathed again – he was only stunned by the fall. It served him right – it would teach him better manners in future. Should I help him to his horse? No. For any other combination of offences I would; but his were too unpardonable. (p. 109)

Gilbert's physical attack on Frederick makes particularly vivid and concrete an opposition between Helen's suitor and her brother that is visible throughout the novel, yet Frederick's importance has been largely overlooked by critics.[12]

Frederick plays an instrumental role in the recuperation of Helen's unhappy history; it is he, not Gilbert, who redeems Helen's faith in humanity after her disillusioning experience with Arthur. She writes in her diary: 'I was beginning insensibly to cherish very unamiable feelings against my fellow mortals – the male part of them especially; but it is a comfort to see that there is at least one among them worthy to be trusted and esteemed' (p. 356). Curiously, Frederick is exactly the sort of man the reader who wants a happier, more appropriate second marriage for Helen would expect her to marry. He, not Gilbert, is the gentle, sensitive, and supportive male that Helen has sought. If we are to look for an optimistic, meliorist plot in the novel, it is more likely to be found in the brother–sister relationship than in the husband–wife one. The opportunity for revision and recuperation lies not in the undeniably disappointing Gilbert, so curiously less mature than his bride, but in the brother. Improvement is effected not so much by Gilbert as a replacement for Helen's first husband as it is by her brother as a replacement for her father.[13] Juliet McMaster notes a pattern of generational improvement in the novel's juxtaposition of characters who embody Regency values with those who embody Victorian values.[14] She discusses this distinction primarily with reference to the replacement of the dissolute Arthur, with his aristocratic associations, by the gentleman farmer Gilbert (elevated to the squirearchy by his marriage to the newly propertied Helen). But that pattern is most marked in the contrast between Helen's irresponsible father and his virtuous son.[15] The framing story is the wrong place to look for a positive alternative to Helen's marriage with Arthur; we must look instead to her diary, to the account of her relationship with Frederick. By shifting attention from the suitor to the brother, we can account for the dissatisfactions of the courtship narrative while revealing Brontë's display of alternate forms of domestic containment. It is Helen's growing relationship with her brother, rather than the burgeoning relationship with Gilbert, that receives the privileged place in her diary after she leaves her husband. The containment of the brother–sister plot within the embedded narrative reflects the turn inward, toward the natal family. The claustrophobic narrative structure, originally linked to an imprisoning marriage, finds an alternate thematic corollary in a potentially incestuous relationship.

II

Poised between Helen's first marriage and her second is the relationship she forges with her brother during her exile. As the person to whom Helen turns for help when she makes her escape, Frederick serves as a buffer between her and the world during her period of disguise. Helen and Frederick's relationship is peculiar for a brother–sister one because they have been raised having only minimal contact with each other. Helen's father, an alcoholic with no interest in daughters, abnegated his responsibility toward her, turning her over to relatives after the death of his wife, while keeping charge of his son. Helen's flight from her husband provides the occasion for building a relationship with her brother that they have thus far not enjoyed. Becoming better acquainted as adults, their relationship is in some ways structurally closer to a courtship relationship than to a brother–sister one. The townspeople, ignorant of Helen's true identity, construe their relationship as a sexual one, and Gilbert sees him as a romantic rival, suggesting, perhaps, the novel's own flirtation with an incest motif. Helen, after all, is fixated on her son's resemblance to the brother she loves. She reconceives her son as the progeny not of her husband Arthur but of her brother Frederick; she says to him: 'He is like you, Frederick . . . in some of his moods: I sometimes think he resembles you more than his father; and I am glad of it' (p. 357). Helen's flight from her husband's to her brother's house is followed, then, by the realignment of her son's lineage in relation to her natal family. Previously, the son's physical likeness to his father was stressed, and Helen has kept Arthur senior's portrait (which had symbolized her physical desire for him) in order to compare the child to it as he grows. In raising her son, she seeks to instill the character she would create into the body she desired. Finding the embodiment of manly virtue in her brother, she redesignates her son's person as 'like Frederick's.'

Rather than exploring sexual overtones in the sibling relationship, however, Brontë's novel foregrounds its relationship to domestic reform; Frederick's virtue compensates for their father's neglectful treatment of Helen, and their comfortable relationship, defined by mutual respect, contrasts with Helen's problematic relationships with her husband and her suitor. The implication that the brother–sister relationship has the potential to redeem a compromised domestic sphere bears some resemblance to Jane Austen's employment of the sibling model of relationships as described by Glenda A. Hudson in *Sibling Love and Incest in Jane Austen's Fiction*. Emphasizing the nonsalacious nature of Austen's treatment of incestuous relationships – 'In her novels, the in-family marriages between the cousins and in-laws are successful because they do not grow out of sexual longing but are rooted in a deeper, more abiding domestic love which merges spiritual, intellectual and physical affinities' – Hudson argues that for Austen, 'the incestuous marriages of Fanny and Edmund, Emma and Knightley, and Elinor and Edward Ferrars are therapeutic and restorative; the endogamous unions safeguard the family circle and its values . . . Incest in Austen's novels creates a loving and enclosed family circle.'[16] The idea of closing family ranks for protective and restorative purposes can be applied to Helen's turn to her brother.[17] Unlike what we would find in an Austen novel, however, no warm relationship is effected between Frederick and Gilbert through the latter's marriage to Frederick's sister. The brother-in-law whose visit Gilbert eagerly anticipates at the end of the novel is Jack Halford, not Frederick Lawrence. The alternate domestic relationships of siblings and spouses remain quite distinct in Helen's experience, rather than the former fostering marital exchange.

The endogamous quality of the brother–sister relationship is exaggerated in the case of Helen and Frederick: formed during her time in hiding, it is necessarily an insular one which cannot incorporate outsiders. And it coexists with a regressive project in which Helen engages upon her flight from her marital home, for Helen's retreat from her husband is followed by a return to her natal family origins, symbolized by her adoption of her mother's maiden name as her alias and her return to the home in which her mother died. Wildfell Hall, though 'no[t] yet quite sunk into decay,' is a previous family home that has been exchanged for a more up-to-date one, so she is not only symbolically returning to her family, but returning to a prior stage in the family history (p. 355).

Together, Helen and Frederick revise their family history. Enjoying frequent contact with her brother, Helen reconstructs the family life she was denied as a child. Frederick's supportive and responsible fraternal behavior compensates for the poor behavior of Helen's father. The contrast between Helen's relationship with her father and the relationship she enjoys with her brother bears out claims made by Joseph P. Boone and Deborah E. Nord about Victorian brother–sister plots. They argue that the '[sister's] investment in the brother figure . . . originates as a means to combat her own devaluation within the family and society,' frequently making up for paternal neglect in particular. They also note that the brother–sister relationship might be used to circumvent problems inherent in a conjugal relationship: '[I]n some cases, the sibling ideal becomes a utopian basis for figuring heterosexual relationships not based on traditional conceptions of gender polarity as the basis of romantic attraction. Theoretically, at least, the idealized union of brother and sister rests on a more egalitarian, less threatening mode of male–female relationship, precisely because the bond is one in which gender difference is rendered secondary to the tie of blood-likeness, familiarity and friendship.'[18] While one might question the assumption that there is something more inherently benign about brother–sister relations than other male–female ones, Helen and Frederick's relationship does seem intended to provide an alternative to the violence and power plays that contaminate the conjugal relationship. Frederick gives her both emotional and practical support and appears to be the only male in the novel who embodies the virtues she seeks in a mate.

Contrary to the case of the brothers and sisters Boone and Nord describe, however, the intimacy of Frederick and Helen is not born and nurtured in the nursery; it is not itself, therefore, cultivated by domestic arrangements. It is, we must suspect, precisely because Frederick and Helen have not been raised together that their sibling relationship presents a strong contrast to the others in the novel, such as that between Gilbert and his sister Rose, who complains of the favoritism with which the sons of the family are treated, and that of Esther Hargrave and her brother, who attempts to pressure her into an unsuitable match. The problem of triangulation within the nuclear family is called to our attention from the first page, when Gilbert commences his account of himself with reference to the competing agendas his mother and father had regarding their son; this is swiftly followed by an exposure to the sibling rivalry between Gilbert and his younger brother as well as that between Rose and her brothers. (The fact that Helen's son is conceived alternately as an improved version of her husband and a younger version of her brother suggests that her family will not be exempt from the kind of triangulation that plagues the Markham family.) Because Helen and Frederick come together as adults, there is no parental mediation to promote rivalry or jealousy. Moreover, due to the early death of his mother, Frederick has not been spoiled by maternal indulgence in the way that both Arthur and Gilbert are said to have been. Thus, their exemplary sibling relationship is also exceptional. While Helen and Frederick's relationship seems to present a model for domestic relations, it is a somewhat utopian one, and its strength, paradoxically, derives from the absence of domestic structures in its formation. Therefore, that model is unable to provide the basis for its own reproduction.

In this respect, Brontë's treatment of the brother–sister motif differs from that of many other nineteenth-century novelists who privilege sibling bonds. Austen and Charles Dickens, for example, both use the sibling relationship as a model for the marital one by having the spouse metonymically connected to the brother (either by being him, as in *Mansfield Park*, or by having a special connection to him, as in *Dombey and Son*). In *Tenant*, this approach is visible only on the margins of the central plot, as, for example, when Helen arranges for Frederick's marriage to Esther Hargrave, the young woman whom she has called her 'sister in heart and affection' (p. 338). The marriage of Arthur Jr and Helen Hattersly, a second 'Helen and Arthur' marriage, is also a sort of fraternal/sororal match, since their mothers' closeness has caused them often to play and take lessons together from childhood, as siblings would do. Gilbert and Helen's marriage, however, does not adhere to the sibling paradigm. In the central plot, Brontë keeps the suitor and the brother steadfastly segregated: they are antithetical types and are, consequently, antipathetic to each other. Moreover, Gilbert is rendered analogous not to Helen's brother, but to her son. Using his friendship with little Arthur as a way of accessing the mother, the petulant and immature Gilbert is, as Shires describes him, the 'boy child who wants to take possession of the mother.'[19] It is Frederick, not Gilbert, whom Helen perceives as Arthur's ideal imaginary parent. This fact reinforces the extent to which Frederick appears to be Helen's only male equal in the novel as well as the only exemplar of manly domestic virtue. Though it is incest that is traditionally associated with the disruption of normal generational sequence,[20] Brontë reverses this association by figuring generational imbalance in the exogamous relationship.

Brontë's treatment of the sibling motif contrasts not only with Dickens's and Austen's, but, closer to home, with her own sister's. Numerous critics have traced the lines of kinship between *Tenant* and *Wuthering Heights*, which contains the more famous representation of sibling love.[21] Paradoxically, while the incest motif appears less transgressive in *Tenant* than in *Wuthering Heights* – it is where family values are housed – it is less translatable into the social sphere. In Emily Brontë's novel (as in Charlotte Brontë's *Jane Eyre*), the notion of kinship is used to figure the romantic love whose promise is a cornerstone of the domestic ideal. In *Desire and Domestic Fiction*, Armstrong alludes to the strategy behind the kind of romantic identification often associated with incest in the novels of the other Brontë sisters: 'In the face of the essential incompatibility of the social roles they attempt to couple, [Emily and Charlotte Brontë] endow their lovers with absolute identity on an entirely different ontological plane.' Working against a critical tradition that 'had turned the Brontës' novels into sublimating strategies that conceal forbidden desires, including incest,' Armstrong associates Emily and Charlotte Brontë's fiction with a development whereby 'sexuality . . . become[s] the instrument of, and not the resistance to, conventional morality.'[22] It is not surprising that Armstrong's account does not include Anne Brontë, for, unlike Emily and Charlotte, Anne seems to juxtapose rather than to collapse kinship relations and sexual ones in *Tenant*.[23] This makes *Tenant* a most unusual example of nineteenth-century domestic fiction, a fact that may account for the relative marginalization of Anne's masterpiece within the Brontë corpus.

Helen's relationship to her brother Frederick cannot ultimately solve the problems or contradictions that cluster around the concept of the domestic, for it apparently cannot be brought to bear on other familial relationships, or on anything outside its own circuit. While in *Wuthering Heights* the incestuous longing of Cathy and Heathcliff is replaced by the more socially acceptable (but, as William Goetz points out, sanguinally more affined[24]) marriage of Catherine and Hareton, in *Tenant*, the sibling relationship seems to exist as an end in itself. The sense of narrative claustrophobia described above is the formal corollary of this self-containment. Helen and Frederick's relationship remains insular, and it remains locked within the field of Helen's diary.

Helen's narrative itself is 'locked,' for, once her diary is turned over to Gilbert, she never again narrates.[25] This means that we have only his word for the success of their marriage. That he is satisfied is clear, but the reader has no firsthand access to Helen's subsequent experience. It also means that in Helen's diary the strongest affective relationship with a man that she describes after leaving Arthur is with her brother, in keeping with Brontë's use of the brother–sister plot to cast a dubious light on Gilbert and his courtship. It is no doubt because the novel privileges Helen's relationship to her brother, the record of which is confined to the embedded narrative, that Gilbert's framing narrative strikes many readers as perfunctory.

But it is more than perfunctory; it is part of a sustained critique of marital domesticity and part of an oppositional structure that segregates the nuptial and the natal forms of domestic containment. *Tenant* is distinctive in its brilliant use of compartmentalized narratives to reflect this thematic opposition. It is even more distinctive in its refusal to reconcile sexual and kinship relations, and in its willingness to sustain the resulting note of unease.

NOTES

I would like to thank Deirdre d'Albertis for her valuable comments on the draft of this essay.

1. Quoted in Miriam Allott, *The Brontës: The Critical Heritage* (London and Boston: Routledge & Kegan Paul, 1974), pp. 272, 262.

2. Anne Brontë, *The Tenant of Wildfell Hall*, ed. Herbert Rosengarten (New York: Oxford Univ. Press, 1993), p. 439. All subsequent citations to this novel refer to this edition and are indicated parenthetically in the text.

3. Others have commented on the novel's ironic stance toward the notion of the woman's role as 'angel monitress,' particularly Maria H. Frawley, who in *Anne Brontë* (New York: Twayne, 1996), argues that Brontë 'challenges the domestic ideology that encouraged women to construct themselves as ethereal agents of morality and virtue' (pp. 133–4). Though Elizabeth Langland, in *Anne Brontë: The Other One* (London: Macmillan, 1989), shows with respect to Helen and Arthur that *Tenant* 'explodes [the] myth' that women 'can serve as redemptive angels to . . . men,' she maintains that Helen's diary 'serves a . . . vital function in *educating* Gilbert' and that the 'Gilbert who marries Helen must accede to . . . the probity of her "harshness" in correcting [male] weakness,' thus suggesting that Helen's reforming mission is realized with her second husband (pp. 141, 134).

4. In a footnote to 'Acts of Custody and Incarceration in *Wuthering Heights* and *The Tenant of Wildfell Hall*,' *Novel* 30.1 (Fall 1996): 32–55, Laura Berry comments, in a similar vein to mine: 'Gilbert Markham's likeness to Arthur Huntingdon is often elided in order to read into Brontë's ending a conditional conjugal equality, and thus to make Anne Brontë's novel a proto-feminist one. This understandable gesture . . . does not always do justice to the complexity of the narrative' (p. 45, n. 19). Berry, however, does not address the role of Frederick and the sibling relationship, arguing rather that Brontë 'abandon[s] hope in marital pedagogy in favour of child training' (p. 47).

5. N.M. Jacobs, 'Gender and Layered Narrative in *Wuthering Heights* and *The Tenant of Wildfell Hall*,' *JNT* 16.3 (Fall 1986): 204–19, 213. [See also Chapter 11, this volume.]

6. Quoted in Allott, p. 272.

7. Linda Shires, 'Of Maenads, Mothers, and Feminized Males: Victorian Readings of the French Revolution,' in *Rewriting the Victorians: Theory, History and the Politics of Gender*, ed. Shires (New York and London: Routledge, 1992), pp. 147–65, 160. Shires explicitly acknowledges her own motivation in putting the slant she does on the novel. 'Although [the text] can be read as shutting down women's independent voices and actions, [it] should be read primarily as instrumental in enabling and promoting the next wave of revolutionary English feminism' (p. 162). What I am underscoring is the connection between this act of recuperating the text for and as a feminist history and a view of recuperation as what is at stake in the novel's double marriage plot, since readings such as Shires's and Jacobs's imply that Helen's second marriage, in contrast to her disastrous first one, is benign.

8. Langland, 'The Voicing of Female Desire in Anne Brontë's *The Tenant of Wildfell Hall*,' in *Gender and Discourse in Victorian Literature and Art*, ed. Antony H. Harrison and Beverly Taylor (Dekalb: Northern Illinois Univ. Press, 1992), pp. 111–23, 111, 112.

9. Langland does, however, argue in her essay that Helen controls Gilbert's narrative to Halford, that her diary 'redeem[s]' his 'bankrupt' narrative (p. 116).

10. Eve Kosofsky Sedgwick, *Between Men: English Literature and Male Homosocial Desire* (New York: Columbia Univ. Press, 1985).

11. Jan B. Gordon, 'Gossip, Diary, Letter, Text: Anne Brontë's Narrative *Tenant* and the Problematic of the Gothic Sequel,' *ELH* 51.4 (Winter 1984): 719–45, 725.

12. For example, though Langland is interested in the way the novel 'critiques the conventional manly ideal [and] criticizes male indulgence,' she does not consider how the exemplary Frederick factors into the novel's representation of male character (*Anne Brontë*, p. 137). Of Gilbert's attack on Frederick she says: 'Thematically and structurally in the novel, this episode develops the insidious effects of an indulgence that leads to masculine arrogance and abuse of power,' without commenting on the juxtaposition of these sharply contrasting specimens of manhood or noting that their opposition factors into the thematic and structural organization of the novel as a whole (p. 133). Langland's approach is typical in seeming to view Frederick's role

in the novel as incidental. Shires notes that '[i]deologically, this text, like *Jane Eyre*, promotes gender and class equality which it figures in heterosexual marriage. Yet nearly every man in the book is susceptible to appearance, sentimental romanticizing, cant, or corruption' (p. 161); she does not consider the counterexample offered by Frederick, focusing instead on Helen's two husbands.

13. If, as has sometimes been suggested, the original of the alcoholic Arthur is Branwell Brontë, then Anne Brontë, in substituting Frederick for Arthur, might be imagining for herself an improved brother. On Anne's relationship to Branwell and her desire to rescue him, see Langland's *Anne Brontë*, pp. 16–8; for the possible influence of Branwell's character and history on *Tenant*, see Edward Chitham, *A Life of Anne Brontë* (Oxford and Cambridge MA: Basil Blackwell, 1991), pp. 137, 143, 146, and 148–50.

14. Juliet McMaster, ' "Imbecile Laughter" and "Desperate Earnest" in *The Tenant of Wildfell Hall*,' *MLQ* 43.4 (December 1982): 352–68.

15. This pattern is iterated in Helen's attempt to make Arthur Jr a better man than the father he risks resembling. Again, improvement is sought within the natal family.

16. Glenda Hudson, *Sibling Love and Incest in Jane Austen's Fiction* (London: Macmillan, 1992), pp. 25, 35.

17. Tony Tanner, *Adultery in the Novel: Contract and Transgression* (Baltimore: Johns Hopkins Univ. Press, 1979), acknowledges the function of incest in maintaining family values when he remarks, apropos of the ending of *The Mill on the Floss*: 'There are cases when the bourgeois novel avoids adultery only by permitting or even pursuing something that is very close to incest' (p. 72).

18. Joseph P. Boone and Deborah E. Nord, 'Brother and Sister: The Seductions of Siblinghood in Dickens, Eliot and Brontë,' *WHR* 46.2 (Summer 1992): 164–88, 167, 165.

19. Shires, p. 162.

20. Marc Shell, *The End of Kinship: 'Measure for Measure,' Incest, and the Ideal of Universal Siblinghood* (Stanford: Stanford Univ. Press, 1988), p. 40.

21. Jacobs, for example, stresses the similar use of narrative layering in the two novels and what she calls 'narrative cross dressing' in both. Other accounts suggest that a Bloomian rivalry is played out in the siblings' novels. Chitham suggests that 'Anne's artistic and moral challenge to the content of her sisters' novels comes in *Wildfell Hall*,' noting, for instance, that she 'parodied Emily's scenes of violence' and arguing that '[a]s *Wildfell Hall* developed from common ground with Emily, Anne used her story to show how very different was her "moral" view from Emily's "poetic" one. This argument, involving matters of realism, morality, and indeed differing world views, began to pervade [*Tenant*, which] does, finally, become Anne's considered "answer" to *Wuthering Heights*' (pp. 134, 145, 142). Gordon discusses *Tenant* as a novel which 'encloses . . . *Wuthering Heights*, as it strives to supplant it' (p. 720). Gordon also suggests that the labyrinthine narrative format of both novels can be related to their shared interest in a potentially incestuous relationship when he comments that

in both *Wuthering Heights* and *The Tenant of Wildfell Hall* '[t]he whole question of belatedness and priority threatens to collapse all the narratives back into a single narrative in much the same way that genealogy threatens to collapse back into the disappearance of difference that produces the monstrous, the ruin, or the fragment – the ontic status of lacking paternity or succession' (p. 737).

22. Nancy Armstrong, *Desire and Domestic Fiction: A Political History of the Novel* (New York: Oxford Univ. Press, 1987), pp. 197, 187, 199.

23. When Armstrong asserts that 'the Brontës . . . had more to do with formulating universal forms of subjectivity than any other novelists' and that 'the Brontës have come to be known for a literary language that allows emotion to overpower convention and become a value in its own right, blotting out all features of political person, place, and event,' her 'Brontës' refers to Emily and Charlotte (pp. 187, 197). Anne is the odd sister out, as she is in Charlotte's biographical notice that accompanied the reissue of *Wuthering Heights*. While Emily appears as the genius championed by her famous sister, Anne's efforts are dismissed: 'I cannot wonder [at the unfavorable reception of *The Tenant of Wildfell Hall*]. The choice of subject was an entire mistake. Nothing less congruous with the writer's nature could be conceived . . . She was a very sincere and practical Christian, but the tinge of religious melancholy communicated a sad shade to her brief, blameless life' ([Charlotte Brontë], 'Biographical Notice of Ellis and Acton Bell,' in *Wuthering Heights*, ed. David Daiches (New York: Penguin, 1985), p. 34).

24. William Goetz, 'Genealogy and Incest in *Wuthering Heights*,' *SNNTS* 14.4 (Winter 1982): 359–76.

25. For a contrasting point of view, see Langland's claim in 'The Voicing of Female Desire' that Helen's voice is present in Gilbert's narrative, that she is the focalizer of his account of Huntingdon's death (pp. 119–20).

CHAPTER THIRTEEN

Diaries and Displacement in *Wuthering Heights*

REBECCA STEINITZ

Rebecca Steinitz is a member of the English Faculty at the Ohio Wesleyan University where she teaches Victorian literature and feminist literary criticism and theory. She is particularly interested in diaries and other forms of life-writing and has written numerous articles on these subjects. In the one reprinted here she focuses on the diaries of Lockwood and the first Catherine in *Wuthering Heights* to explore the potential of diaries as a literary device. She contrasts the two as explicitly masculine and concerned with externals, and feminine as concerned with the inner life. She reads even more into the potential of such diaries as offering the apparent possibility of controlling space as well as time. Both Lockwood and Catherine, it is suggested, are involved in a search for a place of their own: his practical, hers emotional. It is a search in which each is unsuccessful. Steinitz concludes that Emily Brontë's use of diaries in this way opens up new possibilities for their use in fiction.

I t is self-evident, if soon forgettable, that *Wuthering Heights* opens as a diary: '1801 – I have just returned from a visit to my landlord.'[1] Yet, though Lockwood's voice begins the novel, the dated entry, immediacy, and first person account of events and thoughts which characterize the diary soon give way to the recounting, through multiple narrators, of the complex story of the Earnshaws, the Lintons, and Heathcliff, a saga which takes place in the past, albeit a past which grows closer as the

Reprinted from *Studies in the Novel* 32.4 (2000): 407–19.

novel progresses. This diary, it would seem, functions primarily as a frame, an excuse for telling this story. In the novel's third chapter, however, we encounter something more insistently and explicitly a 'regular diary' (p. 16), as Lockwood terms it: Catherine's passionate description of the day of injustices she and Heathcliff have just suffered, 'scrawled in an unformed, childish hand' in the margins of an old religious book and stowed away in the confines of the cabinet bed.[2] These two diaries could not seem more different: Lockwood's appears to function primarily to transmit narrative; Catherine's as revelation of experience and subjectivity. Lockwood's has no physical specificity, no book or pages; Catherine's is emphatically material. Lockwood's moves through time, both the year of his tenantship at Thrushcross Grange and the decades of his story; of Catherine's we receive only the fragments of a single day (or perhaps two). Yet we do not need J. Hillis Miller's image of the novel as a set of 'Chinese boxes of texts within texts' to see Catherine's diary as diametrically engaged with Lockwood's, the inner text to his outer.[3] Indeed, the formal prominence and stylistic differences of these two diaries insist upon critical attention.

Not surprisingly, such attention has been given, sometimes at great length. Yet, almost inevitably, critical narratives have subsumed the novel's diaries under some larger rubric. Often, that rubric has been textuality itself, as one or both diaries take their place among the novel's diverse books, letters and inscriptions. Robert McKibben instances Catherine's marginal scribbles as an example of the misuse of books which the novel's characters must overcome to live in peace with each other and their texts.[4] In contrast, like J. Hillis Miller, Carol Jacobs finds in the insufficiencies of the diary a marker for the unconquerable instabilities of fiction, textuality, and interpretation.[5] Feminist critics Margaret Homans, Patricia Yaeger, and Regina Barreca, reading gendered discourse in the novel, seize upon Lockwood's and Catherine's diaries as emblematic texts.[6] Even Jan Gordon, who offers one of the most sustained treatments of the ontological status of the diaries, particularly Lockwood's, ultimately foregrounds the genre as an instance of textuality in tension with what he argues is the novel's dominant orality.[7] Yet, to see the diaries in *Wuthering Heights* as simply texts among other texts, or as mere thematic vehicles (say, a protest against religion or patriarchy in the case of Catherine's, or a paradigmatic instance of misreading in the case of Lockwood's), is to overlook their particularity as diaries.

In his magisterial *Telling Time: Clocks, Diaries, and English Diurnal Form, 1660–1785*, Stuart Sherman theorizes temporality as the primary locus for understanding both the diary and its appearances in fiction.[8] Diurnal form, he argues, offered diarists, journalists, and novelists a means of enacting the repetitive fullness of time and experience, a means to which, in the eighteenth century, all three kinds of writers reacted ambivalently, drawn to its copious potential, but repelled by its refusal to select and highlight significant details or events, its insistence on equality of representation. In this account, diaries in novels figure as a mode of representing and ordering time, a mode at once embraced and resisted in the eighteenth-century texts he discusses. I want to argue here, however, that in *Wuthering Heights*, materiality becomes the significant locus for the diaristic, a locus foregrounded in particular by Emily Brontë's idio-syncratic reorganization of diaristic temporality. That is, useful for its temporal schema, the diary ultimately works, both thematically and literally, as an object which itself promises a space for the realization of its writer's and readers' desires. Indeed, despite their many differences of status, both Catherine and Lockwood – the marginalized young farmer's daughter, and the gentleman, a socially central figure who insists upon marginalizing himself – use their diaries to deal precisely with their senses of displacement. In the novel, then, the diary itself becomes the proverbial place of one's own, but its very status as such reveals how, psychologic-ally, textually, and materially, one's own place can never be secured.

Brontë's own quasi-diary serves as an effective starting-point for a consideration of her use of diaries in fiction, despite the fact that she is not known as a diarist and her diary is unconventional, especially in its temporality. Using Frank Kermode's distinction between *kairos* and *chronos*, Sherman argues that the temporality of the diary is like that of the watch: the '*Tick, Tick, Tick* – of the *quotidian* as series and structure.'[9] He opposes this aural repetition to two alternatives: theoretically, the clock's '*tick-tock*,' which for Kermode symbolizes the progression of narrative; and, historically, the sound of the church bell which marks 'occasional' time, itself generally subsumed into 'narratives of signal occasions.'[10] Sherman claims that in the seventeenth century, the diary as a genre, once a collection of notations of occasions, became charac-terized by a regular and endless succession of formally identical entries, entries which, in his description, depend upon their dailiness. In nineteenth-century diaries, however, what we might call the '*Tick, Tick, Tick*' of dailiness in fact coexists with the '*tock*' or peal of occasional time; almost invariably, diarists use the occasion of significant dates – New Year's Day, birthdays, wedding anniversaries, anniversaries of deaths – to take stock, to pray, to predict, in short, to mark the developments of their own personal narratives. Brontë's diary, consisting of four entries written years apart in 1834, 1837, 1841, and 1845, one on her brother Branwell's birthday and two on her own, registers only the '*tock*,' the significant occasion.[11] Yet in registering that '*tock*' almost regularly over a dozen years, the diary has its own repetitive sequence, a sequence that insists on the ongoing openendedness of such personal narrative.

The entries themselves display an interest in time, both in the moment at hand, and in its progression. In 1834, for instance, Brontë notes, 'Anne and I have been peeling apples for Charlotte to make us an apple pudding . . . Tabby said just now Come Anne pilloputate (i.e., pill a potato) Aunt has come into the kitchen just now and said where are your feet Anne Anne answered On the floor Aunt.' In 1837, she specu-lates, 'I guess that this day 4 years we shall all be in this drawing-room comfortable I hope it may be so. Anne guesses we shall all be gone some-where comfortable We hope it may be so indeed.' In 1841, she foresees 'that at the time appointed for the opening of this paper we i.e. Charlotte, Anne, and I, shall be all merrily seated in our own sitting-room in some pleasant and flourishing seminary'; four years later, she marks the fact that the 'school scheme has been abandoned.' Even in their temporal pre-occupation, however, these few quotations reveal how time, for Brontë, is in many ways a screen for space. The main question about the passage of time is *where* it will lead the diary's denizens. Will their feet still be on the floor? Will they be in the drawing room at Haworth? In an imaginary seminary's sitting-room? Though the 1841 entry begins with time, it immediately turns to a wide-ranging consideration of precise location:

It is Friday evening, near 9 o'clock – wild rainy weather. I am seated in the dining-room alone, having just concluded tidying our desk boxes, writing this document. Papa is in the parlour – aunt upstairs in her room. She has been reading *Blackwood's Magazine* to papa. Victoria and Adelaide [the geese] are ensconced in the peat-house. Keeper [the dog] is in the kitchen – Hero [a hawk] in his cage. We are all stout and hearty, as I hope is the case with Charlotte, Branwell, and Anne, of whom the first is at John White, Esq., Upperwood House, Rawdon; the second is at Luddended Foot; and the third is, I believe, at Scarborough, inditing perhaps a paper corresponding to this . . .

The Gondalians are at present in a threatening state, but there is no open rupture as yet. All the princes and princesses of the Royalty are at the Palace of Instruction.

What people do matters, but, except for the fictional Gondalians, always already dematerialized, it is consistently secondary to where they are.

Indeed, space is not just a thematic concern for the diary, but a mater-ial one as well. Nineteenth-century British diarists were quite deliberate about where and how they wrote their diaries, arranging and rearranging their sheets of paper, blank books, and printed diary volumes to suit their representational needs. The physical body of the diary thus developed its own iconic import. Brontë composed her entries on single sheets of paper covered closely with text and sketches. In the 1837 entry, for example, she includes a sketch which illustrates the kitchen scene described in the main text, captions the sketch with a dialogue between its figures, and writes lengthwise along the edge of the page about the future. Here the space of the page enables not just the physical reproduction of relationships between people, but a further reproduction of time, specifically in the relationship between the central present and its peripheral but essential future. Brontë herself foregrounds the diary's materiality by titling her 1841 entry 'A PAPER to be opened/when Anne is/25 years old,/or my next birthday after/if/all be well' (her capitalization). As an object, the diary has talismanic significance: here, the very opening of the 'PAPER' will signal that all is well, that is, that the two sisters have survived and the material emblem of the past has arrived safely into the future.

It is easy to see the pervasive sense of emplacement in these entries as a response to anxiety, particularly when it is coupled with the graphically highlighted conditional, 'if/all be well.' As many biographers and critics have pointed out, the loss of the Brontës' mother in 1821, and of their older sisters, Elizabeth and Maria, in 1825, not to mention the location of the Haworth parsonage on the edge of the graveyard, made death a constant in their lives.[12] If people could be placed, and placed actively through what they were doing in the place where they were, their existence, and perhaps their continued existence, could be imaginatively guaranteed. Less mortally, collecting the locations of family members on a single page could psychologically alleviate the anxiety of separation, itself a negative portent: Elizabeth and Maria had gone away to board at Cowan Bridge School where they contracted the typhoid that killed them; economic exigencies had dispersed Brontë's siblings to 'John White, Esq., Upperwood House, Rawdon; . . . Luddended Foot; and . . . Scarborough,' metonyms for their teaching positions. In short, Brontë had tangible reasons to be anxious about where people were and where they belonged.

But if in her diary Brontë responds to anxiety by insistently locating, she threads her novel with dislocation, perhaps enacting more drastically that anxiety's existential depth. The cry of the ghostly Catherine at the window – 'Let me in – let me in!' (p. 20) – articulates most trenchantly the anxiety of place in *Wuthering Heights*. 'I'm coming home, I'd lost my way on the moor!' the ghost tells Lockwood, the stranger sleeping, perhaps dreaming, in her bed. Adrift in the vastness of the frightening world, here the moors, dark and cold, the ghost seeks only to secure a space for herself. The home she seeks, the old house with 'the date "1500," and the name "Hareton Earnshaw"' (p. 4) carved on its lintel, and '*Catherine Earnshaw*,' '*Catherine Heathcliff*,' and '*Catherine Linton*'

(p. 15) scratched in its window ledge, itself memorializes claims for place so strong they are staked in writing on its very walls. Indeed, it seems as if almost everyone – from Catherine and the ancestral Hareton, to Hindley, Heathcliff, Joseph, and Nelly – demands Wuthering Heights for their own. Yet the house consistently refuses such demands. For strangers, like Lockwood, the young Heathcliff, and Isabella, who have inordinate trouble finding seats and beds within its walls, Wuthering Heights itself becomes the frightening and unfamiliar world in which one has no place. Even for those who might think it theirs, the house marks the difficulty, if not the impossibility, of permanently assuring one's own space: Lockwood violently thwarts the ghost's attempt to come in through the window, while at the novel's end, Hareton and Cathy reject the home claimed in their names by their forebears. In *Wuthering Heights*, then, the fundamental experience of place is displacement. The novel can be read as a series of attempts to address the sense of displacement, including, most notably for my purposes, the efforts of Catherine and Lockwood to do so through their diaries.

It should not be surprising that the young Catherine Earnshaw seeks a place of her own. Orphaned, harassed by her older brother, harangued by Joseph, attached primarily to the foundling Heathcliff, not to mention young and female, she finds little space readily available to her at Wuthering Heights, emotionally, physically, and structurally. Unlike Brontë, who uses her diary to articulate her preoccupation with space by locating all of her family members precisely, even to noting that Anne's foot is on the floor, Catherine instead uses hers to detail a series of struggles which replace emplacement with displacement. When rain prevents attendance at church, Joseph creates his own congregation: 'Heathcliff, myself, and the unhappy plough-boy were commanded to take our Prayer-books, and mount. We were ranged in a row, on a sack of corn, groaning and shivering, and hoping that Joseph would shiver too, so that he might gives us a short homily for his own sake' (p. 16). Released downstairs, where Hindley makes clear his power to control the environment – ' "You forget you have a master here," says the tyrant. "I'll demolish the first who puts me out of temper!" ' – Catherine attempts to create a refuge, but fails again: 'We made ourselves as snug as our means allowed in the arch of the dresser. I had just fastened our pinafores together, and hung them up for a curtain, when in comes Joseph . . . he compelled us to square our positions that we might receive, from the far-off fire, a dull ray to show us the text of the lumber he thrust upon us' (p. 17). When Catherine and Heathcliff rebel, Hindley steps in once more: 'Hindley hurried up from his paradise on the hearth, and seizing one of us by the collar, and the other by the arm, hurled both into the back-kitchen, where, Joseph asseverated, "owd Nick" would fetch us as sure as we were living; and, so comforted, we each sought a separate nook to await his advent.'

I quote at length to demonstrate how repeatedly Catherine becomes the object of others, both grammatically and physically, even as she continually attempts to find a space for herself. Though Heathcliff may be aligned with her through much of her trouble, he too works to thwart her efforts: 'I reached this book, and a pot of ink from a shelf, and pushed the house-door ajar to give me light, and I have got the time on with writing for twenty minutes; but my companion is impatient and proposes that we should appropriate the dairy woman's cloak, and have a scamper on the moors under its shelter' (p. 17). Finding 'shelter' together means abandoning the only site which she successfully, at least so far, has carved out for herself. The provisional nature of that 'shelter,' a stolen piece of fabric, emblematizes the impossibility of finding a permanent place for oneself which the entire diary entry dramatizes. It seems not at all coincidental that the excerpts from the diary conclude with Catherine's fears about Hindley's treatment of Heathcliff: ' "He . . . swears he will reduce him to his right *place* – " ' (p. 18, emphasis added).

Hindley's oath, of course, references place as social status or class, not physical coordinate. He wants to return Heathcliff from his once-privileged position as favored adopted son to his apparent origins in the social depths. Yet Hindley articulates his strategy for doing so spatially: according to Catherine, 'Hindley calls him a vagabond, and won't let him sit with us, nor eat with us any more, and, he says, he and I must not play together, and threatens to turn him out of the house if we break his orders' (p. 18). Hindley names Heathcliff as a 'vagabond,' one without a place, refuses him the familial spaces of Wuthering Heights, and asserts his power to render the younger boy homeless. It would seem as if the condition of displacement in the novel is at once material and social, the two inseparable.

Lockwood's sense of displacement, however, renders this preliminary conclusion moot, or at least inadequate. Lockwood is clearly a gentleman of considerable leisure and financial resources. He rambles from the seaside to the moors to London and then North for shooting. He rents capacious homes, complete with servants. Still, like Catherine, Lockwood suffers the anxiety of place and uses his diary to record his compensatory search for a space for himself, albeit fairly ludicrously. Lockwood begins the novel with the conviction that he has found a suitable location:

1801 – I have just returned from a visit to my landlord – the solitary neighbour that I shall be troubled with. This is certainly a beautiful country! In all England, I do not believe that I could have fixed on a situation so completely removed from the stir of society. A perfect misanthropist's heaven – and Mr Heathcliff and I are such a suitable pair to divide the desolation between us. (p. 3)

Clearly, his search for an appropriate locale corresponds to a search for self, and in his exultation at the idea that he has found both, he is just as clearly mistaken, as the ironies of his pleasure in the 'beautiful . . . desolation' and his simultaneous claim to misanthropy and companionship in the final sentence suggest. His own 'dear mother,' Lockwood notes, 'used to say I should never have a comfortable home' (p. 5), a statement whose truth is writ large and absurd in his flight from the seashore where he rejects the interest of the woman he desires, to Thrushcross Grange where he chafes at the constraints of his chosen solitude, and, eventually, back to London. At Thrushcross Grange, over the course of the diary and novel, Lockwood never seems comfortable with his chosen place and persona: despite his claim to misanthropy, he repeatedly visits the clearly inhospitable Wuthering Heights and solicits the company of his housekeeper, Nelly. Lockwood's displacement thus seems exaggeratedly self-selected, even as it is clearly and powerfully felt. At once, then, the novel universalizes the anxiety of place and points to its particularity for the socially dispossessed. Displacement, in all its varieties, becomes the human condition.

It may seem, so far, that my argument about diaries is as thematic as any cited above, that I am merely presenting diaries as vehicles not just for Brontë's concerns with textuality, gender, and class, but also for her interest in place. I want to suggest, however, that in her representation of the novel's diaries, Brontë works specifically with the genre's cultural connotations, in particular its material significance, valorizing these texts' ability to alleviate the anxiety of place, even as she ultimately problematizes that ability. Lockwood's description makes Catherine's diary most emphatically material: kept, in part, in an 'injured tome . . . smelling dreadfully musty,' its 'faded hieroglyphics' 'scrawled in an unformed, childish hand,' it even includes 'an excellent caricature of my friend Joseph, rudely yet powerfully sketched' (p. 16). Though her diary's actual marginality ('a pen and ink commentary – at least, the appearance of one – covering every morsel of blank that the printer had left') may physically replicate her social marginality, Catherine has made the diary into her place, claiming the margins as her own, as it were. Here she can tell her own story; here she can say how she feels; here she can express her opinion by caricature; and here we even find the indexical traces of her own 'hand,' which turn the diary into a rhetorical extension of her body. It seems that the most dispossessed young girl can still find a place for herself in a diary, even if that diary itself recounts a narrative of displacement. Again, then, the novel echoes the imperative found in Brontë's own diary: the urge to secure a space for the self through text written on paper: the diary as place.

Yet, in Catherine's diary, as in Brontë's, that urge surfaces only to be thwarted. Brontë's diary, with its hope that envisioning the future will ensure its arrival, certainly failed dramatically in its prescriptive purpose. Though the last entry ends 'With best wishes for the whole house till 1848, July 30th, and as much longer as may be,' no 1848 entry survives, if any was written. A short year after it would have been written, both Emily and Anne were dead. Obviously, a diary's textual representation of the future cannot ward off death, just as its textual representation of spatial desire cannot provide a social, physical or ontological place for a particular person. Less obviously, its failure to do so is not only literal, but also symbolic and material: creating an object which will persist, like the 'PAPER to be opened/ . . . /if/all be well,' also creates an object which can be threatened. Catherine's diary emphasizes this contradiction. Burned by Lockwood's candle, piled up like bricks against the window, drenched by incoming snow, left behind when Cathy and Hareton vacate Wuthering Heights for Thrushcross Grange at the novel's end, it demonstrates, to an extreme, the potential dangers the material diary faces. Disfigured and abandoned, suffering almost as much as its writer, Catherine's diary finally articulates the frustration of location, making explicit the illusory nature of the diary's offer of a site for the self. Indeed, Lockwood's use of its volumes to keep Catherine's ghost out of her childhood home (p. 20), not four pages after we read her entries, symbolically underscores the immediate refusal of the genre's promise.

But what of Lockwood? Place is clearly a preoccupation of all three diaries, Brontë's, Catherine's, and Lockwood's, even if Brontë articulates her own preoccupation as emplacement, Catherine's as displacement, and Lockwood's as confusion. But, unlike the other two, Lockwood's diary seems distinctly immaterial. We receive no glimpse of the book or paper upon which he writes, not even a reference to the physical act of writing: the act which he performs is retelling, not transcribing, as he explains, 'I have now heard all my neighbour's history, at different sittings, as the housekeeper could spare time from more important occupations. I'll continue it in her own words, only a little condensed. She is, on the whole, a very fair narrator and I don't think I could improve her style' (p. 120). Indeed, Lockwood's violent deployment of Catherine's diary could be seen to mark him as the diary's anti-materialist, that is, as one with no respect for the privileged textual materiality of the genre.

Unlike Catherine, however, Lockwood can procure physical spaces for himself. He can rent Thrushcross Grange; he can respond to the closed door at Wuthering Heights by announcing, correctly as it turns out, 'I don't care – I will get in!' (pp. 7–8); he can order a servant to 'prepare a corner of a sitting-room for me to sup in, and a bed-room to sleep in' (p. 232); he clearly could have settled into a home of his own with the 'real goddess' he meets 'While enjoying a month of fine weather at the sea-coast' (p. 5) before the events of the novel begin. His ability to procure such spaces, of course, derives directly from his more powerful social and economic position, made evident through indicators like the seaside vacation, the rented country house, and the hunting trips, as well as the essential privilege of gender. But what Lockwood lacks, at least in the body of the novel, are two things that Catherine has almost to excess: a family and a narrative. These, the familial and the narrative, are the spaces which he seems most to long for and least able to achieve, as epitomized by his subjunctively-expressed and partially-displaced desire to write Cathy into the heroine of his own romance: ' "What a realization of something more romantic than a fairy tale it would have been for Mrs Linton Heathcliff, had she and I struck up an attachment, as her good nurse desired, and migrated together into the stirring atmosphere of the town!" ' (pp. 230–31).

In this context, the status of Lockwood's diary as frame becomes another key to understanding its apparent lack of materiality within the text. In one sense, the space emphasized by Lockwood's diary is, precisely, narrative space: the diary provides the space within which the story of the Earnshaws and Lintons can be told. Indeed, writing their story in his diary can be seen as a way for Lockwood to claim that story for his own, both to insinuate himself into it and to take material possession of it. But if this may seem yet another abstracted conception of materiality, it ultimately leads us to the most literal enactment thereof. It seems not incidental that frame, the term for narratives which enable the recounting of other narratives, also references the construction and structure of a building. For, in the end, Lockwood's diary can be seen as the most literally material aspect of *Wuthering Heights*. Housing the narrative, his diary becomes the book itself, the cover we hold, the pages we turn as we read. Ironically, while the novel may seem to emphasize the greater urgency of Catherine's need for space, by giving her a material diary within the text, it also points to the significantly greater possibilities Lockwood has for actually achieving a space of his own, by making his diary enclose the text itself. Yet the irony of Lockwood's material triumph is at least partly, if only partly, blunted by the persistence of Catherine's diary as an emotional focal point of the novel. As such, the two diaries once again reflect the gender and class differences between their writers, becoming almost a microcosm of the separate spheres: Catherine's stands for the enclosed world of emotional power, housed within Lockwood's material boundaries, an all-too-familiar structure of Victorian social and familial spaces.

It might be argued that the other texts of *Wuthering Heights* register displacement as significantly as do its diaries, and that they too do so materially as well as thematically. Certainly the carved names in the lintel and the windowsill, as well as Isabella's plaintive epistles, operate on these terms. But the formal and material prominence of Lockwood's and Catherine's diaries, as well as their ascription to the characters who stand at the novel's emotional periphery and center, establish their priority. That is, they reveal how Brontë's formal narrative strategy of enclosing the story of her main characters within the diary of a stranger, a diary which itself ultimately encloses the diary of one of those main characters, is in fact thematically essential to the full elucidation of the novel's concern with displacement.

Though the thrust of my argument has thus focused on the diary's thematic and material enactment of place, I want to conclude by returning to Sherman's frame of reference: time. Like Brontë's, Catherine's and Lockwood's diaries specifically abjure diurnality. While Catherine's text is clearly copious, the reader receives from Lockwood only two interrupted fragments of it. It is not even clear whether these fragments represent one day or two, for both are undated, and Lockwood writes of the second only that 'the next sentence took up another subject' (p. 17). Lockwood's diary itself has only two dates: '1801' (p. 3) and '1802' (p. 231). Years, rather than days, these notations echo Brontë's own quadrennial entries. Within the text, he locates time more punctually and immediately, though still not diurnally. At the end of chapter 9, as the first installment of Nelly's tale ends with Catherine and Edgar's marriage, he references the present moment of diary-writing by the hour: 'At this point of the housekeeper's story, she chanced to glance towards the time-piece over the chimney; and was in amazement on seeing the minute-hand measure half-past one . . . now that she is vanished to her rest, and I have meditated for another hour or two, I shall summon courage to go, also, in spite of aching laziness of head and limbs' (p. 70). When the next chapter begins, he marks the passing of 'Four weeks' torture, tossing and sickness!' He even tries to account for the unrealistic idea that several chapters and many years of narrative could be written down in a single diary entry: 'Another week over – and I am so many days nearer health, and spring! I have now heard all my neighbour's history, at different sittings, as the housekeeper could spare time from more important occupations. I'll continue it in her own words, only a little condensed' (p. 120). Yet all of these temporally-focused entries still evade dailiness, even as they do so self-consciously.

As in the diurnal diary, however, both Catherine's absolute fragmentariness, enforced for writer and reader alike by interruption, and Lockwood's ongoing sense of time passing, pose a resistance to temporal and textual closure. Ironically, as the novel itself reaches closure, in its very last paragraph, the diary is once again our direct means of narration: Lockwood, visiting the graves of Heathcliff, Edgar and Catherine at the edge of the churchyard, writes, 'I lingered round them' (p. 256). This phrase, with its sense of abeyance, suggests at once a suspension of temporality and activity, and a future beyond the close of the book, when he will leave these buried bodies behind and move on with his life. At the same time, this last scene, captured so diaristically, works specifically to foreground the unattainability of place. As the diary, theoretically, continues forever, so does the quest for place which the novel embodies, a quest highlighted, in the transitory moments of this final entry, for all its major characters: Catherine, whose body rests in the churchyard, poised between the two men in her life, as her spirit presumably roams the moors with Heathcliff, the foundling whom she loved first and best; Lockwood, off to continue his restless travels; and Cathy and Hareton, who believe they can escape the legacy of Wuthering Heights simply by leaving the house behind.

Ultimately, I would argue, Brontë at once minimizes diaristic temporality and puts it to use in service of the materiality which is key to the genre's function in the novel. By using temporality to thematize placement and displacement at the novel's conclusion, Brontë returns us to the central concerns played out through materiality, and thus finally renders temporality subordinate. *Wuthering Heights* is not alone among nineteenth-century novels in this generic revaluation. While the temporality Sherman focuses on in the eighteenth century remains a crucial aspect of the diary's function in fiction, the placement and treatment of the material diary becomes a vital element of the genre's significance in a host of other nineteenth-century texts. Just a few such examples include the monster's discovery of Victor's diary in the pocket of his overcoat in *Frankenstein*, the torn pages of the diary Helen Huntingdon gives Gilbert Markham in *The Tenant of Wildfell Hall*, Fosco's inscribed invasion of Marian Halcombe's diary in *The Woman in White*, and Cecily's offer of her diary as a physical guarantor of her (lack of) veracity in *The Importance of Being Earnest*. Though these novels may not share the thematic preoccupations of Brontë's texts, they constitute their own diaries similarly, as physical repositories of character, plot, ideology, and meaning. As such, like Brontë's own idiosyncratic diary, they significantly reflect and reshape the artistic and ideological significance of the diary in nineteenth-century British fiction and culture.

NOTES

1. Emily Brontë, *Wuthering Heights* (New York: Norton, 1990), p. 3. All subsequent references will be made parenthetically.
2. For the sake of clarity, I refer to Catherine Earnshaw Linton as Catherine, and to her daughter, Catherine Linton Heathcliff, as Cathy.
3. J. Hillis Miller, *Fiction and Repetition* (Cambridge: Harvard Univ. Press, 1982), p. 45.
4. Robert C. McKibben, 'The Image of the Book in *Wuthering Heights*,' *Nineteenth-century Fiction* 15 (1960): 159–69.
5. Carol Jacobs, '*Wuthering Heights*: At the Threshold of Interpretation,' *Boundary 2: A Journal of Postmodern Literature* 7.3 (1979): 49–71.
6. Margaret Homans, *Bearing the Word: Language and Female Experience in Nineteenth-century Women's Writing* (Chicago: Univ. of Chicago Press, 1986), pp. 72–3; Patricia Yaeger, 'Violence in the Sitting Room: *Wuthering Heights* and the Woman's Novel,' *Genre* 11 (1988): 203–29; and Regina Barreca, 'The Power of Excommunication: Sex and the Feminine Text in *Wuthering Heights*,' Regina Barreca, ed., *Sex and Death in Victorian Literature* (Bloomington: Indiana Univ. Press, 1990), pp. 227–40.
7. Jan Gordon, *Gossip and Subversion in Nineteenth-century British Fiction: Echo's Economies* (New York: St Martin's, 1996), pp. 97–154.
8. Stuart Sherman, *Telling Time: Clocks, Diaries, and English Diurnal Form, 1660–1785* (Chicago: Univ. of Chicago Press, 1996).
9. Ibid., p. 22.
10. Ibid., pp. 7, 42, 35. Sherman works through the distinction between the temporality of occasion and 'diurnal form' in a comparison between Pepys and John Donne's *Devotions upon Emergent Occasions*. See pp. 36–48.
11. The diary papers, as they are known, can be seen in the museum at the parsonage at Haworth. All quotes here come from transcriptions included in the Norton edition of *Wuthering Heights* cited above, pp. 295–8.
12. For an analysis of the profound effect of those deaths on the surviving Brontës, see Kate Brown, 'Plain and Lovely Bodies: Consolations of Form in the Fiction of Charlotte Brontë,' dissertation (Univ. of California, Berkeley, 1996).

Further Reading

BIOGRAPHICAL MATERIAL

There is a huge amount of this. The most useful works are listed below.

BARKER, JULIET. *The Brontës* (London: Orion, 1994). The fullest and most detailed biography of the whole family and their background.

GORDON, LYNDALL. *Charlotte Brontë: A Passionate Life* (London: Chatto & Windus, 1994).

JAY, ELISABETH, ed. *Elizabeth Gaskell's Life of Charlotte Brontë* (Harmondsworth: Penguin, 1998).

MILLER, LUCASTA. *The Brontë Myth* (London: Jonathan Cape, 2001). A compelling history of the popular and critical traditions relating to the Brontës.

NESTOR, PAULINE, ed. 'Charlotte Brontë's Biographical Notice of Ellis and Acton Bell' in *Wuthering Heights* (Harmondsworth: Penguin, 1995).

OREL, HAROLD, ed. *The Brontës: Interviews and Recollections* (Iowa: Univ. of Iowa Press, 1996). Includes 'Reminiscences of Charlotte Brontë' by Ellen Nussey, her close friend.

LETTERS

SMITH, MARGARET, ed. *The Letters of Charlotte Brontë*, vols 1 and 2 (Oxford: Clarendon Press, 1995 and 2000).

WISE, THOMAS J. and SYMINGTON, ALEXANDER, eds. *The Brontës: their Lives, Friendships and Correspondence in Four Volumes* (1933; Oxford: Basil Blackwell, 1980).

JUVENILIA

ALEXANDER, CHRISTINE. *The Early Writings of Charlotte Brontë* (Oxford: Blackwell, 1983).

PERIODICALS

Brontë Society Gazette

Brontë Society Transactions

GENDER AND CLASS

The two are often discussed together and the treatment of them forms the bulk of Brontë criticism.

ABBOTT, MEGAN E. 'The Servant's Gaze: Nelly Dean's Rise to Power in *Wuthering Heights*', *Women's Law Reporter* 18.2 (1997): 107–34.

BARKER, FRANCIS, ed. 'Women's Writing: *Jane Eyre, Shirley, Villette, Aurora Leigh*', 1848, *The Sociology of Literature* (Colchester: Univ. of Essex, 1978), pp. 185–206.

BOND STOCKTON, KATHRYN. *God between their Lips: Desire between Women in Irigeray, Brontë and Eliot* (California: Stanford Univ. Press, 1994).

BOONE, JOSEPH. 'Depolicing *Villette*: Surveillance, Invisibility and the Female Erotics of Heretic Narrative', *Novel* 26.1 (1992): 20–42.

CARNELL, RACHEL K. 'Feminism and the Public Sphere in Anne Brontë's *The Tenant of Wildfell Hall*', *Nineteenth Century Literature* 53.1 (1998): 1–24.

CIOLKOWSKI, LAURA E. 'Charlotte Brontë's *Villette*: Forgeries of Sex and Self', *Studies in the Novel* 26.3 (1994): 218–34.

CLAPP, AILSA M. 'The Tenant of Patriarchal Culture: Anne Brontë's Problematic Female Artist', *Michigan Academician* 28.2 (1996): 352–68.

DAMES, NICHOLAS. 'The Clinical Novel: Phrenology and *Villette*', *Novel* 29.3 (1996): 367–91.

DOLIN, TIM. 'Fictional Territory and a Woman's Place: Regional and Sexual Difference in *Shirley*', *English Literary History* 62.1 (1995): 197–215.

FEINBERG, MONICA L. 'Homesick: The Domestic Interiors of *Villette*', *Novel* 26.2 (1993): 170–85.

GOUNELAS, RUTH. 'Charlotte Brontë and the Critics: Attitudes to Female Qualities in her Writing', *Journal of the Australasian Universities' Language and Literature Association* 62 (1984): 151–70.

GREENE, SALLY. 'Apocalypse When?' *Shirley*'s Vision and the Politics of Reading', *Studies in the Novel* 26.4 (1994): 350–71.

JACOBUS, MARY. 'The Buried Letter: Feminism and Romanticism in *Villette*', in *Women Writing and Writing about Women*, ed. Jacobus (London: Croom Helm, 1979), pp. 42–60.

JOHNSON, PATRICIA E. 'This Heretic Narrative: The Strategy of the Split Self in Charlotte Brontë's *Villette*', *Studies in English Literature* 30.4 (1990): 617–32.

KENNARD, JEAN E. 'Lesbianism and the Censoring of *Wuthering Heights*', *NWSA* 8.2 (1986): 17–25.

KREILKAMP, IVAN. 'Unuttered: Withheld Speech and Female Authorship in *Jane Eyre* and *Villette*', *Novel* 32.2 (1999): 331–55.

McMASTER, JULIET. ' "Imbecile Laughter" and "Desperate Earnest" in *The Tenant of Wildfell Hall*', *Modern Language Quarterly* 43.4 (1982): 352–68.

MENDUS, SUSAN and RANDALL, JANE, eds. *Sexuality and Subordination: Interdisciplinary Studies of Gender in the Nineteenth Century* (London: Routledge, 1989).

POLITI, JINA. 'Jane Eyre Class-ified', *Literature and History* 8 (1982): 56–66.

PRESTON, ELIZABETH. 'Relational Reconsiderations: Reliability, Heterosexuality and Narrative Authority in *Villette*', *Style* 30.3 (1996): 386–409.

SHAW, MARGARET L. 'Narrative Surveillance and Social Control in *Villette*', *Studies in English Literature* 34.4 (1994): 813–33.

SHUTTLEWORTH, SALLY. *Charlotte Brontë and Victorian Psychology* (Cambridge: Cambridge Univ. Press, 1996).

TAYLOR, HELEN. 'Class and Gender in Charlotte Brontë's *Shirley*', *Feminist Review* 1 (1979): 83–93.

THOMPSON, N. 'The Unveiling of Ellis Bell: Gender and the Reception of *Wuthering Heights*', *Women's Studies* 24.4 (1995): 341–60.

VOSKUIL, IVAN. 'Acting Naturally: Brontë, Lewes and the Problem of Gender Performance', *English Literary History* 62.2 (1995): 409–43.

POST-COLONIALISM

BARRELL, JOHN. 'Death on the Nile: Fantasy and the Literature of Tourism 1840–1860', *Essays in Criticism* 4.2 (1991): 97–127.

DAVID, DEIRDRE. *Rule Britannia: Women, Empire and Victorian Writing* (Ithaca, NY: Cornell Univ. Press, 1995), pp. 77–117.

DONALDSON, LAURA E. 'The Miranda Complex: Colonialism and the Question of Feminist Readings', *Diacritics* 18.3 (1988): 58–77.

GIBSON, MARY ELLIS. 'Seraglio or Suttee: Brontë's *Jane Eyre*', *Postscript* 4 (1987): 1–8.

MEYER, SUSAN L. 'Colonialism and the Figurative Strategy of *Jane Eyre*', *Victorian Studies* 33.2 (1990): 247–68.

SHUTTLEWORTH, SALLY. 'The Dynamic of Culturalism in Charlotte Brontë's Fiction', in *English Literature and the Wider World: Creditable Warriors 1830–1876*, ed. Michael Cotsell (London: Ashfield Press, 1990), pp. 173–85.

ADAPTATIONS AND SEQUELS

MILLS, PAMELA. 'Wyler's Version of Brontë's Storms in *Wuthering Heights*', *Literature Film Quarterly* 24.4 (1996): 414–23.

NUDD, DONNA MARIE. 'Bibliography of film, television and stage adaptations of *Jane Eyre*', *Brontë Society Transactions* 20.3 (1991): 169–72.

NUDD, DONNA MARIE. 'Rediscovering *Jane Eyre* through its Adaptations', in *Approaches to Teaching Jane Eyre*, eds Diane Hoeveler and Beth Lau (New York: MLA, 1992).

STONEMAN, PATSY. *Brontë Transformations: The Cultural Dissemination of Jane Eyre and Wuthering Heights* (Hemel Hempstead: Prentice Hall, 1996). A comprehensive account of all kinds of adaptations and sequels including plays, novels, operas, films.

WILLS, JACK C. 'Villette and the Marble Fawn', *Studies in the Novel* 25.3 (1993): 272–90.

DECONSTRUCTION

DOWNING, CRYSTAL. 'Hieroglyphics (De)Constructed: Interpreting Brontë Fictions', *Literature, Interpretation, Theory* 2 (1991): 261–73.

PSYCHOANALYTICAL INTERPRETATIONS

KUCICH, JOHN. *Repression in Victorian Fiction: Charlotte Brontë, George Eliot and Charles Dickens* (Berkeley: Univ. of California Press, 1987).

SADOFF, DIANNE. *Monsters of Affection: Dickens, Eliot and Brontë on Fatherhood* (Baltimore: Johns Hopkins Univ. Press, 1982).

STRUCTURE AND FORM

BERRY, LAURA C. 'Acts of Custody and Incarceration in *Wuthering Heights* and *The Tenant of Wildfell Hall*', *Novel* 30.1 (1996): 32–56.

FLETCHER, LUANN McCRACKEN. 'Manufactured Marvels, Heretic Narratives and the Process of Interpretation in *Villette*', *Studies in English Literature* 32.4 (1992): 723–46.

JOHNSON, PATRICIA E. ' "This Heretic Narrative": The Strategy of the Split Narrative in Charlotte Brontë's *Villette*', *Studies in English Literature* 30.4 (1990): 617–32.

LAWSON, KATE. 'Reading Desire: *Villette* as Heretic Narrative', *English Studies in Canada* 17.1 (1991): 53–68.

NEMESVARI, RICHARD. 'Strange Attractors on the Yorkshire Moors: Chaos Theory and *Wuthering Heights*', *Victorian Newsletter* 92 (1997): 15–21.

PRESTON, ELIZABETH. 'Relational Reconsiderations: Reliability, Heterosexuality, and Narrative Authority in *Villette*', *Style* 30.3 (1996): 386–409.

Index